KOUME'S WORLD

KOUME'S WORLD

THE LIFE AND WORK OF A SAMURAI WOMAN BEFORE AND AFTER THE MEIJI RESTORATION

SIMON PARTNER

Columbia University Press
New York

Columbia University Press
Publishers Since 1893
New York   Chichester, West Sussex
cup.columbia.edu
Copyright © 2024 Columbia University Press
All rights reserved

Library of Congress Cataloging-in-Publication Data
Names: Partner, Simon, 1958– author.
Title: Koume's world : the life and work of a samurai woman before and after the Meiji restoration / Simon Partner.
Other titles: Life and work of a samurai woman before and after the Meiji restoration
Description: New York : Columbia University Press, [2023] | Includes bibliographical references and index.
Identifiers: LCCN 2023022351 (print) | LCCN 2023022352 (ebook) | ISBN 9780231211840 (hardback) | ISBN 9780231211857 (trade paperback) | ISBN 9780231559102 (ebook)
Subjects: LCSH: Kawai, Koume, 1804–1889. | Kawai, Koume, 1804–1889—Diaries. | Women—Japan—Social life and customs—19th century. | Samurai—Social life and customs—19th century. | Wakayama-ken (Japan)—History. | Japan—Civilization—1600–1868. | Japan—Civilization—1868–1912.
Classification: LCC DS881 .P37 2023 (print) | LCC DS881 (ebook) | DDC 952/.025082—dc23/eng/20230614
LC record available at https://lccn.loc.gov/2023022351
LC ebook record available at https://lccn.loc.gov/2023022352

Cover design: Milenda Nan Ok Lee
Cover image: Kawai Koume, *Kanbai ensō bijinzu* (Portrait of beautiful woman gazing at plum blossoms through a round window), date unknown. Collection of Wakayama City Museum. Courtesy of Wakayama City Museum.

CONTENTS

Preface and Acknowledgments vii
Kawai Family Tree xiii
Monetary Values xv
Chronology xvii

INTRODUCTION 1

1. GROWING UP IN KISHŪ DOMAIN 12

2. A YEAR OF CALAMITIES 41

3. IN THE SHADOW OF THE BLACK SHIPS 62

4. WORK AND FAMILY 94

5. WAR AND REVOLUTION 124

6. THE ARTIST'S LIFE 164

7. ACROSS THE DIVIDE 189

CONCLUSION 227

Notes 253
Bibliography 269
Index 277

PREFACE AND ACKNOWLEDGMENTS

At 10:30 p.m. on July 9, 1945, air-raid sirens howled over the city of Wakayama. At 11:00 a radio alert warned the citizens of Wakayama that as many as 250 American bombers were flying up the coast of the Kii Peninsula, in five waves. Their vanguard had turned over Awaji Island and was now headed toward Wakayama city. At 11:30 the bombs began falling on the coast. Minutes later, the planes were over Wakayama.

The bombing of Wakayama went on throughout the night. By the time the bombers left to return to their base on Tinian Island, more than half the structures in the city were destroyed. Thirty-one thousand homes were lost. More than fourteen hundred people were killed, another five thousand injured. Wakayama castle, which had stood proudly over the city since the reconstruction of the keep in 1848, was reduced to ashes.

After the war, Wakayama was rebuilt along modern lines, with wide avenues designed for auto traffic, and modern high-rise buildings in place of the sprawling mansions of the domain's samurai elite. The castle was reconstructed, but in ferroconcrete. Few traces remain of the Edo-era cityscape. The protagonist of this book, Kawai Koume, lived in a large compound in one of the samurai residential districts of the castle town. Where Koume's house is thought to have stood there is now a small, dated apartment building. Her street still looks south to an imposing view of the castle, but the viewer is distracted by the competing billboards of

FIGURE P.1 Panoramic view of Wakayama castle and surrounding landscape. Photo courtesy of MySecretWakayama.com.

hotels, department stores, and entertainment centers. With the wide Kinokawa River running along its northern edge, the Bay of Osaka to the west, and mountains to the north, south, and east, Wakayama is still a lovely town. But Koume's Wakayama is all but lost.

Or is it?

I first visited Wakayama in April 2017. During my visit, I met for the first time the members of the Society for the Enjoyment of Koume's Diary (Koume Nikki wo Tanoshimu Kai). Since its founding in 2007, this group of twenty or so local historians and enthusiasts has kept alive the memory of Koume's life. The members are mostly retired, pursuing their interest in Kawai Koume alongside a variety of other passions. Each of them helped me in innumerable ways. Inoue Yasuo is a keen historian of Kishū domain with an encyclopedic knowledge of the politics and daily life of the Tokugawa era. He has written and privately published numerous books, several of which became fundamental guides for my research. Watanabe Keiji is a former journalist who is always ready to tackle a difficult question. Tsuji Ken, one of the society's founders, guided me around several of the important sites of Koume's life, showing me how the present landscape of Wakayama maps onto the past. Shiga Junko, who is Koume's great-great-great granddaughter, shared memories and much valuable information about her family.

The current organizers of the society are Nakamura Sumiko and Yamaue Sachiko. These extraordinarily able women, both graduates of a prestigious women's university, know far more about Koume and her diary than I can ever hope to master. In many ways, these women are strikingly like Koume: smart, well-educated, articulate, highly literate, and enjoying to the full the abundant cultural and social fabric of Wakayama. These are people with whom Koume would have felt quite at home. In fact, I think of them as Koume's friends, even though they are separated by 150 years of dramatic and turbulent history. Talking to Yamaue-san and Nakamura-san, I am struck by how well the social fabric of Wakayama has endured. They have been invaluable helpers and guides at every step of my project. Both read the first full draft of this book, providing me with priceless guidance and gentle correction of my many mistakes. My gratitude to them is profound and heartfelt. I will treasure their inspiring support and friendship for the rest of my days.

One member of the society who is not present to see the publication of this book is Abe Takeshi, who passed away in 2019. Mr. Abe wrote the only Japanese book to date on Koume's life.[1] He became an amateur historian after retiring from a successful career in marketing. He had come to Koume through her love of sake. He had already written an entire book on women who drink—a quirky but endearing interest of his. The first time I attended one of the society's monthly meetings, Mr. Abe asked a modest but deeply interesting question: Who *was* Kawai Koume? He had worked for years on her history, but, he said, after all this time he still did not feel that he truly knew her.

That question, which for him was a final reflection, became my starting point.

In addition to the members of the Society for the Enjoyment of Koume's Diary, I am particularly grateful to Kondō Takashi, who, as director of the Wakayama City Museum, arranged two separate showings of Koume's works for me; to the late Suyama Takaaki, who showed me Wakayama Archives' copy of *Strange Things Heard in Foreign Lands*, and who shared with me some of his immense knowledge of Koume and her environment;

and to Fujimoto Seijirō, an eminent scholar of Wakayama history, who led an enlightening walking tour of the historic castle town, and who shared with me many of his insights into the city's complicated social history.

I undertook much of the research and writing of this book while on a fellowship at the International Research Center for Japanese Studies (Nichibunken). My term was supposed to be for one year. But when the pandemic disrupted life in Japan and throughout the world, Nichibunken kindly allowed my wife and me to stay for an additional nine months, during which I was able to complete the book. My deepest gratitude to the director, Inoue Shōichi; to my academic sponsor, Liu Jianhui; and to John Breen, Isomae Jun'ichi, Isoda Michifumi, Matsugi Hiromi, and Takii Kazuhiro for sharing books, encouraging me to write for publication in Japan, and warm conversation. Heartfelt thanks also to the staff of Nichibunken for making my long stay so comfortable. I am also extremely grateful to my cohort of Fellows, who provided comfort and community during a strange and frightening period in our lives. Thanks to James Ketelaar, Astghik Hovhannisyan, Alistair Swale, Liao Chin-ping, and Ryōta Nishino.

I had several opportunities to present my work in progress to receptive and knowledgeable audiences, who gave me precious feedback and support. My thanks to the École française d'Extrême-Orient, the Italian School of East Asian Studies, the Nichibunken Evening Seminar, Walk Japan, and the Triangle Japan Forum. And as always, my deepest appreciation to my wonderful Japan studies colleagues at Duke University, the University of North Carolina at Chapel Hill and at Charlotte, and North Carolina State University. I could not ask for a more intellectually challenging or supportive community. A particular thank you to Gennifer Weisenfeld, who read a draft of chapter 6 and gave me very helpful feedback.

The title of the book pays homage to Gail Lee Bernstein, whose book *Haruko's World* (1983) was an early inspiration in my studies of ordinary people's lives in modern and early modern Japan.

Finally, I would like to thank Anne Walthall and an anonymous reader for their enormously helpful critiques of my manuscript. In the first draft they read, I ended this prologue with a disclaimer that although this book narrates the life story of Kawai Koume, a female artist who lived much of her life in the final decades of the Tokugawa era, I am neither an early modernist, nor an art historian, nor a gender historian. Both readers responded with a similar comment: yes, and it shows! I have spent a year revising the manuscript and, I hope, improving my understanding of the relevant historiographies. The critiques of my work by giants in the field of Tokugawa-era women's history were humbling, but they were also a catalyst to deepening my understanding of this most interesting of eras in Japanese history. Reading manuscripts on behalf of publishers is a laborious and often thankless task. I want both of these readers to know how grateful I am for their deeply constructive and helpful criticism and suggestions.

All that said, I recognize that I am still an outsider to the fields in which this book attempts to intervene. I apologize for any lingering mistakes or misinterpretations, and I hope that the message of the story I tell—that, regardless of shifting gender and status ideologies, a talented and determined individual could forge for herself a creative life of deep satisfaction, a dense social network in which she experienced an absolute sense of belonging, and a measure of economic stability despite numerous challenges—will resonate nonetheless.

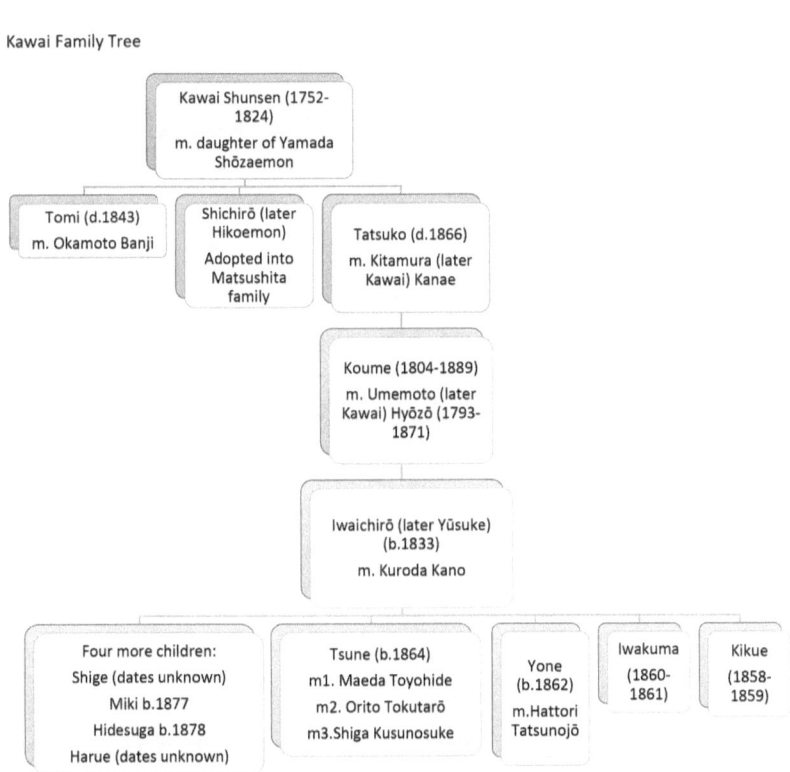

FIGURE 0.1 Kawai family tree.

MONETARY VALUES

Edo monetary values are notoriously complex. In the Kantō region, merchants used the *ryō* as the basic unit of computation. Although this was notionally equivalent to the gold *koban* coin, gold coins were seldom used in merchant transactions. The currencies in common circulation were the silver *bu* and the copper (or iron) *mon*. Due to recoinages, the actual specie content of these coins varied greatly. Hence merchants used the *monme* (a weight of pure silver) as a functional standard. For a fuller explanation, see E. S. Crawcour and K. Yamamura, "The Tokugawa Monetary System: 1787–1868," *Economic Development and Cultural Change* 18, no. 4 (1970): 489–518.

Monetary Values, in Silver Monme

	1859	1860	1861	1862	1863	1864	1865	1866	1867	1868
ryō/koban	73.00	73.00	72.00	75.00	84.00	89.00	101.00	115.00	127.00	216.00
Bu	18.25	18.25	18.00	18.75	21.00	22.25	25.25	28.75	31.75	54.00
monme	1.00	1.00	1.00	1.00	1.00	1.00	1.00	1.00	1.00	1.00
Kan	6.85	6.53	6.26	6.39	6.44	6.46	6.68	7.87	8.80	13.09
Mon	0.01	0.01	0.01	0.01	0.01	0.01	0.01	0.01	0.01	0.01
tenpō	0.69	0.65	0.63	0.64	0.64	0.65	0.67	0.79	0.88	1.31
Koku	121.00	153.00	163.00	147.00	164.00	202.00	347.00	944.00	996.00	565.00
$Mexican	36.00	37.00	35.00	35.00	36.00	33.00	37.00	46.00	48.00	45.00

Relative Values, 1865

	ryō/koban	*Bu*	*monme*	*kan*	*mon*	*tenpō*	*koku*	$Mexican
1 *ryō/koban*	1.00	4.00	101.00	15.12	15119.76	151.20	0.29	2.73
1 *bu*	0.25	1.00	25.25	3.78	3779.94	37.80	0.07	0.68
1 *monme*	0.01	0.04	1.00	0.15	149.70	1.50	0.00	0.03
1 *kan*	0.07	0.26	6.68	1.00	1000.00	10.00	0.02	0.18
1 *mon*	0.00	0.00	0.01	0.00	1.00	0.01	0.00	0.00
1 *tenpō*	0.01	0.03	0.67	0.10	100.00	1.00	0.00	0.02
1 *koku*	3.44	13.74	347.00	51.95	51946.11	519.46	1.00	9.38
1$Mexican	0.37	1.47	37.00	5.54	5538.92	55.39	0.11	1.00

Simon Partner, *The Merchant's Tale: Yokohama and the Transformation of Japan* (New York: Columbia University Press, 2017), 7.

CHRONOLOGY

1804 (Bunka 1)	Kishū daimyo Tokugawa Harutomi founds the Gakushūkan (domain school); Koume's grandfather Kawai Shunsen is a Confucian scholar there.
	Kawai Koume is born in Wakayama, daughter of Shunsen's daughter Tatsuko and her husband Kanae.
1805 (Bunka 2)	Shunsen moves to Matsuzaka to open a branch school.
1808 (Bunka 5)	Kanae dies in Kyoto at age thirty-two.
1819 (Bunsei 2)	Koume marries Umemoto (later Kawai) Hyōzō.
1824 (Bunsei 7)	Shunsen dies at age seventy-four.
1833 (Tenpō 4)	Koume's son Iwaichirō is born.
	Motoori Ōhira, Koume's poetry teacher, dies.
1837 (Tenpō 8)	First surviving year of Koume's diary.
	Ōshio Heihachirō insurrection takes place.
	Tenpō famine occurs.
	Koume copies "Strange Things Heard in Foreign Lands" (*Kankai ibun*).
1839 (Tenpō 10)	Gakushūkan scholars complete "Supplemental Gazetteer of Kii" (*Kii zoku fudoki*).
Around 1844	Iwaichirō changes his name to Yūsuke.

1848 (Kaei 1)	Hyōzō is promoted to rank of Okuzume with stipend of 25 *koku*.
1852 (Kaei 5)	Tokugawa Harutomi dies.
	Date Chihiro and "Wakayama faction" are purged.
1853 (Kaei 6)	Perry mission arrives.
	Hyōzō writes opinion paper for daimyo on foreign threat.
	Kishū domain gives all retainers money to buy weapons, and Hyōzō serves in coastal defense regiment.
	Hyōzō's stipend is increased to 30 *koku*.
1854 (Ansei 1)	U.S.-Japan Treaty of Kanagawa is signed.
1855 (Ansei 2)	Great Ansei earthquake occurs.
1857 (Ansei 4)	Hyōzō and Yūsuke travel to Edo.
	Yūsuke marries Kuroda Kano, daughter of Jinbei and Kise.
	Hyōzō is appointed principal of Gakushūkan; stipend is increased to 40 *koku*.
1858 (Ansei 5)	U.S.-Japan Treaty of Amity and Friendship is signed.
	Koume's granddaughter, Kikue, is born.
	Kishū daimyo becomes fourteenth shogun, Iemochi.
1859 (Ansei 6)	Cholera spreads in Wakayama.
	Kikue dies.
1860 (Man'en 1)	Grandson Iwakuma is born.
1861 (Bunkyū 1)	Iwakuma dies.
	Food shortages appear in Wakayama.
	Antiforeign incidents spread.
1862 (Bunkyū 2)	Shogun Iemochi travels to Kyoto; emperor orders him to expel the foreigners.
1863 (Bunkyū 3)	Chōshū domain fires on foreign ships at Shimonoseki.
	British attack Kagoshima.
	Hyōzō is mobilized to fight rebels near Osaka.
	Hyōzō completes his magnum opus, "Investigation of the Commentary of Zuo" (*Saden kōchō*).

1864 (Genji 1)	Fighting erupts at imperial palace in Kyoto, and much of the city is burned.
	First shogunal campaign to chastise Chōshū domain takes place.
	Granddaughter Tsune is born.
	Kano's father, Kuroda Jinbei, dies.
1865 (Keiō 1)	Second shogunal campaign to chastise Chōshū domain is mobilized; Kishū daimyo Tokugawa Mochitsugu commands shogunal army.
	Hyōzō's stipend is increased to 50 *koku*.
1866 (Keiō 2)	Beriberi spreads among shogunal army.
	Iemochi dies from beriberi.
	Chōshū army defeats shogunal forces.
	Emperor Kōmei dies.
	Koume's mother, Tatsuko, dies.
1867 (Keiō 3)	Tanaka Zenzō is murdered.
	Amulets fall from sky in Kyoto and Wakayama; street dancing and chanting of *eejanaika* begin.
	Satsuma and Chōshū ally against the shogunate; Shogun Yoshinobu resigns and pledges allegiance to the emperor.
	Publication of Hyōzō's book is canceled.
	Hyōzō retires.
	Yūsuke is promoted to Confucian scholar.
1868 (Meiji 1)	Battle of Toba-Fushimi occurs and shogunate collapses; Emperor Meiji moves to Edo, renamed Tokyo.
	Yūsuke becomes family head.
1871 (Meiji 4)	Daimyo return their domains to the emperor.
	Kishū daimyo is relieved of duty and moves to Tokyo.
	Hyōzō dies at age seventy-eight.
1872 (Meiji 5)	Gakushūkan closes.
	Compulsory education rescript is promulgated.
	Western calendar is introduced.

1873 (Meiji 6)	Conscription law is promulgated.
	New land registration and tax system is introduced.
1875 (Meiji 8)	Samurai rice stipends are now payable in cash.
1876 (Meiji 9)	Samurai stipends are converted to one-time issuance of bonds.
	Koume's diary resumes after seven years. The Kawai family own several rental properties; total rent is around 2.50 yen.
	Yūsuke becomes an elementary school teacher, seventh level, and starts to teach at Nishimura elementary school.
	Koume teaches daughter of Lord Mizuno.
	Yūsuke leaves Nishimura and goes to teach in Kandori elementary school.
1877 (Meiji 10)	Satsuma rebellion breaks out.
1878 (Meiji 11)	Grandson Hidesuga is born.
	Kuroda Kise dies.
	Yūsuke is teaching at private academy.
1880 (Meiji 13)	Yone is married to Hattori Tatsunosuke.
	Koume is painting many commissioned works.
1881 (Meiji 14)	Tsune is married to Maeda Toyohide; returns after three months.
1882 (Meiji 15)	Yone has a baby, Koume's first great-grandchild.
	Yūsuke's private academy is forced to close.
	Tsune marries Orito Tokutarō; marriage lasts only a few weeks.
	Koume submits two paintings to the Domestic Painting Competitive Exhibition in Tokyo.
1883 (Meiji 16)	Koume's eightieth year is recognized with gift from former daimyo.
1884 (Meiji 17)	Koume commemorates thirteenth anniversary of Hyōzō's death.
1889 (Meiji 22)	Koume dies.

KOUME'S WORLD

INTRODUCTION

On a midsummer day in 1864,[1] a sixty-year-old woman wrote in the diary that had been her daily companion for the past thirty or more years:

> On the twenty-third of last month, a large band of men marched in front of the gates of Chōshū domain's estate in Osaka. It's said that a headquarters has been established at Tennōzan, and that more and more soldiers are gathering there. There is a company of women soldiers, and also one of monks who eat meat, take wives, and allow their hair to grow. They are wearing armor and carrying pikes and swaggering around with no one to stop them. There are reports of armed clashes in Kyoto. It's said that the emperor has ordered the expulsion of the foreigners, and it's also said that a large band of vagabond soldiers has gathered in Senju in Edo. A thousand of them are said to have gathered at the estate of the Lord of Mito, and more and more are pouring in. It's said that in Edo people are wearing their [winter] kimono linings, and in Nikko it has been snowing. I don't know if it's true. But really, every day we hear nothing but disturbing rumors.[2]

The woman's name was Kawai Koume (1804–1889), an artist, wife, mother, and grandmother in a samurai family in the castle town of Wakayama, 550 kilometers from the shogun's capital in Edo and 130 kilometers from the imperial capital in Kyoto. In Koume's diary entry, we see her fear that unruly forces were tearing apart the political fabric of Japan; we see her struggle to sort out which of the swirling rumors she should believe; and we see her uneasy certainty that something was very wrong in the state of affairs. Even the weather had been turned upside down.

On the same day, Koume also reported that her old friend Tanaka Zenzō was off on a trip to Osaka—she sent him a flask of citrus liqueur as a farewell gift. She wrote that the three pear trees she had planted were still not fruiting. And she wrote of the drought affecting the cotton crops. Life went on, even as the certainties that Koume had enjoyed for most of her life eroded and crumbled.

For those of us living through the Covid-19 pandemic and war in Europe, this mixture of fear and uncertainty with the mundane details of daily existence may feel all too familiar. This, I have come to realize, is what it feels like to *live* history. We are relatively powerless to affect the big events—to *make* history—so we do what we can to see to our own welfare, and we make the most of the choices we have. This book is the account of one woman's experience with those realities.

Kawai Koume left a detailed record of her family's daily activities in the form of a diary, which she kept daily for upward of fifty years. A total of seventeen years between 1837 and 1883 survive in whole or in part. Her entries included comments on the weather; the movements of all the family members throughout the day; visitors to the Kawai house, the food and drink they consumed, and the topics they discussed; gifts received and given; money received and spent, and prices in the local markets; transactions with pawnbrokers; births, marriages, sicknesses, and deaths in the community; popular entertainments such as shrine festivals and traveling theatrical troupes; news and gossip; natural phenomena such as comets, floods, and unusual celestial events; significant events in the lives of the Kawai family, relatives, and friends; goings-on in Wakayama castle town and the domain; orders and instructions coming down from the domain administration in Wakayama castle; and events in Edo, Kyoto, Osaka, and other parts of Japan. Some scholars have dismissed her diary as overly concerned with mundane details: "The preparation of meals, heating the bath, and similar tasks of Japanese women of the time . . . are unlikely to retain the attention of a modern reader for very long."[3] But if we want to know how women experienced history, then we must

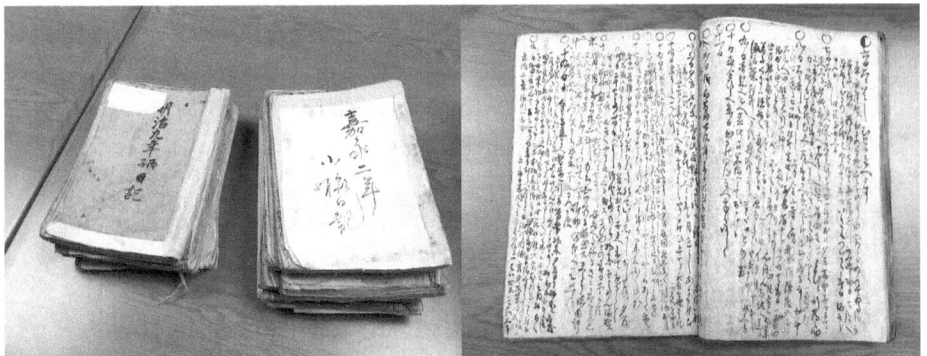

FIGURE I.1 A page from Kawai Koume's diary. Special collections, Wakayama Prefectural Library. Courtesy of Wakayama Prefectural Library.

recognize that meal preparation, laundry, and visits to and from friends and family are inseparable from that experience. Koume lived through some of the most dramatic events in all Japanese history. She wrote about many of them at length, and the diary gives us remarkable insight into how the upheavals surrounding the Meiji Restoration affected a lower-ranking samurai family. But Koume's comments on the volcanic events of mid-nineteenth-century Japan are sprinkled among the granular details of her daily experience. Rather than gloss over the "tasks of Japanese women," we can learn much by trying to understand them.

Anyone trying to understand Koume's life must grapple with understanding her diary: literally, since it is written in archaic Japanese, and metaphorically, as an entry into meaning that must be interpreted with due caution.

A diary may be defined as a document, kept usually by one individual, maintained regularly—usually daily, as the word "diary" suggests—and written (or drawn, or dictated) more or less as the events described happened: certainly not so late that the record might be distorted by the haze of memory.[4] Within this broad definition, though, there are countless variations. Many depend on the intended readership of the document. Diaries can be official records for bureaucratic or business purposes (for example, a ship's journal). Or they can be literary artifacts intended for circulation (for example, Japanese travel diaries such as the *Tosa nikki*).

Or they can be deeply personal reflections or confessions that the authors likely never expected to be read by others (famous examples are those by Samuel Pepys and Anne Frank). Or they can be private journals intended to record everyday interactions, perhaps as a reference to assist the writer in managing an enterprise, or perhaps as part of an ongoing record intended for the next generation.

Each of these categories can, of course, be problematized. How, for example, can we know who the intended audience was for a given document? Did the authors themselves always know? How can we be sure that the entries are in fact contemporaneous, and not added later? How can we be sure that the account is an authentic one, and not written to please an authority figure? How can we be sure that entries are complete, and not redacted? Do we even know the true identity of the author? The *Tosa nikki*, for example, purported to be written by a woman of the Heian court, is thought to actually have been written by the male courtier Ki no Tsurayuki. Similarly, Daniel Defoe's purported *Journal of the Plague Year* is a heavily fictionalized account of events that took place almost sixty years earlier, when the author was only five years old.

For historians wishing to use diaries as primary sources, there are additional complications. If the diary was published after the author's death (as in Koume's case), how accurate or complete is the transcription? Was it redacted in any way? How do we deal with lacunae caused by missing sections, or omission of vital details? How, from the perspective of our own ethics and values, do we understand the author's motives, actions, and worldview? How do we reconcile conflicts between events as recorded in a diary and those documented in other sources? How do we distinguish secondhand accounts or hearsay from directly observed events?

Koume's diary presents us with many of these conundrums. Transcribed by her great-grandson, the bulk of it was published almost one hundred years after her death. Two newly discovered years of the diary were transcribed and separately published by another scholar. The originals of the diary are still available for viewing in the Wakayama Prefectural Library, but a line-by-line check of the script, which is written in a flowing cursive using many irregular kanji characters, would be a daunting task. In practice, I was forced to accept the interpretations and decisions of the transcribers.

Koume's diary most closely fits the final category: a private journal intended to record the everyday activities of her family. Famous surviving examples in this genre include the Sekiguchi diary, which Sekiguchi family heads maintained over five generations, from 1762 to 1901; and the Nishiyama diary, kept by a tenant farmer in Niigata prefecture for more than fifty years. Such diaries focus on circumstances and conditions affecting the family enterprise—the weather for a farmer's diary, for example; social interactions and obligations; business and financial transactions; and news and information as it reaches the diary-keeper. Koume's production of such a document raises many more questions. If the document was the record of an enterprise, what was that enterprise, and who were its constituents? Koume describes the movements and activities of all her family members (often without using names or personal pronouns to clarify whom she was writing about), but her husband was far more active socially and professionally than Koume. Was he the "subject" of the diary? What does her maintenance of such a document tell us about Koume's position in the family? Did such a record (perhaps kept by her mother or grandfather) exist prior to Koume taking up her brush? When, indeed, did Koume begin keeping her diary? And why? Did she imagine a readership beyond her immediate family members? How did that affect her decisions on what to record and what to omit? Overall, Koume's diary seems highly colloquial, matter-of-fact, and businesslike. But sometimes she also transcribed poems she had composed, or sketched objects on the pages of the diary. What is their role, and how do they affect our interpretation? And how did Koume's relationship with her diary, and her approach to writing her daily entries, change over the course of her lifetime, especially after the succession of her son Yūsuke to the family headship?

Some of these questions, such as those concerning Koume's motives, cannot be answered with any certainty. But each problem raised by the diary is also an interpretive opportunity. While it must be approached with care, Koume's diary offers us important insights into the experience of the final decades of the Tokugawa era, the collapse of the Tokugawa shogunate, and the difficult transitions of the early Meiji period.

Koume's diary is particularly valuable because, unlike Kantō-centric personal accounts such as the letters of the Yokohama merchant Shinohara Chūemon, the letters of the runaway bride Tsuneno, or the diary of the shogunal official Katsu Kaishū, it offers a distinctly regional perspective. Koume lived in a domain with close ties to the Edo-based shogunate—its daimyo were from one of the three main branches of the ruling Tokugawa family—but it was located in the Kansai region, more than 500 kilometers from Edo. Events that were dramatic and immediate when they took place in Edo or Yokohama were often garbled and hazy in the recounting by the time they reached Wakayama. On the other hand, local concerns that might have received little attention in Edo loomed large in the lives of Koume and her family members. Recent scholarship has turned attention from center to periphery and "projected a fragmented picture of Japan," while affirming the importance of domains and regional political economies.[5] Koume's position as a resident of a provincial castle town offers significant interpretive possibilities. How did Koume's identity as a member of a Kishū retainer family affect her perspectives on social unrest, antiforeign sentiment, antishogunal agitation, and the establishment of an imperial nation? How did she conceive of "Japan" as a political, economic, or cultural unit? In what ways did she, or did she not, transfer her loyalties to the new imperial nation-state?

Looking at these questions even more broadly, Koume's diary can serve as an entry point into a broader history of a prominent but understudied domain in the nineteenth century (as yet there is no English-language history of Kishū domain or Wakayama city). What were the goals, policies, and successes of Kishū during the decades of the mid-nineteenth century, and to what extent did they coincide with those of the Tokugawa shogunate? To what extent was Kishū, despite being ruled by one of the main branches of the Tokugawa family, able to chart an independent path? This study adds to a body of regional, domainal, and prefectural histories that offer regional perspectives to build a more complex and nuanced understanding of Japan's fragmented political, economic, social, and cultural tapestry around the time of the Meiji Restoration.

Second, Koume's diary teaches us much about the family life of a samurai woman. While there has been a small boom in English-language life stories of Edo-era women, few of them focus on women from the *bushi* (samurai) status group. Yamakawa Kikue's *Women of Mito Domain* is a valuable exception, but it is an oral history based on memories collected decades after the events in question. Sugimoto Etsu's *A Daughter of the Samurai*, written in 1926, is also a memoir recalling events of the early Meiji period, when the author (born in 1873) was a very young child. By contrast, Koume's account of her daily life over five decades spanning the Meiji Restoration is an enormously valuable contemporary resource for better understanding the lives of lower-ranking samurai women.

Recent scholarship has helped us understand the immense diversity of women's experiences in early modern Japan. In the process, it has called into question assumptions about status, and about gender and the oppression of women under the patriarchal Tokugawa system. Studies by Anne Walthall, Laura Nenzi, Amy Stanley, Marcia Yonemoto, and others have emphasized the relative freedom of female actors to live the lives they chose.[6] How was gender lived and performed in a bushi household? To what extent did gender impose real limitations on the lives of Koume and other women in her household?

Third, Koume's diary makes possible an unusually detailed study of a lower-ranking bushi family's household economy, with a particular focus on the role of the wife in her family's economic affairs. My analysis examines the family's finances, both in cash and in kind; the family's social exchanges and their role in the household economy; the daily exchange of gifts as a part of the complex noncash economy; the production and consumption of food and drink; the management of servants and household maintenance; the family's participation in weddings, funerals, and other social rituals; and the varieties of women's work. What forms of labor did Koume undertake? How was her role understood in the family? What, indeed, were the meanings of "family" for a bushi household like the Kawai? And what was Koume's role in managing the family's social economy?

Fourth, Koume's diary offers us a window into the Meiji Restoration as it was experienced by a bushi family. One of the great ironies of the Restoration era is that the very group that was most instrumental in pushing toward the overthrow of the shogunate—namely, lower-ranking samurai from peripheral domains—were also the ones who lost the most from the changes that followed. The loss of status privilege, the conversion of samurai stipends to one-time bond issues, the closing down of most of the domain offices that had provided employment to the bushi, and the introduction of a conscription system and consequent loss of the bushi monopoly over military affairs combined to destroy the livelihood of hundreds of thousands of bushi families. Some sank into dire poverty; a few prospered from new opportunities for government service or business entrepreneurship; and many, like the Kawai family, just muddled through. Koume's diary is a valuable window into the difficulties faced by a bushi family in the aftermath of the Meiji Restoration, the adaptations it was forced to make, and the ways in which its members responded. What was the impact of its loss of privilege? How did the abolition of the domain affect it? How did its identity and loyalties change? To what extent did it embrace the opportunities created by the Restoration? How well prepared was it to adapt and prosper?

Fifth, the diary tells us a great deal about female artists and the economy of artistic production in the late Tokugawa and early Meiji periods. In the last decades of the Tokugawa era, Koume's diary shows us her active participation in the cultural community of Kishū scholars. Koume was an accomplished poet and painter, and she was much in demand as a producer of cultural artifacts. She produced poems and paintings at communal events, sometimes in the homes of fellow scholars and sometimes at outdoor events celebrating spring blossoms or fall foliage. Koume also accepted commissions from family members, colleagues, townspeople, and others. Her cultural production contributed significantly to the domestic economy of the family. This book offers an extensive analysis of a female artist at work before and after the Meiji Restoration. How should we understand Koume's cultural production? Was it a profession? How was she viewed as a female artist? What was the economy of her art? How was it related to her broader responsibilities as manager of the Kawai household? And, perhaps most interesting in Koume's case, how did the social and economic transformations that followed the Meiji Restoration affect her work as an artist?

Finally, there is much we can learn from Koume's diary about the information economy of the bakumatsu era. The diary is Koume's window onto the world of Kishū domain and beyond. In it, she recorded a daily stream of information passing through the Kawai household. Some of the information was extremely local: the movements of her own family members, the people they had encountered, festivals taking place that day, goings-on in the castle, and local gossip or scandal. But Koume also received a steady flow of news and information about events in the domain and beyond. What were the sources of this information? What role did it play in Koume's position as household manager? What is the relationship between news, information, and the diary itself? What can we learn from her commentary about Koume's political views, or indeed her worldview?

And how did all this change in the years surrounding the Meiji Restoration?

This book is an attempt to explore and, where possible, answer these questions, while also paying attention to the unique experience and the individuality of Koume herself. As much as possible, I want to keep hold of my starting question: Who was Koume? What gave her life shape and meaning? How did this one individual experience the startling transformations of her later years? How, indeed, did she "live" history?

This is my fifth book chronicling the life of an individual during extraordinary times. For the past twenty years, I have made it my mission to try to understand the dramatic events and transformations of modern Japan through the experiences of farmers, shopkeepers, and housewives. At times it has been a lonely road. But in turning to the life of an Edo-era woman, I have found myself in excellent company. Given the paucity of archival sources on women who were largely excluded from the public sphere, scholars have found biography (using diaries and letters) to be an entry point into a better understanding of women's experience. Recent examples in English include Anne Walthall's *The Weak Body of a Useless Woman: Matsuo Taseko and the Meiji Restoration*; Laura Nenzi's *The Chaos and Cosmos of Kurosawa Tokiko: One Woman's Transit from Tokugawa to Meiji*; Amy Stanley's *Stranger in the Shogun's City: A Japanese Woman and Her World*; and Bettina Gramlich-Oka's *Thinking Like a Man: Tadano Makuzu (1763–1825)*.[7] Less recent, but still very relevant, are Edwin McClellan's *Woman in the Crested Kimono*, based on a biography by Mori Ōgai; and Kate Nakai's translation of Yamakawa Kikue's *Women of the Mito Domain*, a memoir of Yamakawa's grandmother's life.[8]

The subjects of these studies are very different people in terms of wealth and social status, region of origin, and activities and achievements. The more recent studies deal with women who, while they might for much of their lives have seemed ordinary, were driven to engage with their society, to step outside their boundaries and try to change things, whether for their own economic betterment or for the political transformation of the nation. While they acknowledge the rigid ideologies of class and gender that prevailed in Edo-era Japan, the authors refuse to allow their subjects to be defined or bound by those categories. As Walthall writes, "To become a woman is a process in no sense fixed.... If we begin with the assumption that [women] 'lived in a world as complex, fluid, and riddled with ambivalence as the world of today,' then [their lives become] much more interesting and believable."[9] Stanley's protagonist Tsuneno, who fled her hometown in search of opportunity in the big city of Edo, seized on opportunities for resistance to the destiny apparently allotted to her by the circumstances of her birth. It was women like her who "populated the crowded spaces of the growing city, who provided the essential services, and who used [their] earnings to help expand the city's vibrant consumer economy." In the process, Tsuneno helped "shape the modern world that she would not live to see."[10]

It has been a humbling experience to try to place among these works by giants in the field of Japanese women's history my own work on a woman who, while interesting in many ways, expressed few political views and made no visible attempt to change the course of national (or even local) politics. I am encouraged, however, by Walthall's call for more studies of "how women actually maneuvered" within the limits imposed by a patriarchal social system, and "the leeway they had to craft themselves."[11] Like the subjects of all these works, Kawai Koume was a unique and self-aware individual with her own desires and motives. She lived within a social and political system bound by categories of status, rank, and gender, but she made every effort to take control of her own destiny. Her life was indeed complex and fluid, and within the bounds of her own possibilities, she did indeed help shape the modern world. In this book I explore the ways in which Koume strove to better her own life and those of her family and community members. At the same time, I pay attention to the ways in which her life both was affected by and contributed to the political, social, economic, and cultural transformations of the mid-nineteenth century.

As much as possible, I have structured the book as a narrative of Koume's life. I have tried not to stray farther than necessary from her own story, and from her personal experiences. During the revision of the book, however, I came to understand that there were some aspects of Koume's life that were best understood separately from the main narrative, and without the constraints of a chapter-by-chapter chronology. The two most sustained analyses made possible by the diary are of Koume's work as household manager in a busy samurai household and of her life as an artist in the Tokugawa era and beyond. I have broken each of these into a separate chapter (chapters 4 and 6) that takes some liberties with the chronological sequence of Koume's life story. That said, I could not bring myself to break completely from the narrative format. Wherever possible, chapter 4 uses examples from the 1850s, which is the chronologically appropriate decade for the chapter's place in the book. And although chapter 6 covers Koume's life and work as an artist from the 1830s to the 1860s, my discussion of the transformations in the social economy of her artistic production during the Meiji period appears in the correct chronological sequence, in chapter 7.

1

GROWING UP IN KISHŪ DOMAIN

For two hundred years the great castle, its curved roofs with their leaping carp ornaments symbolizing the pride and power of Kishū domain, had looked down over the city from the summit of the "Reclining Tiger" mountain. In the streets below the massive castle precinct, which occupied fully one quarter of the city, the fifty-five thousand residents had lived in peace through the long decades of Tokugawa rule. Wholesalers, shopkeepers, and peddlers haggled in the crowded streets of the commercial quarters. Over one hundred temples and shrines welcomed the townspeople (and their money) to their worship halls, gardens, and cemeteries. And in the privileged residential quarters, the city's samurai retainers went about their business, far removed from the struggle and strife that had bought them their status two centuries earlier. In one of those samurai residences, in a pleasant and spacious house with a direct view of the castle, a baby girl was born. It was the twenty-second day of the twelfth month of the first year of the Bunka era: January 22, 1805, in the Western calendar. The baby's mother named her Koume: Little Plum.

Koume's mother was Kawai Tatsuko, the wife of a young scholar, Kawai Kanae. Kanae had been adopted into the Kawai family, whose head was Kawai Shunsen, one of the leading scholars of the domain. Kanae's bride, Tatsuko, was Shunsen's only child. In situations where there was no competent male heir to inherit the family assets and name, it was customary for the family to bring a husband into the family—a *muko* (adopted husband). Instead of Tatsuko moving out and changing her name to that of her husband, Kanae moved in and changed his family name to Kawai. Shortly after their marriage, Shunsen moved to the other side of the domain, to the castle town of Matsuzaka, where he was tasked with starting a new school. While living there, when he was almost sixty years old, Shunsen fathered (or perhaps adopted) a son, whom he named Shichirō. This might have complicated the family succession, but since Koume's father Kanae had already become heir to the family headship, Shunsen had Shichirō adopted into another samurai family—a common solution to problems of family stability and succession. Shunsen also had a young daughter, Tomi—again, we do not know if she was his biological daughter or adopted (Abe Takeshi speculates that both children were from Shunsen's birth family and in need of a home).[1] She, too, was sent out for adoption.

Sadly, Koume never got to know her father. Around the time of her birth, Kanae went to Kyoto to further pursue his Confucian studies, and in 1808, when Koume was only three years old, he died there. So Koume was raised by her mother and grandparents. She was to stay in their Wakayama home for her entire life.

KISHŪ DOMAIN

Koume was born in the castle town of Wakayama, the seat of the feudal lord (daimyo) of Kishū domain. The domain was a vast territory, of which the castle town sat on the northwestern tip. To the north were the great commercial and cultural centers of the Kinai plain: Sakai, Osaka, Nara, and Kyoto. To the east was the valley of the Kinokawa River, the domain's rice-producing heartland, while to the south were the fishing ports and citrus-covered hillsides of the peninsula's west coast. On the eastern side of the peninsula were the great religious centers of Kumano and Ise, the destination of pilgrims from throughout Japan. Ise was directly governed by the shogunate, but the surrounding area and the Kumano shrines were controlled by the Kishū daimyo. Inland, the domain was covered in densely forested mountains, a vast repository of timber and other natural resources. Indeed, the name of the region, Kiinokuni or Kishū, may originally have meant "land of the forests." Its forested mountains were centers of esoteric religious cults: in the Ōmine range, *yamabushi* priests and pilgrims wandered the high mountain trails and subjected themselves to austerities, hanging from cliffs and standing under waterfalls, to acquire some of the spiritual power of the mountains. Surrounding the peninsula was the ocean, abundant with every variety of seafood. The domain's assessed productivity of 550,000 *koku* (a *koku* is a measure of volume equivalent to about 150 kilograms) placed it fifth in wealth among the great domains of Japan.

In ancient times, the Kii family had governed the region. They claimed direct descent from the god Amenomichine, and in addition to their political powers, they served as hereditary high priests of the Hinokuma and Kunikakasu Grand Shrines, in what later became Wakayama city.[2] During the fifteenth and sixteenth centuries, the region was caught up in the civil strife that had swept over the archipelago. The Kii family lost its authority, and there were frequent military conflicts between the warrior monks of Mt. Koya and Negoroji temple, other religious warrior bands, and powerful local clans. In the 1580s these fragmented groups were finally crushed by Toyotomi Hideyoshi. Hideyoshi ordered his brother Hidenaga to build a castle in Wakayama, and Hidenaga in turn appointed Kuwayama Shigeharu as his deputy and castellan. At last, it looked like stability might be restored to the region.

But the Kuwayama family was on the losing side in the battle of Sekigahara (1600), which left Tokugawa Ieyasu as the supreme warlord of Japan. Ieyasu bestowed the domain on his retainer Asano Yoshinaga. Then, in 1619, Ieyasu appointed his own son, Tokugawa Yorinobu, as lord of Wakayama. Yorinobu appointed two of his top retainers, Andō Naotsugu and Mizuno Shigenaka, as lords of Tanabe and Shingū subdomains, with a nominal revenue of 38,000 and 35,000 koku, respectively. Both men were designated *tsukegarō*, or hereditary elders of Kishū domain.

For the next 240 years, the domain was ruled by the Kishū branch of the Tokugawa family, one of the *gosanke* or three branch houses of the Tokugawa that were eligible to provide an heir to the Edo-based shogunate. The shoguns Tokugawa Yoshimune (1684–1751) and Tokugawa Iemochi (1846–1866) were both from the Kishū branch. Nor was the relationship strictly one-way. Adoption between the shogun's family and the Kishū Tokugawa line was frequent. This position assured Kishū domain a significant role—for better or worse—in the unfolding political dramas of the era. During Koume's lifetime, two shoguns' sons became daimyo of Kishū domain, and one daimyo (Iemochi) in turn became shogun.

At the time of Koume's birth, the tenth daimyo of Kishū domain was Tokugawa Harutomi (1771–1853). Harutomi had become daimyo while still a teenager, in 1789. An energetic ruler, he was also a noted patron of the arts. He composed poetry, painted landscapes, and was a renowned calligrapher (some of his paintings and calligraphy are still on display in the Wakayama castle museum). He was known throughout Japan as a tea practitioner and collector, and he was also a supporter of the Nō theater, building a performance space in the castle precinct. Under his patronage the arts flourished, with the domain guaranteeing stipends to painters, poets, and scholars. Shunsen was a direct beneficiary of Harutomi's interest in education and scholarship. In 1791 Harutomi had ordered a major renovation and expansion of the domain school, which he renamed the Gakushūkan. Shunsen was one of the first teachers appointed to work in the new school.

THE CASTLE TOWN

Koume's street, which contained about twenty compounds allotted to samurai families, ran from north to south. If young Koume emerged from her gatehouse and turned to the south, she had a direct view of the great curved roofs of Wakayama castle, seven hundred meters away.

The street was an unbroken row of whitewashed walls and wooden gatehouses. The house lots were large, about a thousand square meters (a quarter acre) each.[3] The imposing houses behind the walls were of plain wooden siding, roofed with gray tile. The properties were surrounded on three sides by fencing or hedges, with another small gate facing the rear, and their grounds were large enough to accommodate formal gardens and even small orchards and vegetable gardens.

Koume's house had a formal garden with a small carp pond, overlooked by the reception rooms of the house; a west garden with a fruit orchard; and a south garden with an extensive vegetable plot, where the family and its helpers grew eggplants, burdock root, peppers, and sweet potatoes.

FIGURE 1.1 Samurai residential area of Wakayama, from *Kiinokuni meisho zue* (Famous views of Kii), originally published between 1811 and 1851. Reproduced in Nukada Masahiro, ed., *Jōkamachi no fūkei: Karā de yomu "Kiinokuni meisho zue"* (Wakayama-shi: Nyūsu Wakayama, 2009). Courtesy of Nyūsu Wakayama.

There were both interior and exterior toilets, and the house had both a front and a back well. Inside, the single-story house had an earth-floored work area where food was prepared, and a raised tatami-matted area that included private rooms for sleep, study, and painting, a public reception-room for entertaining, and a classroom for teaching. Although it was closed off from the outside world by its walls and gatehouse, the house was far more of a public space than the word "home" conjures today. All day long it witnessed the comings and goings of domestic helpers, traveling salesmen and representatives from the nearby merchant houses, visitors and guests, and the students who came to study with Shunsen.[4]

Although the samurai residential area was far more tranquil than the crowded and noisy commercial districts to the south and east, it was a prime sales district for the entertainers, peddlers, and traveling salespeople who went door to door for a living. Most days, Koume's street was alive

FIGURE 1.2 Detail of map of Wakayama castle town dated 1855. Koume's house is marked with an arrow. Special collections, Wakayama Prefectural Museum. Courtesy of Wakayama Prefectural Museum.

with the cries of peddlers, each with his or her distinctive call. They carried their produce in baskets hung from poles balanced on their shoulders. Their cries advertised their wares: fish, vegetables, rice-cakes, salt, seaweed, noodles, salt, dried bonito flakes, kitchen implements, cups and bowls, firewood, lamp oil, and countless others. Medicine salesmen from distant Toyama came and left medicines on credit—they would come back months later and collect payment for the medicines that had been consumed. Some would combine entertainment with sales, like the drum-beating *hōnen* dancers who sold noodles. Others offered repairs, of eyeglasses or wooden tubs. There were also traveling sellers of books, paintings, and other collectibles; of cloth from the Nishijin workshops of Kyoto or further afield; and of printed broadsheets containing news, religious exhortations, and human-interest stories. And actors would crisscross the streets beating drums to announce the arrival of a theater troupe in town.[5] Years later, Koume herself described the sounds of her street in her diary: "Recently I haven't heard the calls of the fish sellers, but today I heard them calling out their wares of beltfish (*tachiuo*), bonito (*katsuo*), and sardines (*iwashi*). In the morning I heard the sound of the *taiko* drum. Lately there have been theatrical performances at various locations around town."[6]

The Kawai family house was a substantial property, especially located as it was near the center of the city. Compared to most townsmen's homes in Japan's major cities, it was an aristocratic residence. The size of the property, about 330 square meters (100 tsubo), is particularly striking given that the family's hereditary stipend placed it near the bottom of the samurai income scale. Wakayama appears to have been unusually generous in its property allocations. In Aizu domain in northern Japan, by comparison, samurai in the same income class typically lived in houses of only 80 square meters (24 tsubo).[7]

The samurai districts of Wakayama stretched over much of the city. The house lots allocated by the domain to its 1,200 or so core retainers resident in the city ranged from generous, in the case of lower-ranking retainers like the Kawai family, to the palatial estates of the domain's most senior retainers.[8] Collectively, the samurai residences with their five thousand or so inhabitants occupied a little over a third of the real estate in the city, about the same area as the townsmen's districts, which supported

FIGURE 1.3 Peddlers, from *Wakayama furiurizu* (Illustrations of Wakayama street vendors), illustrated scroll, Tenpō 4 (1833). The trades and associated vendors' cries are (*clockwise from top left*): candles ("rōsoku!"); candy ("amezaiku!"); sake from Mount Fuji ("shirazake! Shirazake!"); and lamp wick ("kinoetōshin"). Special collections, Wakayama Prefectural Library. Courtesy of Wakayama Prefectural Library.

a population of perhaps fifty thousand together with their workshops, warehouses, markets, and retail establishments.[9]

Once Koume was big enough, she might have gone out with the family maid or a nurse to buy fish or vegetables in the market, or to visit a shrine or temple. From the Kinokawa River in the north to the southernmost point of the city was 3.5 kilometers, a forty-minute walk. The distance from east to west was about the same, from the maritime harbor at the mouth of the Kinokawa River in the west, to the far side of the Waka River to the east. From Koume's house in the north of the city it was only a few steps to many of the city's major landmarks.

At the bottom of Koume's street was the extensive compound of the Saginomori Honganji temple, one of the largest in the city. In a town that generally adhered to a grid pattern, Saginomori—"Heron's Woods"—tilted 45 degrees, facing southeast rather than directly east. This was because it was one of the few buildings that predated the development of the castle town. Strategically placed on an ancient pilgrimage route, the temple had been established in the sixteenth century, during the prolonged period of civil war. The temple precinct was still partially moated, a relic of the long-past days of instability and civil strife.

Skirting to the east of the Honganji, and still just a few steps from Koume's home, were the dozen or so neighborhoods comprising the commercial center of Wakayama. The parts of the city inhabited by ordinary townspeople were extraordinarily crowded, with a population density of perhaps fifteen thousand per square kilometer.[10] The contrast to Koume's sedate and walled-off neighborhood could not have been starker. This was a place of intense crowds, an assault of brightly colored clothing, rich displays of merchandise, shouting and jostling, and the powerful odors of fish, tea, soy sauce, and refuse. In the narrow confines of the Burakurichō (a popular shopping street running from east to west), the tiny shops spilled their wares out into the street, their owners calling out to the passers-by to take notice of their tempting goods and low prices. Only 3.5 meters wide, the street was crowded with men and women of all social classes, chatting and jostling among the higgledy-piggledy merchandise as they sought out items of clothing, housewares, or accessories. A block away was the Nishinotana fish market, where vendors did a brisk trade in the rich daily catch of the Kinokawa River, Osaka Bay, and the Inland Sea. A contemporary print shows the fish piled up in baskets

FIGURE 1.4 Nishinotana fish market, Wakayama, from *Kiinokuni meisho zue* (Famous views of Kii), originally published between 1811 and 1851. Reproduced in Nukada Masahiro, ed., *Jōkamachi no fūkei: Karā de yomu "Kiinokuni meisho zue"* (Wakayama-shi: Nyūsu Wakayama, 2009). Courtesy of Nyūsu Wakayama.

in front of the merchant houses while samurai, priests, servants, and geisha vie for the attention of the salesmen, and dogs, cats, and buzzards chase the half-naked peddlers who have just bought their wares for the day. Directly east of the fish market was the fruit and vegetable market, another crowded and pungent center of commerce.

The commercial district also had its more sedate neighborhoods. Fronting the main north-south shopping street, which was also the main entranceway to Wakayama castle, were the grander emporia of the city: the clothing merchants, sake suppliers, and moneylenders to the city's wealthier classes and to the samurai elite. Many of these boasted their status as official suppliers to the daimyo and his household. The wealthiest merchants had their warehouses on the wide street facing the moat of the castle. Here, boats carrying produce from the Kinokawa River and the port to the west, or from the Waka River and the rural villages to the east, tied up and unloaded their merchandise. The clerks of the wealthy merchant houses tallied the merchandise as it was unloaded and supervised as it was hauled by scantily clad laborers into the tall white fireproof storehouses lining the street. Every morning a rice market was held here, where the surplus rice (beyond that claimed as taxes by the domain) was ferried in from the hinterland wrapped in cylindrical straw bales, priced, and sold.

As a stipendiary retainer of Kishū domain, Koume's grandfather Shunsen enjoyed many privileges. But he was not wealthy. Many of the town's merchants, although theoretically of lower status than the Kawai, were far richer than Koume's family. One sour critic wrote of the wealthy merchants of nearby Osaka: "Day and night, they can enjoy pleasures of mind and body in much greater luxury than even a daimyo. The splendor of the rich in our age is unparalleled in history; never has such a thing been seen since the beginning of Heaven and Earth. This is the vice that comes with orderly rule."[11] While the wealthy merchants of Wakayama may not have matched these excesses, they did control much of the wealth of the town. They owned property—sometimes whole tracts of residential rental housing—as well as warehouses full of merchandise. Many of them added to their wealth through moneylending, including loans to the samurai of the town, and even to the domain itself.

Most of the townspeople, though, lived much more marginal lives in the crowded commercial neighborhoods of Wakayama. Even the largest neighborhoods, home to a thousand or more people, occupied the same space as just eight or ten houses in Koume's samurai district. The majority of housing in these neighborhoods was rented, and the living spaces must have been extremely small, perhaps 15–20 square meters each.[12] Even within this world of rental dwellers, there were significant distinctions. The houses facing the street might be larger properties occupied by artisans or small-scale retailers. Behind them were the crowded *nagaya*, ramshackle wooden houses facing the back alleys, inhabited by servants and day laborers with no significant assets and few resources to fall back on in times of trouble.[13] These were the people who came to the Kawai to seek work, to sell small items, or sometimes to beg.

No matter their status, the inhabitants of the commercial districts were the officially sanctioned residents of Wakayama. They were subject to the jurisdiction of their neighborhood, which in turn answered to the higher administrative levels of the city, and ultimately to the city magistrate (*machi bugyō*). To a greater or lesser extent, they enjoyed the privileges of membership in their neighborhood: a voice in local affairs, the right to conduct their businesses, and a claim on the collective resources of the neighborhood in times of disaster. Below them, however, was an underclass of human beings who had none of those rights or privileges, and who by reason of birth or economic circumstance were forced to live in the most marginal of the city's communities, or indeed to inhabit the streets. These were people whom Koume would scarcely have noticed, or if she did, she would have been firmly instructed to keep her distance from them.

They were commonly known as *hinin*, which translates literally as "nonpeople." The most common causes of a fall into hinin status were criminality, disease, or destitution. Over time, though, the hinin also came to be associated with ritual pollution, either because they suffered from disfiguring diseases such as leprosy, or because they carried out the dirtiest and most demeaning tasks in society, such as the disposal of dead bodies, the butchering of animals, the guarding of prisons, and the administration of torture. Others were labeled hinin because they did not easily fit into the conventional categories of respectable society. These included beggars, traveling performers, and peddlers. Since they floated on the boundaries of the underworld, they were often suspected of criminal activity and gangsterism.[14]

The domain government established two communities where the hinin were permitted to live: Okashima on the eastern outskirts of Wakayama, and Fukiage in the southwest of the city. By the early nineteenth century their population is thought to have been around three thousand.[15] The lives of the hinin were restricted by a variety of humiliating regulations. They were not permitted to ask for shelter from the rain in the shops of the town, to drink sake or eat snacks in the city's drinking places, to pray at the Wakayama temples, or to relax in their precincts.[16] On the other hand, the domain expected them to provide important services, and to some extent it guaranteed them a livelihood in exchange for those services (indeed, scholars now argue that hinin are best understood as an occupational status group with its own privileges, and not just as outcastes).[17] Those services included cleaning the castle buildings and premises; the removal of excrement (horse and human) from the castle premises; the collection and disposal of dead bodies in the city; and the performance of various guard duties, including security patrols in the city, prison guard duty, the parading of criminals in the streets, and the administration of torture and executions. Ironically, the major targets of their policing efforts were other hinin, particularly those who had entered Kishū from other domains. These vagrants were periodically rounded up by the hinin guards of Wakayama and expelled from Kishū domain, a practice known as "hinin hunting" (*hiningari*).[18]

WAKAYAMA CASTLE

At the east end of the castle moat, across from the broad jetty where the wealthy merchants conducted their business, a black-sided watchtower stood next to the Kyōbashi Bridge. Those with business in the castle could cross here, entering the outer precinct of the castle (the Sannomaru) through the Kyōbashi gate. After the bustle and noise of the town, the castle enclosure was another world altogether. Its massive stone walls and ramparts were topped with pine trees, behind which, in the outer precinct, were the huge compounds of the senior retainers of the domain. Here were the mansions of the Andō, Miura, and Mizuno families, hereditary ministers of the domain with incomes exceeding those of many independent daimyo. Their expansive compounds were inhabited by small armies of personal servants, wives and concubines and their attendants, administrative staff members, trusted advisers, and platoons of guards. The gates of the great houses lined the main streets of the Sannomaru, but behind them there were also a variety of domain offices, such as the headquarters of the provincial magistrates.[19]

At the south end of the outer precinct was the inner moat, where the Ichinohashi Bridge offered access to the Ninomaru, the administrative headquarters of the domain and its nerve center. Here, retainers would dismount from their horses or descend from their palanquins, and, leaving their personal servants and retainers to wait in an open-sided structure near the bridge, they would enter the gate on foot. Koume must have known a good deal about the geography, architecture, and culture of the inner precinct, but there is no mention in her diary of Koume ever setting foot inside.

The Ninomaru was a small city in itself. Here, and in the Suna-no-maru to the west, were the offices of most of the domain's bureaucrats: accountants, secretaries, archivists, and inspectors (*metsuke*); as well as the bureaus of military affairs, commercial management (*shirabesho*), and financial management (*kanteisho*). For formal events, the premises were equipped with beautifully decorated rooms to entertain distinguished guests (such as emissaries of the shogunate or imperial court); conference rooms and audience chambers; and a series of large rooms where, on ceremonial occasions, the entire body of samurai retainers would gather in their formal clothes, their seating arranged strictly by rank, from the domain elders sitting in the Great Hall (*ōhiroma*), to the chief magistrates (*bugyō*) and departmental managers (*bantō*) in the Peacock Room (*kujaku no ma*), to the Tiger Room (*toranoma*), where the lower-ranking samurai would gather.[20]

Periodically, Shunsen would be summoned for a formal event steeped in the traditions of the domain and its proud heritage. Announcements issued by the inspectors who oversaw samurai daily life would circulate ordering special observances for the birth, sickness, recovery, and death of members of the daimyo's family. On occasions when the retainers were summoned to the castle, a message would circulate the previous day, and Shunsen and the other retainers would congregate in full formal attire of crisply stiffened robes adorned with their family crest, wide hakama trousers of dark silk, and lacquered hats denoting status and rank. Shunsen held the right of audience with the daimyo himself, and perhaps at times he was summoned to lecture Harutomi or a member of his family on one of the classic Confucian texts, or on Chinese poetry. He might also have been consulted at times on political questions. There are certainly precedents for such audiences in Kishū and other domains, but no record has survived of Shunsen's day-to-day activities.[21]

The administrative and reception spaces of the domain were grouped in a part of the Ninomaru called the Omote, denoting public space (though "public" in this case was limited strictly to domain retainers above a certain rank). Adjoining the Omote in the Ninomaru complex was the Nakaoku, the residential apartments of the daimyo. The Nakaoku was an intermediate space: it included private rooms where the daimyo could relax, dine, and sleep, but it also contained audience chambers where he conducted official business, and council rooms where his most senior retainers would gather and discuss affairs of state.

Beyond the Nakaoku was the third building complex of the Ninomaru, the Ōoku. This was the residential quarter for the women and children of the daimyo's household. The Ōoku was accessed by a corridor from the daimyo's personal apartments, with locked doors at each end. Only the daimyo was permitted access through these doors. The daily needs of the women and children were met by an all-female staff of servants and attendants, cooks, and cleaners. Only one room in the complex was accessible to men other than the daimyo: a public room on the edge of the precinct, where merchants from the town would offer clothes, makeup, accessories, and other items for the comfort and beauty of the residents. Many of the residents of the Ōoku, particularly those of lower rank, were allowed into the town for shopping and other business, and they brought back news and gossip to share with those unable to leave. The population of the Ōoku varied greatly, depending on the whereabouts of the daimyo. Like other domain lords, the daimyo of Kishū was required to spend every other year in Edo, and his official wife and children were required to live in Edo permanently. When the daimyo traveled to Edo, he took many of his concubines and their attendants with him, so the Ōoku emptied out during those times. But when the daimyo was in residence in Wakayama, there might be as many as four hundred women and children living in the Ōoku.[22]

To the west of the Ninomaru was the Nishinomaru, or western precinct. Originally built as a residence for retired daimyo, it had transformed over time into an elegant pleasure quarter for the daimyo, his friends, and family. It included formal gardens, tea houses, a Nō theater, and a covered bridge with lovely views over the castle grounds.

At the top of the "Tiger Mount" in the center of the castle precinct was the keep (*tenshukaku*) and its surrounding complex of defensive and ceremonial buildings. Designed as the primary residence and military headquarters of the daimyo, in Japan's long era of peace the *tenshukaku* had fallen into disuse. Its main function in the nineteenth century was as symbolic center of the domain. Sitting atop the mountain with its battlements, multilevel walls of stone and white plaster, and tile roofs topped with sculpted carp and other symbolic beasts, the *tenshukaku* dominated the surrounding area and visually represented the wealth and power of the domain and its lord.

FIGURE 1.5 View of the keep *(tenshukaku)* of Wakayama castle.

GROWING UP "SAMURAI"

The work and family life of the Kawai family were dictated in part by the family's status as lower-ranking bushi retainers of Kishū domain. The family's status assured it a share, however small, in the tax rice the domain exacted from farmers. Shunsen received a hereditary stipend, in addition to his salary as a domain employee. As a domain scholar, Shunsen also had a respected position within the domain's social elite. On the other hand, the family's position brought financial and social obligations. When called on, the men in the family were obliged to provide military service to the domain at their own expense. And family members were obliged to maintain the dignity of their position, for example, by paying a retainer to accompany Shunsen in his formal activities involving domain duty.

The samurai indisputably held the highest status among the four commonly recognized estates in the Tokugawa system: samurai, farmer, artisan, and merchant.[23] In their outward appearance, male samurai enjoyed clear markers of their status: the right to wear two swords, and the right to wear certain types of clothing. Economically, many—though by no means all—received hereditary stipends payable in tax rice. Male samurai also had privileged access to elite education, government employment, and military rank. Samurai identity and status markers were recognized not just locally but throughout the Japanese archipelago. In all these ways, samurai status was a universally acknowledged marker of privilege.

On the other hand, Shunsen's income placed him at the lower end of the economic hierarchy, and although none of his financial records have survived, we can surmise from Koume's own experiences that in her childhood, the family struggled to make ends meet. Wealthy merchants in the castle towns looked with pity on the struggles of the samurai, who were often forced to plead with them for a loan to tide them through until the next payday.

Recent scholarship has revealed much about the complex landscape of status in Tokugawa-era Japan. David Howell has argued that the four "estates" delineated by Confucian orthodoxy had no legal basis, and in practice they operated as two status groups: samurai and commoners. Status groups existed as the main point of contact with authority. Their internal organization was left largely up to them. While the main categories of status (each with visible markers of dress, hairstyle, and deportment) were samurai, commoners, priests, outcastes, and court nobility, in practice virtually every family in the shogun's realm was allocated several, overlapping status affiliations. An artisan, for example, was a classified as a commoner in his dealings with the city authorities, but depending on his trade he might also belong to a guild, which in turn would regulate its members and accept taxes and other service obligations to the daimyo. The daimyo in turn accepted obligations to the shogun. While status might theoretically be considered innate and hereditary, in practice it was primarily a function of occupation and the obligations that each occupation carried in its relations with authority. A change in occupation could lead to a change in status group. A peasant, for example, might enter service as retainer to a samurai, at which point he would adopt the visible markers of samurai status. The daughter of a merchant might marry into a samurai family. A samurai might become a priest or doctor.

There was immense diversity within each status group. The category of "farmer" (or, more accurately, villager, since the village was the interface with Tokugawa authority) included wealthy landowners and landless day laborers; subsistence agriculturalists and specialized cash-crop producers; village manufacturers; merchants and brokers; and a host of other occupations. Similarly, an artisan might belong to one of hundreds of occupation-based guilds, working as anything from a laborer on a building site to owner of a large manufacturing facility. The samurai, too, ranged in rank and social standing, from humble foot soldiers guarding the entrance gates of a lord's compound, to powerful daimyo who controlled the fates of hundreds of thousands. The samurai also incorporated a huge variety of occupations: from soldier to scholar; from brush-wielding bureaucrat to swashbuckling swordsman; from proud retainer to authority-flouting *rōnin*.[24]

Koume's own family is a case study in the porousness of status groups and the dense interactions between groups. Although Shunsen was a hereditary retainer of Kishū domain, his family background bore no resemblance to the warriors whose ancestors had fought their way across Japan with the Tokugawa family. Like Koume's own father, Shunsen had not been not a Kawai by birth. It is not even clear that his birth family had samurai status. His father was a doctor in Takasu, in central Japan (now Gifu prefecture). As a young boy, Shunsen was sent out by his father for adoption into the Kawai family, in the castle town of Hikone. Like Shunsen's birth family, the Kawai were doctors, and the expectation was that Shunsen would take over their practice. But instead, Shunsen turned his back on medicine and went to Kyoto to pursue Confucian studies. In 1779, at age twenty-nine, he came to Wakayama, where he opened a private academy. When Tokugawa Harutomi founded the new domain school in 1791, he appointed Shunsen as one of its founding teachers. Shunsen was allocated a housing lot in one of the town's samurai residential districts and awarded a hereditary stipend as one of the domain's core retainers. But even as a stipendiary retainer of Kishū domain, Shunsen maintained close contacts with doctors, artists, poets, and students who might as easily have come from merchant or farmer backgrounds as samurai. Throughout the long years of the diary, Koume maintained easy and often close relations with local artists, merchants, and shopkeepers from the castle town.

Koume was a woman in a samurai family. What did that mean, and how did her status enable or limit her ability to lead a free and fulfilling life? A woman's status derived from her family, not from occupation or individual right of birth. A samurai woman who married into a merchant family shared her husband's status, and vice versa. One might assume, then, that a woman had no legal personhood; that she was just a chattel to be bartered by the male head of her family. Indeed, nineteenth-century commentators painted a dark picture of women's lives. According to Fukuzawa Yukichi, "Women exist at the mercy of men and their security and their fate are in the hands of men. . . . Women's lives are nothing but a series of services, first to parents when young, then to husbands and parents-in-law when married." Echoing Fukuzawa, Basil Hall Chamberlain wrote that "a woman's lot is summed up in what are termed 'the three obediences'—obedience, while yet unmarried, to a father; obedience, when married, to a husband and that husband's parents; obedience, when widowed, to a son."[25] Yet even a cursory study of Koume's diary quickly reveals that her life showed no resemblance to this portrait of gendered servitude. More recent scholarship, indeed, has shown that women had far more agency and authority than these descriptions suggest. Marcia Yonemoto argued in *The Problem of Women in Early Modern Japan* (2016) that a bushi wife in the Tokugawa period had "a type of freedom, mobility, and authority that would have been nearly unthinkable for a woman of her status in imperial China or Chosôn Korea."[26]

The main reason for the greater freedoms and responsibilities of Japanese women, according to Yonemoto, was the prevalence of the stem family model throughout Japanese society. In stem families, only one child (often the oldest son) remains in the household, together with his spouse and children. A typical stem household might contain three generations: retired grandparents, the oldest son and his wife, and their unmarried children. In most cases, sisters and younger brothers would leave the household, either to marry into another family or to find work in a nearby town or a larger city. The stem family was particularly appropriate for Japanese samurai families because many—including the Kawai—were endowed with hereditary stipends that could be passed on only to a male heir. "Of all the status groups, warrior families were most strictly bound by the conventions of patrilineal descent and thus could only survive if they had male heirs; if a family had no inheriting son, it literally had no future."[27]

The stem family model placed extraordinary power in the hands of the family head, who was almost always male. But it also invested unusual power in women. The reason was the widespread custom of adoption, which often involved designating as heir a man from another family, after marrying him to one of the daughters in the receiving family: a system known as *muko yōshi*. The adoptee (*muko*) would change his name to that of his wife's family, and eventually he would succeed to the family headship. Adoption might be used by powerful families to create or strengthen political ties between families (Tokugawa Ieyasu adopted no fewer than twenty-two daughters from the families of his closest military allies).[28] But its most common use was as a strategy to ensure the family succession by a competent male heir. In commoner families, this might mean the adoption of an apprentice or assistant who was highly skilled in the trade or craft that provided the family with its livelihood. In samurai families, it meant that reliability, common sense, and bureaucratic or other occupational skills were often prioritized over the claims of firstborn sons.

The system of adoption drastically reduced the importance of the bloodline in family identity. Instead, it prioritized competence. It also allowed families that did not have a competent son to keep their daughter in the household, and at the same time to save the cost of providing her with a dowry (indeed, adopted sons-in-law sometimes brought their own dowries).[29] There was a ready supply of young men whose families were in search of an adoptive family, since it was much cheaper to have a younger son adopted (even at the cost of a cash settlement with the adopting family) than to set him up in a branch family. This was particularly true in bushi families, whose younger sons could not take jobs in merchant houses or artisan trades. As the saying went, "An only daughter can choose among eight potential husbands."[30]

Studies by Ray Moore, William Skinner, Wakita Osamu, and others have confirmed that adoption of male heirs was common throughout the Tokugawa period, and increasingly common over time. Adoptions accounted for at least 25 percent, and in some domains as many as 50 percent, of all family successions in the latter half of the Tokugawa period, while muko accounted for about 30 percent of all adoptions.[31]

The wife of a muko was likely to have significantly more authority than a bride in her husband's family. Indeed, women with muko husbands had a reputation for being entitled and dominating. "If you own three gō (600 grams) of rice bran, you should not become a muko" went one popular saying.[32] The women in such families were not only wives and mothers; they were also effectively heirs to the family's name and assets, and they often played a prominent role in managing the business and daily affairs of the household.

The Kawai family made liberal use of the muko system. Tatsuko's husband, Kanae, entered the family as a muko. And her daughter Koume, too, was to marry a muko. As the wife of a muko husband, she was to live her entire life in her natal home, and she retained a strong voice in its management. The greater prestige of a muko's wife may help explain Koume's confidence and authority within her family and also in the family's wider social circle. Her superior education and widely recognized skills as poet and painter also surely contributed.

That said, Koume was far from alone in her ability to chart a relatively autonomous course in her life. An eighteenth-century Kyoto ukiyo-e artist, Nishikawa Sukenobu, in his book *One Hundred Types of Women*, depicts women engaged in a wide variety of occupations and lifestyles, from the empress and courtiers to samurai women, farm wives, maids, entertainers, and courtesans. A popular board game in which women throw dice to find a suitable living had thirty possible outcomes, including maid, midwife, child-minder, shamisen player, bride, brothel keeper, schoolteacher, and acupuncturist.[33] A woman's ability to change her class status through marriage further opened up possibilities for self-advancement. A near-contemporary of Koume, the poet Matsuo Taseko (1811–1894), was able to occupy a conventionally respectable position in society and play a vital role in the economic life of her family, but when she felt the call, she was also able to throw herself into the activist politics of the restoration movement.[34] Amy Stanley's biography of Tsuneno, a priest's daughter from Niigata, vividly illustrates her protagonist's willingness to risk everything in the hope of forging for herself a new and better life in the city.[35] As David Howell argues, "Real life is infinitely complex. Even with all the structures to classify and thereby constrain social relations—household, community, and national status order—people nonetheless found ample space to engage in all manner of activities autonomously of status, however defined."[36]

A GIRL'S EDUCATION

Shunsen's place of work was the Gakushūkan, the domain school. The school occupied an extensive compound to the west of the castle. It was open to samurai retainers of all ranks from age eight to thirty. The older students were generally applicants for positions in the domain bureaucracy who, following the system of the Chinese civil service, had to pass a qualifying exam administered by the school. Younger sons of low-ranking retainers were not permitted to sit the exams, but they were allowed to study at the school. Students who were too poor to buy textbooks were permitted to borrow and copy the school's books. At the other end of the samurai social scale, the sons of the domain's most senior retainers were often tutored at home.

The school's curriculum was strictly limited to Chinese studies. It consisted of the Four Books and Five Classics of the Chinese canon, together with poetry composition and additional texts for advanced students.[37] A set of rules established by the first principal limited the teaching to neo-Confucian interpretations of the texts. This was an intellectual orthodoxy that, following the lead of the officially endorsed Hayashi school in Edo, was widespread throughout Japan. In 1790 the shogunate had gone so far as to promulgate an official ban on all heterodox teaching: a rule that reflected the rapid spread of a variety of new schools—some perceived as subversive—throughout Japan. The domain's intellectual traditions were varied, however, and in practice the intellectual environment remained welcoming to a variety of teachings.[38]

Classes began for the younger students with rote memorization and recitation of the texts (*sodoku*). Students then graduated to the lecture program (*kōshaku*), which included line-by-line interpretation as well as lectures on the meanings of the texts, followed by discussion periods (usually led by senior students) in which the students were encouraged to ask questions. For the next stage, students were divided into three groups based on their social status and placed in classes of ten peers. The student leader would have junior classmates read a section of a text and its interpretation (*kaidoku*) and then would answer their questions. Finally, students would graduate to discussion and debate classes (*rinkō*). Once again, classes were divided by status. In the classes, students would take turns leading class discussion, and the teacher would adjudicate the discussion and resolve outstanding questions.

Recitation classes were daily from around 8 a.m. to 12 noon. Lectures were between 2 and 4 p.m. and took place nine times a month. Interpretation and discussion classes were from noon to 2 p.m. and took place twelve times a month.[39] The daily recitations were the core instructional activity of the school. By their teens, most of the boys would be able to recite the four Confucian classics by heart.

The pedagogy of the school was comparable to that of domain schools throughout Japan. In the early years of Tokugawa Confucianism, scholars had limited their teaching mostly to lectures—some just for the benefit of students, others attended by members of the samurai elite, even by the daimyo. But the renowned scholar Ogyū Sorai strongly criticized lecturing as a way to teach children, arguing that it left little room for independent thinking: "They sit at the teacher's feet and take down every word of his lecture. Word for word, not a syllable out of place, from beginning to end. The worst of them will even mark a pause where the teacher stopped to clear his throat."[40] Sorai pioneered the *kaidoku* and *rinkō* methods, which gave much more opportunity for students to engage in active thinking and debate.

In addition to teaching, the scholars of the school were also expected to undertake research, both independently and by command of the domain. In 1806, for example, Harutomi commissioned the school to prepare a comprehensive gazetteer of Kishū domain, the "Supplemental Gazetteer of Kii" (*Kii zoku fudoki*). The original gazetteer had been produced in the Heian period, almost a thousand years earlier. Work on this massive project continued on and off over a period of more than thirty years, led by successive scholars from the domain school and elsewhere; it was finally completed in 1839, in 192 volumes. The editors surveyed village leaders about the history, population, local customs, and agricultural and other production of their communities. The editors sent out teams of field workers to verify and add to the information.

On top of his teaching responsibilities in the domain school, Shunsen taught Confucian studies in his own home. At any given time, there might be a handful of live-in students in addition to servants and Shunsen's young secretary, Shunzō. Koume's mother Tatsuko was a noted poet and intellectual in her own right, and their home must surely have been one of the centers of Wakayama's vibrant cultural life.

FIGURE 1.6 The Gakushūkan (domain school), from *Kiinokuni meisho zue* (Famous views of Kii), originally published between 1811 and 1851. Reproduced in Nukada Masahiro, ed., *Jōkamachi no fūkei: Karā de yomu "Kiinokuni meisho zue"* (Wakayama-shi: Nyūsu Wakayama, 2009). Courtesy of Nyūsu Wakayama.

What was it like for a little girl growing up in a bustling scholarly household where the focus was almost entirely on educating boys and young men? Through formal schooling, at-home instruction, and martial arts training, boys were expected to acquire the full range of skills—literary, philosophical, practical, and martial—understood at the time to prepare them for membership in the governing elite. For girls, on the other hand, some male authority figures considered such skills to be subversive. The shogunal minister Matsudaira Sadanobu went so far as to assert, "I consider it best for women to be illiterate." Even in cases where scholars and administrators promoted female education, it was often as a method of moral instruction, with a strong emphasis on moral texts such as the *Greater Learning for Women* (*Onna Daigaku*) and the *Imagawa Letter for Women*.[41]

In her memoir of women's life in mid-nineteenth-century Mito domain, Yamakawa Kikue writes that her grandmother, Kiku, despite being the wife of a respected scholar, had not "received much formal instruction in reading and writing; she was simply what she had been brought up to be, a solid, hard-working wife.... She did not know any stories, did not know anything of what was going on in the world; if the wives of the neighborhood gathered together to chat over tea, Kiku never joined them. She simply tended without pause to one chore after another." Yamakawa's mother Chise, despite being the daughter of a scholar, received all her schooling at the local girls' academy, which trained girls in the basic skills of literacy and penmanship, but not much more. "Girls were not expected to master a large number of Chinese characters; it was regarded as sufficient if they could read the Japanese syllabary, and when they reached the age of twelve or thirteen the main focus of their education became learning how to sew." According to Yamakawa, her mother's school reading was restricted to the *Hyakunin Isshu* poetry collection, the *Greater Learning for Women*, and a few other classic moral texts, though she was lucky to study later with her father and another teacher who helped her read some of the Chinese classics. Even women who were well-educated (usually the daughters of prominent scholars) were discouraged from discussing politics. As one such woman reminisced to Yamakawa: "It not being customary at that time to talk to women about politics, I wasn't told anything, and thus didn't understand at all what was happening."[42]

Rai Shizuko, a samurai housewife and poet who was a generation older than Koume, describes in her diary the education of her daughter O-Tō. Although Shizuko was herself the wife and daughter of a scholar, a noted poet, and a teacher of reading and writing to girls in the community, Shizuko emphasized practical skills in her own daughter's education. O-Tō began working in the household from the age of nine, helping her mother with spinning and sewing. There are numerous references in the diary to the different kinds of work to which she put her daughter, while O-Tō's academic education is only mentioned in passing. Certainly O-Tō was taught to read and write, but the diary makes no suggestion that she was educated beyond those basic skills.[43]

Koume was educated far beyond the level suggested by these examples. Some details are unclear. What tuition, if any, did she receive from her grandfather? Did her mother teach her the core skills of reading and writing, or did she attend a girls' school? Most likely Koume did not systematically study the Chinese language, Chinese poetry, or Chinese philosophy. But she acquired an extensive knowledge of kanji (Chinese) characters, as well as an appreciation for Chinese poetry and art. Koume also received years of training in the memorization, interpretation, and composition of Japanese poetry. Her mother placed young Koume with her own poetry teacher, Motoori Ōhira. Ōhira and his school of "national learning" emphasized the study of Japanese, rather than Chinese, cultural traditions. Koume benefited from the emergence and growing popularity of this new focus on Japanese culture because it made cultural production much more open to women. Chinese poetry required years of training, from which girls and women were generally excluded, in Chinese language and philosophical and literary traditions. Although no less challenging to study and practice, Japanese *waka* poetry was written in (somewhat stylized) Japanese, and in the phonetic *kana* syllabary in which many women were educated. Some of the great poets in the *waka* tradition had been women.[44]

Koume was also fortunate that her mother and grandfather recognized her artistic talent and encouraged her to learn music (she played the koto), drawing, and painting from an early age. Koume's painting teacher, Nogiwa Hakusetsu (1773–1849), was one of the most respected artists of his generation. Nogiwa painted in the *bunjinga* or literati style that was particularly popular in the late Edo period. This style, derived from Chinese scholarly traditions, combined poetry and calligraphy with the naturalistic painting of flowers and birds. It was well-suited to the scholarly community surrounding Koume's family. A typical artistic gathering would take place at a scenic outdoor spot, with poetry and paintings often produced collaboratively by the participants. It would usually be accompanied by large amounts of sake-drinking. The artists and scholars would combine conversation, music and song, eating and drinking, painting, and poetry in an event that strengthened the community's social and cultural bonds.

In receiving such a wide education, Koume certainly benefited from her scholarly family background. But she also benefited from the broader educational and cultural opportunities afforded by the urban culture of the Tokugawa era. Townspeople could afford to pay for schooling for both their sons and daughters, and literacy and cultural skills were increasingly valued in women. An educated wife could play an important role in preparing her sons and daughters for their future roles in society. Women in nineteenth-century Japan—including members of the samurai class and the daughters of merchants and affluent farmers—tended to be much more widely educated than their own mothers and grandmothers. There was a boom in educational facilities starting in the final decades of the eighteenth century and continuing unabated in the nineteenth.

As women's education spread across class and status boundaries, authors and publishers responded with an outpouring of new educational materials for the commercial marketplace. Education, including women's education, was an important segment of the booming print culture of eighteenth- and nineteenth-century Japan. The works published in this category included classic moral texts like the *Greater Learning for Women* and the *Imagawa Letter for Women*, but they were often adapted and packaged to a consumer marketplace. The *Greater Learning for Women* was just one volume in a much larger *Treasure Box of Greater Learning for Women*. The *Treasure Box* was not only a moral guide but also a handbook and almanac for many of the daily concerns and interests of women, such as entertainment, childbirth, child rearing, first aid, and examples of popular literature from Japan and China. It was published to be purchased not by men as a means of controlling their women, but by women who were looking for education and useful instruction. And it was popular, going through twelve editions from 1716 to 1863.[45] There were many similar works. The *Record of Women's Great Treasures* (*Onna Chōhōki*), for example, had sections on the correct application of makeup; clothes and fashion; wedding planning and etiquette; poetry composition; playing the koto; "women's illnesses" and their cures; stain removal; techniques of wrapping and folding; and the management of pregnancy. A survey of sixty-four examples of ownership of the *Onna Chōhōki* shows that it was owned by members of every status group and every segment of society, "including court nobles, higher and lower warrior families from various parts of the country, merchant houses in and around Kyoto, doctors, village headmen, scholars, and musicians."[46]

Women also were avid readers of popular fiction. This included classics like *The Tale of Genji* but also current best-sellers, such as Takizawa Bakin's ever-popular *Satomi and the Eight Dogs*, which was the runaway best-seller of the first half of the nineteenth century. Bakin published the first volume in 1814 and continued producing episodes for the next thirty years. The final set comprised 106 volumes. The novel was written in cursive script and printed on woodblocks, allowing a combination of illustrations and text that could flow in and out of each other. The format of the *Eight Dogs* (and countless other popular novels of the period) could best be compared to today's manga. Dramatizing illustrations and hyperbolic text worked together to create immediacy and drama. No inventory survives of Shunsen's library, nor any record of Koume's childhood reading, but the diary of her later years makes it clear that she was familiar with *Satomi and the Eight Dogs* and other popular works of her time.

MARRIAGE

In 1819, when Koume was only fifteen years old, Shunsen—now back in Wakayama—arranged for her to marry Umemoto Hyōzō, a twenty-five-year-old Confucian scholar from Wakayama. Hyōzō was born into the Umemoto family, which until the previous generation had belonged to the lowest rank of samurai retainers, the *dōshin*, barely above the townsmen in status. Hyōzō's father had won promotion to the rank of a full-fledged retainer, but the family continued to live in the townsmen's residential district. Hyōzō's mother came from a merchant family that had only recently been awarded samurai status. Many of Koume's in-laws were not samurai at all, but merchants and townsmen.

Hyōzō had been sent by his family to study with Shunsen as a live-in student. So Koume and Hyōzō had lived in the same household since her childhood. Hyōzō was the oldest son, and his father was expecting him eventually to come home and take up the Umemoto family headship. But the Kawai family conspired to keep Hyōzō with them. One reason was the urgency of appointing an heir to the Kawai family's name and position. Shunsen was in his late sixties (he turned seventy in 1820), and if he did not have a male heir there was a risk that the family's hereditary stipend and honored position in the domain's educational system would be lost. Hyōzō was a promising young scholar with the potential to further enhance the family's standing. But another reason for the match seems to have been Koume's own wishes. According to her great-grandson (and editor of her published diary) Shiga Yasuharu, Koume had fallen for the gentle, scholarly man whom she had known most of her life. There is a poem said to have been composed by the teenaged Koume, as she faced the prospect of Hyōzō returning to his birth family. Anne Walthall has pointed out that love poems like this were often fantasies, since most women of Koume's rank had few opportunities for romantic liaisons.[47] But at least in Kawai family lore, the poem expressed Koume's longing for Hyōzō.

> Kimi to nomi / koi kogaretsustu
> Tezusamini / ura no tanbo de / serinagari
> Burning with love for you only, I while away the time
> Cutting *seri* leaves in the rice fields behind the house.[48]

And so Hyōzō stayed with the family. He and Koume were married, and Shunsen adopted Hyōzō into the Kawai family as eldest son and heir (Hyōzō became the family head before Shunsen died in 1823). In his writing, Hyōzō adopted the pen-name Baisho—"the place of the plum." Koume's name means "little plum." Hyōzō had indeed found his place.

Koume's marriage to Hyōzō meant that education and scholarship, as well as the cultural community of poets and artists, remained central to her life. More than just a workplace, the scholarly community of the domain school formed the basis of the Kawai family's social interactions, gift exchanges, entertainment, and cultural life. And Koume was able to put her education and artistic skills to use as she supported and nurtured that community.

2

A YEAR OF CALAMITIES

A YOUNG FAMILY

In Tenpō 8 (1837), the first year for which her diary survives, a window opens into the lives of Koume and her family members. Koume was a young mother: her son, Iwaichirō, turned four in the first month, and Koume herself was thirty-two years old. The household consisted of Hyōzō, Koume, Iwaichirō, Koume's mother Tatsuko, and a transient population of maids and students. In the early months of 1837, Koume's diary records the family in their large and lively home, interacting daily with family members, colleagues, and friends. Her entries are brief summaries of the everyday concerns of a family living in peaceful times.

> Year of the Rooster, First Month.
> First day. Clear skies. Today Takahashi Saburoemon brought one sake coupon and two writing brushes.

This first entry suggests the purpose of Koume's diary: a factual account of the family's daily business, to be used, perhaps, as a reference to assist the family in meeting its social and financial obligations. The terse language, not prefaced by any introduction, suggests that Koume had been keeping the diary for some time and intended to continue over the long term.

The subdued nature of the day's events is surprising. During the Edo period, New Year's was the biggest holiday in the calendar. Take, by comparison, Francis Hall's description of New Year's Day as celebrated by the samurai of Yokohama:

> In the officers' quarters stately visits are going on with a great deal of ceremony, there are long genuflections, much knocking of the head on the mats, prim fellows in their highly stiffened gala dresses followed by servants bearing umbrella and shoes go about from house to house leaving their cards at the door.... The children of the officials, very pretty in their figured silks and sashes of crimson and scarlet and purple crape, and the little girls with faces artificially whitened till not a vestige of the original color is left, with vermilion lips, hair in great shining coifs of midnight, broad girdles gathered in buns behind half as large as themselves, and socks of spotless purity, are playing in the open streets or in the house areas.... There goes a brave little fellow not more than four years old, he is strutting proudly in his new silk trousers and a gala robe such as his father wears and two swords tied to his side.[1]

There is no mention in Koume's diary of family members dressing in their finest clothes, nor of calls made on neighbors and friends, nor of festive eating and drinking, nor of the games traditionally played on this day. Rather, it appears that the family stayed home quietly, and that they received only one visitor. This might indicate a lack of means to celebrate the New Year in festive style, or it might reflect the austerity of this particular year, at a time when the domain authorities were discouraging extravagance.

The brushes Takahashi Saburoemon brought suggest that he was a member of Hyōzō's scholarly community. They might have been intended for either Hyōzō's writing or Koume's painting. The sake coupon was a paper token, which could be purchased from one of the town's ninety-three sake shops and redeemed for a quantity of sake—usually one *shō*, about 1.8 liters, with a cash value of 1.5 to 3.5 *monme* (6 to 13 grams) of silver, depending on the price of the main ingredient, rice. As with gift cards today, these coupons were a convenient way of giving something close to money but that still felt like a gift. In some cases, sake coupons could also be redeemed for cash.[2] Writing, painting, and drinking were three central activities of the Kawai family—as we will see.

On the third day of the month, "Sent Chūbei to get two coupons. Uchimura Matajūrō came, gave him sake. Koume had a toothache so lay down. Learned how to cast spells from Matajūrō." The coupons were likely for sake, to use as gifts to friends and colleagues. Chūbei was the family's manservant at the time, perhaps a paid helper from the town, or perhaps a student in Hyōzō's school who was working for the family to help pay his board and lodging. As for the toothache, it illustrates the limits of Koume's access to medical care. The only sure solution to a tooth problem was removal of the tooth, usually performed by a traveling practitioner without, of course, the benefit of anesthetic. Perhaps Koume had already tried the common cures of hot pepper, alum, ground incense, or moxa smoke.[3] Casting a spell may have been her best remaining option. Koume offers no details of the spell, other than to mention some days later that it involved roasted beans (which were also used to cast out demons in the popular Setsubun festival). For a while, the spell seems to have worked: on 1/10 Koume went to the local Konpira shrine to offer thanks for her recovery, before walking up to the river to cast the beans into the river.

The fact that Koume refers to herself in the third person is also noteworthy. As we will see, the diary reports the movements of all the family members, but most extensively of Hyōzō, whose professional and social obligations took him outside the house much more frequently than Koume or Tatsuko. When Koume reported on Hyōzō's activities, she usually omitted his name. To her, it seems to have gone without saying that the family head should be the main individual protagonist of her diary.

On the fourth, the family celebrated Iwaichirō's fourth birthday with a traditional festive meal of rice cooked with red beans. They sent out packages of the dish to family members and neighbors. On the same day, "Shin'emon brought potatoes wrapped in straw." Shin'emon, we will learn later in the year, is a farmer from a nearby village who had entered into a contract with the Kawai family to purchase their excrement. Human manure was a valuable commodity for farmers, one of their main sources of fertilizer. Families would collect it in earthenware pots under the toilet, and the farmers would come periodically to cart it away. Shin'emon sent more consignments of sweet potatoes and daikon radishes through the year, and at the end of the year he paid Koume 24 monme in cash.

On the fifth, the priests of two different temples came, each bringing a gift. The gifts were probably to express thanks for contributions the previous year. One of the temples, Myōsenji, contained the Kawai family's graves, and the family would certainly have contributed to the temple. Temple priests were also important members of the Kawai's family's cultural network, the members of which frequently exchanged gifts.

On the seventh, the family's neighbors, the Ikeda, invited them to share their bath (during the year, Koume recorded having a bath at a neighbor's house four times, and the family invited others six times). On other days, Koume's family members visited and received visits from friends and relatives; purchased charcoal, sake, medicine, and picture books; paid visits to temples and shrines; dismantled their New Year's decorations; and ate sweets at home (on 1/5 Iwaichirō was thrilled with a gift of *manjū*, steamed buns stuffed with sweet bean paste, decorated with painted faces).

It was not until the eighteenth that Hyōzō resumed his work life. On that day he received his private students in his home for the start of the new term. Among the new students was his four-year-old son Iwaichirō, who "began reading the Book of Filial Piety." Hyōzō finally started his teaching duties at the domain school on the twenty-third. Hyōzō, now in his forties, was slowly rising through the domain's educational hierarchy. In 1832 he had been promoted to the position of professor (*kōkan*).[4] He now delivered lectures once a week, on average.

Hyōzō's own research was on the *Zuo zhuan*, or *Commentary of Zuo* (*Sashiden* in Japanese). Composed in the fourth century BC, the *Commentary* elaborates the story of the *Spring and Autumn Annals*, which chronicled the history of one of the early Chinese states, Lu, over a period of three hundred years. The *Commentary* is treasured for its style; its narrative, particularly of key moments such as decisive battles; its vivid recreations of notable speeches by historical figures; its strong moral tone, encapsulating the Confucian worldview; and its memorable aphorisms. It was a core text of the Japanese classical educational system and was part of the school curriculum for more advanced students. Hyōzō was working on an authoritative study of the *Commentary*, which he hoped to publish eventually.

On Tenpō 8 (1837)/3/9, "Iwaichirō lost his short sword." As was the custom for samurai boys, his family had bought him the sword for his fourth birthday, just two months earlier. It is not hard to visualize him strutting around the neighborhood wearing his new finery, long black hair grown out and tied in a plume atop his head, dressed in padded jacket and baggy trousers of dark cotton, the sword tucked into his belt a newly acquired limb, not a toy but not yet quite real. Perhaps he found it awkward as he played with his friends and left it on the ground to free up his movement. Children lose things. But for the Kawai family this was a significant financial blow. Replacing the sword cost them 15 silver monme, a large sum given their modest income. Koume does not say if, or how, Iwaichirō was chastised for this carelessness; nor, indeed, does she often mention her duties as parent to this small child. Some of his day-to-day care would have been assigned to one of the family's maids—Koume employed four during the course of the year. Tatsuko also took on some of the duties of caring for the boy. And he spent at least a part of each day studying with his father. Otherwise, he spent his time playing with his Suzuki cousins, visiting temples and shrines with his grandmother, and playing quietly at home. When he seemed under the weather, Koume kept him home, sometimes calling in the family doctor. On 7/8 "Isaburō came bringing boxed lunches. Gave him sake. Iwaichirō also drank some sake, and then lay down." The four-year-old boy had a severe reaction to the alcohol. "In the evening he had a high fever. Gave him various medicines, but at the fourth hour he had convulsions." Koume provided no further gloss on this alarming incident. Iwaichirō recovered and went on to enjoy drinking sake as much as his parents did.

The liveliest period in the year's social calendar was the fourth month, when friends and colleagues held frequent parties to view the spring blossoms. Most of these were men-only events, but Koume also went on expeditions, often with her mother and son. On 4/13 Hyōzō went on a boating party to Wakaura, a scenic location four kilometers south of Wakayama, and the location of several famous temples and shrines. On the same day, Koume, her maid O-Shika, and Iwaichirō went to visit the Nōkawa kannon temple, well-known for its magnificent avenue of stone stairs lined with cherry trees. Later in the day, Iwaichirō came down with a fever, and Koume sent O-Shika to get medicine from Tamiya Shūhaku, the family doctor. The next day, Hyōzō went to a party given by his colleagues. Koume stayed home, where she received a visit from a clothes seller. She bought three pieces of material from him, including one length of silk damask and another of crepe. On 4/15 Koume bought some sweetened rice cakes from a vendor. On the sixteenth one of the tenants in the family's rental property brought a gift of caged fireflies.

FAMINE IN WAKAYAMA

The majority of Koume's diary entries are given over to such mundane family matters: the movements of Hyōzō and Koume; visits to and from friends and relatives; gifts given and received; purchases made and payments received; minor illnesses; observances of birth and death anniversaries; and small dramas. But even as she was recording these trivial details, Koume and Hyōzō were absorbing a constant flow of information coming from outside their family circle. Much of this information came by word of mouth, but there were many other sources, including official announcements from the castle, circulating broadsheets, and letters from friends in Edo, Kyoto, and Osaka. Every so often, Koume wrote about events she observed or heard about in the world around her. Early in the year, she began commenting on the shortages and high prices of food in the local markets. On 2/14 she wrote that "fish is in extremely short supply." And on 3/6 a Mrs. Yoshida showed Koume a letter from her son, who was stationed in the domain's Edo compound. The letter commented on the very high price of rice in Edo: 240 monme per koku.[5] "Here," commented Koume, "it is 100 monme per koku." It would soon catch up.

Koume was surely aware that the 1836 harvest had been among the worst in living memory. It was the culmination of five successive years of disastrous weather, which we now know were caused, in part, by a pair of huge volcanic eruptions: the Babujan Claro in the Philippines in 1831, and the Coseguina in Nicaragua in 1835.[6] The summer of 1836 was cold and wet from Europe to China—so cold in Japan that a contemporary diarist recorded wearing his winter cape in July and reported frost on the roofs of the houses in Edo in August.[7] After the disastrous fall harvest, stores of grain were a fraction of their normal level. By the spring of 1837 they were dwindling rapidly, and the price of rice was spiraling up. The summer brought a catastrophic famine that by some estimates caused over a million deaths throughout Japan.[8]

On 3/18 Koume reported for the first time on the developing food crisis in Wakayama.

> The lord has given [a total of] 1 *kan* [equivalent to about 10 monme] each to the people living in the alleys, and since last winter he has been distributing rice gruel from the castle stables to the needy. Now he will give them another 400 mon [4 monme] each. It will cost over 10,000 ryō [equivalent to 600,000 monme]. They are saying that eight or nine people a day are dying of starvation. They are rounding up the hinin and expelling outsiders. Even those who aren't hinin are begging. These are unprecedented times. . . . It's said that even the lord is eating rice gruel three times a day.

A few days later, on 3/24, Koume gave another report: "It's said that rice is fetching 184 monme [per koku]." Rice prices were always subject to sizeable fluctuation, but historically, the price had averaged around 60 monme per koku.[9] "Truly these are difficult times," commented Koume. "The vulnerable are falling sick, or have become beggars, or they have gone to beg their way on the Shikoku pilgrimage. . . . The news is truly terrible."[10]

Kishū domain did its best to respond to the crisis. In the tenth month of 1836, fearing a further increase in the price of rice, it had implemented special measures to store as much spare grain as possible. Now it called on its subjects to eke out their food supplies with rice gruel, barley, and millet. It banned the export of grains to other parts of Japan, and it strengthened patrols to control the flow of outsiders into the domain. To provide work for the starving, the domain also undertook a river clearance project at the entrance of the Kinokawa harbor.[11] And of course, it exhorted the people of the domain to practice frugality.[12]

For those with no one else to turn to, the domain set up stations in the hinin residential districts for the distribution of rice gruel and cash. But assistance was not easy to get. Supplicants could receive help only after undergoing a thorough investigation. First they had to submit a request to the town officials in writing. The officials would then investigate their living conditions and marketable assets, to ensure they had no independent resources to tide them over the crisis. The officials also investigated the petitioners' family circumstances, to make sure they had no family members who could help them.[13]

On the second day of the fifth month, Koume reported that "today, five dead bodies were taken from the beggars' shelter. There are many reports of people collapsed on the road. Even children are to be seen walking on the road leaning on sticks." And the following day, eight more bodies were removed from the shelter.

On the twenty-ninth day of the fifth month, Koume wrote that some of the city's doctors had visited the shelter in the hinin district where the destitute were housed. The doctors had gone in response to the townsmen's entreaties, but "they found contagious disease there, so they suspended treatment and ordered the huts destroyed."

The next day Koume reported:

> Epidemic is spreading through the land. There are countless dead of starvation, and there are not enough hinin and others to dispose of them. There are reports of women's bodies being eaten by dogs. People are jumping off the Yoriai bridge [in central Wakayama], and by the time they've floated under the bridge they're already dead. The hinin are all walking with the help of bamboo sticks. In Kyoto there are many dead, and there are not enough resources to dispose of them, so they are digging huge square pits and throwing the bodies in. After they have gathered a thousand bodies they are erecting large memorial stupas, and the priests are gathering to pray for the dead. It's said they have dug six of these pits around the city. Six thousand people through the middle of the fifth month. At least seventy people have thrown themselves into the river. There are no words for the tragedy. Rice is 270 monme.

Ironically, while Koume commented with growing concern about the food crisis, her own family enjoyed privileged access to the tax rice collected from the domain's farmers and even benefited at times from the sky-high price of rice. The family members were able to avoid hunger, and sometimes to enjoy the finer things in life: drinking parties, fine clothes, and the exchange of gifts. Indeed, at times Hyōzō and Koume's elegant and seemingly carefree lifestyle contrasted jarringly with the growing suffering in the region.

The contrast is particularly striking in the fourth and fifth months, when both Koume and Hyōzō were enjoying blossom-viewing parties, expeditions to famous beauty spots, and seasonal festivals. For example, on 5/28 Tatsuko took Iwaichirō together with their maid to a shrine festival, where they watched the men, women, and children of the neighborhood parade the streets with the portable *mikoshi* shrine. They reported that the festival had been more subdued than normal, with the participants wearing cotton rather than silk, and that it had ended early out of respect for a curfew imposed by the domain to restrict consumption. But such restrictions did not stop Koume, who stayed home, from ordering that same day from visiting merchants a lacquered portable lunch box for 7 monme, and a piece of silk cloth for 36 monme. Just a day or two later Koume wrote of the spreading epidemic and of thousands of victims of disease and starvation being buried in mass graves in Kyoto.

POVERTY AND PRIVILEGE

In the 1830s, when the diary opens, Hyōzō's stipend was nominally fixed at a "ten-person allowance" (*jū-nin fuchi*). The more "persons" in the allowance, the more retainers the samurai could theoretically keep in his service. In practice, most samurai at Hyōzō's level kept one or two part-time retainers to escort them on formal occasions and spent the rest of the allowance on their own family, consuming the rice they needed and cashing in the rest. The allowance was calculated at 1.8 koku (about 270 kg) per person per year, so the Kawai family's notional stipend was 18 koku, or about 2,700 kg.

The family's actual income, however, was nowhere close to that amount. Typically, Hyōzō lost around one quarter of his notional allowance in deductions and compulsory loans or payments to the domain. The *fuchi* stipend was paid monthly, so Hyōzō should have received 1.5 koku (225 kg) per month. However, in 1837 Koume records getting a maximum of 1.2 koku (three bales, or 180 kg). And of that income, the family was required to deposit one-third with Kawaguchiya Saburō, the domain's licensed rice broker (*kakeya*), for the repayment of existing loans or as a deposit against future advances. Of the remaining two bales, the family typically kept one bale (60 kg) to feed themselves and sold the other for cash. For example, on 1/25 the family received three bales of rice. Hyōzō turned in one bale immediately to the kakeya, retained one bale for his family's consumption, and sold the third to a local rice broker for a total of 66.8 monme in silver. Koume (who managed most of the day-to-day finances) used 15 monme to buy 2.5 *kan* (about 9.4 kg) of whale meat.[14] She used another 30 monme to pay off loans from the Iseya pawnshop, redeeming a silk obi belt. And she used the rest of the cash income to repay debts that had remained outstanding from the previous year, leaving her with no spending money for the next month.

A month later, the pattern repeated itself. Hyōzō received three bales of rice, of which one went to the kakeya, one went to feed the Kawai family and its retainers, and the third Hyōzō sold. Once again, Koume was forced to use almost half the proceeds to redeem items she had pawned. And the third month was more of the same, with Koume getting 84 monme from the sale of one bale of rice, of which 61 monme immediately went to redeem pawned items, leaving only 23 monme for the month's expenses.

In the fourth month the domain held back even more of the Kawai family's stipend. After depositing their quota with the kakeya, they were left with only 3.2 *shō* (about 6 kg) of rice for their family's consumption. The fifth and sixth months brought the usual three bales, but once again in the seventh month the domain reduced salaries, paying the Kawai family only a little over two bales. The stipend also fell short in the tenth and eleventh months.

Even in normal times, Koume frequently had to resort to borrowing or pawning belongings to get the family through the month. This left them highly vulnerable to short-term cash crunches caused by unexpected expenses or charitable giving. Both occurred in the third month of Tenpō 8 (1837). In the third month, Iwaichirō's lost sword had to be replaced at a cost of 15 monme. In the same month, a succession of relatives and dependents came to the family to ask for help as the devastating shortage of rice swallowed their fragile earnings. On 3/8 Moriya Shōsuke, a relative of Hyōzō's mother, came to ask for help. His father's small business was failing, and Shōsuke had resolved to walk the 80 kilometers to Osaka, the economic center of western Japan, to look for a job there to support his family.[15] He came to Koume to ask for a loan of one gold *bu* (worth around 15 silver monme). Koume had to borrow the money to help him. The next day a tenant named Iwaemon came and begged for a few pennies. Koume gave him 24 copper mon. Later in the month another of Hyōzō's relatives, called Hisa, came to Koume to ask for money. Koume gave her 100 mon on the spot, and 2 silver *shu* two days later. Between them these loans and gifts amounted to 18.5 monme.[16] These expenses came in a month when the family's cash income (after repayment of their debts) amounted to only 23 monme.

When it ran out of cash, the family had no choice but to turn to the pawnshop. When Shōsuke came to beg for 15 monme, "to raise the money, Mother went to Kosayo. Returned at noon."[17] Kosayo was a townswoman who specialized in helping samurai families procure funds from the pawnshops. Since a self-respecting samurai, male or female, could not be seen in such an establishment, they needed a reliable intermediary to take their precious clothes, negotiate with the pawnbroker, and bring back the cash. Many used their own maids and servants, but Koume and her mother often used Kosayo's services.

On Tenpō 8 (1837)/4/29, Koume "sent for [a helper called] O-Isa. She came soon after noon, and I asked her to go to the pawnshop for me. She borrowed 49 monme. [Placed] two items of clothing: a short-sleeved kimono (*kosode*) with family crest, and a short-sleeved kimono of silk pongee." On 5/1: "O-Tomi [Koume's aunt] went to fetch Kosayo, who came.... Kosayo once again borrowed 25 monme." In this case, Koume was pawning her *obi* to raise cash to buy a kimono for her mother. And again on 5/3: "Today Kosayo came again. Pawned goods for 700 mon [about 7 monme], to pay [a vegetable seller called] Koben. Sent Iwa[ichirō] and Yasu to pay [Koben] 1 bu [15 monme]." Koume's favored pawnbroker was called Iseya (the House of Ise). Ise was the home of Japan's most venerated shrine, and since Koume used the Iseya's services so frequently, she occasionally referred jokingly to Kosayo's visits there as "the Ise pilgrimage."[18]

The dependence by samurai on the pawnshops of Edo, Osaka, and other cities was well-known. Samurai in popular literature were often forced into debt by spendthrift sons or by financial incompetence. Writing at the turn of the nineteenth century, Murata Seifū noted: "For years now, the samurai have suffered from poverty and their minds have been occupied by making a living: 'Buy this, sell that' and 'pawn this to pay for that' has become all of their lives."[19] A satirical poem (*senryu*) of the same period commented on the shame samurai felt at their indebtedness, which they were forced to hide from all but their creditors:

> Please share this misery with me, my dear keepers of pawnshops
> You are truly the only ones who know of this pain.[20]

On 5/4 Koume wrote about her debts at month-end, many of which remained unpaid: "The vegetable seller Koben and [a merchant called] Kikyōya are fully paid. [Told] Nōkawaya [a clothing merchant], Izumiya [sake shop], Nakajimaya [footwear merchant], Yonekichi [rice merchant], and the rice merchant Kyūbei that I could not pay them."[21]

Koume's family experienced some difficulties because of salary reductions caused by the shortage of rice in this famine year. But most of the issues they faced arose from their marginal economic status. Even in the best of years, three bales of rice were scarcely enough to keep a samurai family and its dependents in comfort. The two bales they actually received ensured a precarious lifestyle.

Nevertheless, thanks to their rice stipend, the family got through the year without ever going short of the essentials for a comfortable life, including rice, fish, vegetables, sake, lamp oil, charcoal or wood for heating and cooking, materials for writing and painting, and cloth or finished clothing. To some extent they even benefited from the severe shortages of the Tenpō famine. In the summer of 1837 the price of rice, which had averaged about 60 monme per koku for much of the past century, soared as high as 263 monme per koku.[22] Even with a reduced stipend, in those months when they had surplus rice to sell, the Kawai were able to get a much higher price than in previous years. In other months, however, they were forced to borrow rice or buy it for cash, just when prices were at their highest. On 3/16 Koume sent the Matsushita's manservant, Tokuzaemon, to the kakeya to borrow back 1.6 *to* (29 kg) of rice. But "the weather has been bad and there's a shortage of rice, so he would only give us one *to* (18 kg)." On 4/25, after receiving only 3.2 *shō* (6 kg) of rice stipend, Koume had to buy an additional 1 *shō* (1.8 kg) from a retailer in town. And on 4/27 and 5/3 the family borrowed another 15 *shō* (27 kg) of rice from the kakeya.

The greatest extravagances of the Kawai family were fine cloth and clothing, and sake. Sake was made of rice, and the rice used to make it was food wasted in the eyes of the domain. Early in the year, the domain further reduced the allocation of rice for sake brewing, from one third (as it had been for the past three years) to one quarter the level of a normal year. Despite these restrictions, through the summer months when the famine was at its peak, Hyōzō used his contact network to buy large quantities of sake. For example, on 5/9 Hyōzō took delivery of 6 shō (11 liters) of "Momijiyama" (maple leaf mountain), a brand from the Kawakami sake-making region around the mountain village of Katsuragi. He sent half of it to the Matsushita family. On 5/17 Hyōzō obtained another 3 shō (5 liters), via a local retailer. This time he sent some of it to his colleague Tominaga. He bought another 5 shō on 6/3 and sent half to the Miyake family. Two days later Hyōzō bought another 3 shō, and the following day another 2 shō. The deliveries continued at a similar pace through the sixth month. On 6/27 Koume calculated that over the past two months the family had purchased a total of 25 shō (45 liters) of Kawakami sake, at a price of 2.8 monme per shō.

THE WRATH OF HEAVEN

The rice that the Kawai family received came from the taxes of farmers who were struggling with the burdens of heavy taxation, land shortage, and debt. Even worse affected in this famine year were the growing ranks of wage workers and day laborers, who at best made a meager living from physical labor, and who were completely dependent on cash earnings that failed to keep up with the steep rise in prices. In that sense, the Tenpō famine underscored deep inequities and vulnerability that had arisen in Japan's social structure. Wealthy merchants, privileged samurai, and independent farmers could ride out the crisis. But marginal farmers and the huge underclass of underemployed and unemployed laborers had been made far more vulnerable by the rise of the cash economy and the widening of social and economic divisions. Koume's diary gives no evidence that she or Hyōzō felt they were themselves part of the problem. Their close connections to the townspeople's community and their own relatively marginal economic status perhaps made them feel more victim than oppressor. But any social system that allows tens of thousands to starve while a privileged few enjoy the fruits of the land is likely to be the target of anger and resentment.

Indeed, just such an explosion of anger occurred in the second month of 1837. It took place in the nearby city of Osaka and was led by a samurai official of similar status to Hyōzō and Koume.

On Tenpō 8 (1837)/2/20, Koume wrote: "The Shinmachi merchant Kanamiya Gohei's wife came to visit. She told us of a big fire and disturbance in Osaka. The houses of Mitsui, Kōnoike and others were burnt. [Umemoto] Tōshirō [Hyōzō's brother] also came to tell us about it."

The report of major disturbances in Osaka, only two days' walk from Wakayama and the economic hub of the entire region, caused intense interest and consternation. The next day Koume reported: "It seems the perpetrator is a police officer [*yoriki*] called Ōshio Heihachi or something. At noon, an official message circulated informing us of the conflagration and turmoil in Osaka. Depending on the circumstances, troops may be dispatched, so retainers should make themselves ready. At present the fires are still burning."

The events Koume was writing about continue to be remembered as a key moment in the chronology of nineteenth-century Japan. The destructive outburst in Osaka, led by a samurai official of lower rank, threw the dire social and economic problems Japan was facing into stark relief. Those problems, and the continuing resentment of lower-ranking samurai like Ōshio, were to play a significant role in the turmoil to come.

Ōshio Heihachirō, born in 1793, had been considered an able official within the Osaka bureaucracy. He was also highly respected as a scholar and teacher. In 1832, at age thirty-eight, he resigned from his position as an officer in the Osaka security establishment and retired to his home, where he opened a school devoted to teaching the philosophy of Wang Yangming.

This philosophy ran counter to the neo-Confucian orthodoxy that the Tokugawa regime had embraced, which continued to be taught in most of the official domain schools. While neo-Confucianism emphasized acceptance of the status quo and obedience to the authorities, the school of Wang Yangming challenged its followers to a more activist stance. If they saw an injustice, they should act, even if that meant confronting the powers that be, and even at the cost of one's own life: "To know and not to act is not to know."[23] Understandably, the authorities viewed this philosophy with suspicion, but it was gaining traction among the ranks of the lower samurai, many of whom were embittered by what they saw as corruption and complacency on the part of the hereditary officeholders, whose positions were denied to them based on the accident of their birth. In keeping with the principle of direct action, Ōshio did not stop at teaching his students philosophy. He also began training a select group of them, mostly officers in the ranks of the Osaka police, in modern warfare, particularly cannonry. In the closing months of 1836, Ōshio built up a small group of dedicated militants who were willing to take their cause onto the streets of Osaka.

Ōshio's motivation in creating this small private army was to try to relieve the suffering he saw among the townspeople of Osaka. He felt that the authorities were doing nothing to help the people, while the wealthy merchant houses were stockpiling rice to increase their own profits. Osaka was the central rice market of Japan, and there were indeed vast storehouses filled with grain even as the people of Osaka starved.

Prior to launching his attack, Ōshio had his followers distribute a manifesto addressed to "headmen, officeholders, established farmers, and landless peasants" of the surrounding villages. Ōshio wrote:

> During the recent upsurge in rice prices the Commissioner of Osaka as well as all the administrators ignored the benevolence that pervades all things.... [The wealthy merchants of Osaka] dislocate all manner of farming lands for mansions, living lives without wants. Knowing of the recent disasters of Heaven, they do not tremble with fear. Although people die of starvation and beg in the streets they refuse to aid them ... they wear silk, hire jesters and dancing girls as if they were enjoying the pleasures of ordinary times.... Day in and day out they manipulate the rice markets, making themselves veritable salary-robbers.... At this juncture, those of us who have watched from seclusion ... unite with those of high purpose, and punish these officials and the luxuriating wealthy townspeople of Osaka. We will attack and kill them, taking the wealth that they have hidden away in holes and storerooms, taking the gold, silver, copper cash and grains that are hidden in warehouses and mete out all of these.[24]

The rebels launched their attack on the morning of 2/19. After torching their own neighborhood of Tenmabashi, they marched on the residential quarter of the city's wealthy merchants. Ōshio's plan had been to break into the merchants' warehouses and seize their supplies of rice and other foodstuffs, which the rebels would then distribute to the people. The merchants themselves would (at gunpoint) be requested to provide generous gifts to the people of the city. The raids on the merchant houses were largely successful. Kōnoikeya was reportedly forced to turn over the enormous sum of 40,000 gold ryō (equivalent to 2.4 million silver monme). But the attacks soon got out of hand. Some of the rebels reportedly broke into the warehouses of the city's sake merchants, drinking themselves stupid before continuing their rampage. As they set fire to buildings around the city, a conflagration rapidly spread out of control. The fires burned fiercely all that night and the next day, only ending in the evening of 2/20. Of Osaka's 620 neighborhoods, 112 were burned to the ground, with a loss of 3,389 houses. Tragically, the fires quickly engulfed the very warehouses that the rebels had planned to empty and distribute to the people. A total of 30,000–40,000 koku of rice was destroyed.

The city authorities sent troops from Osaka castle at noon on 2/19. The two sides, neither of which had experienced combat, fought each other through the afternoon. Ōshio's men were mostly farmers and townsmen, and, despite their training in Ōshio's academy, they were quickly cowed by the large forces of city troops. Through the course of the afternoon most of Ōshio's supporters melted away, and by evening the rebellion was over. Ōshio and his son fled the city.[25]

For several weeks, Ōshio and his followers were the object of a massive manhunt. Although their exact movements are not known, it's believed that Ōshio and his adopted son Kakunosuke returned to Osaka four or five days after fleeing, and took shelter in a sympathizer's house, where they successfully stayed out of sight for a whole month, while Ōshio's fellow activists were rounded up or committed suicide. Eventually Ōshio's whereabouts were discovered, and government troops closed in on his hideout. Rather than submit to arrest, torture, and certain execution, Ōshio ignited the gunpowder he had been stockpiling, and he and his son perished in the flames. Their bodies, when removed from the ashes of the house, were unrecognizable.[26] Koume reported on his death on Tenpō 8 (1837)/3/29: "Ōshio Heihachi died on the twenty-fifth. It's said that he was surrounded in the house of a townsman, a seller of household goods or a stone carver or something, and as the police officers closed in on him, he set fire to the house. Some people say he burnt himself to death, others that he was shot. There are many rumors. In any case, he is dead. It's said that the townsman who helped him was also killed."

Around forty detainees were sent to Edo for an official investigation by the shogunal administration. The detainees came mostly from the more privileged classes: eleven were samurai, and all sixteen of the farmers were from wealthier families with the resources to send their sons to Osaka to study in Ōshio's school. For example, one of Ōshio's chief followers, Hashimoto Chūbei, came from the family of a village headman with agricultural land yielding 50 koku of rice, and extensive interests in regional commerce. The samurai members of the band, meanwhile, were generally junior officers within the Osaka administration.[27]

The significance of the Ōshio rebellion lies not so much in the high rank of Ōshio and the other samurai rebels relative to the poor townsmen in whose cause they took up arms, as in their low rank within the samurai hierarchy. No matter how talented they were, men like Ōshio were helpless to affect the course of events. Other than in a few exceptional cases, their hereditary status precluded them from senior administrative positions within the domains or the shogunal administration. From Ōshio's perspective, he had to watch while greedy, inefficient, and corrupt hereditary officials squandered the resources that might have been used to help the people. Throughout Japan there were thousands of talented, well-educated junior officials like him, seething with frustration as they watched the Tokugawa polity fail to fulfil its basic duties to keep the people safe. In terms of education, wealth, and social status, Koume's own family were not so different.

Koume's final word on the topic was a riddle. On Tenpō 8 (1837)/3/18, several weeks after Ōshio Heihachirō's insurrection but before the news of his death, Koume reported: "According to some people, Ōshio Heihachi wrote a statement in which he says: 'Try adding "one" (ichi, 一) to "rice" (kome, 米), and then try dividing that.' If you add them, you get 'come' (kuru, 来), and [if you divide that] you get Heihachi (平八). So in rice, you can find Heihachi."

The word play suggests that Ōshio's very identity is linked to the provision of rice for the people. It points to the awareness and perhaps even admiration of the people as well as to their humorous cynicism about the events unfolding around them. These sentiments, wrapped in clever word play, were circulating in the media variously known as *kyōka* (crazy verses), *senryū* (comic poems), *rakusho* (graffiti), and *rakushū* (comic poems). For those with few political rights and a limited stake in the political status quo, humor was an outlet to express their awareness of, but also detachment from, the goings-on of those on high.

Ōshio's protest highlighted some of the stresses affecting Japan after two centuries of peaceful economic growth. According to Ōshio, the samurai officials charged with bestowing "the benevolence that pervades all things" were instead "personages of low character, lacking basic moral virtues, totally lacking any human sensitivity." Meanwhile, lowly commoners who had cornered the market in commodities "live as if they were senior retainers of daimyo" and refuse to acknowledge the poverty for which they were themselves responsible, "instead dining on delicacies and feasting extravagantly."[28]

There is no evidence, though, that Koume and Hyōzō saw the strife in Osaka as a warning. Koume's concern was for the immediate threat to life and property. She received daily reports of the devastating fire and conflict in Osaka, a vital economic center for Kishū domain and all of western Japan. She expressed concern that the rebels might escape into Kishū, where it would be the domain's responsibility to apprehend them. Perhaps there was also a touch of excitement, as each day brought more news of the dramatic events. Other than in the riddle she quoted, Koume's mentions of Ōshio are mostly about the threat to law and order. She clearly saw him as a dangerous criminal.

STRANGE THINGS HEARD IN FOREIGN LANDS

The shogunate's inability—or unwillingness—to alleviate the suffering of the poor was not the only sign of stress in the system, for those with eyes to see it. The looming threat of foreign powers with powerful navies also hung over the land. In the midst of the dramas and tragedies of the middle months of 1837, Koume spent three months copying a sixteen-volume narrative of travel in Siberia and Russia, first written in 1803. The title was *Kankai ibun* (Strange things heard in foreign lands). Aside from her diary, it is one of the major works of Koume to survive to the present day.

The book recounts the narrative of the surviving crew members of the *Wakamiya-maru*, a merchant ship trading in lumber and rice along the northeast coast of Japan. In the final month of 1793, the ship with seventeen crew members was on a routine voyage from the northeastern town of Ishinomaki, in Sendai domain, to Edo. The *Wakamiya-maru* was designed to hug the shore as it made its way down the coast on its two-hundred-mile journey. But it was overtaken by a storm, its mast and rudder were broken, and it was swept out into the open sea.

The ship drifted for almost six months, the sailors surviving on fish they pulled from the ocean, the rice they were carrying, and rainwater. Finally, they ran aground on an island hundreds of miles to the north. Establishing themselves on shore as best they could, the crew endured a bitter Arctic winter until they were rescued by Russian fur traders, who took them to Okhotsk on the Siberian mainland. From there, they were taken overland to Yakutsk and then Irkutsk. There, they were astonished to find a small community of Japanese settlers, mostly former castaways themselves, who now worked as instructors in a Japanese language school that had been founded there in 1754. The sailors of the *Wakamiya-maru* remained in Irkutsk for the next eight years. Two of them died; four others converted to Christianity and settled permanently in the region.

In 1803 the remaining castaways were summoned to St. Petersburg. After a long overland journey across the vast expanse of Russia, they were greeted with a royal welcome. The city's aristocratic residents were curious about these exotic men from the East, inviting them to dinners and balls. They were given an audience by the young tsar, Alexander 1 (of *War and Peace* fame). And then they were offered passage home to Japan.

For the Russians, the castaways were a useful pawn. Returning them would be a goodwill gesture to the Japanese government, with which the Russians hoped to establish diplomatic and trade relations. And so, in the summer of 1803, four of the castaways boarded the 450-ton sloop *Nadezhda* for the long voyage back to Japan. They traveled via England, the Canary Islands, Brazil, Cape Horn, the Hawaiian Islands, and Kamchatka, finally landing in Nagasaki near the end of 1804.[29] The voyage was not an easy one, for passengers or crew. The ship's captain, Johann von Krusenstern, found his Japanese passengers to be "lazy, dirty in their persons, always ill-humored and passionate in the highest degree."[30]

Nor did the diplomatic mission go as planned. The Japanese government was resolutely opposed to any sort of ties beyond the tightly controlled relations that it had with Holland, China, and Korea. The shogunal authorities in Nagasaki treated their visitors with courtesy but firmly rebuffed their diplomatic overtures. After six months confined to their ship and, later, to a small compound in Nagasaki, the Russian envoy, Nikolai Rezanov, turned the castaways over to the authorities and left.[31] From there the sailors were sent to Edo where they were returned to officers of Sendai domain, their home province. Eventually they were taken back to Sendai, where they were detained and questioned about every detail of their shipwreck, sojourn in Russia, and return. Despite their generally low opinion of the "undeveloped and ignorant poor creatures" they were questioning, the interrogators (two scholars of "Dutch studies") produced a remarkably detailed narrative of the sailors' ordeal, and the most complete account to date of Russia's geography and society.[32] Because of the inherent interest of the material it contained, their handwritten report soon took on a life of its own, being copied and recopied by scholars and officials throughout Japan.

Koume mentions in her diary that she began copying this work on 5/23. Wakayama was a peaceful provincial city, far from Japan's political center. Kawai Koume was not politically connected, nor was she an activist, nor did she have any background in foreign affairs. Why did Koume, an artist and household manager, spend almost three months copying an account of events that had taken place thousands of miles away and forty years earlier? Koume's work speaks to the interest among the Wakayama scholarly community in books on the world beyond Japan—a world that had been largely off-limits to Japanese people for more than two hundred years. Their interest was strong enough to make Koume and her husband think it worthwhile to devote her time, as well as the expense of ink and paper, to copying a borrowed manuscript for their home library.[33]

The reasons for their interest were not just academic. Throughout the eighteenth century, Russian administrators, military strategists, explorers, and traders had been consolidating Russia's presence in Northeast Asia. It was becoming increasingly clear that Russia and Japan shared common borders, though their exact location had yet to be defined. Russian explorers were mapping Hokkaido, and Russian warships increasingly appeared on the Japanese coast. The Russians were not the only ones arriving on Japanese shores. Russian and British imperial expansion in East Asia, the growing China trade, and the rapid growth of the

American whaling industry were quickly turning the Pacific into a space of global competition: the Japanese, as David Howell argued, were "drawn into the early modern Pacific World."[34] In 1803 two American ships anchored in Nagasaki in the hope of securing trading rights. In 1808 a British warship demanded at gunpoint to be supplied with water and provisions. After Mito domain discovered in 1824 that some of its coastal villages were engaging in barter trade with foreign fishing and whaling ships and their crews, the shogunate issued an order to fire on sight at all foreign vessels approaching Japanese ports.[35] In July 1837, while Koume was still copying *Kankai ibun*, Japanese batteries fired on an American merchant ship, the *Morrison*, as it tried to dock in the bay of Edo to barter three Japanese castaways for trading rights. It was becoming clear by the mid-1830s that foreign ships, both commercial and military, were not going to stop appearing on Japanese shores. The policy of international isolation, which had helped the Tokugawa government maintain peace in Japan for more than two hundred years, was starting to erode. Koume's activity copying the *Kankai ibun* manuscript perhaps reveals her family's awareness of Japan's increasingly uncertain position in the modern world of nationalist expansion and imperialism.

Did Koume and Hyōzō connect the dots and conclude that the Tokugawa system was under threat? Surely not. Koume betrays no suspicion that in her own lifetime, the political and social order that had brought peace and a measure of security to Japan over a period of more than two hundred years was to collapse so completely. The Tokugawa system had brought enormous benefits of peace and stability to Japan. Its authority was still unquestioned; it was impossible indeed to imagine an alternative. And yet it is remarkable in Koume's account of this year that—at least with the benefit of hindsight—the cracks in the foundations of Tokugawa rule were already so visible: the economic inequalities thrown into sharp relief by the Tenpō famine; the growing anger and frustration of lower-level samurai and elite merchants and farmers; and the increasingly evident threat of technologically superior foreign aggression. Koume's diary is missing for the years 1838–1847. When it resumed, it would open a window onto a new world of radical destabilization and conflict that would ultimately sweep away the entire Tokugawa political and social system.

3

IN THE SHADOW OF THE BLACK SHIPS

THE KAEI PURGE

The troubles began with a local event: the illness and death of the former daimyo, Tokugawa Harutomi. Harutomi had been the effective ruler of Kishū domain for Koume's entire life. He had retired as daimyo in 1824, at age fifty-three, but he retained his control over the domain for the next thirty years.

Part of the reason for his continuing grip on the domain was the weakness of his successors. His immediate heir, Nariyuki, was the son of a shogun and had little interest in Kishū affairs. Preferring to live an extravagant life in Edo, he spent only six of his twenty-two years of office in Kishū. Nariyuki's successor, Narikatsu, died after only three years in office, at age thirty, and Narikatsu's successor, Tokugawa Yoshitomi, was only three years old when he succeeded to the position of daimyo in 1849.

Another key to Harutomi's continued grip on power was his control of the domain's two main revenue-producing institutions. Tax rice alone had never been enough to support the expenses of the domain, which included the heavy cost of its retainer stipends; the cost of maintaining the pomp and rituals required by the Tokugawa daimyo, including the maintenance of large estates in Edo; and the lavish lifestyles of several of the daimyo. The domain began introducing cost-saving measures as early as 1646, when it reduced the rice stipends payable to its retainers. But it also began borrowing from wealthy merchant houses and others, piling up heavy debts by the start of the eighteenth century. In 1705 the fifth daimyo, Tokugawa Yoshimune, began the process of mending the domain's finances. He passed a series of laws that enforced frugality by samurai and commoners and encouraged industry and trade. Yoshimune also introduced major land reclamation projects to expand the domain's productive base. His policies were partially successful in reversing the deficits that had plagued the domain administration, and when he moved to Edo to become shogun in 1716, he began implementing similar reforms throughout the shogunal administration.

When Harutomi became daimyo in 1789, he adopted a variety of policies to build on Yoshimune's legacy. Some were successful; others aroused bitter resentment. Under Harutomi's leadership, the domain increased taxes on commodities including rice and sake. It tightened supervision of villages, implementing inspections to make sure that newly improved land was assessed and taxed. Harutomi spread the pain to his samurai retainers, who were one of the heaviest drains on the domain's resources. Starting in 1806, the domain once again began reducing stipends. Officially, the cut was a form of savings plan for the samurai themselves: the domain would hold the rice in escrow, either as a loan to the domain or as repayment of accumulated debts to the domain.[1]

Harutomi's most notable success was his development of two obscure institutions, the domain investment office (*oshiirekata*) and the Kumano shrines lending office (*Kumano sanzan kashitsuke*), into financial powerhouses on a national scale.

The domain investment office was founded in 1700, with the goal of supporting the regional economy of Kishū's poor mountain villages by selling their produce in the region's commercial centers. It was conceived as a welfare measure to help relieve the deep poverty of the region, but over time the advance of trade became more for the profit of the domain than for the benefit of the locals. In the financial reforms of 1806 the office greatly expanded, establishing branches throughout the domain, with sales offices in Edo, Osaka, Kyoto, and Sakai. The office effectively became controller and broker for the domain's trade. And its products, which had originally been mostly lumber-related, expanded to all sorts of agricultural products as well as manufactures, including charcoal, textiles, and soy sauce. In addition to its trading profits, the office also imposed a variety of taxes and fees on producers, so that by the early nineteenth century it had, ironically, become a major burden for the agricultural and manufacturing producers of the domain—but a major income source for the domain itself.

The Kumano shrines lending office had started as a small fund to support the maintenance of the buildings and facilities of the three major shrines of southern Kishū, which were a popular pilgrimage destination. Over time the endowment had increased with the gifts of benefactors, and from the 1830s Harutomi and his staff began investing its capital in moneylending. At its peak, the fund's capital reached 200,000 ryō, making it one of Japan's most important financial institutions. Its main office was in the domain's compound in the Shiba district of Edo, and it had branch offices in Osaka, Hyogo, Kyoto, Otsu, Nara, and Sakai as well as Wakayama, Shingū, and Hikata. Its main business activity was moneylending to daimyo, wealthy merchants, and temples and shrines, with interest at 10 percent monthly. If payments were late, the office was backed by the power and authority of the Tokugawa shogunate, which had granted it special status in light of its ostensible mission of protecting some of Japan's greatest shrines.[2]

Although Harutomi was successful in improving the domain's finances (and also in financing his own lavish lifestyle), his financial innovations came at a heavy cost. The social inequities of growing wealth among the merchant and landowning classes, and increasing dispossession and poverty among the laboring classes, began to threaten the domain's social fabric. The tax burden was so high that many poorer peasants were forced to sell their land and make a living instead as day laborers. A failed harvest in 1823 triggered widespread unrest. In the sixth month, an army of almost 100,000 peasants marched on Wakayama, beating drums and blowing on conch shells. The domain mobilized its foot soldiers and deployed musket brigades and artillery, blocking the routes into the town and promising a response if the peasants would submit their demands in writing. In the end, the domain ignored most of their demands, and, following an investigation, it arrested three hundred instigators of the rebellion, putting thirty-three of them to death.

The uprising in 1823 was the greatest threat to the domain's authority in two hundred years. It was also a damning indictment of Harutomi's policies, which had succeeded in enriching his coffers but had amplified the growing divide between wealthy landowners and merchants and destitute peasants and laborers. In the wake of the rebellion, Harutomi resigned as a gesture of responsibility, though he remained the de facto ruler of Kishū until his death in 1853.[3]

During the 1840s, Harutomi's chief administrators were Yamanaka Toshinobu, a high-ranking retainer, and Date Chihiro, a brilliant scholar and manager who came from a middle-ranking samurai family and had risen to prominence through his own accomplishments. Yamanaka was of Harutomi's generation, but Date was a relatively young man. In 1844, at age forty-two, Date had taken control of the domain's two key financial offices, and he had presided over a rapid expansion of their activities. Date was said to be a born salesman. According to one account, on a visit to Edo he had noticed the popularity of a yellow cloth that was in fashion that year. When he got back to Kishū, Date took samples and had the cotton weavers of Wakayama imitate it. He sent a large shipment to Osaka and threw a big party for all the prominent merchants of the city, entertaining them with geisha dressed in this new fabric. He also hired a famous kabuki actor to attend the party dressed in yellow and perform a dance extolling the virtues of the material.[4]

Koume and Hyōzō had some personal connections to these leaders. Hyōzō was private tutor to Yamanaka's son, attending him in the Yamanaka family mansion. The Kawai family often received gifts from the Yamanaka family, and on one occasion Koume sent a gift of fifteen paintings "for the young people in the family."

When the elderly Yamanaka died in the ninth month of Kaei 5 (1852), Harutomi's enemies struck a lightning blow against Harutomi's administrative leaders. The anti-Harutomi faction spread rumors that Yamanaka and others had been caught out in financial misdeeds. On Kaei 5/12/12, Date Chihiro was stripped of his positions and his stipend and sent to confinement in the Tanabe castle, on the charge of "suspicious handling of goods." As he wrote in his memoir, "Transported there in a bamboo cage like a common criminal, I felt as if a mountain wind had blown me, an autumn leaf, down to the bottom of a dark valley."[5] The chief priest of the Kumano shrine, Tamaki Nui, was sent to jail in Shingū. A few days later, Date's adopted son Gorō and other family members were exiled. Only Date's wife, daughters, and young son, Munemitsu, age nine, were allowed to remain in Wakayama. Even Chihiro's father was stripped of his rank and imprisoned in Tamaru castle in Ise, where he died later in the year.

Date and his associates were accused of profiting from the money flowing through their hands, living extravagant lifestyles quite unfitting for their lowly rank. There is some justification for the accusations. In his own memoirs, Chihiro described "the pleasures he had enjoyed in the Gion entertainment area of Kyoto."[6] After their downfall, lurid stories quickly spread about the outrageous extravagance of the disgraced officials. Date was said to have a pond underneath his house filled with koi fish, so that the entire house remained cool throughout the summer, while Tamaki was said to take baths in sugared water.[7]

Koume's diary is missing for Kaei 5 and only picks up again on New Year's Day of Kaei 6. The purge of Date and his followers was in full swing. On Kaei 6 (1853)1/9, Koume reported that the town's merchants and artisans had been left with large unpaid debts as a result of the extravagant spending of Date and his followers. On 1/21 she wrote: "It's said that Date embezzled 170,000 ryō." Koume also transcribed a satirical poem that was circulating in Wakayama:

> Chū no ji wo wasureta take no suzume dono
> Odori ga sugite ami no norimono
> Lord bamboo sparrow has forgotten how to write "loyalty"
> After the dancing, a meshed palanquin

This was a play on the Date family crest, which included the characters for bamboo and sparrow. The "meshed palanquin" was the cage used to transport Date into exile.

Koume was extraordinarily interested in the purge of Date and his followers. In addition to her diary, Koume kept notebooks in which she copied news, rumors, satire, and other information she received on the scandal. She copied most without attribution, but it is likely she was copying broadsheets circulating in the consumer market. For example, when Koume told the story of the craftsmen and sake merchants who went unpaid owing to Date's arrest, she used rhetorical flourishes that differ markedly from her normal writing style, suggesting she was copying from a printed source. The satirical poems she copied also must have been circulating in writing. In her notebooks, Koume copied in full the text of a *chobokure*, a humorous monologue meant to be recited by a traveling entertainer (*yomiuri*) but also printed and available for purchase.

> Hey, hey, everyone, listen, don't you want to hear about Chikugo [Yamanaka Toshinobu]'s behavior? It was really bad. Now, at first he supported all sorts of performing arts, whether old or new. He followed all the rules, he gave money, he followed the samurai code, and he encouraged everyone to exert themselves. But then in recent years he changed. He lived only for himself, surrounding himself with greedy men regardless of their rank or experience. Isn't that foolish?[8]

Amid the drama of the purge, a bigger drama intruded. Harutomi himself had fallen ill. Starting in the final weeks of Kaei 5 (1852), the inspectors (*metsuke*) began issuing regular bulletins on the state of his health. At year's end, both retainers and townsmen were prohibited from holding the normal New Year's festivities, and the area around the castle was declared a quiet zone in which conversation and bright lights were not allowed. On New Year's Day Koume wrote "Today no one came to offer New Year's greetings. Only ten or so people wrote anything in the notebook in front of the house." Three days later she added: "After consulting, the decision was made not to exchange New Year's greetings this year. Only ten or so passed by the front gate. We left a greeting book outside, but not a single samurai wrote in it. Moreover, today was Yūsuke's birthday, but we just made celebratory rice [with red beans] at home, without inviting any of our neighbors." (Yūsuke was Koume's son Iwaichirō's adult name. Like most young men, he changed it on reaching full adulthood around the age of twenty.)

In the following days, the retired lord's condition worsened. On Kaei 6 (1853)1/17, Koume wrote: "At the eighth hour [around 2:00 p.m.] a circulating notice came. Since the Lord of the First Rank [Harutomi] is sick, there will be gathering [of retainers] tomorrow at the fourth hour [10 a.m.] to enquire after his health." Hyōzō did not attend that gathering, but three days later he was summoned to another audience to "enquire" after the retired daimyo's health. Just as Hyōzō was setting off for the event, "Kishi Kakunosuke brought another notice. It announced that immediate attendance was required at the castle. We passed it on to Iwahashi, and [Hyōzō] left soon after."

Later that day, Koume copied an urgent bulletin from the domain administration: "The Lord of the First Rank has been unwell, and was unable to recover. This evening at the hour of the tiger, he passed away. His Buddhist name will be Shunkyōin. [Signed] Tanaka Kyūemon."

The city was plunged into deep (and compulsory) mourning. On 1/22 Koume reported: "Fine weather. Everything is quiet, no voices can be heard. Yesterday, all the neighborhoods closed their gates in the evening. It is said that there has been nothing like this before."

The funeral was held on 1/26, at the Tokugawa family mausoleum in Chōhōji. The streets along the route of the procession were strictly patrolled. Unless they had official business, townsmen were not permitted to go out. "Woke at the 6th hour (6 a.m.)," wrote Koume of her husband's movements, "and dressed [in formal clothes]."

> Before the 5th hour [8 a.m.] proceeded to the Nishihama palace to see off the procession. Yūsuke went to invite [Iwahashi] Tetsunosuke. Stopped in front of Lord Kano's house to watch. The orders are that no one should be out, but many people were out watching, even women.... The procession was 6 or 7 *chō* in length [700–800 meters]. At the head of the procession was Wagōin [Harutomi's consort]. The coffin was carried in a palanquin, but not covered in white. It was just like a normal funeral procession. My husband paid his respects at the garden entrance of the Nishihama palace. There were thirty-six ladies in waiting there, all dressed in white.

The next day the shops were finally allowed to open, although noisy activities such as construction and music-making were still not allowed.

Harutomi had been eighty-one years old. He was the only real ruler Koume and Hyōzō had ever known, and he commanded enormous respect and affection from both samurai retainers and the townspeople of Wakayama. The solemn ceremonies and displays of mourning were a sincere reflection of the emotion many were feeling at the loss of this commanding figure.

Except that unknown to Koume and the townspeople of Wakayama, Harutomi had already been dead for almost two months. His sickness and death as described by Koume were an elaborate fiction.

Such fictions were not unusual. Luke Roberts has described numerous examples in which the senior retainers hid the death of a daimyo or top-ranking official, sometimes for years. Often, the reason was to ensure that a suitable heir was in place once the death was officially announced. The fiction embraced not only the daimyo's subjects—both commoners and lower-ranking samurai—but also the shogunate, which had to certify the domain's succession plans. The officers of the shogun were often willing collaborators: as long as the rituals and formalities were observed, they were willing to turn a blind eye to the domain's machinations to ensure a smooth succession. Roberts describes one example in which the shogunate sent a senior official, three retainers, and five doctors who joined two of the daimyo's own doctors in the daimyo's sick room. The doctors "examined" the daimyo (who was hidden behind a screen) and pronounced that he was of sound mind, although "he suffers from coldness and has trouble eating." This was a major understatement: the daimyo had been dead for more than three weeks.[9]

In the case of Harutomi, the issue was not succession (Harutomi had passed on the family headship almost thirty years back). Rather, it was a mammoth internecine struggle, which revealed the castle and the daimyo's court to be a viper's nest of intrigue. During the decades in which he exercised control over the domain, Harutomi and his closest advisors had made some bitter enemies. Chief among them was the lord of Shingū domain, Mizuno Tadanaka. Shingū was a subordinate domain within Kishū, and Mizuno was a hereditary advisor to the Kishū daimyo. Mizuno had been sidelined by Harutomi, but he had been a father-figure to the domain's sixteen-year-old daimyo, Tokugawa Yoshitomi. He was also well-connected among the Edo elite.

When both Yamanaka and Harutomi died within a month of each other, Mizuno seized his opportunity. Hiding the fact of Harutomi's death, Mizuno had his agents round up Date, Tamaki, and their followers, accuse them of corruption, and imprison them—all in the names of Harutomi and Yoshitomi. It was a brilliantly orchestrated coup that played on the resentments of the Kishū retainers, who had been forced to tighten their belts in the name of economy and frugality even as they witnessed senior officials leading extravagant lifestyles.

Koume had little sympathy for Date, Tamaki, or the senior officials accused of corruption. But the purge quickly spread to much lower levels of the domain bureaucracy. Over the next several months almost two hundred officials were arrested, demoted, or transferred, and thirty were imprisoned, exiled, or otherwise punished. On Kaei 6 (1853)/6/7, Koume described how a friend, Yamaguchi Hyōma, rushed to hide his assets as the officers approached to arrest him. He hid his money under a pile of letters in a box, and he "gave" many of his wife and daughters' valuable kimonos to the servants, for safekeeping. Yamaguchi was arrested and confined to a three-mat (10-square-meter) room, while his son was dismissed from his job in the Kumano shrines' finance office in Osaka. On 6/17 Koume wrote:

> Last night Miyazaki, Noguchi, Hashimoto, and Nishioka were all exiled to 20 *ri* outside the capital. They were sent to Shimizu, while Nagasawa Seiemon was placed in the custody of his parents, and his stipend confiscated. Yamanaka [the son of Harutomi's chief advisor] has had his income reduced by 1,000 koku. Ochiai and nine others will be punished, of whom three are *metsuke*. This was on the evening of the sixteenth day. And on the evening the seventeenth day, Yamanaka Tokunosuke and Atsumi were also included. No one knows what will happen now.

THE FOREIGN THREAT

What actually happened over the following months was as frightening as it was unexpected. The events that were to rock Kishū and all Japan came not from the tortuous internal politics of the domain, but from an unexpected and deeply alarming outside force: the United States of America.

On Kaei 6/6/15 (July 20, 1853), Koume reported on an uneventful day. It was "very hot." She dispensed sake and food to her Umemoto in-laws, Tanaka Zenzō, and others. Hyōzō, with Yasubei as his retainer, went to a moon-viewing party on the riverbank. The only event that was at all out of the ordinary was the arrival of a circular notice from the castle, announcing: "Recently French ships have arrived, and everyone is to be alert." As little as Koume and Hyōzō expected it, this event was to send a shockwave through the domain that was to dominate their lives for months to come.

News bulletins soon clarified that the ships were not French but American. Commodore Matthew Perry and his fleet of warships had traveled around the world from Norfolk, Virginia, via Cape Town, Colombo,

Singapore, and Hong Kong, arriving on July 8 in the Bay of Edo, within view of the wooden houses and castle ramparts of the shogun's capital, to demand the abandonment of Japan's isolation policy and the initiation of diplomatic relations. The government had dealt with repeated incursions by foreign ships but had never faced an organized naval force showing up in Edo Bay and refusing all efforts by the Japanese to send them elsewhere. Perry backed up his refusal with a volley by his ships' seventy-three guns—ostensibly in observance of Independence Day.

The overwhelming superiority of the Americans' weapons—Perry made it clear that he could destroy Edo without ever needing to land a soldier—woke the Japanese authorities to their vulnerability. Wakayama was hundreds of miles from Edo, but the arrival of the black ships stirred up a hornet's nest in the castle town. Just two days after her initial report, Koume wrote in alarm of the erupting crisis. "Again and again, the foreign ships are causing disturbances. As a result, forces are being mobilized to resist them. The foreigners asked to lease Oshima off the Izu coast, and if this is refused, there will be conflict. They have ninety ships carrying three thousand men each, and the ships are said to look like mountains." The details are wildly inaccurate. Perry had only four ships and a small body of marines. But (allowing for the twelve days it took for news to arrive from Edo) the effect on Kishū domain was immediate: "The thirty men of the Kanazawa . . . troop have been mobilized, and in response to the situation seventy suits of armor have been issued, two for each man. The cost of these is being loaned to the men. They are being loaned 10 ryō each. Many men are receiving them. Shishido, Watanabe Ikkaku, and Chimoto are all departing this evening. Lord Kuno has also been summoned. They gathered in the Chrysanthemum Room. It was just like in a book. After making their preparations they will set off for Edo."

Two weeks later, on 7/2, Koume reported on preparations in the Edo region: "If something happens, then beacons will be lit. In that case, the fire alarms will be sounded and on that signal, all daimyo of 10,000 koku or greater, without exception, will be called up." Meanwhile in Kishū, many of Hyōzō's colleagues in the domain school were being mobilized: "First Iwahashi, and then Tanaka, Noro, Asanosuke, and others have been called up."

On 7/8 Koume received accurate news of the death of the shogun on Kaei 6/6/22 (July 27, 1853), but a wildly inaccurate account of the cause.

According to rumor, he had been at the top of a tower, watching the British fleet through a telescope, when he had fallen and died. Koume also reported inaccurate rumors about the demands of the foreigners. "Four English ships have arrived, and another fifty have been seen approaching at a distance of fifty *ri*. . . . The English ships are said to be requesting 50,000 koku of rice per year. As yet, they have received no response. Here and there, ships continue to appear occasionally. The government is making rigorous preparations."

The next day, Koume reported two scurrilous riddles:

> Someone left a pole for carrying a wooden chest [*nagamochi*: the word, used to describe stout chests, literally means long-lasting] at the gate of the shogun's castle as a riddle. After five days or so, someone solved the riddle. It's that the *kubō* [the word means shogun but could also mean "a pole at the shogunal court"] has no *nagamochi* [i.e., will not last long]. It was extremely disrespectful. Later, two [*ni-hon*] daikon radishes were found, each with moxa applied to it. The meaning was that Japan [Nihon] is in great difficulty [*daikonkyu*, which can also mean a daikon receiving moxa treatment]. They are well done, but certainly insolent.

Although Koume comments on the disrespect and insolence of the authors of these riddles, her enjoyment of their cleverness is palpable. No matter how closely an issue affected the vital interests of her domain or of Japan, Koume was always interested in witty or clever satirical verses or riddles, most likely circulating in underground broadsheets.

The inaccuracy of Koume's information is surprising, given that news she received on shogunal affairs was often accurate. She does not specify her sources, but it seems likely she was listening to rapidly spreading rumors, as well as reading some of the enormous flood of printed and handwritten materials circulating in the immediate aftermath of Perry's visit. The number of printed broadsheets (estimated by William Steele at five hundred, with an average run of two thousand, for a total of one million sheets) is testament to the deep alarm felt by the people of Edo in particular at the arrival of the foreign ships.[10] According to Steele, the broadsheets were "filled with inaccurate information," but the reality of the emergency was clear. The shogunal government ordered the people of Edo to prepare for an invasion, and "the broad streets of the shogun's capital are packed with people running about in panic as they carry furniture and possessions. Such a state of things breeds wild rumors and the people have no peace of mind."[11] Ōta Tomiyasu details the flood of information received by the Hayashi family of Akao village in Musashi province. Noting the extremely large volume, Ōta concludes that in the early days after Perry's arrival, much of the news the family head, Hayashi Shinkai, received was by word of mouth, and it was inaccurate. But over time, much more accurate information arrived in the form of written communications from reliable sources, including shogunal government officials.[12] The news reported by Koume follows a similar pattern: wild rumors in the early days, followed by more authoritative information.

Given the death of the shogun, Perry recognized the impossibility of concluding an immediate treaty. On Kaei 6/7/20 (August 24, 1853), he withdrew his ships from Edo, promising to return in a year to receive a reply to the American president's letter demanding the opening of diplomatic relations. The immediate crisis was over, but the incident had revealed Japan's deep vulnerability. The challenge of securing Japan's extensive coastline was overwhelming, and it underlined the weakness of Japan's fragmented political system. Each domain was responsible for its own defense, but a breach in one domain could affect the entire country. As a Tokugawa family domain, Kishū was obliged to set an example in the installation of robust new defenses along its coast. But its implementation highlights the unpreparedness of the domains to deal with the threat posed by a sophisticated modern navy.

Although the retainers of Kishū were nominally warriors, they had seen no military conflict for generations. The teachers in the domain school were scholars, thoroughly unprepared for fighting. But within the school, the burning topic was how to prepare to fight the foreigners. Suddenly, teachers and students were clamoring to purchase armor and weapons. The choices available to them were the tools of conflict from the sixteenth century, when Japan had last been at war: suits of armor, swords, bows and arrows, pikes, and muskets. And even these were enormously expensive relative to the straitened incomes of the lower-ranking samurai.

Kishū domain authorized immediate loans of 10 ryō for each samurai family, to be used for purchasing armor. Domain officials, including several of the teachers at the domain school, drew up detailed defense plans including building coastal batteries and blocking the river mouth. The domain's younger samurai plunged themselves into intensive training in swordsmanship and gunnery. Yūsuke and Hyōzō both rushed to purchase armor and weapons. Hyōzō spent over 12 ryō on his purchases of sword, helmet, and accessories, borrowing some of the money short-term from friends and the balance long-term from the domain. In the seventh month, the domain gave 100 ryō each to the domain's schools of swordsmanship, spearmanship, archery, horseback fighting, cannonry, and military studies. The Gakushūkan also received a grant of 100 ryō, to produce scholarship on military arts. Five of the domain school's teachers, including the head of the school, Yamamoto Hikojūrou, were assigned to senior roles in coastal defense preparations.

From the ninth month, Yūsuke, now twenty years old, began a program of intensive military training in gunnery, archery, and spear-fighting. On Kaei 6 (1853)/10/13, Koume reported: "Yūsuke went for gunnery practice. Tamenosuke followed later. Yūsuke didn't hit a single target. Tamenosuke hit one." Yūsuke also began purchasing armor piecemeal—a helmet from one seller, a sword from another. The cost was high: just for his helmet, he paid over 7 ryō (Kaei 6/10/19).

The domain established thirty-two coastal guard posts along its extensive coastline, mobilizing six thousand soldiers to serve in them. All samurai retainers holding official rank were included in the draft. Hyōzō, sixty-one years old and with no military experience, was mobilized along with everyone else. He was assigned to a brigade under the command of Lord Miura, a young man of twenty whom Hyōzō had taught in private tutoring sessions just a few years earlier. The brigade was assigned to the stretch of coastline in the Kada district, a few miles north of the castle town. Unlike those sent to guard the southern coastline, Hyōzō's assignment was close enough to home that he could continue to live in Wakayama. Several of Hyōzō's close relatives joined him in the unit: his cousins Enomoto Seizaemon, Uchimura Matajūrō, and Naitō Jingozaemon. The brigade was equipped with three gun batteries, with two large, one middle-sized, and ten small cannons. It comprised 852 soldiers, of whom 152 had firearms of some sort. The rest were armed with just swords and spears. Many of these foot soldiers were farmers and fishermen. There were not enough samurai to meet the manpower needs of this military emergency, so the domain created a special unit of commoners, called the *uragumi* or unofficial army. All villagers between the ages of fifteen and sixty were declared eligible for the draft.[13]

Military service was not the only duty required of Hyōzō. In the seventh month, the shogunal government in Edo issued an unusual request. Usually, the Edo government was anxious to assert its authority over the domains, and it tended to lead by command, not consultation. But the arrival of the black ships threw it into a completely new situation. The shogunate was unable to defend the entire Japanese coastline using its own resources. It needed the consent of the domains to mount an effective strategy against the foreign threat. The chief minister in Edo requested all the daimyo to submit memorials stating their opinion about how the government should respond to Perry's demand. On Kaei 6 (1853)/7/20, Koume wrote: "The shogun has ordered Confucian scholars to submit their ideas without reservation. The teachers at the school have been ordered to write their ideas by the twenty-seventh day, so they gathered to discuss the matter. They divided up a sheaf of paper and copied the American letter. Luckily Yūsuke showed up so he too copied the letter." Koume commented on one suggestion on 8/22: "Some people are saying we should send an ambassador to the foreign countries and ask them to wait thirty years. That would be fine, but it would be enormously expensive for the authorities, although one couldn't say it's impossible."

Hyōzō and his colleagues spent a month of intensive work over the seventh and eighth months of 1853 working on a response to the shogunate's request, and the memorial they produced was sent on to the shogunal authorities in Edo. Their letter has not survived, but of the sixty responses the shogunate received, two-thirds advocated some degree of compliance with the demands of the foreigners for foreign trade and diplomatic relations. The remaining third called on the shogunate to defend the existing system. Given the closeness of the Kishū Tokugawa family to the shogun, it is likely that the domain would have supported the shogunal government's approach, which leaned toward accommodation of the foreigners' request.

As a gesture of thanks for the scholars' work on this response, the domain gave the school a gift of 100 ryō, although, as Koume commented on 8/22, "this will be given to the accounting office, and the interest is to be used each year to purchase weapons.... If you divide up the annual interest it comes to 50 monme per person. There's not much we can do with that." Hyōzō, though, was subsequently rewarded for his work on the memorial with a salary increase to 30 koku and promoted to the military rank of *orusuimonogashira* (musketeer captain of the palace guard). Following this effort, the scholars started work on a *Chronicle of the Foreign Ships* (*Isenki*), which was completed the following year.[14]

Regardless of the shogunate's response, the arrival of the black ships was a wake-up call for Kishū to prepare for its own defense. As one of the domain elders, Abe Ise no Kami, wrote in a memorial dated Kaei 6 (1853)/11/1:

> Many opinions have been submitted in response to the letter from the United States of America, and after careful consideration, although there are many differing opinions, they can be reduced to two words: Peace? Or War? However, among the various opinions, there is agreement that even in peacetime, the preparations for our coastal defense are far from complete. Next year [the black ships] will return, and they will demand a response to their letter. Even if we respond that we would like to manage the matter peacefully, they may not permit that. If we are not prepared for that eventuality, it will be a disgrace to the domain. And so we must loyally throw ourselves with wholehearted commitment into the defense of our coast. We can then observe the actions of [the black ships], and if they should open hostilities, then all of us, high and low, old and young, must expend all our strength and perseverance in this loyal endeavor.[15]

In the twelfth month, Koume added her own patriotic commentary on the turbulent year, in the form of a poem:

> Kage ni nomi kakuroi mosede hi no moto ni
> Kitaraba tokuru Amerika no fune
> If they stop hiding in shadows and come into the light of the land
> Of the rising sun, they will melt, those ships from America.[16]

This is one of the few places in the diary that Koume expresses patriotism not for her domain of Kishū, but for an imagined national community of "the land of the rising sun," or Japan. Throughout Japan, the sense of a national crisis created by the arrival of aggressive foreigners, as well as the insistence of the foreigners on dragging Japan into the system of nation-states, helped foster the foundations of a national identity.

The following year Koume reported on another upheaval in Wakayama: this time, a natural disaster. On Ansei 1/11/4 (December 23, 1854), a massive earthquake, with a magnitude of 8.4 on the Richter scale, struck the Tōkai region of Japan. The earthquake triggered a tsunami. Izu and Suruga provinces (now Shizuoka prefecture) bore the brunt of the earthquake, with the Izu Peninsula the worst hit. The Treaty of Amity and Commerce (1854), signed just nine months earlier between Japan and the United States, had opened the port town of Shimoda as the site of diplomatic relations and shipping supplies. Shimoda was engulfed by the tsunami and virtually destroyed. A Russian fleet, which had arrived a few days earlier to begin negotiations for a treaty similar to the American one, was sunk in the disaster.

The Tōkai coast of Japan is one section of the Nankai Trough, an interconnected series of faults that often trigger one another. Thirty-two hours after the Tōkai quake, a second quake of similar magnitude struck the Nankai region, including Shikoku and Kishū. Once again, a tsunami followed. Koume's diary for 1854 has not survived, but an account that she wrote of the earthquakes has survived in a separate group of papers.

> A little after the fifth hour [9 a.m., on 11/4] we felt a big shaking, and we ran out into the back garden in bare feet. The roof on the west side of the house abruptly crumbled, and tiles fell to the ground. The most shocking and terrifying moments lasted for about the time it would take to take five or six puffs of a pipe. Yūsuke, Manjirō, and the others were on their way back from Toyama's house. They had gone about 2 chō (220 meters) and were in Yakatamachi [when the earthquake hit]. The girls came running out of the houses holding hands so they wouldn't fall. While we were still terrified [from this experience] the next day, the fifth, at the seventh hour [about 5 p.m.] another huge earthquake shook the ground. Once again we dashed out into the garden. The shaking was worse than the previous day—we could hardly stand up. While we were holding onto the trees [to keep our balance] we were startled by the crash of falling tiles from the second floor [the family had added this in 1847], and the eaves of the house collapsed. There was a crash like the sound of a cannon, and the noise reverberated seven or eight times. We had no idea

what the noise was. At first we thought it must be thunder. The sky had suddenly gone black—it was a sudden transformation like nothing we had ever experienced before. All we could do was call on the names of the Buddhas and kami, until eventually it stopped.

This quake was ten times stronger than yesterday's.... The sound of the nearby houses collapsing was enough to make your heart stop. We spent the whole night in the garden. We had not yet made the evening meal, and I brought a stove and earthenware pot out into the garden. It was terrifying just to set foot in the house, and I ran back out as fast as I could. We gathered some futons together, but as soon as we lay down the day broke. The ground shook five or six times before morning.

Apart from this single entry, there is no record of Koume's life from 1854 to 1858. With Iwaichirō's name-change to Yūsuke, Koume's responsibilities as mother came to an end. Yūsuke's role in the family increasingly came to resemble that of his father: as scholar, teacher (he was hired by the domain school sometime in the late 1850s), family representative in social and cultural affairs, and family head-in-waiting. Koume supported him in the same ways that she supported Hyōzō: recording his movements, entertaining his guests, and ensuring the smooth running of the household.

Yūsuke's position as adult heir to the family headship was cemented by his marriage, probably in 1857, to a young woman called Kuroda Kano. The Kawai and Kuroda families were already connected: Hyōzō and Kano's mother Kise were first cousins. Like the Kawai, the Kuroda family were in the lower-middle ranks of the samurai hierarchy, although they were not scholars. The Kuroda lived in the Kukenochō district, just a few blocks from the Kawai. Unlike the Kawai family, though, the Kuroda had been retainers of the Kishū daimyo since the establishment of the domain in the seventeenth century. The current family head was the sixth generation to take the name Kuroda Jinbei.[17]

In the same year, 1857, Hyōzō and Yūsuke were posted to Edo, where they stayed for a year.[18] We know nothing about their stay in Edo, but shortly after their return, Hyōzō was promoted to principal of the domain school, and Kano became pregnant with her first child. Her daughter, Kikue, was born at the end of 1858. Koume, who started the decade of the 1850s as a mother, ended it a grandmother.

CHOLERA IN THE CASTLE TOWN

As principal of the domain school, the sixty-four-year-old Hyōzō was now one of the presiding figures in the rich culture of the Wakayama scholarly community. At the school, his official duties included supervising the educational program; representing the school to the domain authorities; submitting memorials recommending promotions or celebrating cultural achievements; and participating in official cultural activities at the castle. Fifteen year earlier, in 1837, Hyōzō's duties had been light. On average he had teaching duty at the school once a week, reported for duty at the castle once a month, and attended a study group three times a month. Now, as principal, Hyōzō only occasionally reported for teaching duty at the school, but he performed five or six administrative and ritual duties per month at the school, and about five times a month he performed administrative duties at the castle. He also attended roughly double the number of study groups and work-related social events compared to his days as a junior scholar.[19] Hyōzō also expanded his lecturing at the houses of the great families of the domain: the Miura, Andō, and Kanō. These scholarly house-calls took place on average three times a month.[20]

By the time Hyōzō became principal, the domain school seems to have fallen into a state of decay. With around thirty scholars and administrators, the school was well-staffed—perhaps overstaffed—for its student body of around three hundred.[21] Most teachers showed up only occasionally for teaching duty. The educational emphasis at the school was on rote learning and memorization, and only a few scholarly students pursued Chinese studies with any passion. For most, the school with its exam system was just a required stop on the route to an official position in the domain.

On Kaei 4 (1851)/5/22, Koume had commented on the condition of the school, after the death of a valued teacher: "The school at present is in a deep decline. It's so sad. [Yamamoto] Shōtarō, for whom we had so much hope for the future, is dead, and with his death the principal's authority will inevitably decline. Itō Taizō has also been bedridden since last autumn.... Iwahashi [Tōzō] too has requested to withdraw from the school to deal with financial problems. Now the active ones are [Umemoto] Asanosuke, [Kuge] Umanosuke, [Egawa] Gennosuke, and Kishi [Junnosuke]. Not a single one of them can be relied on." The problems continued into Hyōzō's term as principal. Horinouchi Makoto, who attended a class at the school in 1865, wrote that out of nineteen students studying the reading of Chinese texts, only two or three asked any questions at all. There was no academic discussion or debate, and Horinouchi wrote that the class he attended felt more like a ceremony than a learning experience.[22]

Hyōzō faced the challenge not only of improving morale and restoring the prestige of the school's educational program but also of responding to a sea change in educational philosophy. For centuries the mastery of the Chinese classics had been considered necessary and sufficient for the domain retainers' academic education. But with the rise of radical new schools of thought, and with the challenge of Western science and technology, the focus of education was shifting.

Under Hyōzō's leadership, the domain did its best to respond to the challenge. It opened schools of national learning and "Dutch" (Western) studies in the 1850s, as well as an institute of military training, and Hyōzō moved to strengthen its programs in all these areas, and to greatly expand access to the core educational curriculum. In Keiō 2 (1866) the school, which had previously been open only to the sons of stipendiary retainers of the domain, was opened to academically inclined boys from farming and merchant families. The domain had come to understand that in the modern world, advancement must be based on ability and not on the accident of birth. To house its expanded student body, the school was moved to the location of the military training institute, on the hill known as Oka, just south of the castle walls. The original school buildings west of the castle became a Confucian temple.

Hyōzō's most burdensome task as school principal was his representation of the school to the domain administration. At least once a week, Hyōzō donned his formal clothes and went to the castle to submit petitions for the promotion and advancement of teachers and students, to receive official communications, and to consult about the policies of the school. For example, on Ansei 6 (1859)/5/15, Hyōzō went to the castle to request permission to hire two new teachers, Matsudaira Saburōtarō and Tamiya Heishirō. Both were young men who were hoping for positions as instructors. Like bureaucracies everywhere, the castle administration was slow to respond. Hyōzō had to resubmit his request twice over the next six months, before the petition was finally accepted on Ansei 6/11/20. After submitting three petitions and waiting six months for a response, Hyōzō went to the home of the responsible domain official to offer his humble thanks. He also went to the houses of Matsudaira and Tamiya to offer his congratulations, taking gifts with him. The two young teachers in turn came to visit Hyōzō numerous times to offer thanks and gifts, starting with the original submission of Hyōzō's petition, and continuing until they were installed as teachers in the school. The process did not end until 12/16, when Hyōzō attended a party at Matsudaira's house to celebrate the appointments.[23]

When Koume's diary picks up in Ansei 6 (1859) after a five-year gap, she had a great new joy in her life: her baby granddaughter, Kikue. Koume took a major role in the baby's care, carrying Kikue to doctors' appointments, celebrating her milestones, worrying about her health, and sometimes just carrying her around the streets for the pleasure of it.

In the spring the entire family came together to celebrate their new member on the occasion of her first girls' festival. Kikue herself, only a few months old, would have been quite unaware of all the joyful activity around her. On 2/29 the Kawai family held a big party at their home. Twenty-three family members and close friends attended. A few days earlier, a carpenter had been in to build a shelf to display the dolls that girls are given for this festival, and on 2/25 Koume went shopping to buy dolls. At Matsuya she bought a pair of courtiers, representing ministers of the right and left, together with a pair of lampstands. She also stopped at Iseya to buy clothes for the occasion. Koume bought new dishes and hired five helpers for the party. The party was extravagant, costing more than 125 monme. In her diary, Koume entered a list of the gifts her guests had brought. They included sake coupons, a large quantity of fresh fish, and dolls for Kikue's spring solstice display.

Just three days later, the family hosted another celebration, this time inviting the faculty of the domain school. Twenty-six guests came. Kikue's grandfather, Kuroda Jinbei, took charge of the catering, bringing two helpers. Koume hired two more helpers for the cleanup. She also hired a musician and a pair of dancers, mother and daughter. Koume does not give a full accounting of the event, but she does record that the guests consumed 1 *to*, or almost 5 gallons, of sake; 1.1 *to* (about 35 pounds) of rice—half going to make sushi, the other half colored with red beans; a large quantity of fish, both purchased and received as gifts; as well as vinegar for sushi, and fruits and vegetables. The family also received substantial gifts in return: a total of 2.7 *to* (11 gallons) of sake in the form of coupons and a barrel brought by one guest; and gifts of sweets and money. The following day Koume hosted yet another party, this time for a few close relatives. Once again, she summoned a pair of dancers. The guests ate leftovers from the previous day's event, so the expense to Koume and Hyōzō was modest—only 5 monme.

The parties for Kikue were not the only celebrations taking place in this auspicious season. On Ansei 6 (1859)/2/22, the Kuroda family married Kano's younger sister, Kan, to her cousin Suzuki Yoshitarō. And on 2/28 all the retainers of the town were summoned to the castle for a great celebration of the coming-of-age ceremony for the young daimyo, Tokugawa Mochitsugu. He had become daimyo just the previous year when the reigning daimyo, Yoshitomi, had been installed as shogun (he became the fourteenth shogun, taking the name Iemochi). The ceremony marked the beginning of a busy spring season of pleasure outings and cultural events. Through the third and fourth months, Koume, Hyōzō, and Yūsuke went to spring solstice celebrations, flower-viewing parties, poetry gatherings, boating trips, and excursions to scenic temples and shrines.

On 3/18 Dr. Hayashi came to the house to discuss Kikue's smallpox vaccination. Vaccination techniques using the cowpox bacillus had entered Japan via Nagasaki some years earlier, and by this time the treatment had become widely known, although practiced by only a minority of educated people in Japan's urban centers.[24] Koume took Kikue for her first treatment on 3/27. Dr. Hayashi made five scratches in each of Kikue's arms and painted a little of the bacillus into each scratch, warning Koume that the wounds might suppurate a little, and telling her to be sure to bring Kikue back in four days. Two days later Koume took her granddaughter back to the doctor: the blisters were not developing as they should. Dr. Hayashi reassured her. He promised to come and check up on Kikue in a few days, which he did on 4/5, pronouncing her well. Two days later the family cooked red-bean rice to celebrate the successful treatment, sending a portion to Dr. Hayashi. The second round of treatment came a month later: on 5/1 Dr. Hayashi made a total of seven scratches and reapplied the vaccine.

Through all these happy domestic events, Koume scarcely mentions goings-on in the outside world. On Ansei 6/6/2 (July 1, 1859), a new chapter opened in Japan's relationship with the Western nations, as the government opened the ports of Nagasaki and Hakodate, as well as the brand-new port town of Yokohama, for trade under treaties signed the previous year with Great Britain, the United States, France, Holland, and Russia. The treaties had been highly controversial. Many Japanese had been vehemently opposed to the opening of trade and diplomatic relations, and they saw the shogun's acceptance of the foreigners' demands as a sign of inexcusable weakness. In response, the shogunal chief minister, Ii Naosuke, was carrying out a brutal purge of the shogunate's critics, including the daimyo of Mito domain, Tokugawa Nariaki, who was placed under house arrest. Among the issues under dispute had been the question of who should succeed the shogun Iesada, who died in 1858. Activists favored Tokugawa Yoshinobu, one of Nariaki's sons. Ii Naosuke, however, succeeded in placing the young (and pliable) Kishū daimyo, Yoshitomi, as shogun. These events must have been widely discussed in Wakayama, but amid the joyous events in her own family, Koume largely ignored them through the first half of the year.

By the middle of Ansei 6 (1859), however, ominous reports were spreading of a more immediate threat. A terrible disease had entered Japan with the foreign ships: cholera. It had started the previous year in the southwestern port city of Nagasaki, where dock workers fell ill with severe stomach pains, diarrhea and vomiting, seizures, and sudden death. The disease spread along Japan's ports and highways, and by mid-1858 it had reached Edo, where an estimated fifty thousand people died over the next eighteen months.[25] Although the disease died down in the winter months, it surged again in the hot summer of 1859. Cholera arrived in Wakayama in the fifth month and quickly spread. Kishū was particularly vulnerable to the spread of the disease, since several of its ports were stopping points along the main Inland Sea shipping route between eastern and western Japan.

For Koume, the first portent came on Ansei 6 (1859)/5/18, as the rainy season set in. On that evening, word came that Hyōzō's cousin, Umemoto Asakitsu, had died of a vomiting disease. As soon as they heard the news, Hyōzō and Yūsuke oiled and arranged their hair and set off to pay a formal call on the family. Koume followed soon after, commenting that the atmosphere in the house was "dreadful grief, and extreme pity." A few days later, on 5/24, Koume and Hyōzō were invited to the Buddhist memorial ceremony for Asakitsu. They were told that his widow Hisano was planning to bring a medium, since "she would dearly love to hear his voice one more time." Thinking this was "too sad," Koume declined to attend. Hisano also sent a request to Koume: Would she paint a portrait of Asakitsu—not in death, but as he was when he was alive? Koume commented that "I had no choice but to say yes."

One month later, on 7/3, it was the Kawai family's turn to be affected by illness. "Kikue is not well," reported Koume. The family sent for Dr. Hayashi, who left three packets of medicine.

The next day the doctor came again. Kikue was doing much better. But on the night of 7/7 the baby was fussy and sleepless, and in the morning she was vomiting. Dr. Hayashi came again, and meanwhile Yūsuke consulted with his friend Arima Son'an, who was also a doctor. Dr. Arima suggested a different medicine, and Yūsuke sent the family handyman, Zōkichi, in search of it. Meanwhile Dr. Hayashi brought yet another doctor, Dr. Kuge, to examine the baby. Kuge prescribed yet another medicine, and shortly after they left, Dr. Arima came to administer the medicine Zōkichi had purchased. After consulting about the medicines Drs. Hayashi and Kuge had prescribed, Arima advised holding off on the new medicine to give those she had already taken a chance to work. In the meantime, Kikue herself seemed to be doing better than she had in the morning.

But by 7/10 Kikue was seriously ill. Dr. Hayashi came once again, and Kikue's grandmother Kise and aunt Kan came. Kise stayed overnight. The next morning Kise went to the Konpira shrine, where she drew a divination straw that assured her all would be well. And indeed, during the day the baby seemed better. But that night Kikue was worse than ever, clearly in great pain. Dr. Hayashi suggested they try yet another medicine, which was supposed to act on the nervous system to calm a patient down. It had no effect. On 7/15 Kikue's grandfather Kuroda Jinbei brought still more medicine, recommended by a Dr. Tanaka. Dr. Hayashi came to visit later in the day, and he, too, brought another new medicine, this one made of antelope horn. The family decided to wait and see how the medicine Jinbei had brought worked before trying Hayashi's prescription.

None of the medicines relieved the baby's intense pain. Koume wrote that "it is hard to bear." On 7/17 Moriya Rihachi came with yet another medicine for the family to try. The family added it to all the other remedies they were feeding the little girl, who in the meantime was suffering one convulsive attack after another. That evening another doctor, Imai Zuian, came to examine the child. He thought Dr. Hayashi's prescription was the best cure available and advised them to stick to it and not try any others. And in the night, the little child seemed a bit better, suffering only two attacks. The next morning Dr. Arima came again, bringing candy for the child to suck on and gain a little nourishment.

As Kikue's conditioned worsened and a cure seemed further and further out of reach, cholera continued to spread through the town. On 7/20 word came that a family friend had died suddenly of the disease. The next day, for the first time, Koume acknowledged that an epidemic was underway:

> Presently cholera is spreading. It's worse than last year, just like a dream.... In the town, every house displays a condolence register. Just among the ones I have heard of, there are Mr. Toda, Mr. Okada, Higashi's older daughter, Motosaki Bōsuke, the retired Noguchi, Enomoto's wife, three people in Kukenocho, Yamahata's son, Master Tada, Uchimura Matasuke, Mr. Kamatari, both Kamashis, even though he was a doctor, and Mrs. Shimamoto. I can hardly count them all. Mr. Toda was out fishing in the river just yesterday. While he was in his boat his stomach felt bad. Three hours after he got home, he started having attacks. He suffered seven attacks altogether.

Meanwhile, Kikue continued to decline. On 7/23 Dr. Hayashi examined her and pronounced her much better, but the next day she suffered more bouts of severe pain, and on 7/26 she had more seizures. Her grandfather Jinbei brought in yet another doctor, Nakura Hachizō. When Dr. Hayashi stopped by later in the day, he once again advised against trying any more medicines. The doctors were very worried by the seizures.

On 7/29 a great purification ceremony was held at the Kawara shrine, to cleanse the town of the epidemic. Yūsuke went to participate, but there was a huge crowd there and he was so worried about his child that he turned around and came home. And indeed, Kikue was much worse.

During the day she suffered eight attacks. Koume, worn out and suffering dreadfully to see her grandchild in so much pain, wrote: "Today Kikue is very, very gravely ill. . . . If it goes on like this we can see the end coming. I could see the movement of her hands getting weaker." And the next day, "The only comfort is that she went all day with no convulsions." Her suffering was nearly over.

By 8/1 Kikue was unconscious. She had not been able to hold down any food for twenty days. At the same time, Wakayama was prostrate in the grip of the epidemic and an oppressive heat wave.

> The cholera is spreading, and in 1-chōme, 2-chōme, Burakurichō, and Urahashi it is very widespread. At night, they are not letting people pass through even if they have business there. Everyone is calling on the gods, and the neighborhood groups are starting to dance in the streets. This evening they are dancing in Komeyamachi and 4-chōme. It's said that they are wearing gorgeous costumes in Komeyamachi. In 4-chōme they are wearing *kanmuri* [tall hats] like Shinto priests, [otherwise] going naked except for red loin cloths and wearing geta [wooden clogs] [on one foot] and *zōri* [straw sandals] [on the other], taking the form of the god Uzume no mikoto. Some are also wearing O-Fuku [plump-cheeked goddess of fortune] masks. I could hear the banging of drums and bells. They are starting at the Ujigami shrines, then dancing on to seven other shrines, and ending up at the Nichizengū shrine.

On 8/2 the baby was still unconscious, and her hands and feet were no longer twitching. A few days earlier the family had hired a nursemaid, Masu, from one of the shops in the commercial district. But over the past three days both her aunt and her uncle had died of cholera, and she had to take time off to attend their funerals. Meanwhile a family friend, Kihei, came to call, to inform them that his father Wakaemon had also died of cholera.

The next day the heat remained intense. Kikue's breath was very rapid, and when Dr. Komatsu came to examine her, he suspected that the family had been giving her too many different medicines—which they denied. Meanwhile, in another ominous sign, Hyōzō too fell sick with diarrhea and stomach pains. Rather than acknowledge the possibility that he had come down with cholera, Koume preferred to attribute his illness to the fried eggplant he had eaten earlier in the day.

On 8/4 the heat was unbearable. The baby's breathing was now rapid and shallow, and increasingly harsh. And Hyōzō too was very unwell. Later in the day, Hyōzō's colleague Yasoichirō came over and urged Koume not to forget her husband. "There's nothing you can do for the young Miss," he said, "so from tonight please devote yourself to Sensei [Hyōzō]'s care." Koume asked her sister-in-law Kise to take care of the baby, and she followed Yasoichirō's advice. Anyway, "It's hard to be at Kikue's side." After a while, though, she was called back to her granddaughter's sickroom and found baby Kikue once again convulsing.

> It went on for a long time, and just wouldn't stop. There was something about it that was different from before, and I suspected she was approaching a critical point. But I thought it would be bad for my husband if he worried, so I didn't say anything. As we pushed on her, her breathing gradually got weaker, and her fingers went cold. It was so sad, but what can one do but say but that life is fleeting? . . . The end came at the eighth hour [about 2:00 p.m.]. There was nothing to be done.

Koume added: "DREADFUL DAY."

Koume never mentions cholera in relation to Kikue, and it is unlikely that she had the disease, which usually causes severe diarrhea and kills within a few days. Kikue's symptoms—pain, vomiting, and seizures—are not specific enough for a diagnosis. Death in early childhood was very common in nineteenth-century Japan: between 10 and 20 percent of children died before their first birthday. One thing that jumps out from Koume's diary is the large number of different medicines Kikue was given: a total of eight, prescribed by five different doctors. The family was confused about whether to give all these medicines simultaneously or to wait and try them sequentially. But at any given time it seems that Kikue was being given at least two or three different medicines. The two ingredients specified in the diary are antelope horn and pear extract. They sound harmless, but we know nothing about the manufacturing processes of these drugs, nor about the ingredients in the other medicines Kikue was taking. It seems likely that they did more harm than good.

The family buried Kikue the next day, Ansei 6 (1859)/8/5. The funeral arrangements were hampered by the extreme conditions prevailing in the town. Throughout the town, workers and artisans were preparing for a massive outpouring of prayer and supplication. All the neighborhoods were planning processions for the following day, with brightly dressed dancers and groups of young men carrying portable shrines. Kuroda Jinbei did the rounds trying to organize priests, pallbearers, and implements for the hurried funeral. A family friend, Jinsuke, tried to arrange a coffin, but

> the carpenters are all busy building portable shrines, and they were not willing to undertake such an inauspicious task. Eventually he got someone he knows in Shironokuchi to make us one. He had it made to Kikue's length of 2.1 shaku, and width of one shaku, but [Jinnosuke] forgot to tell [the carpenter] how deep to make it, so it ended up being too big. If we had told him it was for a coffin, he would have refused to do it because of the ritual pollution, so [Jinnosuke] told him it was a medicine box. We couldn't find an appropriate palanquin [for the coffin], so again we ended up renting one that's much too big. Nor could we find anyone to wash the body, until Jinbei finally found someone. That person is doing seven [bodies] today so is very busy. The day laborers did not want to interfere with their work for tomorrow, so they came late too. Everything is confused.... We wanted to replace our lantern, and we asked around, but because they are all needed for the floats tomorrow, there are no lanterns to be found. So we had no choice but to use our old and torn lantern.

Koume concluded: "I am feeling so weak, I'm no use for anything."

Despite the obstacles, the family was able to put on a respectable funeral. Koume described the order of the procession: a lantern carrier; a man bearing the family's crest on a pole; priests of the temple; a man carrying Kikue's mortuary tablet; a man carrying burning incense; a man carrying a naginata spear; a man carrying a white funeral lantern; two men carrying the coffin; another man carrying the family crest; and two female mourners, one provided by the Kawai family and one by the Kuroda. The total cost of temple and priests, bearers, equipment rental, and hired mourners came to about 50 monme.

For several days, Koume's diary fell silent. She was too exhausted to pay attention to the processions and prayers on the streets of Wakayama. Hyōzō was still sick, and Koume herself was not feeling well. She was only brought around by the outpouring of support from her close network of friends and family, who came in a constant stream with food and sympathy. On Ansei 6 (1859)/8/8, Hyōzō was finally starting to recover from his bout with the disease (most likely, he had a mild case of cholera). The doctor came by with medicine for him, and "I too was feeling a little tired, so I got five packets of medicine." Yūsuke went to the temple to pray. Throughout Kikue's sickness and death Koume makes no mention of Kikue's mother, Kano. Perhaps one reason was that Kano was once again pregnant. Maybe she needed to be protected from the stress of her daughter's illness and death.

Meanwhile, the people of Wakayama responded to the crisis by taking to the streets in frantic displays of dance and prayer. On 8/10 Koume reported that "in town, the dancers have been fighting in the streets. Stores are closing, and all the people are doing is dancing. This evening, too, there are seven or eight rival groups out on the streets." And the next day, Koume went out to see what was going on. She watched big crowds milling around in the Kitamachi district. That day, she commented on portents visible in and around Wakayama:

> The wells are running dry even though it is constantly raining. Five or six days ago the sky from the shoreline was red—people said there must be a great fire in Osaka, but there was nothing like that. There is no explanation for it. People are frightened by these signs. The dancers are fighting for no reason. Six or seven groups are going out every night, processing around the city. At least three of them have even gone past our gate. People are going out without caring a bit about how they look. . . . Even old and retired people are joining in.

This combination of evil omens and threatening, frenetic dancing in the midst of a deadly epidemic is strikingly reminiscent of popular outbreaks in Europe, such as the "dance plagues" that broke out in Strasbourg and other cities in the sixteenth century. Until recently the phenomenon, which has been named "choreomania," might have seemed irrational and archaic to modern observers, but the Covid-19 pandemic has shaken many of our convictions about the rational behavior of modern society.[26]

On 8/13 the woes of the town were compounded by major flooding, as the banks of the drainage channels running through the town burst. On 9/8 Koume wrote, "My goodness, it is a dreadful time. The cholera continues to spread. It seems that [Hyōzō's colleague and drinking partner] Yasoichirō and his mother both have it." And on 9/9 an earthquake shook the town: "We started to run out of the house, but then it stopped." Koume then went into the town to watch the festival floats being paraded through the streets.

> All the different parts of the town were beautifully decorated. Children were playing the shamisen and beating drums by lantern-light. Some of them had ten or more lanterns hanging from their foreign hats. Their faces were powdered white. Four or five of them were wearing improvised wigs. There is no sign that there is sickness, the night was so lively. But I was unable to enjoy it. Seeing the people holding their children, I was reminded of Kikue. Certainly, seeing all this lively play makes my feeling of loss grow, but perhaps it's better than just staying home. I went to several districts of town, and in all these places fifteen- or sixteen-year-old girls and children were everywhere out and running around.

Amid all these heartbreaking events, the arrival of foreigners in distant Yokohama and other ports was not a central concern for Koume and her circle. But news was circulating of their arrival, and of the political controversy it had unleashed. On 8/28 Koume reported that children were throwing stones at foreigners on the streets of Edo. "They have been scolded by the authorities. It's also said that a *dōshin* [low-ranking samurai] has wounded three foreigners. One of them was cut from his forehead to his mouth. One was cut in the shoulders, while the other escaped with a cut to his hand. The whereabouts of the assailant is unknown."

The inability of the shogunate to prevent the establishment of foreign enclaves triggered a profound instability in Japanese politics. The job of the shogun was to protect Japan (his formal title meant "barbarian-quelling great general"), and many people felt that he was failing. Restive samurai were taking matters into their own hands, attacking foreigners and attempting to undermine the shogunate. The political instability contributed to a widespread feeling that Japan was on the brink of a catastrophe. On 8/28 Koume reported a conversation with Mr. Okano over dinner:

> At the beginning of the month the northern sky went red. People were saying there must be a great fire in Hyogo or Osaka, but there was none. People are talking about it. Some say it's a sign there will be another great earthquake, followed by [another] epidemic—in any case, nothing but calamities. But Okano thinks they're all wrong. According to the Tsuchimikado [an aristocratic family in Kyoto family known for its skills in divination], the red sky is an omen of civil war.

Okano went on to discuss a massive political purge taking place in Edo. He also reported a visit by thirteen Russian naval vessels, to discuss the status of Ezo (Hokkaido and Sakhalin). If Japan did not take Ezo, the Russians said, then the Americans or British would. If Japan wanted to act, Russia would not stop them. On the other hand, if Japan did nothing, Russia would step in and take control of the islands. Okano did not know what answer the Japanese officials had given but concluded that "these are difficult times." He added: "In the Yōwa era before the Genpei war, there were all sorts of calamities such as earthquake, storm, starvation, and fire. Then came the war. I, too, have witnessed unpleasant, even terrible things. But now on top of that we have a terrible epidemic, and even worse we have this threat from foreigners. And it also looks like there will be a civil war. . . . We shouldn't be praying for long life, just that we will get through this unharmed."

Koume ended this entry with a poem:

> Kono koro wo usa no kagiri to nari yukaba
> Nagara furutomo kai ha arubeshi
> Even if this period is gloomy, the end is in sight
> It is worth living for the better times that will come

Meanwhile, the epidemic continued unabated. On Ansei 6 (1859)/9/11, "[Hyōzō's colleague] Noro Seikichi's wife fell ill yesterday morning and was dead by the evening. She had a baby at the breast. It is so sad." And on 9/13 Koume listed eight more people who had died of cholera, including the mother of their servant Zōkichi. Noro's wife's medical expenses had left him in debt, and he had no idea how to take care of his young baby. Koume and Hyōzō lent him money and persuaded several friends to help him out too. Meanwhile his baby was taken in by a nursing mother in a neighboring family.

Through the sickness and suffering, shrines all over the area continued to hold festivals, and Koume commented again on the lovely clothes worn by the young people participating in the processions. But she also noted that the horses at the Nōkawa Inari shrine were refusing to eat. "Cholera is even affecting the horses. . . . It's affecting the crops too. There has been a poor fruit harvest, and cotton is bad too. The rice crop is good, but the insects are out of control and they are damaging the crops. Many of the birds have disappeared."

On 9/24 Koume made o-hagi rice cakes in observance of the forty-ninth day after Kikue's death—the day on which the deceased is said to complete her journey to the afterlife. Meanwhile, she reported:

> The man who sells us our salt was carrying his load home when he collapsed. Also, [a cooper called Kintoki] lived with his wife and child. While he was at the shrine festival, he suddenly fell ill. His son was sent for, to take him home. But while the son was coming to get him, word came that the mother too had fallen ill. He left his father, and set off home to take care of his mother, but when he got there, she was already dead. He went back to fetch his father for the funeral, but found that he [too] had died. In every province, the situation is terrible.

After a spate of particularly lavish festivals, the castle issued a ban on further extravagance. "They say that 40,000 ryō has been wasted in the town."

On 12/8 the castle issued a set of proclamations, about a variety of topics related to the opening of the country. One of these was about the changing of gold and silver: after the opening of Japan to trade, there had been a sudden and devastating drain of gold out of the country, as foreigners rushed to take advantage of its low price in Japan relative to the silver currency. Kishū domain subjects were forbidden to speculate in these markets. After commenting on the unfortunate consequences of the attacks on foreigners by rogue Mito samurai, the proclamations went on to explicitly forbid throwing stones at or otherwise molesting foreigners. If anyone heard of or saw such an act taking place, they were to report it immediately to the authorities.

On the last day of Ansei 6 (1859), Koume commented on this tragic year. Koume's first grandchild had died. The entire domain had been devastated by the rapid spread of cholera. And, as Koume wrote, the prices of core commodities such as rice and textiles were quickly increasing. The high price of silk on the international market was putting it out of reach of the Japanese. Six hundred Kyoto weaving shops had reportedly been forced to close. On top of that, "Since the autumn there has been a craze for dancing. Even day laborers have been dressing in undergarments of *chirimen* silk without a thought for tomorrow. Of course, as year-end approaches they are in [financial] difficulties." However, the domain had launched several construction projects near the end of the year, and that had put money into the pockets of the townspeople. "As a result, [the year] has ended reasonably calmly. The shoe shops are usually open till Sunday, but when I went at the ninth hour, they were already sold out, and I returned without buying any. The used goods shops are also said to be doing well. It's cause for celebration."

Koume ended with a reflection on the loss of Kikue. "In the autumn, I lost my beloved granddaughter Kikue, who was like a flower in my hair. There is no help for my feelings of grief." But amid all the suffering of this dreadful year, there was one small ray of comfort for Koume and her family: Kano was expecting another baby in the new year.

4

WORK AND FAMILY

In an essay on the scholar's wife Rai Shizuko, Yoshida Yuriko argues that, while women in farming and merchant families might have an active economic role to play in their families: "In a samurai household, the husband was the income producer.... The wife's job was to care for the household, and to bear and raise children. In the samurai world, the man was in charge of relations with the outside world (*omote*), while the woman was in charge of the inner quarters (*oku*) and did not show herself to the outside." Yoshida uses as an example a list of tasks and exhortations which Shizuko's husband Rai Shunsui wrote out for her when he was about to leave for Edo, leaving Shizuko in charge of the household. The list included daily observances at the household shrine; making sure the fireproof storehouse was opened in the morning and properly closed at night; taking care of their son Kyūtarō (later to become the renowned scholar Rai San'yō); practicing reading with their son; copying poetry and other literature; watching out for and taking precautions against fire; avoiding overfamiliarity with neighbors and others; enforcing a ban on smoking in the house; receiving stipend rice and checking the amount; and avoiding extravagant expenditures.[1] Shunsui entrusted his wife with some elements of the financial management of the household, but broadly these instructions emphasize the management of the home and the avoidance of unnecessary engagement with the outside world.

How does this compare with Koume's experience? And what conclusions, if any, can we draw about the nature of a bushi wife's work, or her role in her family?

With an elderly mother to take care of, a busy husband and son, a new daughter-in-law, a new grandchild on the way, servants to manage, and live-in students to care for, Koume in the 1850s was as busy as she had ever been. While Hyōzō focused on his duties in the school and castle, Koume occupied herself with the smooth running of the Kawai family's busy household. Her duties included taking care of her family members; managing the family's complex extended family and social networks; managing servants and helpers; maintaining the family's property; providing food and drink for family members and guests; managing the family's day-to-day finances; and participating in the ritual and cultural life of the family and community. She was helped in these activities by her high standing in the community, her intelligence and eagerness for information, and her close relationship with her husband. Her diary affords us an unusually intimate look at a samurai wife's activities and responsibilities, and at the conditions of her family's daily life.

FOOD AND DRINK

The most frequent references to Koume's management of the household relate to food and drink. Koume was responsible for keeping her family and guests fed, and on most days she recorded the details of food and drink purchased, given or received as gifts, prepared, and consumed in the Kawai household.

The staples of the Kawai family diet were rice, fish, and vegetables. Rice was generally plentiful in the Kawai household because it was the basic currency of samurai privilege. On payday, Hyōzō and his retainers took physical possession of bales of rice at the kakeya warehouse and carried them home, and periodically Koume had a helper polish one or more bales using a large mortar and pestle. Sometimes they had to supplement this with purchases in the marketplace, but more often, they were able to sell some for cash and still keep enough for home consumption.

The diary contains few direct references to the cooking of rice, and most of those are in relation to parties held at the Kawai home. But we may speculate that every two to three days, Koume or one of her helpers would have risen early, stoked and lit the furnace, washed and soaked the rice, and steamed it in one of the family's large cauldrons. Cooking rice was hard work and consumed valuable fuel: a family of Koume's economic status would be unlikely to cook it every day. Rice was, however, served in one form or another with almost every meal. Once cooked, a cauldron of rice could be eaten over the next two to three days, both hot and cold. Koume often offered her family and guests sushi, *kayu* (rice soup), rice balls, or rice cakes, none of which needed freshly steamed rice.

Wakayama was on the ocean, and fishing boats set out daily into Osaka Bay and the surrounding waters. Their catch was on sale in the fish market a short distance from Koume's home, and traveling salesmen often passed by Koume's front gate. But fish was expensive, and cash was scarce. Koume sent her servants out to buy fresh fish only on special occasions—either to send out as a gift in celebration of some event in a colleague's life, or to offer at a celebration held in the Kawai family home. When alone, the family members generally ate fresh fish only when they were given it.

More commonly, the family ate preserved fish in the form of sushi. The typical sushi of nineteenth-century Wakayama was different from the perfectly fresh slices wrapped in crisp seaweed that we associate with the word today. Sushi for Koume was a lightly preserved product, using cheaper cuts of fish salted and steeped overnight in vinegar, and mixed with vegetables before folding it into rice—somewhat like today's *chirashi-zushi*. It could be eaten cold for two or three days, even without refrigeration.[2]

When the family ate fresh fish, it came in enormous variety—as it does in Japan today. A close friend or colleague might give them a package of five or ten small horse mackerel (*aji*), an everyday fish then as today. On the other hand, one of the aristocratic families whose children Hyōzō taught might send a basket of premium fish such as red snapper (*tai*) and lobster. Many of the fish that passed through Koume's hands (often only to be passed on as a gift to another family) were local to the area and had names that appear in no dictionary today.

The Kawai family had a vegetable patch in the back of their house, and we may assume that seasonable vegetables had a prominent place on their table. But the references in the diary are more commonly to pickled vegetables, which seem to have been served with most meals. Koume bought substantial quantities of vegetables in preparation for the winter months, particularly dried beans and pickling vegetables such as daikon radish and eggplant. In winter, most of the vegetables the family consumed were either dried or pickled, since there were no greenhouses or other distribution systems that might bring off-season vegetables to the market. The family also had a substantial orchard in the rear of their house, with a variety of citrus trees as well as plums, which they again pickled.

The picture that emerges is of a somewhat repetitive diet, brightened by frequent gifts of fresh fish and other delicacies. The diet must have been more monotonous for the women, who had many less opportunities to eat out or be entertained. Rice, plain or in the form of rice balls or sticky rice cakes, soup (Koume mentions rice soup, mushroom soup, whale soup, and noodle soup, among others), sushi with vinegared fish, and pickled vegetables, particularly radishes (*takuan*), were the mainstays of the Kawai table. These were the everyday items that Koume would also offer to guests who dropped in throughout the day. The pickled foods the family ate daily would have been extremely salty (to prevent spoilage) and, as they aged, pungent. The powerful taste (and smell) of aged *takuan* is, once experienced, not easily forgotten.

One benefit of this diet was that it placed a relatively low burden on Koume. Cooking rice was hard work, but it could be done every second or third day, and if the family had a live-in maid at the time, she could be tasked with the job. The servants could also help with pickling vegetables, which was a heavy and dirty job. Rice, sushi, and pickled vegetables could be put on the table at a moment's notice and required little preparation. For someone like Koume whose heart was in art and culture, this was surely a relief. For the family and guests, though, it suggests a tedious diet of mostly cold food, often strong-tasting after sitting in a fermenting tub for weeks or months. On the other hand, the family probably ate ample fresh vegetables during the prime growing months, many of them grown in their own garden.

There are around sixty references to food in Koume's diary in the eleventh and twelfth months of Kaei 2 (1849). During those two months, the family received gifts of food and drink on twenty-five separate occasions. The gifts included rice cakes and other sweets, *sōmen* noodles, beans, sugar, sushi, celebratory red bean rice, miso, fresh and preserved fish, beef, wheat germ, and coupons exchangeable for sake. The family also offered food items as gifts a total of six times: citrus from their garden, sweets, *sōmen* noodles, pickles, and a part of the chicken they had been given a few days earlier. The surplus of gifts received over given suggests that Hyōzō and Koume were providing services, such as teaching, and were being paid in the currency of gifts.

Koume and her helpers purchased food items a total of thirty times during the two-month period. In addition to sake (which comprised more than a third of all purchases), they bought sticky rice, tobacco, sweets, whale meat, soy sauce, fish, tofu, salt, and daikon radishes. While the whale meat was for family consumption, their purchases of fish were almost exclusively for entertaining. On Kaei 2/12/15, for example, Koume ordered three shō (5.4 liters) of sake as well as seven fresh fish, to serve at a party they were giving that evening for six colleagues from the domain school. The sticky rice was for the upcoming New Year's celebrations, which they would celebrate with rice cakes. Most of the other purchases were small quantities, except for the daikon, which was in its harvest season. Koume bought 120 daikon radishes on 11/21, and another eighty on 11/29. Koume and her helpers pickled the radishes on 12/7 and then again on 12/20. Given the family's precarious cash flow, Koume took every opportunity to substitute home-produced goods for those purchased in the market.

One notable feature of the gifts they received is the smattering of exotic or unusual items: for example, beef and chicken. Neither of these was an item Koume would have bought for her own family. The beef was a gift from Sakai Baisai, a doctor and artist. This was the first of a dozen times he would give the Kawai family beef, even offering it as a take-home gift at his own father's memorial service. It is unclear in what form the meat came: raw, cooked, pickled, dried, or salted. A few days later, on 12/3, Koume offered some of the beef, together with sushi and sake, to Endō Ichirō as they discussed a painting commission. And on 12/5 Koume once again offered beef to her guests at a party for Hyōzō's colleagues. But, she wrote, "I ate three slices, and in the middle of the night I had stomach pains and diarrhea." Chicken was more commonly available in the markets of Wakayama, but it was an expensive product and not one regularly consumed by the Kawai family.

Koume's consumption of beef at this date is a little surprising, since beef-eating is often associated with the new, Western lifestyles that entered Japan after the opening of the ports. While animal husbandry for meat was rare in early modern Japan, there is ample evidence that wild animals such as deer, bear, wild boar, and rabbits were consumed, especially by communities with a tradition of hunting. Domesticated animals, particularly horses, were also eaten, though usually as a by-product of their main function. Excavations in the former Edo quarters of Kii domain revealed bones of cows, deer, horses, and wild rabbits, with knife cuts indicating they had been prepared and cooked.[3] Cookery books and illustrations of Edo street scenes confirm that by the nineteenth century deer and wild boar were established components of Edo food culture—though often euphemistically referred to as "mountain whale." From the 1850s, some establishments were offering "Ryukyu hotpot," which was made with pork.[4]

Beef seems to have been eaten much less frequently. Cattle husbandry was uncommon, though oxen were sometimes used as draft animals, especially in western Japan. But there are records dating back to the eighteenth century of dried beef being sent by regional daimyo as a gift to the shogun's palace. It is possible that meat-eating, including beef, was more widespread, and more acceptable among samurai than other groups, since animal flesh was assumed to enhance the eater's martial spirits.[5] Owing to the stigma attached to the handling of animal carcasses, however, meat-eating was also associated with the poorest and most despised members of Japanese society. In his autobiography, Fukuzawa Yukichi (himself from a samurai background) recalls as a medical student eating beef in "the lowest sort of places." "No ordinary man ever entered them. All their customers were *gorotsuki*, or city bullies, who exhibited their fully tattooed torsos.... Where the meat came from and whether it was of a cow that was killed or that had died, we did not care."[6]

By the 1860s, once foreigners had been resident in the new treaty ports for several years, eating meat became widely fashionable. In 1867 the Kishū administrator Date Chihiro wrote that farmers were increasingly selling oxen, deer, and wild boar to the townspeople of Wakayama "who have become extravagant and whose customs are becoming more foreign."[7] Perhaps Baisai's gifts were an early sign of this trend. But for the Kawai family, they were an exception. Meat never became a regular part of their diet.

A key feature of the life and culture of the Kawai family was the free flow of sake. The family's entire circle of friends, colleagues, and family seem to have been prodigious drinkers. Visitors were offered sake almost as a matter of course, no matter what the time of day they stopped by. Both men and women drank, but the men drank more. Again and again, Koume records Hyōzō staggering home drunk. This sometimes led to friction. On Ansei 6 (1859)/6/14, "in the evening, Yasoichirō came over. As usual they talked of all sorts of trivial things, [and] it made me angry. Both of them were talking and laughing their heads off. Between them they drank one shō (1.8 liters) of sake." And on 8/14, "in the evening [Hyōzō] sent for Yasoichirō, and he came. As usual, they got very drunk. I was furious."

Hyōzō was not the only one who loved sake. Yūsuke also participated in the drinking culture, and from an early age. The first mention of him drinking sake was at the age of four, though on that occasion it made him severely ill (see chapter 2). By his mid-teens, his social interactions often involved drinking. On Kōka 5 (1848)/7/22, for example, the fifteen-year-old Yūsuke (still called Iwaichirō at the time) went with Hyōzō to watch a firework display. After it was over, they went to visit Tanaka Zenzō, where the drinking began. Then they moved to Iwahashi Tōsuke's house, where "Iwaichirō got drunk, and went to sleep under the mosquito net. [Hyōzō] left him there and came home alone."

Koume describes several riotous parties at which she drank as freely as the men. On Kaei 4 (1851)/3/7, for example, Hyōzō (who had been at a party the night before) "had a hangover. Stayed in bed. Gave everyone the day off. He got up before noon but couldn't look at his books." On that day, the family had been planning to go on an excursion to the riverbank. It was the peak of the spring flower-viewing season. The following day, pleasure outings were to be banned owing to memorial observances at the castle, so Koume was eager to seize the moment. In the early afternoon she set off with Yūsuke and Tatsuko, leaving a student to take care of Hyōzō. Koume, Tatsuko, and Yūsuke were joined by several friends and relatives, making a party of eleven including Gonshichi, their servant, who carried their things. This time it was Koume's turn to get very drunk. After staggering home, "I lay down as soon as I got home, and I remember nothing before or after. At the eighth hour of the evening (around 2:00 a.m.) my husband got up and lit the stove, and made me some tea. After that I finally sobered up. Really," she reflected, "this sort of behavior is inexcusable."

Compared to Hyōzō, Koume had many fewer opportunities to drink socially. But she also sometimes liked to drink alone, especially when she was tired or frustrated. On other occasions, she offered sake to the female members of her household. After a long day of laundering at the river, for example, she might share a gourd-full of sake with her helpers.[8]

Koume and Hyōzō also sometimes distilled sake into liqueurs using flowers and fruits from their garden. On Kaei 2 (1849)/8/1 Koume records the purchase of two *ranbiki*, one large and one small, for 25 monme. The *ranbiki* was a charcoal-fired, three-layered distiller made of glazed earthenware. The name and design were derived from the European alembic (from the Arabic *al-inbīq*) introduced to Japan by the Portuguese in the sixteenth century. On that day, Koume bought 1.5 shō (2.7 liters) of sake and made a liqueur using *bushukan* citrus fruit from the garden. During the month she made three more batches of liqueur, two with *bushukan* and one with *shiso* (Japanese basil) leaves. She records making liqueurs at least a dozen more times in the pages of the diary. The family drank some of them at home while giving others to friends and relatives.

THE HOUSEHOLD ECONOMY

Koume played a central role in the family's financial management. In the pages of the diary, she recorded most of the family's financial transactions, from salary received, to loans made and given, to daily purchases, to the costs of commodities in the marketplace. Koume seldom clarifies whether discussions and decisions about finances were made by Hyōzō, Koume, or both together. It seems, though, that Koume oversaw the day-to-day management of the family's cash resources. She took responsibility for most purchases, sending Gonshichi or another helper to the shops to pick up merchandise. She made and repaid small loans, paid servants and workers, and took charge of the family's obligations to its social network. These might include buying a gift for a colleague who had been promoted, had a child, or recovered from sickness, or helping a needy relative.

Occasionally, Koume entered a rough summary of the state of the family's finances. On Kaei 2 (1849)/12/30, for example, she summarized the family's income and expenses for the year:

> This year, we had a good income. But our expenses, too, were unexpectedly high. Here is a summary:
>
> 2 bu gold, lent to Seikichi
> Also a considerable sum for making a sword
> 2 gold bu, repayment by same of a previous loan
> 1 bu, given to Ryōzō as a celebration gift
> 2 shu, Takimoto
> 300 *hiki* to Koume
> 2 shu to Asanosuke
> 2 shu and 6 monme to Iwaichirō
> 2 gold bu, lent to Bunsai
> 11 monme worth of books, to Jintatsu
> 9 monme, to Iwaichirō for poetry collection

Including payments, repayments, and gifts, total income: 1 kan, 612 monme, 3 bu, 7 *rin* [1,612.37 monme].

> Annual Expenses:
>
> Rice. 3 *to* of sticky rice, about 260 [mon]me
> Sake. 1 koku 9 to 2 shō [1.92 koku, about 346 liters]
> Firewood. 113 monme 9 bu [113.9 monme]
> Soy sauce
> Oil
> Vegetables
> Gifts. 371 received, 276 given
> Clothing
> Rice. 3 *to* of sticky rice
> 4 shō of millet
> Oil. Around 4 monme 3 bu
> Daikon. 2 *kanmon* [2,000 mon] worth
> Sticky rice. 98 monme

Salt
Brown sugar. 1 *kin*. 1 monme 9 bu
White sugar, top quality, 5 monme 3 bu
This year Iwahashi Kusumatsu and Nogiwa Saichō died.
[Illegible]. 3 monme 6 bu.
Sake. 1 monme 8 bu per 1 shō
Shōyu. Purchased 8 shō for 11 monme 5 bu.
Tea. Purchased at 1 monme per *kin*.
Daikon. Around 4.5 mon each.

If we apply the standards of modern accounting, Koume's "summary" is thoroughly confusing. What looks like the "income" side seems to consist mostly of expenses. Perhaps it is better seen as a cash flow statement. But what does the 1,612 monme total mean? Is it the family's net cash income after deducting all expenses? Or it is a statement of total income, before expenses but net of lending activities? And where is the income from the family's main source: its official stipend?

The "expenses" are no clearer. They include repetitions. "3 *to*" of sticky rice appears twice: is it the same item? The list sometimes states the quantity of items and other times the cost. Is the "98 monme" for sticky rice a payment for the 3 *to* listed a few lines above? Sometimes Koume lists the total price paid, other times the price per unit. And the expense side includes no summary of the total cost for the year, so we are left in the dark as to the family's total expenditure and net balance.

The confused account most likely reflects Koume and Hyōzō's own naiveté about money and accounting. At the turn of the nineteenth century, samurai men and women were seldom trained in financial matters or in the use of the abacus. By contrast, merchants were increasingly training their daughters in financial affairs, and by the mid-nineteenth century, training in the abacus had become much more normalized across all classes. But Koume had no training in the abacus, as she herself admitted later in life.[9]

Some things, however, do become clear from Koume's statement of accounts at the end of 1849.

First, the range of expenditures was consistent with the patterns of consumption revealed by the day-to-day entries in the diary. Most expenses were for necessities, and there were very few luxuries. The range of foods purchased was narrow: sticky rice, sake, soy sauce, vegetables, millet, daikon, salt, sugar, and tea. There is no mention of fish, which implies that this was not a regular item for the family unless received as a gift. The only vegetable specified is daikon, which we know Koume used for pickling. It is likely that many of the other purchases were bought to be dried, pickled, or otherwise preserved. Even the sugar, the only luxury item on the list, seems to have been purchased as a gift.

Second, a large portion of the family's economy depended on the giving and receipt of gifts. Given the cash difficulties the family so often found themselves in, it is unsurprising that noncash transactions made up an important part of their economic life. Although the family had to purchase some gifts, this was not a major item in the family's budget despite the large number of gifts exchanged—suggesting that many of the gifts they gave were either home-produced or gifts they had received that they recycled and put back into circulation.

And third, the family spent a very large amount of cash on sake. Applying the price per shō mentioned in the summary to the quantity purchased, the family would have spent 288 monme on sake during the year, making it the largest single item of consumption specified in the summary. Koume does not specify the amount spent on clothing, but clothes were considered an investment since they retained their value and could be used to raise money at times of cash shortage. Sake, on the other hand, was purely for consumption. Why, when they were so frugal in their use of cash, particularly when it came to nonessential foods, would they spend so much on a consumable like sake? The obvious answer, undeniably true, is that the whole family loved drinking. But sake can perhaps be better understood as an essential lubricant of the family's social network, helping Hyōzō and Koume build the social capital that was so essential to their status and position in the Wakayama scholarly community.

Koume and Hyōzō's cash flow continued to be precarious. At the turn of the 1850s, Hyōzō's rice stipend was 25 koku: only a modest improvement over the previous decade (it increased to 30 koku in 1853, 40 koku in 1857 with Hyōzō's promotion, and 50 koku in 1865). Faced with frequent cash crunches, the family resorted to the pawnshops, as well as to their friends and relatives, to tide them over short-term financial difficulties. On Kaei 4 (1851)/7/13 a relative of Hyōzō's, Endō Ichirō, arranged a loan for the Kawai family of 500 monme. The next day Koume gloomily reflected: "We owe 200 *[mon]me* to Yukawa. Also 3 ryō and 100 *me* to Fujita Ryōkichi. Altogether that's 600 *me* in debts. Now we have borrowed 500 *me* through Endō Ichirō. Adding that, we have a total of 1,100 monme in debts. We also have some loans. [We lent] a little each to Iwahashi, Noro, Umemoto, Murai, and others, but we cannot get the money back from any of them. Asanosuke, too, still owes us 300 *me*, but he is not saying anything [about repaying us]. . . . Each year the prices are going up, and our expenses are rising. Our outgoings are gradually increasing."

Koume often faced a cash crunch when it came time to pay her retail suppliers. In most cases accounts were to be settled monthly. But on Kaei 2 (1849)/9/8 she wrote: "Refused [payment] to various [suppliers]. I was out most of the day. It's very difficult. I must try not to borrow any money. I must not forget!" Only a month later, on 10/30, she wrote: "Bill collectors came from various places. Paid 30 [monme]. Refused most." Hyōzō, too, sometimes had the job of placating creditors. On the last day of Kaei 2, for example, when families were supposed to settle all their debts, he made the rounds of several retailers to persuade them to accept only partial payment.

Faced with pressing cash needs, Koume resorted again and again to sending her servant Gonshichi on the "Ise pilgrimage" to the pawnshop, to borrow money or to redeem pawned items. In Kōka 5 (1848) alone, Koume sent him to Iseya fifteen times.[10] Among other items, she pawned a summer kimono made of raw silk, a *haori* jacket, and a pair of swords, one long, one short. Generally, Koume pawned her own clothes. There is a pattern throughout the diary of Koume buying nice clothes when money was available and using them as security when times were harder. Fine clothes kept their value, sometimes for generations, if they were properly cared for. Silk cloth was high-value, portable, and easily stored. And fine clothes were also beautiful—and necessary for a woman of Koume's social position.

Lower-ranking samurai families throughout Japan experienced similar financial struggles. As one example, Constantine Vaporis writes about the Tosa domain scholar Tani Tannai. Tani's income and social background were very similar to the Kawai family's. The Tani family's nominal income was 42 koku, but after various deductions for interest and deposits with the domain, the family was left with under 18 koku, equivalent to a cash income only a little over 800 monme. Like the Kawai, the family was forced to resort to borrowing to make ends meet. And like the Kawai, Tannai's limited understanding of money and accounting prevented him from effectively managing the household's cash flow.[11]

Isoda Michifumi came to a similar conclusion in his study of a middle-ranking retainer from Kaga domain. The Inuyama family struggled to make ends meet even with an annual income of 51 koku. The Inuyama owed debts equivalent to two years' income. In a related study, Isoda found that in Tottori domain, the average indebtedness of a large sample of samurai retainers also averaged about two years' income. Isoda concludes: "In the late Tokugawa period, the samurai were for the most part engulfed in high-interest debts, and the high interest rates left them no room to breathe."[12]

Despite her own family's limited financial resources, Koume was always aware that others were worse off. Koume diary suggests an easy intercourse between Koume and the shopkeepers, handymen, laborers, and tenants with whom she came into daily contact. Koume often invited her servants and their families to join her for a drink. She enjoyed the gossip that she picked up through these encounters. And she was usually willing to help a family in need. She had a soft spot for young women, taking an interest in their stories and offering them help and hospitality when they were in need.

Indeed, Koume's own family were not so far removed from the poverty she saw all around her. Hyōzō's older sister, Kane, was married to Moriya Shōbei (who was also their first cousin on their mother's side). Shōbei was a small-scale merchant who struggled with constant financial difficulties, his business always on the edge of ruin. At the turn of the 1850s, both Shōbei and his son Shōsuke came repeatedly to ask the Kawai family to buy small items from them to help raise cash. Many of the items were paintings or other artworks, perhaps possessions left over from a period of greater prosperity. But they also came to sell petty items, such as tobacco. Two years later, in Kaei 4 (1851), Shōbei was still needy, and still getting himself into trouble. During the first month of the year, Shōbei and his wife came over repeatedly to ask Koume to help them out. On 1/16 Shōbei brought over a painting and a hibachi floor heater and asked Koume to buy them both. She commented: "I don't need either of these items, but recently Shōsuke has a lot of debts, so I bought them from him." On 3/19 Koume once again helped him out: "He is very hard up at present."

SOCIAL NETWORKS AND GIFT EXCHANGE

Koume's diary describes intense, daily interactions between the Kawai family and their networks of friends, colleagues, and extended family. There was a constant stream of visitors into the Kawai family home, none of whom was sent away without first being offered a cup of sake and a few simple snacks. Often, Koume prepared more elaborate entertainments for the many events the family hosted, including study groups, family and school celebrations, poetry gatherings, and drunken parties for Hyōzō's colleagues. Throughout the day, Koume gathered information from visitors, passers-by, shopkeepers, domain officials, servants, and others, recording it all in her diary. She supplemented it with information her family picked up on their excursions outside the house and subsequently related to her.

In the final month of Kaei 6 (1853), for example, Koume received guests on fifteen of the twenty-five days recorded in the diary: sometimes with Hyōzō present, but also in his absence. On 12/16 Hyōzō hosted a study group at home, with six participants. Koume served them snacks and sake, and they were "drinking until the fourth hour [10:00 p.m.]." On 12/12, by contrast, Koume received a visit from a Mr. Numano while Hyōzō was out. Numano came to return a part of a loan the Kawai family had extended to him. Koume not only entertained him with sake, she also handled the details of the business and carefully recorded the transaction in her diary. Other visitors came in Hyōzō's absence bringing news and gossip. Other than students, workmen, and household servants, all the visitors mentioned by Koume were men in Hyōzō's circle. There is no record of Koume receiving or paying visits during the month to or from female friends or relatives in her own circle.

As Hyōzō's position in the domain school became more prominent, the Kawai family home became a central point in the dense network of relations among the scholars of the school community. Their closest ties were with the Tanaka, Iwahashi, Noro, Yamamoto, and Tominaga families—all faculty members in the domain school. The Tanaka family were closest. During a single year (1848), Koume recorded more than ninety encounters between the two families.[13] Koume also took care of the guests at Hyōzō's intellectual gatherings. The school's faculty met in study groups centered on the scholarly work of a faculty member. Hyōzō's own group was known as the "Zuo group" (Sashi no kai). It met three times a month, over a period of at least ten years, to support Hyōzō in his work on the *Commentary of Zuo*. The study group meetings were ostensibly to discuss the *Commentary* and to support Hyōzō in his great intellectual endeavor. But they were also an excuse for convivial drinking, with Koume responsible for supplying the guests with food and drink.

The Kawai family maintained near-daily contact with its extended family network. Koume's immediate family was small, but the extended family reached beyond the scholarly community into the lower ranks of domain officialdom and beyond. Hyōzō's mother was from a merchant family, and of his three Umemoto siblings, two had in turn married commoners. Hyōzō had six first cousins, with whom he remained close through his life. Koume, too, was close to the Kitamura family (her father's birth family) and the Matsushita, which had adopted her brother Shichirō. After Yūsuke's marriage to Kuroda Kano, the Kawai and Kuroda families also maintained close ties.

At the heart of the social networks over which Koume presided was the culture of gift exchange. The samurai society in which Koume and Hyōzō moved was cash-poor, and samurai who received stipends from domain governments might want to avoid the appearance of engaging in overtly commercial activities. Gift-giving was a way to obscure differences in wealth, and to recognize value without any monetary exchange. Of course, it also served many other social functions. It showed caring and thoughtfulness. It allowed members to share in the milestone events in one another's lives. It was a subtle messaging system to indicate hierarchy and respect. It flattened the difference between those who had enough money and those who did not. And it was a measurable proxy for the complex system of mutual obligation, equity, and parity that governed social interactions between the members of the community. Scholars have pointed to the vital role gift exchange played in social interactions and power relations in medieval and early modern Japan. Among the samurai elite, the bestowal or exchange of cultural artifacts of great value might help reinforce governmental authority, display power and wealth, and reinforce hierarchical difference.[14] For lower-ranking families like the Kawai, gifts were a vital component of the household economy.

In Koume's diary, almost every entry includes some record of a gift received or given, including enough detail to assess its rough value. It was Koume's responsibility to manage the family's participation in the culture of gifts, in such a way as to keep the ledger of service and obligation roughly in balance.

Gifts given and received fell into several overlapping categories. The most common was "celebration" (*iwai*) on the occasion of births, marriages, promotions, recovery from an illness, or a significant birthday. Families celebrating such an event would often distribute packages of red beans in rice—a symbol of good fortune—to their network, and in return they would receive gifts of sweets, fish, or delicacies. On the other hand, the Kawai family would also send gifts to families in which a member was sick or had died (*mimai*).

A third category was gifts of thanks or payment in recognition for services received (*rei*). Gifts were more acceptable than cash payments in a samurai culture that disdained commercial transactions, and more elegant (if home-produced or recycled, they were also less costly). The Kawai family received many more "thank you" gifts than it gave, in recognition of Hyōzō's prominent position as a teacher and school administrator. The most substantial were clearly a form of payment, either for teaching services provided by Hyōzō and Koume, or for Koume's painting. For example, on Kaei 2 (1849)/12/17, Endō Ichirō, who was one of Koume's chief patrons, sent two bags of azuki beans, three dried bonito fish, and three sake coupons "in recognition of all of your work on a *gassaku* collaboration." And on 12/7 Hyōzō received five sake coupons from Lord Miura, whose son he had been teaching. Miura explained: "Since classes ended today we had been planning to offer you sake, but in the current environment of frugality, please enjoy a drink in your own home." Sake coupons were among the most frequent gifts received by the Kawai family.

Other categories included gifts given in return for those previously received (*o-kaeshi*), and recycled gifts, which the family often sent to close friends or family members after receiving perishable produce. For example, on Kaei 4 (1851)/4/23, Koume sent a pair of lobsters and a conger eel over to the Kitamura family. They were part of a basket of seafood that the Kawai family had received that day from Hyōzō's colleague Niida Genichirō, who was celebrating his son's commendation by the daimyo. Without refrigeration, fish and seafood must be eaten quickly, so it made sense to share such a gift with family and friends.

HOUSEWORK

At the core of Koume's work as household manager was the maintenance and smooth operation of the house and its daily routines. For many bushi wives, such work was a daily drudge of physical labor. Yamakawa Kikue describes the daily life of her grandmother, Aoyama Kiku, who was born in the second decade of the nineteenth century in Mito domain: "She took care of the household chores quickly and efficiently, the sort who, getting up while it was still dark, would manage in the space of a day to take the quilts apart, wash the covers and stretch them to dry, and then sew them back together so that they would be ready, all fresh and clean, to spread out to sleep on that night." In the kitchen, she "knew how to prepare a variety of delicacies. She enjoyed taking care of the vegetable garden and would work away in it energetically, her sleeves tied back, skirts tucked up, barefoot, hoe in hand. She took pleasure in putting eggplant and cucumbers she had grown herself on her own dinner table and also in giving them to others."[15] When she had no other task at hand, Kiku turned to spinning. She was never idle.

By contrast, Koume spent much less time on physical labor and more on intellectual, social, and cultural activities, such as entertaining guests, recording events in her diary, painting, and composing poetry. As a literate consumer, Koume would have had access to numerous published guides and manuals on housework and household management. Kaibara Ekiken's *Treasury of Various Mundane Matters* included chapters on the care and cleaning of clothes; construction and home improvement; the use and care of tools and utensils; the use and care of writing implements; sharpening and care of swords; horticulture, flowers, and flower-arranging; perfumes and incense; fire-lighting and heating; stretching paper for shōji screens; dyeing; prevention and treatment of infestations;

divination and selection of auspicious days; seasons and crop management; health and wellness; preparation and correct use of medicines; and moxibustion treatment.[16] Koume mentions few of these activities in her diary, and entries that do touch on them are usually about hiring and managing the labor to carry them out. Hyōzō and Koume employed servants, day laborers, construction specialists, maids, and nurses to do much of the physical labor of housekeeping.

Among the physical tasks that Koume did perform herself, the most common was cooking and food preparation, which for her was a near-daily responsibility. Other tasks, such as housecleaning and laundry, she seems to have undertaken much less frequently. For example, on Bunkyū 1 (1861)/5/24, Koume went down to the river to wash, together with Kano, their maid Tsuru, their student helper Kamezō, and Kano's baby son Iwakuma. "We washed thirty-five or thirty-six items. We took a kettle and boiled river water to make *ochazuke* [a rice soup made with hot tea]. They also brought leftover sushi to snack on, but "we were so exhausted he couldn't even eat." On other occasions, Koume sent her servant or her daughter-in-law Kano. For example, on Kaei 4 (1851)/5/24, Koume's servant Yasubei spent the day washing the women's summer kimonos, while Koume stayed home offering food and entertainment to a string of visitors. And on Ansei 6 (1859)/5/11, Kano took the washing down to the river with her three sisters. They were accompanied by Koume's servant Zōkichi. Koume, meanwhile, was able to stay home and prepare for an evening's entertainment of poetry readings.

Koume mentions washing only two or three times a year. Does that mean that the family wore unwashed clothes the rest of the year? Or was the washing of small items too trivial to mention in her diary? Rai Shizuko, a samurai scholar's wife of Koume's mother's generation, similarly describes expeditions two or three times a year for seasonal laundering of clothes about to be put into storage. Like Koume, Shizuko does not mention clothes-washing other on than these big occasions. Her chronicler, Yoshida Yuriko, suggests that the maid must have done the daily washing of small items, but as with Koume, there is no evidence as to who did such routine washing, or if it was done at all.[17]

As with washing, Koume only occasionally mentions housecleaning. Near the end of the year, Koume sometimes records herself and all the household staff doing a thorough cleaning for the New Year (e.g., Kaei 3

[1853]/12/19). But it seems from the diary that most of the daily cleaning work was done by her maid or a male servant.

Like all houses, the Kawai family home needed constant maintenance and repair. At various times, Koume hired workmen to repair the family's two wells, the house's walls and fences, the roof, and the toilets and bathroom. Koume also had workmen come and repair some of the house's furnishings and appliances, such as on Bunkyū 3 (1863)/9/11, when "Kichiemon came to repair the mortar and pestle," or on Kōka 5 (1848)/2/12, when Yasubei came with two helpers to work on building a room divider (*mikakushi*). Koume's son helped with the painting. Roof repairs were the most common work the family had to do on their house. Tiles frequently needed replacing, and storms often caused damage. The family also occasionally undertook major structural work on their house. The largest was in 1847, when they added a second floor to the house. The diary for that year is lost, so we have no direct record of the project.

Koume's helpers also took care of most of the heavy or skilled work in the garden: pruning the fruit trees, digging and planting, and harvesting. For example, on Tenpo 8 (1837)/2/29, Chōshichi came to plant seeds. Koume paid him 300 mon. On Kōka 5 (1848)/9/6, Koume's son dug holes for tree planting, together with the family's helper Ryōzō. And on Kaei 4 (1851)/4/5, Yasubei came to plant potatoes. On other days Yasubei planted eggplants, burdock, and soybeans.

SIDE EMPLOYMENTS

Given the relatively low stipend of the Kawai family, it is not surprising that family members engaged in side employment to make a little extra. Most scholars, artists, and teachers supplemented their income by taking in private students, and Hyōzō is no exception. Based on the limited accounting in the diary, Hyōzō's private teaching does not seem to have augmented the family's cash income significantly. The few references to payment for such services are mostly in kind: gifts, sake coupons, and, for students from farming families, food staples. The exception is the mid-1860s, by which time Hyōzō was privately tutoring several of the sons of the domain's most powerful families. In 1865 Koume recorded 1,300 monme in income from supplementary teaching, about 15 percent of the family's total cash income.

As an artist, Koume was also painting for patrons from all ranks of society, sometimes based on specific commissions, and certainly she would have expected some sort of compensation. The diary is extremely reticent about payments received for Koume's art. Koume's reluctance to discuss this topic openly in the diary, in addition to some references to her embarrassment at receiving cash, suggest that there was a stigma attached to commercial activity for an artist of Koume's gender and rank (see chapter 6).

By contrast, Koume is less self-conscious when she refers to employments that are less directly connected to her work as an artist in the bushi cultural milieu. For example, on Tenpō 8 (1837)/3/29, Koume wrote: "On the twenty-seventh, I bought three pieces of *chirimen* cloth, a total of three *shaku*, for 3.6 monme. I received this money from Yasuda as payment for making *haribako*." A *haribako* is a box made of wood or thick paper, over which is stretched decorative Japanese paper. Such boxes were typically used for accessories or jewelry. It appears that Koume was producing these boxes for Yasuda to sell into the commercial market. Koume was still working on *haribako* more than a decade later, in the ninth and tenth months of Kaei 6 (1853). By this time, she was working on a larger scale, with several young relatives coming regularly to help her out. Unfortunately, she does not offer any details on the economics of this activity. It appears to have been a regular, income-producing side-employment for Koume, but there is no mention of it in any of the periodic statements of account in the diary.

Koume also worked at a number of tasks that, if not income-producing, at least reduced expenses by producing goods that the family would otherwise have to buy. The scarcity of cash meant the family must do all it could to provide for its own needs. Fresh and pickled fruits and vegetables, and distilled liqueurs, would all be a part of this economy. In 1861 Koume bought several consignments of raw cotton, which she and her daughter-in-law Kano spun into cotton thread, either for sale or (more likely) for family clothing.[18] But this example of spinning is an isolated case: it does not seem to have been a regular feature of Koume's work life.

Given the family's marginal income and its constant indebtedness, why did its members not participate more actively in cash-producing side employments? In a memoir, Fukuzawa Yukichi wrote that in his home domain of Nakatsu (now part of Ōita prefecture in Kyushu), in lower-ranking samurai families with stipends of 10 koku or less, "everyone in the family capable of work, both men and women alike, eked out a poor livelihood by odd jobs such as spinning and handicrafts. These jobs might in theory be mere side work, but in fact the samurai came to regard them as their main occupation, relegating their official clan duties to the position of side work." However, Fukuzawa ranked his domain's Confucian scholars, whose stipends were typically above 25 koku, in the middle to upper ranks of the domain's samurai hierarchy. Such families "were not troubled over the necessities of life such as food or clothing," they "were able to provide their children with a fairly decent education," and they "had plenty of leisure time to devote to the arts, literary and military. They would read the Confucian Classics and the Books of History, study military strategy, practise horsemanship, spearmanship and swordsmanship, and generally indulge in all the branches of art and learning which were considered at the time to be cultured and noble."[19] All these activities sound close to those portrayed in Koume's diary.

By contrast, Yamakawa Kikue notes that in Mito domain, "The domain permitted retainers of the less-than-100 koku category to engage in side jobs, and as they could not manage on their stipends alone, members of their families, and the retainers, too, if they did not hold government positions, undertook various kinds of work for pay." Yamakawa's grandfather was a domain scholar of similar rank and status to Koume's family, but Yamakawa recalls of her grandmother that "throughout the year, anytime she had some minutes to spare, Kiku would turn to spinning the yarn to be used for the family's clothes. Before she had children Kiku also wove the yarn into cloth. However, as one child after another was born and as her husband's social position rose, her time was taken with other things, and although she continued to spin, she sent the yarn out to be woven into cloth. Weaving for others on commission was a standard side job of bushi wives and daughters."[20]

Kären Wigen gives an example from the seventeenth century of a feudal lord ordering his "lesser retainers" to take up side employments. The daimyo of Iida domain (in present-day Nagano prefecture), Hori Chikasada, ordered his lower-ranking retainers to manufacture paper hair ornaments for sale in urban markets. This in turn prompted local entrepreneurs to set up papermaking facilities, and the availability of locally made paper then prompted a neighboring lord to mobilize his own retainers to make paper umbrellas. Wigen concludes that these samurai employments "were established in the Ina valley primarily to address the fiscal imperatives of the local elite: not only the mercantilist requirements of generating export income for the domains but also the need to augment the stipends of hereditary retainers."[21] But Wigen does not specify the stipend levels at which retainers were expected to do this sort of work.

Ujiie Mikito writes that Edo-based shogunal retainers with a stipend of 100 *hyō* (about 35 koku) or less were forced into a variety of side-occupations to eke out their income. Indeed, there was a saying in Edo: "100 hyō, 7 family members, a life of tears." Lucky retainers obtained jobs (often sinecures) in the shogunal bureaucracy, which brought additional salary and benefits. Those without such positions were forced to undertake side-employments to make ends meet: document copying, making bamboo skewers, making paper cords and pins for tying up hair, making paper lanterns, or making hempen thongs for sandals.[22]

Isoda Michifumi gives the example of the Oka, a low-ranking bushi family in Okayama domain with a stipend of 12 koku. According to a memoir written by his son, the family head, Oka Shōgorō, had "no debts, but also no assets." Shōgorō's wife spent her days spinning for a little extra income, and his son spent much of his day tending the family's vegetable plot. His brothers spent their evenings making straw sandals and their days collecting used nails for resale. They were able to make only two pairs of sandals a night, which they could sell for 10 mon each. The family ate only two meals a day, mixing barley with their rice, and thinning it with hot tea in order to stretch out their supply. Other than rice, they were able to eat only a small quantity of vegetables and a little tofu. They ate a little fish four or five times a month and added taste to their food with a salty soup made of miso flavored with sake lees.[23]

Given the discrepancies among these sources, it is hard to assess how many families like Koume's, with an income of 20–50 koku (depending on the decade), might have been dependent on side employments. It is clear from the diary that Hyōzō's private teaching and Koume's art were side employments that brought significant material benefits to the family and helped keep its members free from want. Hyōzō and Koume were able to live reasonably comfortably on their domain-provided stipend. They supplemented this with cultural labor for their community, which was compensated mostly in kind, or in other intangibles such as cultural capital or prestige.

SERVANTS AND RETAINERS

Servants and household helpers were an integral part of the smooth operation of the Kawai household, for which Koume was responsible. The family generally employed one manservant, either a young man from the town (who would attend the family during the daytime) or a student who offered his services in exchange for board and lodging. Despite the Kawai family's relatively low income, as a samurai man Hyōzō needed a personal retainer to accompany him on visits outside the house. Yamakawa Kikue comments in her memoir of Mito domain that "as *bushi* became impoverished they kept fewer and fewer retainers. Instead of maintaining hereditary retainers they made do with short-term servants, employed for a year or six months at a time, and when, for ceremonial purposes, it was necessary to muster the full number of attendants appropriate to their status, they hired them for the occasion."[24] This was exactly the Kawai family's situation.

At the turn of the 1850s their servant was Gonshichi. Hyōzō used Gonshichi as his retainer when he went to the castle on official duty, as a lantern-bearer at funerals, and as an escort for guests on their way home after visiting the Kawai family. When Gonshichi was not with Hyōzō, Koume used him for a variety of errands. Many of these were connected to the extensive borrowing of clothes, raingear, books, and other items that went on daily between members of the samurai community. On Kōka 5 (1848)/3/27, for example, Koume "had Gonshichi return the lantern [that Hyōzō had borrowed the previous evening] to Niida. Returned another one to Shōjūji [temple]. Returned a pot to Tanaka, and had him pick up [our] umbrella there." And on Kaei 4 (1851)/3/14 Koume had him "take a *haori* (jacket) back to Tanaka. Had him take seven oranges [as a gift]." Koume also sent Gonshichi on small shopping errands, to pick up an item of clothing she had ordered, or to buy fish, soy sauce, or (most frequently) sake. And sometimes she or Tatsuko had him accompany them when they ventured out into the town—women of their class were not expected to go out unattended.

For heavier jobs or those needing a handyman's skills, Koume used the services of Yasubei. Yasubei was a middle-aged man who was as handy planting a tree as mending a roof. When a job was bigger (such as the time in early 1851 when he rebuilt the Kawai family toilets, a job that took three days), Yasubei brought his own helpers: either his son Kumagorō or a hired hand called Ippei. Koume used Yasubei for most of the heavy jobs like milling rice and splitting logs, but she also sometimes sent him on small errands, to buy food and drink, or to take a message to another family. Yasubei and his son also occasionally acted as Hyōzō's personal retainers, accompanying him to funerals or to the domain school.

The Kawai family also usually kept a live-in maidservant. These young women were either residents of the *nagaya* (rental dwellings) in the nearby neighborhoods or were from the villages surrounding Wakayama. In the latter case they often came from wealthier farming or merchant families, who wanted to give their daughters a little urban polish by placing them with a cultured samurai family. For example, on Kaei 4 (1851)/1/26, Koume hired Toyo, whose father was a rice merchant in Kuroe, a coastal village a few miles south of Wakayama. The arrangement was quirky from the beginning.

While Toyo went to work for Koume, her sister, Koiku, was also looking for a job in Wakayama. Koiku shows up in Koume's diary almost as much as Toyo herself, often inviting herself to eat or stay the night with the Kawai family. For a while Koiku got a job at a rice-cake shop, but after three weeks she was fired. Koiku's frequent visits left Koume nonplussed— she seemed to enjoy the young girl's company, but she also recognized that "she's a strange person."[25] Meanwhile, Toyo was turning out to be a mixed blessing. She had a habit of returning to her village or taking to her bed just when she was most needed. On Kaei 4/4/9, for example, when Koume was forced to stay in bed with a bad cold and headache, Toyo "lay down, saying she feels dizzy." And on Kaei 4/6/25, Koume was in bed feeling sick for the third day running, and Toyo too "is in bed with stomach pains." As a result, Koume's elderly mother had to go "to the pharmacy to get medicine for us, and then she had to cook for us all." The next day

Koume was feeling better, and so was Toyo. Koume mentions that she flew into a rage that evening, though she does not specify whether the target was her husband or her maid. In any case, Toyo's service with the Kawai family was coming to an end. On 7/15 Koume gave her two painted fans as a parting gift, and Toyo set off for home. Even after Toyo's departure, she and her sister Koiku still sometimes visited with Koume. On 7/25 Koume gave them both lunch, and Koiku stayed the night. Despite her maid's quirkiness, Koume seems to have been fond of her, her strange sister, and her family. Toyo's parents often sent gifts of rice cakes or shellfish from the bay near their home, and the visits and gift-giving continued for some time after the maid's departure.

Indeed, Koume and Hyōzō treated their servants and helpers as members of their extended family. They were usually willing to lend them a little money if in need. And they often included them in family entertainments, offering them meals or sake when they visited, and sometimes taking them along to theatrical and other performances. On one occasion, Koume describes Hyōzō getting "extremely drunk" with his retainer Yasubei. Yasubei also came occasionally to soak in the Kawai family's bath.[26]

In addition, a succession of students took up temporary residence in the household. Most of the students who studied privately with Hyōzō (now assisted by Yūsuke) came only during the day. But usually there were one or two whose families lived far away, and who needed accommodation. On Kaei 2 (1849)/8/2, for example, Tokura Ryōzō came to live with the family. He paid for his board and lodging in part by helping around the house. "He will bring one *to* [18 kg] of rice, and he will help with the cooking. He will come with only the clothes on his back," and "he will borrow an old futon from some relatives." Soon after, he was joined by a boy called Wada Jintatsu, from a village in the Okukumano region.

RITUAL LIFE

Koume's duties as household manager also included ensuring that her family would be properly represented in the ritual life of the domain. She was responsible for the correct observation of the numerous holidays and religious rituals in the annual calendar of the domain. Many of these doubled as family celebrations: the New Year's holidays, for example, when the family ate celebratory rice cakes, drank plenty of sake, and put on their best clothes to call on their neighbors. Others involved visits to temples and shrines.

Most of Hyōzō and Koume's connections to temples and shrines, however, seem to have been more for pleasure than out of duty or for ritual observance. All the Kawai family members were frequent visitors to the temples and shrines in Wakayama and the surrounding country. Sometimes they went to pray, usually for something specific such as for a friend or family member to recover from illness. For example, on Kaei 4 (1851)/2/1, Yūsuke was invited by his friend Noro Seikichi to go to the Itakiso shrine, east of the castle town, to commission prayers for the recovery of a school colleague, Yamamoto Shōtarō (who unfortunately died soon after). On Kaei 6 (1853)/4/8, Yūsuke and several of his friends once again went to the Itakiso shrine. "Since they requested an exorcism (kitō), they didn't stop anywhere on their way home."

More often, though, Koume and Hyōzō visited temples and shrines for their beautiful gardens, their delightful locations in natural settings outside the town, their famous buildings and artifacts, and their splendid festivals. Temple priests were often leisured men of culture, important figures in the cultural life of the town who hosted poetry gatherings, flower viewings, study groups, and drinking parties in their halls and gardens. Ozaki Sekijō, a samurai from Oshi domain, was friendly with many of the priests in his small town, and in his diary he describes nightly drinking parties at one temple or another.[27] Koume and Hyōzō, too, were close to several priests around Wakayama. They were particularly friendly with the priest of Shōjūji temple, who often commissioned Koume to paint for him (one of her works is still housed in the temple).[28] A number of temples in the area also invited Hyōzō and his colleagues, and sometimes Koume too, to flower-viewing parties on their premises.

The family's ancestral temple was Myōsenji, where the graves of the Kawai ancestors (dating back to Koume's great-grandparents) were located. Koume enjoyed warm relations with the priest of Myōsenji, with whom she exchanged occasional visits. But Myōsenji was only one of many temples and shrines with which the Kawai family had close relations.

A SAMURAI WOMAN AND HER FAMILY

At the beginning of this chapter, I cited Yoshida Yuriko's argument, based on a study of the samurai scholar Rai Shunsui's wife Shizuko, that samurai women's lives were inherently more restricted than those of merchants or farmers, and that, in the patriarchal structure of bushi society, "the man was in charge of relations with the outside world, while the woman was in charge of the inner quarters and did not show herself to the outside." The evidence from Koume's diary suggests that she enjoyed much more autonomy and independent agency than this model implies. There is no suggestion that Hyōzō laid down the law or instructed Koume on avoiding extravagance, or on what she should do from day to day. On the contrary, Koume sometimes had to remind Hyōzō of his obligations as he lay at home too drunk or hung over to keep his appointments. Koume did sometimes worry about her excessive spending, or her inability to manage the monthly budget. But her resolutions to try harder came from Koume herself, not her husband. Koume certainly took responsibility for the smooth management of the household, but those responsibilities involved her in virtually every aspect of her family's social, cultural, and economic life.

Moreover, while Koume undoubtedly stayed home more than Hyōzō, she was far from secluded. She presided over near-constant interactions with the family's social and professional networks, recording news and information, noting (and often managing) financial transactions, and entertaining visitors. The breadth and scope of her activities as household manager suggest a far more prominent role in the maintenance and preservation of the Kawai family's reputation and assets than Yoshida's case study suggests. Indeed, I would go so far as to question whether any meaningful distinction can be made, at least in the mid-nineteenth century, between the scope of activities of a bushi wife of Koume's rank and a merchant or farmer's wife.

Moreover, Koume's role as household manager describes only one part of her life and contribution to her family. Koume was also a sought-after artist who was producing creative content throughout her life and placing much of it in the Wakayama community and beyond. This work, discussed in more detail in chapter 6, made a significant contribution to the family's financial and social economy and further raised Koume's visibility and status in Wakayama society.

Yoshida's case study of the Rai family suggests a relationship between husband and wife that mirrors the patriarchal structure of Japanese society. Again, Koume's diary suggests a very different relationship. While Koume seldom mentions her personal relationship with Hyōzō (except a few times when she was angry at his drunken behavior), the diary suggests a harmonious partnership with separate but overlapping spheres of authority and a high level of mutual trust. Undoubtedly one important reason for this was the fact that Hyōzō had been adopted into the family as a *muko*. Koume's status as the birthright heir to the family's name and assets assured her a measure of authority. Her education and cultural qualifications must also have contributed.

One piece of evidence for Koume's partnership with Hyōzō is the diary itself. Each day, Koume faithfully recorded the movements of each family member, providing the most detail for Hyōzō's movements. She listed the time of his departure, his destinations, and the nature of his business. She recorded the people he met with, and how they entertained him. If he heard something while he was out—for example, news about the illness or death of an acquaintance—she recorded it, so that an appropriate gift could be given or visit made. When Hyōzō discussed business transactions, Koume recorded the details, often down to a fraction of a silver monme. If he submitted memorials requesting appointment or promotion of one of the school faculty, she recorded the number of memorials, and on whose behalf Hyōzō had written them. When guests visited in Hyōzō's absence, Koume discussed matters of family and domain business with them, recording the information in her diary so she could pass it on to Hyōzō. On at least one occasion (Ansei 6 (1859)/6/4), Koume even stood in for Hyōzō in his administrative duties as school principal. On that day, "Koume wrote five memorials." Koume also took it on herself to respond to business letters at times, when Hyōzō was busy with other work. And of course, Koume also wrote in detail about her own movements.

Koume's diary also functioned as a repository of news and useful information, which she recorded as the family learned of it. The information ranged from news of births, marriages, illnesses, and deaths, to reports of accidents and natural disasters such as floods and earthquakes, to stories of strange happenings or phenomena, to news of the political events that were shaking the Japanese administrative structure. Whether the family received information in the form of letters, messages from the domain administration, or word of mouth, Koume recorded it in detail, often copying the written communications word for word.

The diary also recorded details of the family's financial affairs: salary received, loans made and repaid, items sent to the pawnshop, purchases of clothing, food, and drink and their costs, and the costs of household repairs and hired help. It offered detailed descriptions of outings, scenery, and entertainments in which family members participated. It described visits to shrines and temples, or to public entertainments such as shrine festivals. It recorded the poems and paintings Koume and Hyōzō produced, together with their context. And it kept a daily record of gifts given and received.

Hyōzō must have trusted Koume to be a responsible keeper of such detailed and often sensitive information. The fact that Koume and Hyōzō shared information on family finances, work-related concerns, news and gossip, and sensitive political matters speaks to the level of trust and collaboration that must have existed between them. For her to compile such a complete record, she and Hyōzō must have spent significant time together going over his movements, the financial transactions of the day, and the flow of information. Although Hyōzō often went out for social activities, to teach at the school, or to perform his duties at the castle, he spent a part of each day—and sometimes several days at a time—at home with Koume. Did they eat and drink together? Did they sit and chat? Or was each in his own room, working on his or her own projects? We do not know. There is little in the diary, though, to suggest conflict or friction between them. Although their activities were broadly divided based on gender, the division left ample room for collaboration.

The picture that emerges from the pages of Koume's diary is of a husband and wife working closely together to manage the affairs of their household, both business and social. Although Koume's duties gave her fewer opportunities for going out into the community, Koume contributed to the family's economy through home production, through her careful management of cash flow and gift exchange, and, as we will see in a later chapter, through cultural production. Koume and Hyōzō were, in many ways, equal partners in the complex business of managing the Kawai household and maximizing its family members' well-being.

According to a memoir written by Koume's great-grandson, Shiga Yasuharu, Koume and Hyōzō had only a platonic relationship after the birth of their only child. Shiga writes that the couple tried for years to conceive a child, until unexpectedly, after thirteen years of marriage, she became pregnant with Iwaichirō. After a terribly difficult labor in which Koume nearly died, she resolved never again to risk pregnancy. She encouraged Hyōzō to take a mistress, but he refused. So the couple poured their energy into raising their only child, while their own relationship remained affectionate—but celibate.[29] Certainly the diary never hints at physical intimacy, though it would be very surprising for such a document to do so. But there is ample evidence of companionship.

5

WAR AND REVOLUTION

PROSPERITY AMID CHAOS

The 1860s opened with a new life, once again bringing the joyful sounds of a growing young family into the home. Yūsuke and Kano's son Iwakuma was born in the first month of Man'en 1 (1860). Perhaps because the memory of the loss of Kikue was still vivid, Koume's references to the baby are subdued. If she felt the need to protect herself in case something terrible happened once again, she was right to do so. Baby Iwakuma died in the seventh month of Bunkyū 1 (1861), barely a year old. That entire month is missing from Koume's diary—either because she was too distressed to write, or because she later removed those pages. But in 1862 Kano had her third child, a daughter called Yone, and her daughter Tsune was born two years later. Over the next twenty years, Kano was to have four more children, for a total of eight, of whom six survived into adulthood. Her only surviving son, Hidesuga, was not born until 1878 (it is possible that Yūsuke and Kano adopted him, since the family lacked a male heir). Had she lived, his sister Kikue would have been twenty years older than him.

By the mid-1860s the Kawai house was once again filled with the sounds of childish laughter and play. Hyōzō continued his busy life as head teacher. Koume, Tatsuko, Yūsuke, and Kano were living with two-year-old Yone and baby Tsune, a wet nurse for the baby, and their servant Kamezō, with daily appearances by various maids and helpers. There was a constant stream of visitors: relatives who came to greet them or to discuss family business; friends and colleagues of Hyōzō and Yūsuke who came on school business, to discuss Chinese philosophy, or just to chat and drink; friends of Koume, Tatsuko, and Kano; collaborators and patrons of Koume who came to talk about painting; students who came to take private lessons; and merchants and tradesmen who came to show their wares.

As always, their lives were punctuated by family milestones. In the ninth month of Genji 1 (1864), Koume attended the marriage ceremonies of Hyōzō's niece Umemoto Yae to Kano's brother Ushinosuke, eldest son and heir to the Kuroda family. Koume had managed the negotiations. The marriage united two families that each had deep connections to the Kawai. Ushinosuke himself was absent. He had been called up for military duty in Osaka back in the third month, and by the ninth month there was still no sign that he would be allowed home. Since 9/10 was deemed an auspicious day, the families decided to go ahead with the marriage ceremonies even with Ushinosuke absent. Thirteen families were represented at the marriage celebration at the Umemoto home. In the evening, Koume and Kano escorted Yae to visit her prospective in-laws.

Just a few days later, on 9/18, the Kawai family got word that Ushinosuke's father, Kuroda Jinbei, was gravely ill. He had suffered a sudden attack of severe diarrhea and was now said to be close to death. The announcement came in the midst of a dramatic day. Hyōzō and Yūsuke had come home late the previous night after an evening of drinking, and they were still fast asleep when, early in the morning, there was a violent knocking at the gate. A fire had broken out at the house of a neighbor. Yūsuke ran out into the street to see people running to and fro carrying lanterns. The alarm bells were also ringing. Yūsuke hurriedly put on his firefighting clothes and made his way through the crowd to the site of the fire. Luckily, it was limited to one house, and the neighbors were untouched.

Later in the morning, Kano went to the Kuroda house, where she learned of her father Jinbei's sudden illness. The Kuroda family members were debating: Should they summon Ushinosuke home from Osaka?

On the twentieth, with Jinbei still hanging on by a thread, the decision was made to summon Ushinosuke home. A letter was sent by courier the next day. When he received the news, Ushinosuke got permission from his commanding officer and set off immediately for Wakayama, walking right through the night and arriving on the morning of the twenty-second. Now that they had Ushinosuke home, the family decided to move ahead immediately with the completion of the marriage ceremonies. They were held on the twenty-fourth and twenty-fifth, with Koume as go-between, and Yae moved into her new home in the Kuroda household. Jinbei was able to see his daughter married, but just a few days later, on 10/3, he died, leaving Koume's dear friend Kise a widow. Jinbei had been seventy-two years old.

Two years later Koume would lose her own mother, Tatsuko, with whom she had lived her entire life. Tatsuko had lived into her mid-eighties and outlived her husband by almost sixty years. An accomplished poet, she had forged a path that her daughter had followed, as a valued participant in the rich cultural life of the scholarly community of Wakayama.

Hyōzō, too, was now in his seventies. As he approached retirement, Hyōzō's greatest personal commitment was to publish his mammoth thesis on the Commentary of Zuo. The completed work, which he finally submitted in 1863, was an expansive study in fifteen volumes of sixty pages each (about 440,000 characters total), drawing on a bibliography of 183 classic texts and theses, most from the Chinese canon. The main thesis of Hyōzō's book was an argument against the interpretation of a third-century scholar, Du Yu. The project had been Hyōzō's life work, bringing both struggle and joy over the years, as he worked with the support of his study group to complete it amid many competing obligations.

On Keiō 1 (1865)/3/19, the domain finally agreed to finance publication of Hyōzō's book out of its Edo office. Hyōzō was asked to prepare a clean copy of the manuscript and appoint a colleague to carry it up to Edo. Hyōzō and Yūsuke hired a student, Keizō, to make the copy, while Yamamoto Kanzō, Tsukayama Gakuzō, and Ichikawa Hitoshi helped check the content for accuracy and consistency. The copying, checking, and revising went on for over a year, and it was not until the third month of Keiō 3 (1867) that Hyōzō submitted the final copy to the governor of the school, Mizuno Tamon.

Hyōzō retired from the domain school in 1867 at the age of seventy-two, and although he did not formally pass the family headship to Yūsuke until 1870, it is likely that Yūsuke took over many of his responsibilities before that. Yūsuke himself was promoted to a senior position in the domain school in 1867. His career was following a similar path to that of his father.

The 1860s brought relative prosperity to the Kawai family. Gone are the references to pawning clothes and borrowing from relatives. Instead, Koume was able to spend quite freely, sometimes to the point that she worried about her own extravagance. On Bunkyū 1 (1861)/1/16, for example, Koume ordered an *obi* (kimono sash) for 66 monme—the price of enough rice to feed a man for three months, even at the current high prices. On 3/1 she paid for the obi after it was delivered (with an extra 4 monme in interest for the delayed payment), and at the same time she ordered a short-sleeved jacket for 65 monme. The following day Koume commented, "I'm worried about my shopping. I spent 200 monme, 97 of it in cash."

During the 1860s rice prices rose to unprecedented highs as global trade, poor harvests, and political instability fed inflation. Although Koume was shocked and disturbed by the high prices, her own family once again benefited from them. Hyōzō's stipend had increased to 50 koku of rice per year, which at the prices prevailing in 1861 would be worth upward of 13,000 monme (by contrast, the family's nominal income a decade earlier was 2,300 monme per year). The domain's retainers never received their full allowance. But the Kawai family had access to additional sources of income, mostly from extracurricular teaching. Koume's diary offers only glimpses into the state of the family's finances, and no comprehensive picture. But a summary at the end of Keiō 1 (1865) lists the family's total income for the year as 8,796 monme, composed of rice stipend (7,154 monme, or about 24 koku of rice at the average market rate of 300 monme per koku); fees from teaching (1,298 monme); and extra compensation for editing services (344 monme).[1] In spite of high prices and a spate of clothes purchases, the family's total expenses for the year were only 4,650 monme, leaving a surplus of 4,150 monme.

Scarcely a week went by without one of the downtown shopkeepers coming to call on Koume with samples of their clothing. Often Koume obliged by purchasing something. As the decade went on, she sometimes expressed shock at the high prices, as on Keiō 3 (1867)/5/23, when she bought a summer kimono of *Echigo kasuri* (splash pattern from the Niigata area) for Yone for 208 monme. "Really, the prices have become outrageous," she wrote. Yone at the time was only four years old. Two years earlier (Keiō 1 (1865)/11/26), Koume had recorded without comment that they spent 57 monme on a haori jacket for two-year-old Yone, with the family crest sown into the sleeves, which were made of imported cotton and black velvet. Koume's urge to spend on fine clothes, however, clashed at times with her instinct for thrift. On Keiō 3 (1867)/2/7, Koume and Kano refused to pay 1.5 monme to repair a neighbor's doll that one of the Kawai children had damaged. Instead, Koume and her helper did their best to mend it at home. The difference perhaps is that fine clothing was regarded as an investment. In an era of cash shortage and unstable monetary values, a fine garment was a durable item of value which, if cared for properly, could retain its value for many years. And indeed, in earlier years Koume had often converted her clothing into cash—at the pawnshop.

As an older woman freed from many of her responsibilities, Koume had more time for pleasure and entertainments. With her friend and sister-in-law Kuroda Kise now widowed, the two often met for shopping, musical performances, or other entertainments. On Bunkyū 1 (1861)/7/15, Koume and Hyōzō hosted a house party and invited a female shamisen player in to perform for their guests (she was probably going door to door). "We gave her 1 monme. She said that at one time she was the wife of a money broker called Okagi, in the Minato district. She said that she's fifty-one years old. She was not a good shamisen player." On another occasion (Keiō 1 (1865)/4/1), Koume went with Kuroda Kise to the Tokudas' house to hear a noted koto performer named Kikueda. The Tokudas had requested the performance because their daughter, together with Kise's granddaughter, had begun learning the koto. The Kurodas' adopted son Kojirō and his wife were also amateur musicians. After starting with some set pieces suitable for children to learn, Kikueda moved on to play some of the popular songs of the day. Koume, who enjoyed the performance tremendously, mentioned six of the songs by name, including "Nebikimatsu," a popular New Year's song named for the pine fronds used to decorate house fronts. The song combines congratulatory lyrics with extensive solo passages.[2] On another occasion, Koume "was invited to the Kuroda house after noon. It was only the mothers there. We enjoyed ourselves [playing and listening to] the koto and shamisen."³ Shamisen playing had been an art of the entertainment districts and popular theaters, but over time it had come to be accepted as an appropriate accomplishment for a girl of the townsmen and even samurai classes.⁴ And on Genji 1 (1864)/5/22, Koume "was invited to Kuroda to hear a *jōruri* [musical story-telling] performance."

Koume also had more time to go out on excursions. Most of these were nearby, often to local temples or shrines. But on Keiō 3 (1867)/9/4, Koume set off on an extended visit to friends in the village of Umatsugi. It was the first time she had recorded such a long expedition in her diary. She went with her five-year-old granddaughter, Yone.

Umatsugi was a village on the south bank of the Kinokawa River, about 11 kilometers from Wakayama. The family who had invited her were old friends of the Kawai. Sakai Baisai was an artist and poet who now lived in Wakayama, and his sister, Tsuneno, was a close friend of Koume's. Tsuneno had married into the Nishikawaya, an Umatsugi merchant house that handled freight on the Kinokawa River.

Koume and Yone walked to Umatsugi on the afternoon of the fourth, together with Tsuneno's adopted daughter Haru (Haru's biological father was Tsuneno's brother Baisai). On the fifth Koume went with the Nishikawaya family to watch the horse racing at the Zaō Gongen temple on a hillside near Kanaya village. Koume was enthralled by the spectacle. "There were forty-five or forty-six horses" participating in the contest, she wrote:

> Nishikawaya had hired a rider, and there were four others from Umatsugi. I had never been to a horse race before, and I was a little nervous that it might be dangerous. When I saw the horses all lined up I said that I'd seen enough and suggested we go home. But the people who had brought me calmly said that I should see for myself how dangerous it really is. After that we climbed a little higher to watch the race. The riders were all wearing red military surcoats (*jinbaori*). The winner from last year had attached a pole with paper streamers [used in Shinto ceremonies] to his horse. The riders had the name of their place displayed on their backs, and they carried flags as they began the races. It was splendid to watch. Four or five riders pressed on the winner from last year, to try to take

his pole. It was very exciting. The one in possession of the pole galloped ahead, brandishing his stick to stir up the people behind him. It was much more enjoyable than I expected.

And Koume wrote a pair of poems:

> Kakeuma no isamashiki kanaya to koe no / Omowazu agaru oi no sakamichi
> The brave cries of the horse races at Kanaya / Rise unexpectedly on the old mountain road.

> Umatsugi ni kyō umakake wo umare dete / Hajimete mimasu koto zo ureshiki
> At Umatsugi, today for the first time in my life / I watched the horses race. What a happy event!

Later that evening, Yūsuke arrived from Wakayama and stayed the night. The following morning (Keiō 3 [1867]/9/6), their servant Sakichi came to accompany them home. But Koume did not want to go home. Instead, she decided to take Yone to accept her friend Yatsuzuka Magosaburō's invitation to visit him in Kokawa village. Yūsuke and Sakichi had to go home without her.

Kokawa is about 13 kilometers from Umatsugi, and 24 km from Wakayama. As Koume and Yone set off, the sky was threatening rain. And indeed, "within one *ri* (4 km) it started to drizzle. We arrived in Kokawa at around the fifth hour (8:00 p.m.), and we asked the way to Yatsuzuka. Luckily Magosaburō was home, and he entertained us lavishly, the whole family going out of their way to take care of us." After a bath, sake, and an excellent dinner, the family laid out five or six brightly colored silk futons for them, but it was so humid that Koume threw them off and had to fan herself to sleep. In the night she heard it raining hard, and she worried about getting home the next day.

And indeed, the next morning it was still raining. It was impossible to return home, so Koume spent another day with her hosts. They entertained her by bringing out their family treasures, scrolls with calligraphy and paintings from famous Chinese and Japanese artists. "All of them were wonderfully executed. Really, there are no words to describe it. It's not that they were particularly desolate (*wabishii*) in themselves, but gazing at the mountains, I felt my chest tighten."

Later in the day the rain stopped, and Koume's host took her to visit the famous Kokawa Kannon temple. This very large temple, which was patronized by the Tokugawa family, was one of the landmarks of the region. Visiting it was "the fulfillment of a wish I had long held." Magosaburō showed her round the extensive temple grounds, then took her to the main worship hall where the priest offered them tea and sweets. While they were in the hall it started to rain again. They had gone out without umbrellas, so Magosaburō sent his maid running home to fetch some. While they waited, they walked around the hall and its adjoining rooms, admiring the objects on display, as well as the four mausoleums on the premises.

The following day, 9/8, the sun finally came out. "We made our preparations to leave, but they plied us with food, and we did not get off till late morning." Magosaburō sent a manservant to carry Yone. Koume's one disappointment was that she had not been able to meet up with Mr. Kogaku, a well-known poet who lived in Kokawa. The previous day her hosts had twice sent a messenger to see if he was available, but he was in bed with a stomach ailment and couldn't meet her. She had been hoping to give him a portrait of himself that he had requested some time earlier, as well as a painting of a koto. Now he was feeling better, and he in turn had gifts waiting for her: a bag of sugar, and some matsutake mushrooms and persimmons from Mount Kōya. But Koume calculated that if she went to meet with him, she would have to spend yet another night on the road. The weather was still unsettled, and there was no telling what the following day would bring. So instead, her small party walked back to Umatsugi, where Tsuneno greeted them warmly and offered them a bath, food, and drink. Koume decided that if she relaxed too much she would never make it home, so she said goodbye to the manservant who had accompanied her this far and set off with Yone for home, arriving at the fifth hour (8:00 p.m.). Koume, a sixty-two-year-old grandmother, had walked 25 kilometers in the course of the day, and five-year-old Yone had walked at least 11 kilometers. After arriving home, Koume immediately resumed her duties. Hyōzō was entertaining guests, and the moment she had changed out of her travel kimono, Koume hastened to prepare and serve food and drinks for them.

ECONOMIC TURMOIL

While the Kawai family was able to live in relative comfort during the 1860s, Koume clearly did not think everything was fine with the current state of politics and the economy. On Bunkyū 1 (1861)/2/5, Koume commented on the continuing rise in prices and the accompanying hardship and insecurity:

> The retail price [of rice] is 3.25 monme per shō [equivalent to 325 monme per koku]. Wheat is 2 monme and 10 mon. In Hidaka [a coastal district of Kishū domain, south of Wakayama] they are requesting and receiving government assistance. They are making rice soup with eight parts water to one of rice. A moneylender called Mikeya is said to be donating four monme to every family in his neighborhood, and making rice soup for the destitute. There are many robberies. In Hirose [a district east of Wakayama castle], some people are waiting to accost the *eta* [outcaste] women who have been going around collecting leftover food in buckets, and stealing it from them. They're said to be samurai. . . . According to Seizō, when he was on the road by the river in Tainose [the ferry landing for the Kyoto-Osaka highway], he encountered two women of about thirty who had collapsed on the road. He thought it was tragic but there was nothing to be done about it. However, the ferryman gave them something to eat from his lunch. Now one of them is recovering. So long as they are fed, they will not die. But if this increases, we will not be able to help everyone.

The price of rice continued to rise through the decade. On Keiō 1 (1865)/7/25, it was selling at 390 monme per koku. "Now it's impossible to get workers, even if you pay them 3.5 or 4 ryō. Builders are being paid 10 monme each [per day] by people like Lord Kanō—it used to be 8 monme. Even sardines are a monme for twenty on a bad day." On Keiō 1/10/5, Koume wrote that eggs were selling for 5 monme each. By Keiō 3 (1867), on the heels of two successive poor harvests, rice had reached over 800 monme per koku. On Keiō 3/6/15, Koume commented: "Some people are selling large-grained rice from somewhere or other. It's reddish in color, and watery. It swells, so five *go* of rice become almost one shō (10 *go*). They say that if you eat that for three years, you will die." Koume is probably referring to the emergency imports of Southeast Asian rice that the Japanese government brought into Yokohama to alleviate the famine.[5]

On Keio 3/5/2, Koume wrote of a heartbreaking local tale of distress caused by a rapid rise in food prices. Made desperate by his inability to feed them, a poor father living in a tenement district of Wakayama took his three children to the beach at Arahama and threw his three-year-old son into the waves. When the boy floated on his billowing kimono, the father grabbed him, stripped him naked, and threw him back into the water. Then he threw in the seven-year-old, but this time the boy's older sister ran into the water and rescued him. She raced home with the boy on her back, and told her mother what had happened. The distraught mother ran with some neighbors to the beach, where they found the body of her young son, naked and pecked by crows. Koume concluded: "When the price of rice is high, all sorts of things can happen."

On Keiō 3 (1867)/3/22, Koume wrote:

> Today a young woman came to our gate, carrying a package in a *furoshiki* cloth, and asked if we have any work for her. She had recently been at the employment agency at the harbor, but she had sold three kimonos to pay for five days of living expenses, and now she had decided to go home to Tanabe [100 km down the coast from Wakayama]. She asked if I knew where she could get a boat, but in the meantime, it would be a relief if we had some work for her. She had had nothing to eat since yesterday. I felt sorry for her, so I invited her in and gave her some rice balls. She had a very good appearance, and she carried a recommendation letter from her local temple, so I let her stay the night. She is the daughter of one Tomiya Zensuke of Egawa in Tanabe. Her childhood name was Suya, but now she goes by O-Take. She is seventeen.

The Kawai family received many other requests for help. In most cases, they gave something if they could, though often much less than the person had requested. These requests were hardest to refuse when they came from family members, and the most pressing of these was Hyōzō's relative Moriya Rihachi. Rihachi was the son of Shōbei, who had been a persistent beggar from the Kawai family in the 1850s. After Shōbei's death in 1851, his younger son Rihachi took over the family business, as well as its financial woes. Rihachi was as needy as his father. Through the 1860s he continued to importune the Kawai family for loans to tide him over his frequent financial crises. In Keiō 3 (1867), his financial troubles came to a head. In the third month, the Kawai family lent him a total of 450 monme to tide him over his cash flow problems. He repaid 300 monme, but 150 monme remained outstanding. Four months later Rihachi's affairs took a further turn for the worse. Desperate for more financial help, he took the drastic step of writing to one of the domain's great lords, Toda Kinzaemon, to ask for a loan. Rihachi had a family connection with the Toda, since his sister Nao had been placed by their father into service as a concubine to Kinzaemon's father, Toda Korekiyo (who had been a victim of the cholera epidemic in 1859). She had three children by him. Kinzaemon was not happy to be importuned by the brother of his late father's concubine. Rihachi's relatives—the Kawai and Umemoto families—were horrified to learn of this embarrassing faux pas, and they implored Lord Toda to ignore the letter. Rihachi had written that he needed at least 500 monme to survive. In the end, the Kawai family stumped up 200 monme in addition to the 150 monme they still had outstanding from previous loans. The Umemoto family committed to finding another 100 monme, and, after listening to their explanations of the situation, Toda himself unexpectedly sent a contribution of 5 ryō (worth about 600 monme). The situation was resolved, but from that point on, Rihachi was effectively expelled from the family. When he is mentioned again, it is as a servant or helper rather than as a family member.

For those without family connections to fall back on, the domain responded with a mixture of public assistance and exhortations to frugality and thrift. On Bunkyū 1 (1861)/9/2, Koume wrote that "the people have been ordered to be frugal. Two days ago, near Seikanji in Mikura, some people were arrested and stripped of their clothes. The young girls are on the lookout for being stripped and they are removing their embroidery. Children as they pass the temples are removing their hairpins, and if they are wearing nice geta they are removing them and hiding them in the sleeves of their kimono. Eight or so people a day are being taken to the city office because of extravagant hairstyles." A month later, on 10/17, she added: "The people have been commanded to be frugal. Patrols are confiscating things from girls in town. It's okay for samurai to wear silk, but townsmen must wear cotton and not do their hair fancily. That's why

Kano and I didn't meet a single person when we went to Narutaki last month."

Koume is referring to an expedition she made on 9/29 with her daughter-in-law Kano and some members of the Umemoto family to the Kannon temple at Nogawa and on to Sōsenji temple at Narutaki, both locations in a scenic area two hours' walk to the north of Koume's house. Indeed, on that day she recorded in her diary that Nogawa "felt a little lonely" and that Sōsenji was deserted. After eating a picnic, she and her companions picked some wild mushrooms and then hurried home. A few days later Koume recorded a pair of poems that she had "written without thought":

> Oshinabete asa no koromo ni Narutaki no / Momiji ni hitori dare
>   ga yuruseshi
> When everyone is wearing hemp, who permitted the bright
>   autumn leaves at Narutaki?
>
> Kite mireba okitemo yosoni Narutaki no / Mine no Momijiba
>   nishiki kasanuru
> Visit and you will see: the waterfall's ever-distant peak is swathed
>   in silk brocade.[6]

For every comment Koume made on the hardship being suffered by the people of Kishū, however, she also commented on the luxury and extravagance that she saw all around her. For example, on Keiō 3 (1867)/1/10, Koume and Kano went into town on a shopping expedition. Koume commented: "There is no sign of the prohibition [of extravagant clothing]. It was very lively. The geisha, maiko, and low-class people were gorgeously dressed in kimonos of silk crepe, and woven obi. The young people were all wearing obi of striped satin. There was no sign of thrift. Nor was there any sign that the price of rice has gone over 1,000 monme [per koku]. These are strange times."

And on Keiō 3/9/3, Koume and her young granddaughter Yone went to watch the celebrations at the Tōshōgu shrine in Wakaura on the completion of the new shrine hall. "As we approached Wakanoura, the streets became very crowded and lively.... The girls of the town were gorgeously dressed, baring their shoulders to show under-kimonos of crimson crepe, and waving matching yellow handkerchiefs as they walked in front of the cart carrying the rice cakes. The girls of the used clothes shops of Okeyamachi and Kitamachi were also in the procession. . . . The teachers of the sewing schools were leading their students."

When times are hard, people tend to look for someone to blame. The foreigners were an obvious target. Koume was very concerned about the baleful effects of the foreign presence, even in Kishū, where foreigners were not permitted to live. The opening of Japan to trade triggered a rapid inflation as the economy adjusted to global prices. Most people lacked the analytical tools to tie the cost increases directly to the foreign presence, and indeed that was not the only cause (excessive government spending and currency debasement also contributed). But for Koume, as for many others, there was a simple logic in tying the large-scale export of Japanese commodities to shortages, and price rises, in Japan. The disruptive impact of foreign trade fed into a xenophobic narrative of greedy and arrogant foreigners sucking precious resources out of Japan, with the shogunate doing little or nothing to stop them.

For example, in the summer of Bunkyū 1 (1861), Japanese cotton producers began selling into the global market to take advantage of rising prices caused by the American Civil War.[7] While many merchants profited from this trade, Koume saw a darker side.

> This year there has been an excellent cotton harvest, and everyone was joyfully expecting that the price would go below 1 monme. However, the farmers have pleaded with the authorities to allow them to sell their cotton to the foreigners—otherwise they will not be able to pay their taxes. The authorities permitted this, and twelve ships came to Osaka to buy cotton and sell it to the foreigners. As a result, the local people are losing their hope, and after all prices are rising. . . . Now the price has reached above 2 monme, and they are saying it will go as high as 3 monme.

The foreigners were an easy target to blame for Japan's troubles. Few Japanese had met or spoken to one, so they remained a vague and undifferentiated "other," undoubtedly threatening but mostly unknown. Stories circulated of their arrogance, drunkenness, aggression, uncouthness, and above all greed. On Bunkyū 1 (1861)/8/16, a friend relayed to Koume several stories he had picked up. In one account, a foreigner had tried to persuade a shopkeeper to charge 5 mon for an item worth only 1 mon and asked for a commission on the additional profit. On another occasion, "going into a copper workshop and seeing the craftsman at work, a foreigner said something, which of course no one understood. Eventually someone who could translate came along. What they finally understood he was saying was: Didn't you know you could extract gold from that copper?"

In another story, "a foreigner was looking into a house that had many *hibachi* [porcelain charcoal braziers]. He asked if he could buy some, but the owner, who had an independent mind, refused to sell them to him. They say that [the foreigner] stepped over the threshold [onto the clean tatami] in his shoes and threatened the man." On another occasion, "someone had raised a monkey, and taught it various tricks. Seeing this monkey, a foreigner asked its price. The seller asked for 5 ryō, and the foreigner paid it and put the monkey in a box. Then . . . he poured boiling water in the box and killed the monkey, pulled out its hair with some sort of brush, and ate it. The seller regretted his act so much! Truly this was terrible cruelty. Even the [foreigner's] cook, who was Chinese, would not eat such a creature."

In yet another example of the baleful influence of foreigners, plus a dash of the supernatural that Koume enjoyed so much, Koume reported the story of an Osaka merchant who was in his shop when a stranger walked in and asked him to take care of a box for a short time. He assured the merchant that it contained nothing of value, but something about the way he said it excited the merchant's curiosity, so he opened it. It contained a white doll.

Repulsed, he quickly shut the lid and pretended he had not looked.

Later, the man came back and asked for his box. He started to take it away with him, but after a minute he brought it back. "Even though I told you not to open it, you did, didn't you?" he asked. The merchant said, "No, of course I didn't," but the man said he had proof. "Come here and I'll show you." The merchant went to him, and when he put his ear close to the box, he heard [his own] voice saying "I want to open it, I want to open it." It was so strange, he was astounded. The man said, "Whatever you say, there's no doubt that you opened it." And he left. But from that moment, the merchant kept hearing the voice, saying "I opened it, I opened it, I opened it" in both his ears. At a loss, he sent for the man to come back, and he told him,

"Actually I did open it. Please forgive me, and please stop this voice in my ears."

The stranger agreed to help the merchant stop the incessant voice if the merchant would give him a hair from one of his eyebrows. The merchant plucked out a hair and gave it to the stranger, and the voices immediately stopped. But "now the place where he had plucked his eyebrow started to hurt, and gradually it became unbearable." The merchant once again sent for the stranger, who said: "The only way you can cure your pain is to destroy both your *kamidana* [Shinto altar] and your *butsudan* [Buddhist altar]. Unless you do that, you'll never be cured." The pain was so unbearable that the merchant destroyed both his *kamidana* and his *butsudan*. The conclusion to the story, wrote Koume, is that the stranger was a Christian who was using deceitful methods to convert people.[8]

On Bunkyū 1 (1861)/9/2, Koume reported an actual sighting of foreigners in Kishū domain. "An English ship came to Kadaura and has been surveying. Recently many people have been going to see it for pleasure, and a girl of fourteen or fifteen disappeared. After two days she was sent back from the ship. The castle has ordered that even if foreign ships visit, they are not to be regarded as sights to go and see."

On 9/7 Koume reported on the British ship's departure: "The foreign ship has weighed anchor and left Kadaura. The foreigners behaved very roughly when they drank. Because of this, the authorities ordered the people not to go and see them.... Two of them flung [a fisherman] in the ditch.... It seems that if they get drunk they are out of control, grabbing women and generally behaving disgracefully."

GREED, CORRUPTION, AND POLITICS

On Bunkyū 1 (1861)/5/29, Koume wrote:

From the evening of the twenty-fourth, a 4 or 5 ken [7–9 meters] long comet has been observed going from north to southeast. It appears starting in the evening. According to Jinbei, he was up at the sixth hour of the morning [around 6:00 a.m.], and he went out to look at it. It was moving to the west, he said. A few people are rejoicing, saying it presages a good harvest. On the other hand, others are saying that it means the shogun has been poisoned. . . . According to astrological divination, it's not a good sign. We must be on our guard against either a great earthquake or great floods. Frivolous people are claiming it is a star of good harvest. They are doing harvest star dances in the streets as they walk around selling harvest star sweets.

Koume drew a half-page sketch of the comet in her diary. She was always interested in portents, and usually she was willing to believe the most pessimistic interpretation.[9] On 6/16 she added: "There is a rumor that for the last three mornings there have been two suns. The comet is getting higher and higher in the sky." Indeed, Koume wrote several times about reported sightings of two or three suns in the sky. On Genji 1 (1864)/11/29, she wrote about a sighting of triple suns in Ise province. "Two of them were a little purple in color. Many people don't believe this story, but I think it's true. There have also been many other strange things happening: terrible rains, and people being struck by lightning." Two weeks later, on Keiō 1 (1865)/1/13, she added: "The public opinion is that it would be a good thing if an earthquake came."

As the political and economic conditions worsened, Koume often linked them to unusual phenomena and natural disasters. She reflected a palpable sense that some great calamity was at hand. On Bunkyū 1 (1861)/8/25, she wrote of a particularly severe storm: 'We didn't notice [it] so much, but in Matsue it caused great damage apparently. In one temple called Gokurakuji, recently an evil monk murdered his disciple and servant. Now this wind destroyed both of their gravestones. It is certainly a sinister wind. The heavens have been taken over by dragons."

Commenting on a particularly inauspicious day in the astrological calendar, she wrote on Keio 3 (1867)/7/3:

Yesterday was an unlucky day [*akunichi*] and indeed people died in strange circumstances. In a sake shop in Kajibashi called Nakuraya, some youths went to play in the water, and two of them drowned. A third was saved. In the Tanaka area, a boy was run over by an ox cart and died. It ran right over his face. His mother has gone crazy and spends the whole time crying his name. And in yet another incident, the main hall of Kan'ōji temple burned to the ground. It's a terrible shame, but understandable. [The priest] said he had heard sounds coming from the hall of the seven-faced Buddha, and he believed that some foxes were playing at doing military drills, but he didn't dare go and look. He said that the foxes are always playing games there. But this time, they came out from the hall [where they usually played] and passed down the corridor to the main hall, and then to the bell tower. And as they moved about, flames burst out here and there. Already there have been five such incidents. We may say that it's a sign of the times.

But while Koume may have attributed the ills besetting Japan to evil spirits or ominous portents, she also commented on the popular anger at the price rises, corruption, incompetence, and greed of wealthy merchants and complacent officials.

In the second month of Bunkyū 1 (1861), a rice broker, Nogawaya Yahei (known locally as Noya), was arrested and imprisoned for price gouging. He had been abetted by a government official called Mizuno Tōbei, who was reduced in rank for his role in the crime. To make an example of Noya, the domain confiscated his stores of rice and offered them to the public at below-market prices. On 2/17 Koume copied a story about Noya and Mizuno that was circulating in the town:

[A doctor] called Kuroiwa has both Nogawaya Yahei and Mizuno Tōbei among his patients. Recently, Noya sent a messenger to Kuroiwa from the jail. He said, "I'm sick, so please come and visit me." Although Kuroiwa had no desire to go, he felt it would be cruel not to accede to this request, so he went. Noya stuck his hand out of the window and asked the doctor to feel his pulse. Kuroiwa felt it, and he pronounced that Noya had a fever of the fluids. Noya said: "There are many different fluids; which one are you talking about?" Kuroiwa replied, "Blood fluid" [kesshō. A similar word, kessho, means confiscation of assets]. And he went home. [The doctor] thought that was the end of it, but then a messenger came from Mizuno, saying that his master was sick, and to please come as soon as possible. And so he went. . . . Once again, Kuroiwa diagnosed a fever of the fluids. Mizuno asked which fluid [*eki*] he was talking about, and this time he said "*kaieki*" [reduction in rank].

Koume was sympathetic to the townspeople who were suffering from high prices, and she certainly did not sympathize with a profiteering rice broker. But she also enjoyed the clever word play in this little story.

Like many domains, Kishū was thrown into economic and political turmoil by the financial instability, price inflation, and the need to create an effective military deterrent against the foreign threat. And like many domains, Kishū was riven by internal conflict over proposals for reform of the domain's finances and military. Reformers were often able samurai of junior rank who had little prospect of gaining positions of power in the existing system. For the most part, the conservatives stayed on top. They responded to the growing unrest among talented young samurai by cracking down on dissent and purging anyone they felt threatened or challenged their authority. Koume commented on one of the frequent purges on Bunkyū 1 (1861)/8/26: "[Hyōzō] went to visit Kitamura [Koume's cousin]. In a recent proclamation . . . he was rebuked for his outrageous (*furachi*) behavior and placed under house arrest. . . . Many people at present are being chastised. Eight people, including Yamabayashi, Nakajima, and Iguchi, were summoned during the day. . . . Kitamura and others in the evening. In each case, however, we have not heard the details. That's why [Hyōzō] went to visit him. He took a gift of *yōkan*."

As a result, talented younger samurai joined a growing stream of exiles fleeing their domains and joining the revolutionary factions in Kyoto, Chōshū, and Edo. A generation earlier, abandoning your domain and the daimyo to whom your family had sworn loyalty would have been unthinkable. Now, many saw it as their only choice as Japan needed a radical new path to deliver it from the multiple threats besetting it.

The Date family were among them. Frustrated with the continuing conservatism of Kishū domain and their own persecution, at the beginning of 1863 Date Chihiro and his sons Gorō and Munemitsu fled the domain and made their way to Kyoto. There, they were quickly taken up by anti-Tokugawa activists, many of them courtiers who were working for greater political power for the emperor.

Indeed, resistance was growing throughout Japan to the shogunate's conciliatory response to the demands of the foreign powers. By 1863 a powerful movement was agitating for their outright expulsion. At the same time, new ideologies were extolling the emperor as the true legitimate ruler of Japan. From the turn of the nineteenth century, scholars of national learning, including Kishū's own Motoori Norinaga, placed new emphasis on the study of Japan's native traditions, including the supposed divine origins of the imperial family. Scholars, including Hirata Atsutane and Aizawa Seishisai, developed more explicitly pro-imperial and antiforeign critiques—though neither directly criticized the shogunal regime. Their messages were in turn taken up by younger scholars such as Yoshida Shōin, who, prior to his arrest and execution by the shogunal administration, drew on the populist anger and Wang Yangming–inspired commitment to direct action of Ōshio Heihachirō and others. Out of this swirl of intellectual currents arose a new, more radical movement, coalescing around the twin goals of *sonnō* and *jōi* (revere the emperor and expel the barbarian). Popular unrest was further fueled by the rampant inflation.

Some members of the imperial court in Kyoto were caught up in the movement. Seeing the potential for a new, politically powerful role for themselves, they collaborated with activist samurai from Chōshū and other domains. Their goal was to mobilize the emperor himself in the expulsionist cause.

The emperor Kōmei was sympathetic to the antiforeign sentiment. But he was also deeply committed to the existing political status quo. He had agreed to marry his own sister to the shogun, and he supported a political arrangement in which the imperial house lent its prestige to the shogunate in return for a respected position in the shogun's counsel. In early 1863, in a further attempt to solidify ties between shogun and imperial court, the shogun Iemochi embarked on a grand progress to visit the emperor in Kyoto—the first such visit in over two hundred years. Kōmei welcomed the visit as a gesture of unity between court and shogunate, but his advisers persuaded him to demand that the shogun fix a day for the expulsion of the foreigners—a task that the shogunal delegation knew they would not be able to accomplish. British, French, and Dutch naval ships had recently arrived in Japan, tasked with chastising Satsuma domain for the murder by its samurai of a British merchant. The British also demanded an enormous indemnity for the murder. Faced with the threat of attack by the foreign warships, on Bunkyū 3 (1863)/5/9—one day before the date by which the shogun had committed to expel the foreigners—the shogunal authorities paid the indemnity in full. This was hardly the kind of firm measure envisioned by the activists. A month later the British force set out to chastise Satsuma by bombarding its capital city, Kagoshima.

Koume's diary is missing for 1863, so we do not know how she reacted to the shogun's visit to Kyoto; or to his promise to expel the foreigners; or to the indemnity payment to the foreigners; or to the attacks on foreign ships by Chōshū domain, which, seeing the failure of the shogunate to fight the foreigners, resolved to take action on its own; or to the British naval bombardment of Kagoshima. We know, however, that in the eighth month, Hyōzō was mobilized to participate in a military campaign. The fight was not against foreigners, but against a local uprising in the area around Nara.

On Bunkyū 3 (1863)/8/17, a group of thirty men attacked the shogunal office in Gojō and announced the restoration of direct imperial rule in the Nara region. Calling themselves the Tenchūgumi (Heaven's Wrath Band), they promised the local farmers a large cut in taxes and relief from their economic burdens and social humiliation under the Tokugawa regime. Within a few days, they had been joined by over a thousand supporters. The shogunate quickly mobilized its forces in the region.[10] Kishū provided a force of over two thousand samurai, farmer-soldiers, and even some monks, under the joint command of Shibayama Torazaemon, Sakanishi Sōroku, and Mizuno Tamon. Mizuno was, among his other duties, the supervisor of the domain school, and hence he was Hyōzō's boss.

Mizuno's force consisted of some five hundred men, Hyōzō among them.[11] After a decade of preparation, at long last the samurai of Kishū were going to war. It was not against the foreigners, but against people who in many ways resembled them: educated, lower-ranking samurai and village leaders who were motivated by passionate idealism and their own idea of loyalty.

Despite the alarm bells rung by the incursion of foreigners with their advanced military technology, the Kishū army was still structured on the principles of sixteenth-century warfare. The warriors left on horseback and on foot, accompanied by their foot soldiers and servants, wrapped in armor of lacquered blues and reds, helmets topped with gorgeous ornaments in gold leaf and white horsehair, banners streaming, and conch shells blowing.

Why did the seventy-year-old Hyōzō need to join this military force? He wrote that the army under Mizuno included a battalion of Confucian scholars, to which Hyōzō, as the senior scholar of the domain, was assigned. The scholars, like all Kishū samurai, were also military retainers of the daimyo. Hyōzō himself held a military rank in the domain hierarchy. And the chief of their unit was also their boss in the domain school. Perhaps the scholars were expected to function as a general staff for Mizuno. Or perhaps they were expected to chronicle the campaign: indeed, Hyōzō subsequently penned the only surviving firsthand account of the military disaster that followed.

According to Hyōzō's account, the Kishū army left Wakayama on Bunkyū 3 (1863)/8/18, marching first to Osaka and then on to Kyoto.[12] On 8/26 Mizuno was ordered to attack the rebels in their stronghold at Gojō. His forces left Kyoto and camped in Futami village outside Gojō. They were preparing for an attack on the rebels, but on the morning of 8/30 the rebels launched a preemptive strike. Despite superior numbers, the Kishū soldiers were inexperienced in warfare, and they were completely unready for the assault of the rebels, many of whom had resolved to die rather than submit to the shogunate. The Kishū troops quickly scattered in disarray, and Mizuno himself abandoned his troops and fled back to Wakayama. Hyōzō wrote:

> He left written orders entrusting the army to a subordinate officer. I knew nothing of this, and early in the morning I sought him out to discuss the plans. That's when I learned of his disappearance.... Knowing nothing of what was going on, the soldiers became uneasy until generals Koide and Nagasaka succeeded in calming them. Meanwhile ... I and several others returned to Wakayama to counsel Lord Mizuno to return to the field. But his Lordship would not listen. On the fourth [Bunkyū 3/9/4] Lord Mizuno retired to his residence due to illness.

The domain leadership was furious at Mizuno for his cowardice and dereliction of duty. "On the twenty-eighth [Bunkyū 3/9/28] a letter arrived from Wakayama. The gist was that Lord Mizuno had disobeyed the military code, and he was to receive stern punishment. All of us were grief-stricken. His Lordship was to be reduced from his current rank of domain elder with a stipend of 3,000 koku to the second officer class with a stipend of 1,500 koku."

The Tenchūgumi debacle clearly illustrated the unpreparedness of Kishū for a military conflict. In the following years, the domain launched a prolonged campaign of military modernization and reform that by the end of the decade had begun to remake the Kishū army into a Western-style fighting force. The Tenchūgumi was finally suppressed after a month of fighting by a shogunal force of thirteen thousand troops.

The uprising was only one episode in the turmoil afflicting the Kyoto region. After the emperor's expulsion edict, activists poured into Kyoto, determined to take matters into their own hands in defiance of the shogunal authorities. The shogunate responded by mobilizing its most loyal domains, and troops from all sides poured into Kyoto. The shogun himself remained in the area, shuttling between his Kyoto palace and Osaka castle. In the early months of Genji 1 (1864), the sense of an ongoing crisis is palpable in the pages of Koume's diary. On 2/21 Kishū domain circulated a directive (which Koume copied) calling on its samurai to respond to the crisis with loyalty and forbearance. "We know that the mobilization of so many people is causing hardship," said the memorial. "But the times are out of joint. There has been one difficult incident after another, and you must understand the current situation. We must not panic, but must respond with dedication, remembering the many years of blessings we have received as the gift of the domain." And on 2/24 Koume copied a long message from the shogun, explaining the current political circumstances and asking for the cooperation and loyalty of all the domains as he responded to the crisis.

The domain most committed to the "revere the emperor and expel the foreigner" movement was Chōshū, in the far southwest of Honshū island. In the sixth month of Genji 1 (1864), Chōshū sent a large and well-disciplined military force to Kyoto. Koume described the arrival of the Chōshū men as witnessed by a friend who was stationed in Osaka: "On the twenty-third [Genji 1/6/23], one thousand Chōshū men under the domain elder Fukuhara Echigo no Kami passed in front of the Kishū mansion at Tenjinbashi in Osaka, on their way to Kyoto. They were lined up in formation, with silk and cotton flags, each borne by a company of 40 men numbered from one to 8, with drums beating, with absolute discipline in the ranks. Truly we are living in uneasy times."[13] The loyalist domains, including Kishū, responded with mobilizations of their own. "Well, I must say," commented Koume, "the times are not calm.... Lord Miura has been mobilized, and we don't know when he will depart. Classes [Hyōzō had been teaching Miura's sons at the Miura residence] have been canceled."[14]

The Chōshū forces were determined to take direct action in support of the imperial cause. On 7/19 the Chōshū forces attacked the Hamaguri ("clam") gate of the imperial palace, which was defended by warriors of Aizu and Satsuma domains. A battle followed in which the Chōshū forces were soundly defeated. During the conflict, however, fires erupted that destroyed much of central Kyoto.

Koume reported on the Hamaguri gate incident the next day, 7/20. Rumors were flying in Wakayama, and several people brought accounts of the ongoing battle. Tanaka Zenzō reported that since the previous evening Wakayama castle had been in a commotion. Key retainers were being summoned, and Tanaka had been at the castle all night. Shortly after, Matsushita Hikoemon's servant came over and reported that his master had been summoned to Osaka and would leave immediately. Then, in the evening, Sakai Baisai stopped by and told them that "Kyoto is in an uproar." He had heard that Lord Miura's retainers were all being called to arms and would set off for Kyoto. Finally, in the evening, Umemoto Keizō came to visit and told them that "word is there's a battle going on right now in Kyoto. It's said that the castles in Fushimi and Yodo have been taken. But it's very uncertain. All of a sudden there is no communication from Kyoto.... In our neighborhood, Nagasaka, Wada Yoshirō, Kashiwara, Motozaki, Yokomachi, and Tamagawa have all been mobilized today. Mr. Shibuya of Nakanochō has also been mobilized. Oura and Habu have been mobilized, and all [eligible] men have been called up. But it's all very unclear."

Two days later Koume wrote: "The domain is mobilizing.... Armor and spears are being distributed at the gate of the Arima compound. My husband does not know whether he or his students will be mobilized. [Mizuno] Tamon will depart at the eighth hour." And the next day, Genji 1/7/21, Koume reported that sixteen thousand men had assembled, and more were arriving.

The immediate crisis was resolved with the expulsion of the Chōshū troops from Kyoto by the forces of Aizu and Satsuma, and on 7/27 Koume reported that "the security conditions are [back to] normal," and "we should continue with the work of the school." On 7/23, four days after Chōshū's attack on the imperial palace, the emperor issued a rescript commanding the shogun to chastise Chōshū. The shogunate, stung by the attacks on its own troops, was happy to comply. It appointed Tokugawa Mochitsugu, the Kishū daimyo, to command the campaign. Such an appointment was a very undesirable honor: leading a major military campaign would incur enormous expenses. Luckily for Mochitsugu and the domain, the shogunate recognized his inexperience (he was only nineteen years old) and quickly replaced him with the retired lord of Owari, Tokugawa Yoshikatsu, while Mochitsugu was given a lesser position as commander of the shogunal bannermen in charge of the rearguard.

Before the shogunate could launch its offensive, the foreign powers in Japan made their own move against Chōshū. The foreigners had been planning a strike against Chōshū since it began shelling foreign ships in the strait of Shimonoseki a year earlier. They waited until they could amass a sizable fleet of British, French, Dutch, and American ships. On Genji 1/8/5 (September 5, 1864), the fleet sailed into the strait of Shimonoseki and began a systematic bombardment of Chōshū's gun emplacements, before landing marines to storm the Chōshū positions. The battle was a decisive victory for the foreigners, and it greatly weakened Chōshū just as it was under threat from a shogunal invasion. Koume reported the battle on 9/3, concluding that neither Chōshū nor the shogunate gained from the foreign victory "Chōshū must pay a large amount of money, and Japan has been humiliated and forced to take guidance from the foreigners." In the same entry she passed on a rumor (which turned out to be untrue) that the emperor himself would lead the attack on Chōshū.

On 11/3 the army of Kishū domain staged large-scale exercises in preparation for the upcoming campaign against Chōshū. Koume went to Arahama to watch with her friend Tamae. They watched a thousand of Lord Andō's troops parading with conch shells blowing, drums beating, and cannon firing. In the evening they stopped to admire the files of warriors stretching into the distance, their lanterns flickering in the dusk. On 11/8 Koume went out after breakfast to a strategically placed shop, the

Kappaya, from where she could watch another division of the army "set off to chastise Chōshū. They were a magnificent sight.... Among those we know, [Kano's brother Kuroda] Ushinosuke is in the 'killing hand' brigade [*sattetai*]," and Koume mentioned a dozen others whom her family knew well. She went on: "They will march 5 *ri* (about 12 miles) a day. It's said that after Osaka, they will march with spears at the ready. They marched to the beat of a drum." On 11/27 the Kawai family were jolted by a huge explosion. They thought is must be cannon fire, but it turned out to be the domain's gunpowder magazine exploding. Eight people were killed, including a young child, as well as several cows that were kept in the compound. The explosion damaged houses throughout the district, causing some to collapse. The total damage was estimated at 50,000 ryō.

The Chōshū campaign was short and (for the shogunate) sweet. Chōshū capitulated without a fight, and in a brokered agreement at the end of the year, Chōshū agreed to punish antishogunal activists in the domain (three were made to commit suicide and their heads taken to Edo), to suppress such activism in future, and to return several antishogunal court officials who had taken refuge in Chōshū the previous year. The Chōshū daimyo also accepted some personal humiliations, but Chōshū did not lose any soldiers, land, or wealth, and indeed the events of the year prompted Chōshū to move forward with the radical modernization of its military.[15] For the Kishū samurai, though, the quick resolution of the conflict meant demobilization and return to Wakayama. The first of them arrived on Keiō 1 (1865)/1/16, with Kano's brother Ushinosuke in the first batch of returnees. Yūsuke and Hyōzō went straight out to welcome him home.

Unfortunately, the respite was to be short-lived. Although Chōshū had been temporarily subdued, its antishogunal, reformist faction remained very active. It included some of the most intelligent and far-sighted men in the domain. In early 1865 the reformists in Chōshū launched a military attack on conservative hold-outs, and the outcome of the brief civil war within the domain was to place the reformists in top positions in the domain administration. Their priorities were military reform and accommodation with the foreigners, to create an effective antishogunal alliance. The move to befriend the foreigners was an ironic turn, given the antiforeign origins of the movement. But it reflects the growing sophistication of the leaders, and their recognition that the best hope for the long-term independence of Japan was to overthrow the shogunate and unite the country under a modernizing administration.

The shogunate quickly recognized that the settlement it had agreed to a few months earlier was not really a settlement at all. Indeed, it had triggered a revolution in Chōshū that had made the domain even more defiant. Chōshū was now buying large quantities of high-technology foreign weaponry, and the threat it posed was growing by the day. Almost as soon as the soldiers were home, the shogunate embarked on plans for another, more decisive expedition.

Once again, the shogunate asked the lord of Owari to lead the expedition, but this time he refused.[16] And once again, the shogunate turned to Mochitsugu, lord of Kishū, who was forced to accept. The supreme commander would be the shogun himself.

On Keiō 1 (1865)/4/28, Koume wrote that "The daimyo has been commanded to subdue Mōri Daizen [daimyo of Chōshū] . . . [who] still shows no sign of repentance. . . . This has been commanded by the government in Edo." Once again, the troops gathered to depart for war. Lord Andō's force of 2,600 men left for Osaka on 5/17. Koume went to Honmachi to watch the soldiers marching. The daimyo himself left the next day, on horseback, accompanied by only a dozen retainers. At the harbor he boarded the domain's steamship, the *Meikō*, to take him to Osaka. Meanwhile, the shogun, Tokugawa Iemochi, left Edo on 5/16 and arrived in Osaka on 5/22.[17]

The Kishū daimyo Mochitsugu's stay in Osaka was to last a whole year, while shogun Iemochi's advisers struggled to put together a powerful enough coalition for a decisive attack on Chōshū, while also trying to deal with repeated demands from aggressive foreign powers to open more ports, including Hyogo and Osaka itself. The cost of this delay was enormous. The shogunate was said to be spending 175,000 ryō a month to keep the shogun and his army in Osaka.[18] The domains were also suffering from heavy expenses. Kishū ended the year with a deficit approaching one million ryō.

While they were stationed in Osaka and Kyoto, soldiers began falling ill with diseases caused by malnutrition and poor hygiene. On Keiō 1 (1865)/6/20, Koume wrote: "Kanamori Genzaemon, who had returned [from Osaka] suffering from beriberi, has died of heart failure caused by

FIGURE 5.1 Portrait photograph of Tokugawa Mochitsugu, date and artist unknown. Image in public domain, from the collection of Chokkyū Kansōbun, Tokyo, Japan. Reproduced from Wikimedia: https://commons.wikimedia.org/wiki/File:Tokugawa_Mochitsugu.jpg.

the disease. He was twenty-two." A few weeks later, on 8/17, she wrote: "Recently many in Osaka have fallen sick. Many have died of heart failure caused by the [beriberi]." Koume recounted the story of a young Aizu samurai who had fought heroically during the Hamaguri gate incident. "This person was one of twenty or more who have died from beriberi. Everyone is saying what a tragedy it is.... Truly Aizu is a domain that never gives up, a strong domain, but it could not beat the beriberi." Iemochi himself was never to leave Osaka. He succumbed there to beriberi on Keiō 2/7/20 (August 29, 1866), aged only twenty-one. In the same year, the emperor Kōmei died, depriving the shogunate of a crucial supporter.

Koume's diary does not report on the departure of the army from Osaka to Chōshū in June 1866. The domains made a show of support, but most, including the Tokugawa daimyo of both Owari and Kishū, disapproved of the war.[19] And the campaign quickly turned into a military disaster for the shogunal forces as they found themselves outmaneuvered by the newly modernized forces of Chōshū. By this time, Chōshū had the secret support of its powerful neighbor Satsuma, which had helped Chōshū buy over seven thousand of the latest English guns. Fortunately for Mochitsugu and his retainers, the campaign was brought to a halt by the unexpected death of the shogun, which provided an excuse for the shogunal forces to abandon the campaign and go home.

WAR AND REVOLUTION

In the final months of Keiō 3 (1867), a series of crises combined in an explosion of unrest and conflict. They culminated in the decisive battle of Toba-Fushimi, which marked the end of the Tokugawa era.

On Keiō 3 (1867)/8/11, Koume reported on news she had heard from the mother of the nursemaid who was taking care of the children: "In Osaka, the site of the former boat landing was to be turned into residences for the foreigners. However, after Satsuma intervened, the plan was abandoned. Nowadays, the shogunate has lost its strength, and as a result Kishū is in a very difficult position." In this exchange, passed on to her by a humble townswoman, Koume shows the political awareness of the people of Wakayama. The shogunate was being increasingly squeezed by the competing demands of the foreigners and the western domains in alliance with radical factions in the imperial court. And Kishū domain, which was ruled by a senior member of the Tokugawa family, was increasingly beleaguered as it was unable to disengage itself from the losing side.

At the same time, Koume noted a decline in the security situation in Wakayama. On 8/30 she described a bold robbery that had taken place at a neighbor's house. There had been other reports of crimes around the city. In one case, a group of ten robbers had knocked on the servants' door of a house, and when a maid answered, they had tied her up. The same gang had robbed a merchant of 13 ryō. Similar reports were coming in from around the country, as law and order broke down and renegades organized themselves into criminal gangs.[20]

On 5/1 Koume copied out a long list that she simply headed "satirical poems" (*rakushu*). Most of them referred to local politics, though some were on national topics. They included:

> The man who will hand over the sacred country [Japan] to the foreigners: Hitotsubashi [Tokugawa Keiki, the fifteenth shogun]
>
> Even the daikan [regional governors appointed by the shogun] have lost their authority and are now selling fish
>
> The man who is most conceited: Tsuda Matatarō [Tsuda Izuru: a reforming bureaucrat recently appointed to a powerful position by the daimyo]
>
> The man with sinister designs: Tanaka Zenzō [another reforming bureaucrat, and close friend of the Kawai family—he was murdered soon after this]
>
> The *ōzeki* [a top rank in sumo wrestling] of standing by and doing nothing: the samurai administrators
>
> The one we should feel sorry for: His Lordship [the daimyo]

These quotes, which Koume must have copied from a circulating broadsheet, once again illustrate the political awareness of the townsmen of Wakayama. They also illustrate the vibrant culture of satirical writing, often couched in riddles, parodies, and witty epithets, that was circulating in cities throughout Japan, with little regard for censorship or government suppression.

On Keiō 3 (1867)/10/14, recognizing the inevitability of a new political system with the emperor at its head, the newly appointed shogun, Tokugawa Yoshinobu, renounced his title and swore submission to the emperor. The gesture was not enough to appease the reformist leaders of Chōshū and Satsuma. Together with Tosa domain, Satsuma and Chōshū had been planning for the last year to launch a military assault on the shogunate, and to destroy the Tokugawa once and for all. Now, with Yoshinobu still retaining all his lands and wealth, they decided the time had come to act. On 11/13 the Satsuma daimyo, Shimazu Tadayoshi, set off for Kyoto at the head of a powerful army. On 11/18 he met with Mōri Takachika, the daimyo of Chōshū, and they formalized their military alliance. On 11/23 the Satsuma forces entered Kyoto. The Chōshū forces with Mōri at their head arrived a few days later.

While many of these developments were shrouded in secrecy, the Tokugawa family understood that it faced an existential threat. In Wakayama on 10/27, without warning, all the domain's retainers were summoned to the castle—"no one knows why." The next day Koume reported that four hundred men had already been mobilized, and "in the evening my husband took a gift of fish to Suzuki Kantarō, who will depart tomorrow morning." The main body of troops left the following day, 10/28. They were to proceed separately to Kyoto but were to gather at the Honganji temple after their arrival. On the same day, Koume copied in full the shogun's letter returning his powers to the emperor, together with a message from the Kishū domain government informing the retainers that "hereafter, we can expect to see and hear things never before experienced," and exhorting them to follow the path of discernment and morality and to avoid improper actions, so that "we will be able to live in the enjoyment of safety." Koume commented: "Whether or not it is in response to these developments, we have heard that there have been disturbances in Kyoto on the nineteenth and twentieth, what sort we don't know. According to rumor, a large number of men from Satsuma carrying cannons came to Kyoto, and Aizu tried to stop them from bringing those cannons [into the city] . . . the situation sounds very difficult."

But if Koume's attention had been caught by the developing crisis in the capital, it was soon distracted by more immediate events at home. On 11/12 the Wakayama samurai community was rocked by a dramatic murder. The victim was the Kawai family's former colleague and close friend, Tanaka Zenzō.

On the day of the attack, Koume confined herself to reporting the facts. A headless body had been left at the castle gates. Witnesses had seen four men attack and kill the victim, decapitate him, and carry off his head wrapped in a cloth. Most of the samurai men in town had been at the parade grounds, drilling for possible mobilization to Kyoto. The victim had been identified as Tanaka Zenzō.

Zenzō was a scholar in the domain school, and for a decade and more, he had been at the very heart of the Kawai family's social and scholarly circle. Although he was thirty years younger than Hyōzō (he was closer to Yūsuke's age than to theirs), he and his family were connected to the Kawai by three generations of friendship and professional ties, as well as by a shared love of art and poetry. The diary records hundreds of exchanges between the two families during the 1850s, from flower-viewing and poetry-writing excursions, to drunken parties at each other's homes, to helping each other out by lending servants. The relationship was not confined to the men. Zenzō's mother Hisano was Koume's close friend, sometimes staying overnight with the Kawai family. Koume attended events at the Tanaka home, relishing the sharing of artistic and poetic composition. And Zenzō's grandmother had been a friend of Koume's mother.[21]

Sometime in the 1860s, Zenzō had stepped down from his teaching duties, on his appointment to a position in the domain's central decision-making body, the "peacock council." Zenzō was charged with furthering the domain's program of reform. To help pay the enormous expenses incurred by the daimyo for the Chōshū campaigns, Zenzō proposed abolishing many of the hereditary stipends paid by the domain, instead paying all its retainers a fixed stipend of 1.5 koku per household member, regardless of rank, in addition to a salary for any official position they held. This measure was naturally unpopular with the upper-class samurai who depended on generous stipends. Zenzō was also a proponent of radical military reform, arguing for the creation of a Western-style, uniformed army composed of both samurai and commoner soldiers. The inclusion of commoners (other than in support positions) was a red line for many samurai in the domain, who had been raised on the assumption of their exclusive right to dominate military affairs.

Tanaka's murder was part of the complex and fraught political situation in Wakayama. There were at least four different reform factions in and out of the government, each representing a markedly different vision of Wakayama's future. Their rise and fall were in turn linked to factional politics at the very top of the domain hierarchy. Tanaka's had not in fact been the dominant vision in 1867: rather, the leader had been Tsuda Izuru, who had proposed a much more moderate program of financial and military reforms, including an across-the-board 35 percent reduction in samurai stipends, and a status quo policy with regard to military affairs. But at the end of November Tsuda was abruptly dismissed.

Koume was pleased by the dismissal of Tsuda, which on Keio 3 (1867)/11/6 she called "good news (*medetashi*)." But she was also concerned that the dismissal would lead to another wholesale purge, like that of Date Chihiro's supporters a few years earlier.

At this point Tanaka's more radical plan came to the fore. A series of negotiations followed between Tanaka and the domain elder Hisano Lord of Tanba, who strongly disapproved of Tanaka's proposals. Tanaka accepted his superior's demands, agreeing to help implement a policy very similar to that of the dismissed Tsuda. But the next morning, Tanaka was set on by five assailants and killed.

Tanaka's death evoked mixed reactions in the domain. On one hand, he had been a friend to many, and there was widespread condemnation of the assassins for taking the law into their own hands. On the other, there was sympathy for the goals of the assassins—who had immediately turned themselves in. Indeed, Koume notes in her diary that "even low people are rejoicing at the killing."[22]

The following day (11/13) Koume gave a much fuller account. The five murderers had been apprehended and jailed in various places, each under the care of a senior domain official. One of them was placed in the house of Lord Kanō, where Hyōzō was a regular teacher. Koume commented on 11/15 that the prisoners were all being well-treated. Lord Kanō was giving his prisoner the freedom to bathe and to chat with the household staff, but he was being guarded by ten men, day and night.

The day of the murder, Zenzō's son came to the Kawai house with the details of the funeral. Hyōzō attended on behalf of the family. A few days later it was Koume's turn to represent the family at a wake held for Tanaka. She was one of twenty-three people in attendance, most of whom were family members. Koume deliberately sat outside the family circle, not wanting to draw attention to herself. The dinner went on late, and Koume commented that "the people at home were very worried. The situation here is so unsettled. They were wondering: 'What if there were another murder?'"[23]

Despite her fear and her close personal connection to the victim, Koume continued to show her enjoyment of scurrilous or satirical verses. On 11/27 she transcribed several more satirical poems that were doing the rounds in Wakayama:

> In the world today, Tsuda [Izuru] is flying and Tanaka has fallen
> Everyone in the house should rejoice! A quarter [of our
>   stipends?] will be forgiven, *yai, yai*!

While Wakayama was being rocked by these dramatic events, Koume reported on yet another unprecedented phenomenon. On 11/13 Haru, the daughter of Koume's close friend Tsuneno from Umatsugi village, came to visit with a letter she had received from her father Sakai Baisai, who was in Kyoto. "It's all so strange," Haru said. "I want you to read it."

The letter reported that in towns and cities all over Japan, divine amulets had started dropping from the sky. The amulets were of wood, clay, and even stone and depicted all sorts of divinities, both buddhas and native Japanese deities. In one case, "a stone Jizō [Ksitigarbha Bodhisattva] weighing 7 or 8 kan [25–30 kg] fell on a roof and made no noise. Nor was a single tile broken. When people touched it, their bodies trembled." In another, "a woman from Edo descended naked from the sky in Nagoya."

In response to this sudden outpouring of divine portents, people were taking to the streets and dancing. "Now it has begun in the south part of Kyoto," wrote Baisai. "Divine images have been falling from the sky, and there has been great excitement. Even in fine weather, they have been falling from the sky."

> In the houses on which the divine images have fallen, they are displaying decorations of bamboo grass, erecting sacred ropes, and making offerings of rice cakes, sake, fish, and sweets. Family members are gathering in the towns, wearing layers of clothes—winter jackets [*hanten*], Yūzen silk, and dappled *kanoko* cloth, all costing 11 or 12 ryō each.

Wealthier people are wearing five or six layers at once! Their bright red clothes cost over 100 ryō! Women are dressing as men, and men as women. And they are behaving in all sorts of strange ways, it's enough to widen one's eyes. They are playing flutes, shamisen, and drums, ringing bells, cheering, and dancing as they shout "*Yoi ja nai ka yoi ja nai ka*" [it's okay isn't it?]. Everyone, even strangers and samurai, are holding the hands of the people they meet in the street and saying "let's dance, let's dance," as they dance through the streets. The sound of their celebrations starts around noon, and continues till the seventh or eighth hour [2:00–3:00 a.m.]. . . . You would never think that we are expecting a war here. Since this is such an extraordinary event, I wanted to send you a rough description.

On Keiō 3 (1867)/11/20, Koume's servant Sakichi told her that the strange happenings had spread to Wakayama. A few amulets had fallen in the Tatamiyamachi district, and near Kawakami an image of a lion-dog had fallen from the sky. Spooked by the strange and disturbing events, Koume wrote, "At the end of the world, there will be turbulent times and many ominous events, but all we can do is endure."

Three weeks later, on 12/7, Koume wrote:

Amulets are falling here and there. The domain has asked that they should be turned over to the authorities. First they fell on Kawafune. One also fell on Daifukuya in Surugamachi. When an amulet fell in Kukenochō, it's said that a servant inadvertently threw it down the drain. Near the harbor, an amulet fell on the potted plant of a woman who lives alone. Overjoyed, she wanted to make an offering of sacred sake, but she had no money. So she took one of her kimonos to the pawnshop, and she went and bought sake and made her offering to the gods. She went to sleep, and when she woke in the morning the kimono she had pawned the day before was there in her house, as well as 50 ryō in money. Finding this very suspicious, she went back to the pawnshop and told them what had happened. [At first] they would not listen to her, but when they went to look at the shelf where they had left the kimono, it was gone. And so was the money. They were more and more amazed. Whether it's true or not I don't know. . . . At Beniya, when they looked at the hand towels they had dyed, they found that many of them were printed in red with the word "*o-kage*" [thanks to the gods].

For the next three weeks, Koume reported on the strange sights and even stranger stories of the falling amulets. On 12/23 Kuroda Yae told Koume of a conversation she had had with Tsuji Bungo of Nango village. The amulets had just started falling in his village. His daughter Takano had told him about it. She said that "some had fallen near her house, and everyone put on red undershirts and went out dancing. She asked Bungo to lend her a shirt, which he did. She said that this evening she would dress as a man. Men are dressing as women [too]." Bungo told Yae a story about events in the boat-building district of Wakayama:

> At [a shop called] Shinkoya ... an amulet fell from the sky. But just as everyone was rejoicing, the younger son was possessed by a fox. A relative called Moriya came and tied up his arms and legs. They bathed him in incense smoke, and the fox left him. But then it possessed his older brother's wife. The same happened to the wife of a shopkeeper near the Nakahashi bridge. The two [wives] met each other in the street, and the wife from Shinkoya prostrated herself. Apparently the fox possessing the lady from Nakahashi was of a higher status.... Truly, the things you see and hear nowadays are unprecedented.

And on 12/12: "In Okiyachō, an old woman was selling charcoal. Behind her, an image of the Kannon bodhisattva fell [from the sky]. She found one in the mouth of her stove too. Rejoicing, she decorated her entrance with sacred bamboo grass and made a small shrine for the images. She made an offering of rice wine and lit a lantern as a thanks offering. Now people are offering money and praying to the shrine."

But the revelry and unexpected happenings had a darker side. Also on 12/12, Koume wrote of revelers who "kicked over boxes of turnips, and when the shop owner complained, they ignored him, singing '*Yoi ja naika, yoi ja naika.*' ... At a secondhand clothes shop, two red undershirts were stolen. When the owner reproached the people, they said, '*Yoi ja naika, yoi ja naika.*' Everyone's gone crazy, but they all seem to be overjoyed."

The authorities did their best to control the sudden outpouring, as Koume reported on 12/13:

> At Wakaya in 7-chōme, sacred paper and images of *Daikoku* have been falling. The people have been drinking sake and from early evening they

FIGURE 5.2 *Keiō yon hōnen odori no zu* (Dancing in the year Keiō 4). Illustrated calendar by Kawanabe Kyōsai. Collection of National Diet Library, Tokyo, Japan. Public domain image reproduced from Wikimedia, https://commons.wikimedia.org/wiki/File:EeJaNaiKaScene.jpg.

can be heard dancing in the streets. It's said that the authorities have scolded them. When they catch people dancing they are fining them. . . . Women are dancing with their hair finely decorated, but when the officials scold them [for the extravagant display], they take their hands and say "Instead of saying such things, why don't you dance with us?"

And in Kyoto, "the newspapers report that a certain Yokota, a policeman of Fushimi, was on his way to work on the eighth of this month. In front of his own gate, two men disguised as participants in the dancing that has been popular lately grabbed his sword and cut him down. Taking up his head, they tied it with bamboo grass and dumped it on the Takeda highway."[24]

Amid all this, on 12/9 Koume watched as the Kishū daimyo, Tokugawa Mochitsugu, departed Wakayama with a small retinue for yet another military campaign. The main body of his troops had left a few days earlier, followed by those of Lord Andō, and Lord Mizuno's would depart shortly thereafter. This time, their mission was to save the shogunate itself. "It was very cold, with snow . . . the first real winter weather this year. We are worried that his lordship will get cold and ill in his palanquin, and his arrival in Kyoto will be delayed." In fact, Mochitsugu never made it to Kyoto. On 12/7 Koume wrote: "Kyoto is unsettled, so the daimyo is staying in Osaka for now." Two weeks after his appointment, Mochitsugu diplomatically resigned his commission as head of the Tokugawa army, on the grounds of sickness. He quietly returned to Wakayama on 12/20, thus avoiding any involvement in the shogunate's climactic defeat two weeks later.

Amid these troubles, Hyōzō had some bad news from the domain authorities. The publication of his book had been canceled. Confronted by its worst financial crisis in living memory, the administration had to do everything it could to curtail expenses. Hyōzō must have been deeply disappointed that his life's work had fallen victim to the political and economic crisis. But he also recognized that the time for publishing long works of abstract speculation was gone. In an epilogue to his manuscript, Hyōzō reflected on the changes that had made his work obsolete:

> The shogun has embarked on trade with foreign countries, and the samurai are all training with guns. Everyone is devoting themselves to the study of foreign books, and those interested in studying the teaching of the sages have almost disappeared. These are the times that we live in. To whom will this book now be of service? . . . Since I have been absorbed in this work for many years, I do believe that some use must be made of it. So I have kept a copy which I will store in my home. I will be very happy if it can help a future generation of students who have once again returned to the study of the Commentary of Zuo.[25]

Hyōzō's comments reflected the growing sense of changing times. New intellectual currents had been seeping into the Japanese scholarly world for decades, but the political crises of the nineteenth century accelerated their spread, as educated people looked for new solutions to the problems

Japan was facing. Scholars in Japan had been studying Western science for more than a century, but they had faced obstacles arising from conservative reaction as well as xenophobia. Now, military science was an urgent need, while knowledge of Western systems of government, philosophy, and medicine was increasingly seen as an avenue to advancement.

By this time Koume was getting her information not only from letters from friends and word of mouth but also from newspapers. On Keio 3/1/26, she wrote that "today a newspaper came. We had it taken over to the Senjutsusho (military training ground)." Several months later, on 5/15, she once again mentions receiving two newspapers, from Hyōzō's colleague Noguchi Junsuke. The newspapers, which were several months out of date, were "produced by the Englishman, Bailey." Koume is referring to the *Bankoku shinbun* (News of the world), founded by Reverend M. Buckworth Bailey at the beginning of 1867, and thought to be the second Japanese-language newspaper to be launched in Japan after Joseph Heco's *Kaigai shinbun*, which was founded in 1865. The *Bankoku shinbun* was a compendium of foreign news from around the world, arranged by country. The newspaper was short-lived, ending when Bailey abruptly left Yokohama at the end of the year.

Koume continued to report on the "unsettled" conditions in Kyoto, where some Kishū samurai had been in a brawl and two had been killed. Considering the events unfolding at the time, "unsettled" seems like an understatement. At the end of Keiō 3 (1867), a large army of soldiers from Satsuma and Chōshū domains had marched into Kyoto. On 12/9 they took control of the imperial palace and issued in the emperor's name a rescript stripping the ex-shogun of all his lands and estates.

On 12/18 Koume copied out an account that a family friend brought over, summarizing the dizzying changes of the past few days. The shogunate was to be abolished, as were all the official positions of the shogun. Prince Arisugawa was to be appointed to the new position of *sōsai* (prime minister), and many other new appointments were announced.

Tokugawa Yoshinobu had not intended to fight: he had resigned his office in the interest of unifying Japan so that it could withstand the pressures of Western imperialism. But now, faced with a coup d'état and the loss of his wealth and influence, he mobilized his forces in the Kyoto area to challenge the western domains' control over the emperor. Ostensibly, Yoshinobu merely wanted to present a petition to the emperor asking him to reverse his harsh edict. But Yoshinobu accompanied the petition with a large military force, and on Meiji 1 (1868)/1/3, the forces of the ex-shogun collided with those of the western alliance in a four-day battle at Toba-Fushimi outside Kyoto. The battle ended in a decisive defeat for the Tokugawa shogunate.

On Keiō 3 (1867)/12/18, the Kawai family received another long letter from their friend Baisai in Kyoto, describing the dramatic events of the past few days. Baisai wrote of the general mobilization of the shogunal forces on the entry of the Chōshū army into Kyoto on 12/8; the pardoning of the Chōshū rebels by the emperor; the abolition of all official government positions on 12/10; and the appointment of a new national government led by Prince Arisugawa and supported by military leaders from Satsuma, Chōshū, and Tosa. On 12/9 he wrote:

> Inside the imperial palace around thirty thousand troops gathered from Satsuma, Tosa, Echizen, and Aki. The officials of the imperial family ... were all expelled from the palace compound and relieved of their positions. Prince Arisugawa alone remained as protector of the emperor. The five senior retainers of Chōshū, as well as other court officials who had previously been dismissed, were all reinstalled in their positions. This affair will not easily be resolved. Altogether there are around fifty or sixty thousand men, and there have been many clashes.

On 12/12, according to Baisai, the shogun and all his senior retainers had been forced to leave the shogun's residence at Nijo castle in Kyoto, and all the shogunal institutions in Kyoto had been abolished, including the police forces that had been helping to maintain order. "The noticeboards detailing regulations were removed from the bridges. All the officers who were appointed to control outlawry were purged." Baisai explains that the people of Kyoto disliked the shogunal police: they "were wicked and cunning, and the townsmen had become frightened of them."

Baisai went on to outline the program of the new government: "It is said that men of ability will be employed without regard to rank. . . . The rule will be restored to the descendants of the emperor Jinmu, and there is no knowing what the future holds. The [new government] has proclaimed that it will aid the masses of poor and destitute by reducing prices." But despite these heartening proposals, Baisai concluded: "Truly there is nothing to compare with these pitiful events. It is also very worrying what will befall the nation.... Even men of great wisdom and thoughtfulness have no idea what will happen. No one is able to live calmly."

This was the final comment that Koume was to make on political affairs through the end of the Japanese calendar year, except to mention the daimyo's return to Wakayama on 12/26.

The diary stops at the end of Keiō 3. The final entry is on Keiō 3/12/30—January 24, 1868. Three days later, Japan would be shaken by the momentous battle of Toba-Fushimi, which spelled the permanent end of the shogunate and launched Japan's dramatic new era of imperial "restoration," national unification, and modernization. But Koume's diary falls silent. The volumes between 1868 and 1875 are missing. We cannot share the Kawai family's experience of the fall of the shogunate, the abolition of the domains, or indeed of the abolition of the samurai class itself. When her diary reopened on January 1, 1876, it would be in the brave new world of the Meiji era.

6

THE ARTIST'S LIFE

THE *BUNJINGA* TRADITION

Throughout the eventful years recorded in her diary, Koume never stopped painting. When she was at her busiest managing the Kawai household, entertaining guests, hiring and managing servants and helpers, and caring for her young grandchildren, Koume found time to paint only once or twice a month. Later in her life she worked much more consistently, sometimes completing dozens of works in a month. There can be no doubt that her art and her cultural status were central to her identity and sense of belonging in Wakayama and Kishū domain. They were also a significant contribution to her family's domestic economy.

Koume was trained in the Chinese *wenrenhua* (literati painting) tradition known in Japanese as *bunjinga*. The tradition on which the Japanese bunjinga artists built dated back to the fourteenth century and represented one of the major branches of Chinese painting. Chinese practitioners were often trained as scholars, calligraphers, and poets. Many held official positions in government, and they cultivated an intellectual esthetic of the passionate amateur, distancing themselves from the precision and technical mastery of professional painters, emphasizing instead their creativity and spontaneity. As Tokugawa Japan developed a tradition of scholar-bureaucrats among the governing samurai elite, the ideals and esthetics of Chinese painting quickly gained currency.

The pioneering practitioners of Japanese bunjinga were clustered in the Kansai area, and several indeed were from Kishū domain.[1] Gion Nankai (1676–1751), for example, was an eminent scholar and a well-known poet with no formal training as an artist. Nankai encountered *wenrenhua* in printed books such as the *Mustard Seed Garden Manual of Painting*, originally published in China in the 1670s and available in Japanese reprints from the early decades of the eighteenth century. It contained volumes on painting landscapes, bamboo, plum blossoms, and birds—all classic themes of *wenrenhua*. James Cahill suggests that because Nankai and others were viewing Chinese paintings in woodblock reproductions (most of which were in black and white), essential characteristics of the originals were lost or distorted in translation. For example, petals and leaves that might have been textured and free-flowing in the original Chinese paintings appear two-dimensional and stylized in Japanese renditions. As a result, Japanese artists developed a distinct and original style.[2]

A second Kishū-born artist with a national profile was Kuwayama Gyokushū (1746–1799). Gyokushū was born into a wealthy merchant family in Wakaura. He made a large personal fortune before retiring at the age of twenty-six and devoting himself to painting. He studied in both Edo and Kyoto, where he fell under the spell of the innovative painter Ike no Taiga (1723–1776), who was known for his landscapes based on travel and close observation, rather than on the idealized images created by earlier artists.[3] Gyokushū was not only a well-known artist but also an influential theorist of the bunjinga style. He flourished as a painter later in his life. In 1793 he was part of an influential group of painters who, in the tradition of Ike no Taiga, traveled to Kumano and executed many paintings of the region. Their collective work is considered one of the great creative bursts of Kishū's bunjinga painting tradition.

A third founding father of Kishū bunjinga painting was Noro Kaiseki (1747–1828). Kaiseki studied under Ike no Taiga, and later in his life he became an official painter to Kishū domain, with a retainer's rank and stipend. With Gyokushū, Kaiseki was a participant in the 1793 visit to Kumano, which was a formative experience for both painters. By the late eighteenth century, painters like Kaiseki had access to many more original Chinese works of art, and Kaiseki led a reversion to a more authentic Chinese style modeled on recent works of Qing dynasty artists.[4]

Koume was trained in the painting tradition established by this lineage. Her own teacher, Nogiwa Hakusetsu (1773–1849), had been a leading disciple of Kaiseki and was himself an official painter to the domain and a central figure in the domain's cultural life in the early nineteenth century.

Like their Chinese counterparts, Japanese bunjinga painters valued diverse intellectual talents, including not only painting but also philosophy, music, poetry, and calligraphy. Poetry and calligraphy were seen as intimately linked to painting, and the three were often combined in a single work, a *gassaku* (collaborative work), which might combine classical or newly composed Chinese or Japanese poems written in an artistic hand, with a painting in ink or color on a related theme. According to a Chinese practitioner: "What is not used up in poetry overflows to become calligraphy and is then transformed to become painting." Poetry, calligraphy, and painting formed a "trinity of expression" that each added power and meaning to the others.[5]

Literati artists of the samurai elite tended to idealize painting as an escape from the administrative burdens of their daily lives: the "spontaneous and direct expression of the self rather than aesthetic or representational perfection."[6] This escapist esthetic encouraged a playful spontaneity that often went with alcohol-infused social interaction. The scholars in Koume and Hyōzō's circle loved to congregate in parties that combined drinking, poetry composition, calligraphy, and drawing or painting. These events allowed them to combine their love of social connection and good food and drink as they sought collective creative inspiration. Indeed, the visual or verbal portrayal of inspired behavior such as drunkenness or playful antics helped lend authenticity to their work as literati artists.[7]

Kōno Motoaki, Yukio Lippit, and others have argued that the presentation of bunjinga as spontaneous, unpolished, amateur, and noncommercial was a carefully constructed ideal, hiding the diverse realities of "individual and local practices that were only loosely related and all significantly marked by differing historical and regional contingencies."[8] As much as they admired spontaneity, scholars who participated in bunjinga production also revered antiquity and tradition. In practice, they developed a tradition of imitation, allusion, and subtle variations on standard themes. Successful artists in the bunjinga tradition might—ironically—cultivate a spontaneous, amateur style as a mark of their professional skill, developing what Yukio Lippit calls "sophisticated techniques of de-skilling in order to cultivate an amateurity of expression." But there was nothing amateur about the prices paid for the work of fashionable artists. Indeed, Lippit points out that the myth of amateurishness masked a deeply transactional cultural milieu, in which "literati artifacts acquired meaning and value [within] complex economies of obligation and exchange."[9]

Even taking the genre at its face value, not all Western critics have been enamored with the Japanese craze for bunjinga. The influential nineteenth-century popularizer of Japanese art, Ernest Fenollosa, expressed amazement at the ubiquity of the bunjinga genre, which he called a "washed-out style of work," and by the extremely high prices it fetched. Of the practitioners whose work was in greatest demand, such as Ike no Taiga and Yosa Buson, he wrote that "from any universal point of view their art is hardly more than an awkward joke."[10]

GASSAKU AND THE SCHOLARLY CULTURE OF KISHŪ DOMAIN

The culture of bunjinga creation was essentially collaborative and participatory: a social act as well as one of individual creativity. For Koume, it was a doorway into participation in the rich cultural life of her domain's scholarly elite. Koume was excluded from many of the cultural events in which Hyōzō participated, either because they were male-only, or because they were specific to Hyōzō's workplace, or because they clashed with Koume's duties at home. But in the spring and autumn, when scholars, poets, and artists gathered at scenic spots to enjoy spring blossoms or fall colors, Koume was sometimes included.

A painting by Noro Kaiseki illustrates a gassaku event held in 1811 in Wakayama. The painting illustrates fourteen members of the Kishū scholar-artist community (all male, in this case) sitting together in an outdoor location, surrounded by pine trees and bamboo. The participants, many of whom have sake cups at their side, are variously engaged in painting, musical performance, playing games, or exchanging poetic verses (the painter in the center is assumed to be Kaiseki himself). The painting emphasizes both the natural setting and the spontaneously elegant,

FIGURE 6.1 Noro Kaiseki, *Gajin shūkai zu* (Illustration of a gathering of people of taste). Painting of scholars and artists at a gassaku party, 1811. Collection of Wakayama City Museum. Courtesy of Wakayama City Museum.

cultured, and creative pursuits of the participants. The creative spirit of the event is enhanced by the collaborative sociability, as well as by the liberal flow of sake.

Koume describes such an event on Ansei 6 (1859)/3/7, when she attended a party at Shōjūji temple at the invitation of the priest, who was an old friend of the family. She went in a party of eight, including three women: Koume, her mother Tatsuko, and the mother of one of Hyōzō's colleagues. After stopping at a friend's house along the way for tea and sake, they were welcomed by their host, and they spent some time enjoying the cherry blossoms. "We enjoyed creating gassaku with paintings, [Chinese] poems, and [Japanese] *haikai*. The cherries were in full bloom and the colors were really lovely. We climbed the [bell] tower and had a gathering there, gazing at the blossoms in the sunshine under a blue sky. It was very delightful. We were entertained lavishly, with grilled tofu and many other dishes."

However, "At around the fourth hour a sudden storm came up, bringing the party to a sudden end." While their clothes dried out the guests finished their meal indoors. The priest lent them all geta clogs to make their way home through the wet streets, the two elderly mothers supported by their grandsons. Koume completed eleven paintings at the gathering: four full size paintings of chrysanthemums, peonies, cherry blossoms, butterflies, and bamboo, one of them complemented by poems and other writing from three of the scholars; and half a dozen smaller paintings: sketches of citrus trees, pomegranates, and comical faces. Given the short time she spent at the temple, this was a very large output. It is easy to imagine the intense and satisfying burst of creativity that Koume would have put into this production.

Although painted much later in Koume's life, a painting of chrysanthemums in the collection of the Wakayama City Museum is representative of the kind of work Koume might have produced at an event like the spring party in Shōjūji. Executed in black ink on paper, the painting shows rapid brushwork and an impressionistic approach to sketching the flower's stem, leaves, and petals. The painting is on a full-size (80 cm by 25 cm) sheet of paper, and the vertical growth of the chrysanthemum complements the long, narrow composition space. The plant carries two sets of blossoms: one on a smaller stem, with small, quickly sketched blossoms; the other a composition of three large blossoms at the top of the painting. The stem emerges from the bottom right of the painting and forms a diagonal line toward the top left, until the blossoms fill the center of the composition near the top. The whole is surrounded by ample white space. Although the brushwork is entirely in black ink, the clever manipulation of the brush, with darker strokes near the center of the blossoms and lighter stroke for the outer petals, suggests the lush coloration of the chrysanthemum. Overall, the composition suggests many of the classic

FIGURE 6.2 Kawai Koume, *Kiku no zu* (Painting of chrysanthemums), date unknown. Collection of Wakayama City Museum. Courtesy of Wakayama City Museum.

themes of bunjinga painting: a spontaneous style, a standard poetic theme (chrysanthemum blossoms in season), and a simple, unfeigned pleasure in the beauty of nature.

There are, however, several elements that suggest the painting is not quite as fresh or in-the-moment as the bunjinga ideal might suggest. First, the chrysanthemum is not generally considered a spring flower. Rather, it is associated with the autumn season. It is possible that Shōjūji was cultivating spring-flowering chrysanthemums, but more likely that Koume's paintings at the Shōjūji event were based on standardized models that she carried in her head. Despite the emphasis on spontaneity and direct observation pioneered by leading artists such as Ike no Taiga, students of bunjinga painting more commonly learned by copying from books of model illustrations, usually prepared by their teacher. The process of painstakingly copying models again and again until the student could execute them perfectly reflected the philosophy of one of China's founding teachers of painting theory, Xie He (sixth century), who advocated "transmission through reproduction." The method mirrored the *sodoku* rote learning of the Confucian classics that occupied the first few years in the classroom. The Kano school treated its models as a trade secret, imparting them only to selected pupils. But by Koume's day, printed copy-books were widely available.[11] Koume spent long hours later in her life preparing such books for her own students (see chapter 7). A trained artist would most likely "see" an object not primarily from direct observation, but from long practice in copying such models.

The stylized character of the painting is further emphasized by its abstraction from any natural setting, and by the highly simplified leaf details, which show none of the serrated margins, complex vein structures, or variegated blade shapes typical of chrysanthemums. Structurally, it seems unlikely that this long, thin, and top-heavy plant could stand as it is portrayed without artificial support. While the initial impact of the work is in keeping with the ideology of bunjinga painting as fresh, spontaneous, and natural in its expressiveness, a closer examination suggests a careful adherence to tried-and-true models, and an emphasis on the idea of the thing more than the thing itself.

Koume participated in artistic gatherings not only as a painter, but also as a poet. On Kaei 4 (1851)/3/11, she joined an excursion to the seashore at Arahama. Arahama means "rough shore," but Koume commented, "It was calm, an Arahama only in name." Koume spent the afternoon painting and composing poems:

> Arahama wa / sono na nomi shite / haru no umi.
> Nami mo shizukeru / tatsu mo wasurete
> The ocean in springtime / Arahama only in name
> The waves are quiet, as though / they had forgotten how to stand up[12]

Afterward, Tanaka Zenzō invited them back to his house, "where we amused ourselves" composing linked verses. Each participant was given a kanji character to place at the start or end of a poem. Koume was given the place-name "Yoshino" to start, and the character *aru* (there is, there are) to end. "The flowers were in full bloom, with just one or two petals fluttering to the ground. The moon was shining its white light on the flowers, and the view was beautiful. But the lines would not come, and our spirits just got flustered. It had been a long day, and eventually we all fell silent from exhaustion." Finally, as they were about to give up and go home, Koume found her inspiration. "To the east of this house there is a pure water stream that runs through the garden. . . . I wrote and recited the following:

> *Yoshino* ni mo / masu-uo no shimizu / soko sumite.
> Teraseru tsuki ni / hana no kage *aru*
> In Yoshino too / The trout-filled streams are / Pure to the bottom
> In the moon's shining light / *There are* the shadows of flowers"[13]

We can sense Koume's satisfaction that it was she, rather than the eminent men in the gathering, who had found the inspiration for this atmospheric poem.

A surviving gassaku painted by Koume depicts a pair of traveling comedic storytellers identified as *manzai* performers. The inscription at the top is a Chinese poem brushed by Hyōzō:

> New Year's Day
> Singing and dancing
> Vine-decorated fan
> Echo of the *manzai*

The painting illustrates a performer dancing to the rhythm of the drum and manipulating his fan for dramatic effect as he delivers his recitation. The other performer, in the background, is beating a hand-drum. The sharp, jagged lines of the foreground performer's clothing create a sense of dynamic movement, while the lines in the background are softer and more fluid. The performers' comic facial expressions suggest the simple light-heartedness of the performance. The effect of rustic simplicity is augmented by the depiction of the performer's feet, wearing only a pair of straw half-sandals. The black-ink composition is gently enhanced with light wash tints of blue and brown.

Like the chrysanthemum painting discussed earlier, this work achieves a fresh, spontaneous, and charming effect. But the *manzai* painting is a true gassaku: a combined work of poetry, calligraphy, and painting. And unlike the chrysanthemum painting, this work shows a careful attention to composition and detail and a subdued but harmonious color scheme that suggest that, even if it was originally executed at a gassaku party, it was finished with more care in the studio.

Indeed, there is evidence from the diary that Koume and Hyōzō sometimes produced gassaku works at home and not always in the creative and spontaneous environment of a gassaku party. For example, on Bunkyū 1(1861)/2/5, Hyōzō and Yūsuke went to Tsukayama Gakuzō's house, where "they worked on a gassaku." The next day Tsukayama came to ask Koume to add a painting to the composition. In this case, although the poetry and calligraphy were executed by Yūsuke and Hyōzō, respectively, at a gassaku party, the painting was added by Koume later, in her studio.

KOUME'S PAINTING: BUNJINGA AND BEYOND

During the first half of Kaei 4 (1851), Koume mentioned painting on average two or three times a month. The recipients of her work came from all over the social spectrum: courtiers, patrons, colleagues, friends, family members, and servants. On 1/22 a friend requested her to execute a painting for one of the ladies-in-waiting at the retired daimyo's residence. On 1/27 she decorated a folding fan for the priest of Ennyoji temple. In the second month she worked on several paintings of young dancing girls for Noro Seikichi, a colleague of Hyōzō's. On 3/8 Hyōzō hosted two friends

FIGURE 6.3 Kawai Koume, *Manzai no zu* (Illustration of Manzai performers): a gassaku work by Koume and Hyōzō. Collection of Wakayama City Museum. Courtesy of Wakayama City Museum.

for an evening of gassaku poetry-writing and painting. Koume was happy to contribute but commented on the stress of managing their guests' entertainment while also painting and composing poetry. At the end of the day, she "rested, exhausted by being pressured by everyone." On 3/20 she was painting and reciting poems with a bookseller called Kusumotoya. And on 3/25 she composed some poems and painted chrysanthemums for a scholar's sixtieth birthday. In the fourth month she did a series of paintings on silk for Ichikawa Hitoshi, to go into an exhibition he was helping organize. A courtier who saw her work proposed to send them to the Edo residence of Andō Naohiro (1821–1885), daimyo of Tanabe (a subdomain of Kishū). In a panic, Koume asked for the paintings back so that she could work on improving them. In the sixth month she created a series of eleven paintings for a patron, Mr. Taya. And in the seventh month she gave two painted fans to her maid Toyo, to take back to her family in her home village.[14]

With such a wide variety of recipients, it is not surprising that the content of Koume's work should also be diverse. Although Koume herself used the word *bunjinga* to describe her artistic training, the diary shows her painting in a variety of genres that defy easy categorization. Koume was asked to decorate sets of sliding screens (*fusuma*) that were used to divide the rooms of a house, or smaller versions (*kofusuma*) for ornamental shelving used in reception areas. She painted military surcoats (*jinbaori*) as the warriors of the domain prepared for war in the 1850s and 1860s.[15] She painted fans, and she painted designs for cloth-covered boxes. She painted classical Japanese themes, such as portraits of warriors from the *Tales of the Heike*. She painted portraits of living and dead friends and family members. She sketched birds and flowers for her students to use as study aids, as well as a variety of trivia: "O-Fuku" masks (portraying a popular female figure associated with good fortune); comic sketches of fish and animals; and portraits of popular deities such as the "seven gods of good luck."

The largest surviving collection of her work is a copy of the sixteen-volume *Kankai ibun* (Strange things heard in foreign lands), which Koume made in 1837 (see chapter 2). *Kankai ibun* was richly illustrated with dozens of color paintings. The text and illustrations in Koume's possession were probably the result of multiple iterations of copying over the thirty years since the original appearance of the manuscript, though a

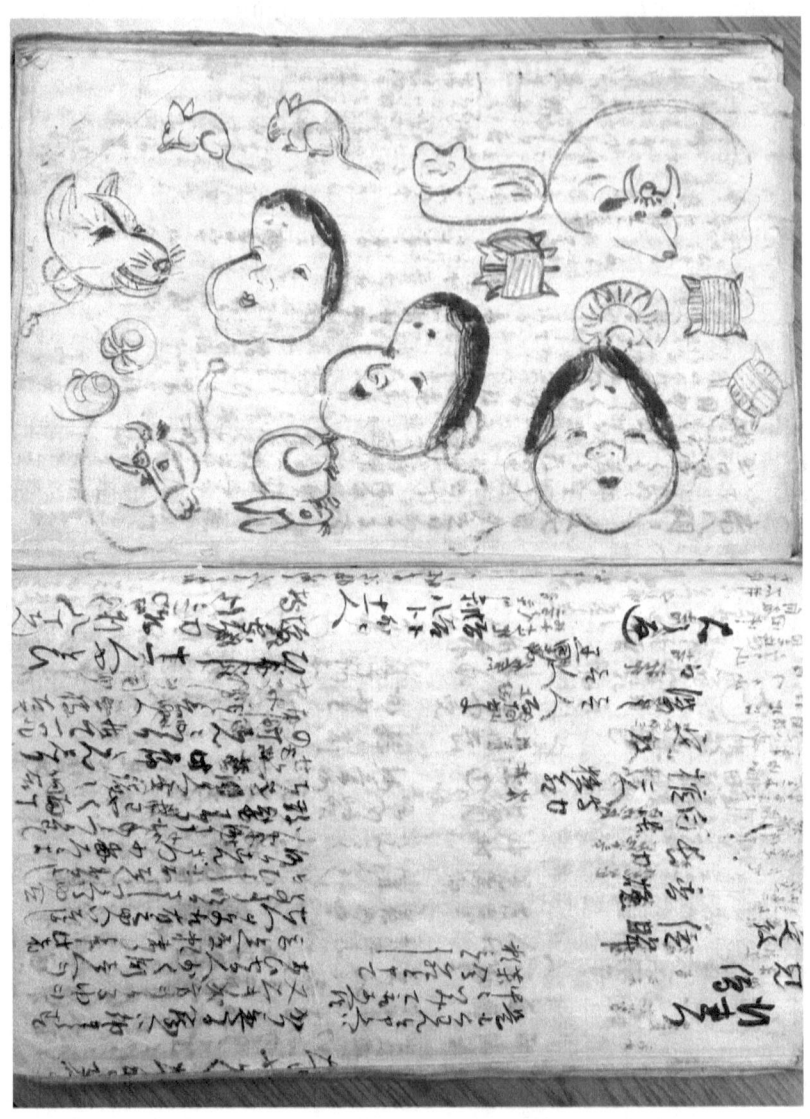

FIGURE 6.4 Kawai Koume, sketches of O-Fuku faces and animals: pages from Koume's diary. Special collections, Wakayama Prefectural Library. Courtesy of Wakayama Prefectural Library.

comparison with early versions shows little distortion. While copying the text may have been a chore, copying the pictures was surely a pleasure for Koume. The illustrations provide a rich depiction of life in a very exotic and fascinating society. They include images of tribal life in Siberia, Russian flora and fauna, architecture and furniture, boats and ships, clothing and uniforms, churches and bell-ringers, flour mills and furnaces, military equipment and fortifications, the court life of St. Petersburg, and the famous Gottorf globe, known as the world's first planetarium. Altogether there were close to one hundred color illustrations, all of which opened new windows onto what must have seemed like a fabulously remote land.[16]

The style of Koume's illustrations for *Kankai ibun* is very different from the elegant, mannerly bunjinga paintings for which she is better known. An untitled painting in this series depicts a crew of eight men wearing red hats preparing for the ascent of a hot-air balloon. Seven of the eight are holding onto the balloon with ropes, while the eighth stands by inside the gondola with a torch to provide heat to adjust the ascent. A single customer stands in the gondola, waiting to take off. The painting is composed in a style similar to the ukiyo-e prints of the time, with simple, cartoon-like line drawing using a thin brush, the interior spaces tinted with a total of five different colors. The gondola is decorated with an indistinct scheme reminiscent of European jewelry. The appeal of the painting lies in the novelty of its topic, the exotic clothing and decoration of the gondola, and in the amusing expressions on the faces of the participants: impassive in the case of the crew, apprehensive on the part of the customer. Of course, Koume would have had little creative input in the execution of this image, since she was copying an already extant manuscript. But she seems perfectly comfortable painting in this cartoon-like style reminiscent of the commercial art of the commoners, and indeed there are many sketches in her diary that use similar techniques. At the least, the painting speaks to her versatility as an artist, extending well beyond the bunjinga genre.

In addition to the surviving copy of *Kankai ibun*, around thirty of Koume's paintings have survived, most owned by the descendants of friends and family members. The largest collection, which includes nine paintings, is in the Wakayama City Museum. The works include portraits,

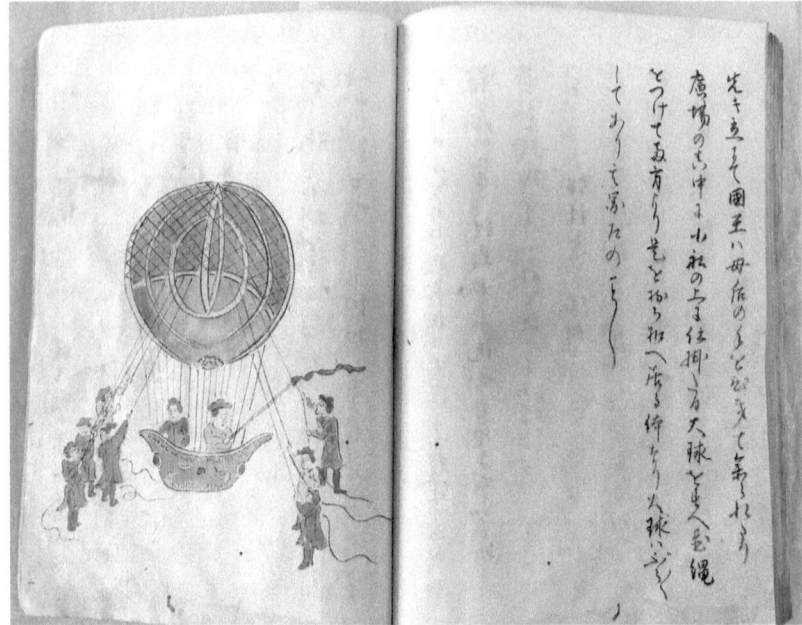

FIGURE 6.5 Illustration of balloonists, in Kawai Koume, manuscript copy of Ōtsuki Gentaku et al., *Kankai ibun* (Strange things heard in foreign lands). Original 1804; copy completed in 1837. Special collections, Wakayama Prefectural Library. Courtesy of Wakayama Prefectural Library.

humorous sketches, a representation of the deified poet Sugawara no Michizane, and several flower paintings.

A portrait of Miwa Bunkō's parents from 1853 (figure 6.6) helps illustrate why Koume's work was in such demand. Bunkō (the pen name of Miwa Saijirō) asked Koume to paint a portrait of his parents for him to carry with him to Edo, where he was about to go for a period of residence. The portrait shows an older couple sitting companionably side by side. The details of their old age are vividly but sympathetically drawn: wrinkled skin, thinning hair, slightly bent stature, wispy eyebrows, and loosely worn, informal clothing. The wife has a cushion resting on her lap and a cup of tea in her hand. She is sitting on the floor with one knee raised, as though in readiness to take care of her husband. He is depicted smoking a pipe, a look of calm satisfaction on his face. In front of him is a small flask of sake, and in his right hand he holds an *inro* box (most likely a tobacco container) ornamented with a *netsuke* in the shape of a disk. The colors are subdued but expressive of peace and calm. Both subjects are looking into the middle distance outside the frame of the painting, and the wife's right hand is raised, perhaps suggesting a farewell gesture as their son sets off on his long journey. This work represents at the same time a charming domestic scene; the peace and calm of a well-earned retirement; an homage to family conventions; an endearing depiction of old age; and an acknowledgment of the separation that was about to take place. The portrait owes less to any particular school of painting than to Koume's deftness of portrayal and her warmth of expression.

Koume wrote about this painting in her diary. On Kaei 6 (1853)/8/3, she wrote:

> On the fifteenth of last month, Miwa Saijirō from Miwa village asked me to paint a portrait of his parents. Today, he came to pick it up. He will shortly set off for Edo in the entourage of Mizuno, Lord of Tosa. He is one of fifty men who will accompany the lord.... Ostensibly they're going to guard the daimyo, but secretly Miwa thinks the reason is to defend the country against foreign ships. Saijirō suggested he write a poem at the top:
>
> > Shikaribito ha / hoka ni ha arazu / chichi no omoi
> > There is no other / person who will scold me / thoughts of my father
>
> He said that it would be nice to hand that message down to his descendants. I thought that was a bit colloquial, so I suggested:
>
> > Muchiukeshi / oshiewasurenu / fubo no omoi
> > Receiving the stick at their hands / is a teaching one cannot
> >   forget / thoughts of my parents.

A grateful Bunkō added the calligraphy, creating a *gassaku* work that combines charm and emotional impact.

A particularly striking work in the Wakayama City Museum collection is the undated *Kanbai ensō bijinzu* (Beautiful woman gazing at plum blossoms through a round window, figure 6.7). In this painting, a richly

FIGURE 6.6 Kawai Koume, *Miwa Bunko fubo no zu* (Portrait of Miwa Bunkō's parents), 1853. Collection of Wakayama City Museum. Courtesy of Wakayama City Museum.

FIGURE 6.7 Kawai Koume, *Kanbai ensō bijinzu* (Portrait of beautiful woman gazing at plum blossoms through a round window), date unknown. Collection of Wakayama City Museum. Courtesy of Wakayama City Museum.

dressed woman with a Chinese hairstyle is staring dreamily out of a circular window at a flowering plum branch. The wintry scene of the plum tree over a background of horizontal banded gray clouds (all executed in black ink and wash) contrasts with the vivid colors of the woman's clothing. Kondō Takashi speculates that this painting represents the story of a sage of the Sui dynasty who lived on Mount Luo Fu, famous for its plum blossoms. One day, the sage entered a drinking house and began carousing. After a while a beautiful woman appeared, accompanied by young dancers and musicians. The woman and the sage talked and drank long into the night, until eventually the sage fell asleep. When he woke up, he found himself in a plum grove, lying at the foot of a beautiful plum tree. He realized that in his dream he had been talking to a sprite of the plum trees. Kondō suggests that this painting, when hung in the *tokonoma* (alcove) of a reception room, would be an evocative image to accompany a scholarly drinking party.[17]

One of the seals Koume used to stamp the painting reads "Rafudōsen," a pseudonym Koume sometimes used, which could be translated as "the cave-dweller of Mount Luo Fu." The scene of plum blossoms associated with Mount Luo Fu suggests an autobiographical nuance. Did Koume (whose name means "Little Plum") want to suggest that she herself was the plum sprite sitting inside the window? The references to Chinese legends, plum blossoms, drinking, and dreams are all characteristic of the bunjinga style. It is tempting to see this dreamy scene of a beautiful woman and blossoms as particularly feminine, a representation of Koume's gendered esthetic. But women had no monopoly on *bijinga* (images of beautiful women), which were equally popular among male painters. Patricia Fister, author of the standard English-language work on Japanese women painters, commented in an interview that looking for "feminine" traits in paintings is a futile exercise.[18] Gender was embedded in the social context of Edo-era paintings more than in the images themselves.

ART, GENDER, AND THE HOUSEHOLD ECONOMY

In the basement of Wakayama castle, there is a display of a half dozen famous citizens of the prefecture. They include Matsushita Kōnosuke

FIGURE 6.8 Detail of figure 6.7

(1894–1989), founder of the National/Panasonic electronics empire; Mutsu Munemitsu (1844–1897), one of the great statesmen of the Meiji era; and Kawai Koume. We learn from this exhibit that Koume's grandfather, father, husband, and son were all teachers in the domain school; that she married early; that she kept a diary; and that her substantial body of work "was not merely a housewife's hobby, but was an accomplishment that earned her the name of artist." Similarly, the most comprehensive work on Kishū artists of the Edo era devotes three-quarters of its brief, quarter-page entry on "The Female Artist, Koume-san" to her pedigree. Each of the male members of her family—grandfather, father, and husband—is introduced, as well as her (male) teachers of poetry and painting. The entry mentions Koume's diary. Only at the end does it describe in a few words two of her paintings (e.g., "a standing woman is depicted manipulating a doll"), before concluding: "Koume was particularly good at these kinds of paintings of beautiful women, and of flowers and birds."[19] As an artist, Koume's most distinctive features as described in these texts are not her style or the quality of her work, but her (male) scholarly pedigree and her gender. Even today, it seems that Koume is defined to a great extent by those social markers, neither of which she chose.

But to see Koume's art merely as a hobby or a feminine accomplishment would misinterpret its meaning for Koume and her family. For Koume, painting was work. While she certainly enjoyed contributing to the cultural life of Wakayama's scholarly community for its own sake, her painting also contributed significantly to the Kawai family's economy. In a world in which financial capital was scarce, intangible assets such as cultural prestige were a meaningful currency for social and career advancement. By contributing to the family's cultural standing, Koume was helping her husband and son build their positions as valued members of the domain's educational community. Their value was recognized with successive increases in Hyōzō's official stipend, culminating in his appointment as principal of the domain school.[20]

Koume's art also contributed to the family's complex economy of non-cash exchange. Koume often used her art as currency in this economy, giving paintings to friends and acquaintances, and accepting requests to produce sketches or more formal works without any direct expectation of payment, but rather as part of a complex economy of gift-giving, obligation, and exchange. In Koume's case, the complexity of her painting's role in the family economy suggests that her life as an artist cannot easily be separated from her work as a household manager.

After completing a painting at a gassaku gathering, Koume might give it to one of the participants as a marker of her cultural accomplishment, thereby accruing to the Kawai family's cultural capital. More often, though, Koume "gave" paintings away in the expectation of some tangible return. In most cases, this was in the form of a "thank you" gift (*rei*), such as fresh fish, sweets, or sake coupons. For example, on Genji 1 (1864)/9/9, a messenger came bringing three sea bream, some tobacco in an elegant box, and a stick of *yōkan*, as "thanks" for a set of paintings Koume had executed for an acquaintance. A high-quality fresh fish was worth anything from 2 to 5 monme, so the total value might have been around 10 monme.[21] As a comparison, on 8/13 Koume had paid 14 monme to two gardeners for two days' work.

In addition to painting for friends and acquaintances, Koume also accepted commissions from several regular patrons: people who repeatedly requested paintings from her, often to pass on to other collectors within the community. Most prominent among these were Sakai Baisai, Endō Ichirō, and Ichikawa Hitoshi. Sakai Baisai was an old family friend, perhaps a former pupil of Hyōzō's, and an amateur painter himself. Endō was a domain official and an avid patron of the arts, and Ichikawa was a teacher in the domain school. We do not know why these men were so keen to promote Koume's work, but they continued to support her for decades, placing her art with dozens of collectors throughout the domain. Most of these final owners were strangers to Koume. In such cases, she seems to have been more willing to accept cash. On Genji 1 (1864)/3/5, for example, Sakai Baisai came to visit, bringing 200 *hiki* as thanks for Koume's painting on a fan. Koume wrote: "I tried to refuse it, but [Baisai] left it anyway."[22] A *hiki* was originally a length of cloth, used as a measure for gifts presented by the emperor. This gave it an elegant aura that distinguished it from cash. By the late Edo period, however, a *hiki* had in fact become a quantity of money: 10 mon.

Did this make Koume a professional artist? The answer is ambiguous at best. Koume painted for a variety of reasons, most of which contributed in one way or another to the family economy. But only occasionally does she mention accepting cash for her work. And the value of both gifts and cash payments was usually quite low.

Despite the amateur esthetic of the bunjinga tradition, wealthy collectors and patrons were willing to pay generously for work by famous artists. According to a study by Timon Screech, works of art by well-known male painters sold in Edo and Kyoto for anything from 200 to 2,000 silver monme in the late eighteenth and early nineteenth centuries.[23] The highest prices were commanded by the very few artists who had secured leading reputations in the major cities of Japan. Even in provincial Wakayama, there was a market for works of art. Collectors were willing to pay for high-quality literati art, and people of all classes widely consumed mass-produced materials such as ukiyo-e prints, illustrated books, and decorative accessories. Wealthy, well-educated merchants and townsmen helped bid up the values of fine art objects that had traditionally been the perquisites of the samurai class: tea implements, lacquerware, *fusuma* screens, and hanging scroll paintings. Koume was able to produce this type of work, which represented the high culture to which many townsmen aspired. Her work may even have been bought and sold in the commercial marketplace. But there is only the occasional hint that Koume interacted directly with that marketplace during the Tokugawa era.

For male artists, there were opportunities to paint for a living, even within the domain's bureaucratic structure. Koume's teacher, Nogiwa Hakusetsu, for example, held an official position as a court artist, and he received a salary comparable to Hyōzō's.[24] He enjoyed ready access to a variety of male-only cultural events, from poetry and painting gatherings at the castle or the retired daimyo's residence, to drinking parties at which art and poetry were produced, to entertainments to welcome visiting artists and poets. These in turn put his work in public view and created opportunities for sale in the commercial market. By contrast, Koume was much less visible. And it was much harder for bushi women to establish professional careers.

In other parts of Japan there were a few striking examples of successful female artists from similar social backgrounds to Koume. But those women often achieved professional success at the expense of the security and comfort of a traditional family structure. Ema Saikō (1787–1861), one of the best-known female painters in the bunjinga style, lamented toward the end of her life that she had never married, asking, "Why should it be the lot of talented women to end up like this? Most of them in empty boudoirs, writing poems of sorrow."[25] Okuhara Seiko (1837–1913), a highly successful artist of the late Edo and early Meiji eras, also renounced the traditional family, cutting her hair short, dressing like a man, and living openly with a woman.[26]

Only once in the pages of her diary, in Ansei 6 (1859), did Koume record an encounter with another female painter. At a picnic by the seashore, Koume met Sakagami Tatsu, who "is Kaiseki's student, and she paints plum blossoms." Tatsu went by the pen-name Sogyoku. She was older than Koume, and although they both loved to paint plum blossoms, Koume sounds a little intimidated by her new acquaintance. Perhaps the age difference was one reason. But another may have been their relative social status. Sogyoku was from a wealthy merchant family. With the spread of education and literacy, girls and women of the merchant class had acquired the tools to participate in the high culture of the elite, including the practice of literati art.[27] Unlike Koume, Sogyoku could affort to paint in the tradition of the "passionate amateur," without having to worry about how her work might support her family.

Rather than discuss Sogyoku's art or compare it to her own, Koume in her diary focused on the disparity in wealth between the two women. She plaintively compared the picnics each brought. Koume's, which she described as "extremely frugal," included "mazesushi [sushi rice mixed with inexpensive fish and vegetables], bamboo shoots, dried tofu, boiled citrus fruit, and dried fish." By contrast, Sogyoku's maid opened up a lavish lacquered lunch box with one tray packed with top-quality sushi, and another with fluffy egg (an expensive ingredient that Koume never mentions eating), fish cake, udo (a luxury vegetable related to ginseng), and awabi (abalone, an expensive shellfish). "The quantities were small," Koume enviously wrote, "but it was very elegant."[28] Sogyoku was able to enjoy the life of a refined literati artist who had no need to profit financially from her work, while Koume, who really could have used a little extra cash, remained bound by the conventions of her status and her gender.

Koume was fortunate to have received an excellent education, and to have acquired skills in the fine arts. But still she prioritized marriage and the domestic duties of a wife and mother. As an artist, Koume accepted and even embraced her designation as a *female* painter, usually signing her work "Koume joshi" (the woman, Koume). Much of her artistic work was in the tradition of the "passionate amateur" and contributed to the complex culture of exchange rather than to her family's cash balance. But other aspects of her work suggest a more commercial orientation. Was Koume operating as a professional even while maintaining the guise of a literati amateur? Her diary is too reticent to give a definitive answer. It seems likely that she was bringing in a small cash income. But the bigger picture is clear. Through her art, as through her household management, Koume was adding to the family's material well-being as well as its intangible capital.

7

ACROSS THE DIVIDE

SURVIVING THE COLLAPSE

After the disastrous defeat at Toba-Fushimi and the ex-shogun's flight to eastern Japan, the Kishū daimyo, Tokugawa Mochitsugu, found himself in a very difficult position. As a close relative of the shogun, he could not evade his connection to the Tokugawa shogunate. Mochitsugu had cleverly avoided any direct involvement in the final battle between the Tokugawa and imperial forces, but he was suspected of having helped the ex-shogun to escape.

The leaders of the Satsuma-Chōshū faction offered a solution: Mochitsugu should give them 150,000 ryō as compensation for his support for the Tokugawa cause. Mochitsugu's retainers offered a compromise: 30,000 ryō in cash, and a significant military commitment to fight on the imperial side in the ongoing campaign in northern Japan, where pro-Tokugawa loyalists were mounting strong resistance. As a result, Kishū domain sent 1,500 of its men to northern Japan to fight against the Tokugawa loyalists—an extraordinary development for a domain that just a few months earlier had been considered synonymous with the Tokugawa regime.

Meanwhile, Mochitsugu and his advisers searched for other ways to show conspicuous loyalty to the new government and its goals. One of those goals was a thorough reform of Japan's administrative systems.

Kishū domain had struggled with repeated attempts at reform, each of which had been choked off by conservative reaction. Now, Mochitsugu acted decisively. In the eleventh month of Meiji 1 (1968), while still in Kyoto, he appointed Tsuda Izuru as the chief administrator of the domain. Tsuda had been in office before, and he had attempted to initiate an ambitious reform program, but reactionary forces had quickly worked to discredit him, and in 1867 he had been dismissed from his post and imprisoned. Mochitsugu, however, had never lost his faith in Tsuda, and now Mochitsugu looked to him to implement the far-ranging reform program that both he and the central government felt was needed. Tsuda had a powerful friend and ally in the person of Mutsu Munemitsu, the son of Date Chihiro. Mutsu was a radical reformer who had fled Kishū domain in the 1860s and who went on to hold high office in the Meiji government. Mutsu briefly returned to Wakayama after the Restoration, and he was able to use his influence with the new government to support Tsuda's program.

Tsuda's first move, on Meiji 2 (1869)/1/27, was to make public the formerly secret accounts of the domain. Tsuda's first challenge was to put the domain's finances on a sound footing, and he felt that a policy of transparency would help secure the support that he needed for painful reforms. Insisting that the daimyo must lead the way in making sacrifices, Tsuda persuaded Mochitsugu to personally donate 5 percent of his income to the general budget. Then, on 2/15, Mochitsugu announced across-the-board salary reductions for all retainers in administrative positions and with stipends over 24 koku. Tsuda took this a step further by substantially reducing the salaries paid to senior retainers for their administrative positions. Those in senior positions were paid eight hundred bales of rice a year (about 300 koku), while midlevel administrators were paid three hundred bales. These salaries would be on top of the retainer's hereditary stipend, which the domain was unable for now to take away. Tsuda further undermined the hereditary status system by opening administrative positions to all men of talent, and by encouraging retainers who did not have administrative positions to engage in agriculture and trade.[1]

Tsuda also resumed his quest to modernize the domain's military. Tsuda had studied Western military science in Edo, and he had long recognized that Japan's time-honored warrior traditions were wholly inadequate for the new, technology-driven world of mass conscript armies and powerful navies. Building on his experience developing farmer-soldier units in 1867, Tsuda reorganized the domain's military into divisions of the army, navy, and traditional martial arts—effectively sidelining the last. In 1867 Tsuda had hired a Prussian military officer, Carl Koeppen, to reform the Kishū military. Koeppen had not yet arrived when Tsuda was fired and imprisoned, but in 1869 Tsuda was able to reinstate Koeppen's appointment, and he arrived later in the year. Working with Koeppen, Tsuda implemented far-reaching reforms, replacing swords and spears with German carbines, and implementing intensive Prussian-style military drills.

Tsuda's most far-reaching reform, though, was the introduction of a compulsory conscription system. In Tsuda's system, all males reaching age twenty were required to submit to a physical exam, and, if found physically fit, they would be put into a pool of men who might be summoned for up to three years' military service. Once conscripted, soldiers would be paid an annual salary of twelve bales of rice (about 4 koku), and they were subject to a strict discipline, including a total ban on alcohol consumption. The number of conscripts were fairly small at first—the first batch call-up was for only six hundred men. But the conscription system greatly complicated the position of the bushi, whose status as an elite warrior class had justified their privileges through the past two and a half centuries of peace. Not only did it call their skills into question, it also undermined their economic basis, making it much harder to justify their stipends, which were paid from the harsh labor of the peasantry.

At first, military service remained open to the bushi: the Kishū army staffed its officer class with well-educated samurai graduates of the domain school, and its ranks were also open to samurai volunteers, who were meanwhile exempted from the draft. But after 1870 Tsuda revised the system to include all young adult men, regardless of status, in the conscript system. Young samurai men were forced to stand alongside peasants and townsmen, and once conscripted into the military, they had to compete on an equal footing with their commoner peers. Tsuda did not rely on conscripts alone. The conscript force was supplemented by a standing army of permanent recruits, many of whom were from warrior families.

By the end of 1871, the Kishū military had built up a total force of 17,500 men, equipped with modern weapons, and many of them conscripts. The domains' armies were disbanded at the end of 1871, but Tsuda's conscription system provided a model for the national system that was implemented in 1873. Meanwhile, many of the career soldiers moved to the newly formed prefectural police force, which began recruiting officers from 1872.[2]

Starting almost immediately, Kishū domain was forced to participate in other major reforms aimed at strengthening the central government and weakening the power of the feudal lords. On Meiji 1/12/2 (January 14, 1869), under the influence of their reformist advisers, the four daimyo whose domains had brought about the Meiji Restoration—Satsuma, Chōshū, Tosa, and Hizen—formally offered to return their domains and retainers to the emperor. Using this gesture as an example, the government quickly pressured the rest of Japan's 262 domains to follow suit. The daimyo were offered a generous settlement: they could stay in their castles, they were given the title of governor, and they received a generous personal stipend, equal to 10 percent of the assessed revenue of the domain. By the end of the sixth month, all but thirteen domains had completed the process. Those few holdouts were then ordered to return their domains to the emperor under threat of military action.

Two years later, in the seventh month of Meiji 4 (1871), the government reneged on parts of this settlement. The emperor issued an edict abolishing the domains. Renamed prefectures, they would now come under the full control of the central government. The former daimyo were ordered to relinquish all their official positions (though they could keep their generous stipends) and move to Tokyo. Mochitsugu left Wakayama on Meiji 4/9/13 and arrived in Tokyo on 10/22. Shortly after that an outsider, Kōyama Kunikiyo, was appointed governor of the new prefecture. Kōyama was a Tosa samurai with an impressive administrative background. He would remain governor of Wakayama for the next ten years.[3]

In 1871 the government introduced a new household registration law, requiring all Japanese family heads to register with their local authority. The new registers recorded the place of residence, births, marriages, and deaths of all members of the household. To extend them to all the families in Japan, the government introduced several radical new policies, including the requirement that all Japanese should have family names (which, though widely used in practice, had theoretically been a privilege limited to the samurai and wealthier classes during the Tokugawa era).

Households continued to be registered based on their former status—*shizoku* for the samurai and *heimin* for commoners. But the new system left no privileges of professional or educational access, mode of dress, or housing. Samurai continued to wear the topknot hairstyle and carry swords for the first few years of the 1870s, but during the decade the traditional samurai style began to seem increasingly outdated. And the government was concerned about the potential for disruption if the samurai were armed. Accordingly, carrying swords was increasingly discouraged, until it was banned altogether in 1876.

At the same time, the government moved to place landownership on a firmer legal basis, ordering surveys and valuation of all real property throughout Japan, and issuing title deeds to those deemed to be the legitimate owners of the property. This in turn prepared the way for the implementation of a new tax code, which required cash payment based on a percentage of the property's assessed value. This assessment, which fell most heavily on the landowning peasantry, was to provide the basis of the government's revenue for the next several decades. It also led, however, to considerable resistance and strife in the countryside. Villagers had to bear many new burdens under the new government, including the loss of land for many who had been denied ownership deeds; the new cash-based tax system that was often based on unfair valuations and made no allowance for poor harvests; the expensive new schools that also deprived families of their children's labor; and the conscription system that took able-bodied young men away from the land and put them in danger.

The changes that swept over Japan in the first decade of the Meiji era were dramatic and far-reaching. For the Kawai family, they meant the abolition of the domain school that had provided employment and status to four generations; the end of samurai privilege, which had provided both social standing and a degree of financial stability; the end of the feudal system, which, through its position as the seat of one of the senior branches of the Tokugawa family, had placed Wakayama in a prominent position national affairs; and the end of many of the certainties that had provided stability for a bushi family like Koume's over a period of generations.

Of all the reforms implemented by the new prefectural and national governments, perhaps the educational policy had the most impact on Koume's family. In the eighth month of Meiji 5 (1872), the central government implemented a new directive requiring universal compulsory education for at least four years from age six—for boys and girls alike. This ambitious policy required prefectures to open thousands of new schools throughout Japan and to find ways to make their educational offerings accessible even to poor peasant families. The central government had no money to support this policy, nor did Wakayama prefecture. The burden fell on the villages, which had to find the money to build or convert schoolhouses, buy materials, and pay teachers.

The prefecture established a policy requiring one school for every 1,500 residents. This meant every village of more than a few hundred households had to open a small school. Students were required to pay fees, but at a rate of only 0.065 yen a month for the first two children in a family—the third child could attend free. Poor families could attend for reduced fees based on a means test. The rest of the financial burden fell on the wealthier villagers. A survey in Meiji 14 (1881) found that school fees covered only 13 percent of the running costs of the Wakayama prefectural schools. Government assistance provided another 6 percent, but most of the schools' income—almost 60 percent—came from special levies that the villages had to make on their inhabitants. Of course, village elites paid a hefty share of these, but even poor village families were expected to contribute, whether or not they had children in the school.[4]

By Meiji 8 (1875) there were 362 schools in the prefecture, with a total enrollment of 21,900 students, or about 60 per school. This represented only 22 percent of eligible children (i.e., those between the ages of six and fourteen): 9 percent of eligible girls, and 34 percent of boys. Despite the best efforts of the prefecture, it was a sacrifice for poor families to pay school fees and to forfeit the labor of their able-bodied children. The situation was worst in the economically precarious mountain villages, where schools were fewer and where the teachers, often barely educated villagers themselves, might have to rotate among three or four schools.

As a tenured Confucian scholar, Yūsuke had enjoyed a privileged position in the domain school system, with a status closer to that of college professor than elementary school teacher. But with the abolition of the domain school in 1872, Yūsuke found himself jobless. His samurai stipend amounted to only 4 yen a month, and even that was under constant threat given the poor state of the prefecture's finances. Yūsuke eked out a living by taking private students, but payment for his services was uncertain at best, often coming in the form of gifts rather than cash. Now, with the opening of dozens of new schools around the prefecture after the new education law was passed, teachers were suddenly in high demand.

Koume's diary resumes in Meiji 9 (1876) after eight missing years. Koume was now a widow: Hyōzō had died in 1871, at age seventy-eight. As the diary opens, Yūsuke was in the midst of negotiations to start a new job as teacher in an elementary school. Some acquaintances were planning to open the school in Nishimura village, 13 kilometers from Wakayama, and they wanted Yūsuke to be the teacher at a salary of 4 yen per month. Yūsuke applied for and received a government teaching license, picking it up from the prefectural office on January 31 (by this time Japan had adopted the Gregorian calendar).

Yūsuke's new school opened in the Saihōji temple. The journey from Wakayama involved a 7-kilometer walk to the Tainose ferry crossing, a short boat ride across the Kinokawa, and then another 6 kilometers northeast, past the village of Nango, where the Kawai family had many friends, toward the base of the mountains. It was familiar territory, but it was also too far from Wakayama for a comfortable commute. Yūsuke would need to find a residence in the village.

On February 22, 1876, Yūsuke set off with a helper carrying futons, blankets, cushions, clothing, portable tables, kitchen and dining equipment, and a case full of books, along the dirt road to the river crossing, and then on the village lanes to Nishimura.

A week later, on February 28, Yūsuke took Koume with him to help set up house in Nishimura, leaving Kano in Wakayama with their four daughters: Yone, age thirteen; Tsune, eleven; Shige, age unknown; and Mikiyo, age unknown. Yūsuke hired a rickshaw to carry his seventy-two-year-old mother as far as the river (the cost was 0.06 yen), but she still had to walk the rest of the way. They arrived in the early afternoon. Yūsuke went out that evening and got drunk with some of the villagers. And the next morning, classes began. Around fifty students showed up, and in the evening Yūsuke taught an evening class for five students who were unable to attend during the day.

Yūsuke had rented a dilapidated house and hired an elderly servant called Yasujirō. In the first days of March, Koume and Yasujirō worked together to replace the *shoji* windows and screens and the *fusuma* partitions throughout the house. They also got the local builder in to help get the kitchen in working order. On March 3 Koume noted that in the old

FIGURE 7.1 Nishimura elementary school. Photo by the author.

calendar it was the *hatsu-uma* festival marking the end of winter. "The temples at Kokawa and Nagata are said to be very lively," she remarked a little wistfully. Koume and Yasujirō prepared a few rice cakes, and they threw them into the corners of the house to ward off evil. In the evenings, they were invited to bathe at the neighbors' houses.

Although Yūsuke was the Nishimura schoolteacher, he was not the manager of the school. The driving forces behind its creation and operation were the headmen of the village and its hamlets, and a few wealthy landowning families. Yūsuke and Koume were welcomed and cared for by these families: the Iida, the Kamata (hereditary headmen of Nishimura village), and the Yukawa of Ueno hamlet, who also had two sons studying at the school.

On March 10 Yūsuke received his first salary payment: 4 yen for the month, plus 0.50 yen to cover part of Yasujirō's 1.50 yen salary. Yūsuke also received an allowance of rice, delivered to him by Mr. Iida. On the same day, the students brought their fees for the month: 0.05 yen per student, and 0.08 yen for the ten evening school students, who had to pay a little extra for the cost of lamp oil. Yasujirō's son and nephew were allowed to attend for free.

The school held a formal opening ceremony on Sunday, March 12. Yūsuke and his helpers spent Saturday cleaning the building and getting everything in order. In the afternoon Mr. Iida and his son came, and Mr. Kamata joined them with a flag on which he had written "小学校" (*shōgakkō*, elementary school) in bright red. They had Yasujirō hoist the flag above the school building. The next morning Yūsuke handed out uniforms to the students, and in the afternoon the mayor and headmen of several of the attached hamlets came to celebrate. Yūsuke and Koume received a gift of twenty flavored rice cakes (*kusamochi*). That evening they returned to Wakayama together with two boys from the school, Tokutarō and Shigetarō, who carried their bags. They arrived home in the dark, Koume's feet painful from the long walk. She had promised to take the boys to see the castle, but she was feeling exhausted, and it had started to rain, so they all went to bed instead.

Over the next few weeks, Koume kept house for Yūsuke during his stays in Nishimura, getting to know the village families and their children, and teaching painting and drawing to some. They generally stayed in the village through the week, returning to Wakayama on Saturday afternoon or on Sunday, which was now a holiday for schools and government offices. While in Nishimura, Koume became gradually absorbed into the villagers' lives. She became intimate with the Yukawa and Iida families. She shared the small dramas of the village and the school, dramas that would be familiar to teachers in any part of the world: "April 6 [1876]: Yesterday Kanekichi stole a boy called Buntarō's inkstone. Today there was an investigation, and it was found in Kane[kichi]'s stationery box. Kane[kichi] ran home, and did not come back. Today Kane[kichi]'s father Yasujirō came and cried. Since [Kanekichi] was unwilling to come back, [Yasujirō] brought the stationery box with him."

The situation was particularly awkward since Yasujirō had been Yūsuke and Koume's servant (although he had quit shortly after the beginning of the term). Two weeks later, on April 20, Yasujirō came once again to apologize for his son's behavior. This time, Kanekichi had lost the needle and thread that Koume had lent him. Yasujirō brought a replacement, even though he grumbled that it should have been his son who came.

Although Koume dutifully accompanied her son to Nishimura and helped him with the management of his household there, she found the village community a little stultifying. On April 13 she wrote: "Fine weather. Nothing happened. Every day I am being pressed by the children to draw for them." And on April 18: "Fine weather. Nothing happened. The children never stop their noisy fighting."

Koume's stay at Nishimura did not last much longer. On April 21 a villager returning from Wakayama reported that Koume's granddaughter, Tsune, had smallpox. Although it seemed to be a mild case, he suggested that Koume might want to go home to keep an eye on things. The next day was Saturday, and after classes finished at 2:00, Koume and Yūsuke set off for home. They got there at 5:00, and "went first to see the little one. Thankfully, she has only four or five spots on her face, and even those you must wear glasses to see. It was a huge relief, and now we could rest. There was a bath waiting. Even though I have a cold, I got in."

From that point on, Yūsuke mostly stayed in Nishimura on his own. Koume resumed her activities in Wakayama, teaching, painting and drawing for friends, visiting temples and shrines, and spending time with the families most closely connected to the Kawai.

Yūsuke's job at Nishimura school did not last much longer. At the end of October, he took a new job at the village school in Kandori, just across the river from Wakayama city. The location was certainly more convenient. But this job too turned out to be short-lived, lasting only till the following April. It is not clear why these teaching jobs proved so unstable. Was it because the schools themselves were not yet on a firm footing? Or was Yūsuke looking for more rewarding work? Yūsuke was involved in several other efforts to open new schools. The most ambitious was an effort to start a new school in Wakayama, funded with gifts of as much as 1,500 yen pledged by some of the wealthy families of the city. The school was to be divided into three sections, devoted to Chinese literary studies, Dutch studies, and English studies. The organizers were planning to hire two foreigners to cover Western studies, and they had strong math teachers lined up. But they needed a Chinese studies teacher, and they thought Yūsuke would be just right for the job. Yūsuke was enthusiastic, but the project never got off the ground.

Instead, at the end of the decade, Yūsuke went back to taking private students, although he also taught part-time at other private academies around the city, notably a school run by the family's close friend, Ichikawa Hiroshi.

For all the challenges that he faced, Yūsuke benefited from the education boom of the early Meiji era. The spread of formal schooling to every village expanded the demand for a service he was well-qualified to provide. Many samurai with less transferrable skills found it harder to adapt. But Yūsuke was also faced with a reality that his father had recognized a decade earlier. The trends of the times were moving away from the Chinese classics of philosophy, history, and literature. The new educational curricula developed by successive governments largely shut out Chinese studies in favor of English, global history, mathematics, and science. There was still a demand for traditional Chinese studies among the wealthier ex-samurai, farmers, and merchants, who continued to aspire to the culture and values of the old samurai elite. But even they tended to view the kind of instruction offered by Yūsuke as an enhancement to the practical skills of the modern educational system, rather than as a substitute.

The government added to the challenges of Yūsuke's school. The proclamation of the new education system in 1872 introduced the principle of compulsory education, but it said little about the medium or content. The new Ministry of Education issued guidelines for school curricula and textbooks, but there was little enforcement. Private schools were allowed, and the curricula offered by schools varied widely. In this system, Yūsuke with his government accreditation could teach a curriculum based on Chinese studies without fear of interference by the government, either in the Nishimura village school or in his own private academy. But in 1880 a new Education Ordinance introduced stricter government controls. Teacher qualification requirements were tightened, and new, more coercive standards were introduced for curricular content. The result was a steep drop in the number of private academies throughout the prefecture, from a peak of eighty-two in 1881 to only twenty the following year.[5] On April 28, 1882, Yūsuke was notified by a prefectural official that "Chinese studies had definitely been abolished," and he would not be allowed to continue operating his school. And on May 5 Yūsuke "took down the signboard from the gate of the house." That day, he went "secretly" to the houses of two pupils to give them lessons.

Nevertheless, Yūsuke adapted. His academy officially closed, but he continued teaching, sometimes at students' homes and sometimes in his own. His instruction was a supplement to the children's education rather than the main source.⁶ Margaret Mehl has shown that schools of Chinese learning adopted a variety of strategies to survive and even flourish in the new era. Some, like Yūsuke, offered Chinese studies as a supplement to the education students were receiving in the public schools. Others offered postelementary education in areas with no easy access to middle schools. Others broadened their curricula, teaching Chinese history, philosophy, and literature using Western methods.⁷

According to Wakayama prefectural records, the family was still receiving a rice stipend of 20 koku per year in 1870. At some point in the early 1870s, this was converted to a cash stipend of 48 yen per year. Then, in September 1878, the annual payment was commuted: in a final settlement from the government, Yūsuke received a 617-yen government bond, which paid 6 percent interest: 37 yen per year.⁸ It was the last official support he would receive from his hereditary status as the head of a samurai family. From the late 1870s prices went into an upward spiral in Japan, with the price of rice doubling between 1877 and 1880, and the market value of the Yūsuke's bond sank proportionately.⁹

The family's income was enhanced by rent from several tenement houses (*nagaya*) that they had purchased at the beginning of the Meiji era. In 1878 they had a total of sixty residents, probably living in crowded conditions, several families to a house. The income from the properties was modest: about 2.5 yen per month. The family was able to increase its income from the sale of the night soil (toilet waste) generated by their tenants. Remarkably, this provided about as much income as the rent itself. In 1878, for example, a farmer called Tokubei was willing to pay 0.48 yen per person per year for the tenants' night soil. With sixty people living in the family's rental houses, that came to 29.40 yen in 1878. The price of night soil contracts varied from year to year, from a high of 0.65 yen per person per year in 1880, to a low of around 0.40 yen in 1881. The family also owned a little rice-producing land, which they added to when they could. The diary records a purchase in 1876 of 7 *tan* (0.7 hectare) of rice fields in Sakaetani village, for 65 yen. Yūsuke borrowed the money to buy it, at 10 percent interest.¹⁰

Combining the interest on the government bond, Yūsuke's income as a teacher, and the rental income, the Kawai family took in around 150 yen per year in the late 1870s. By comparison, the family had recorded 8,796

FIGURE 7.2 Japanese government bond issued to ex-samurai, 1876. Collection of Bank of Japan, Tokyo. Public domain image reproduced from https://www.imes.boj.or.jp/archives/digital_archive/bonds/pages/kinrokukousai01.html.

monme of income at the peak of its prosperity, in 1865, enough to buy 22 koku (4,000 kg) of rice. In 1876, 150 yen would buy 19 koku of rice.[11] Yūsuke had a family of seven (soon to be eight) to feed and clothe, a large house to maintain, and several big expenses on the horizon, including the marriage of his two oldest daughters. His employment was unstable and his income precarious, and prices were going up (by 1880, 150 yen would buy only 14 koku of rice). He could not have found it easy.

The successes and failures of the ex-samurai to adapt to their loss of privilege and income is a complex topic, which I discuss in more detail in the conclusion. While Yūsuke may have struggled, he was able, owing to his skills and qualifications as a teacher, to maintain a middle-class lifestyle for his family. Others fared much worse. It was a particularly bitter pill for many bushi from the southwestern domains, who had fought for the overthrow of the old system, to find themselves seemingly cast aside by the new. Even military affairs, the traditional monopoly of the warrior class, had moved on. The new leaders placed more faith in a disciplined, conscript army of commoners led by a technically trained officer class than in the bravado and derring-do of the old warrior ethic. And they preferred modern rifles and artillery to the swords and bowmanship valued by the samurai of the Edo period. Ironically, samurai values were to make a strong comeback at the end of the nineteenth century, but that was too late for many who had struggled to adapt to the new realities of the Meiji era.

Koume records several examples of samurai bitterness in the diary, and she herself was occasionally resentful of the treatment the warrior class had received. But in Wakayama, samurai unrest did not lead to violence. In other parts of the country, it was a different story. Uprisings of ex-samurai broke out in southwestern Japan, where large numbers of samurai struggled to feed their families after losing their status and income. The southwestern domains had enjoyed a greater degree of independence from the Tokugawa government during the feudal era, so there was more resentment of Tokyo's attempts to exert control—despite the fact that, ironically, most of the top government officials in Tokyo came from those same southwestern domains. Between 1874 and 1877 disturbances and rebellions sprang up in Saga, Hagi, Fukuoka, and Kumamoto. All were severely repressed. The Saga rebellion of 1874, which recruited a disillusioned ex-cabinet minister, Etō Shinpei, as its leader, was suppressed with relatively little fighting. But the so-called Shinpūren attack on Kumamoto castle in October 1876 resulted in more than two hundred deaths.

The greatest rebellion by far broke out in early 1877, when the government confronted twenty thousand men of the far southwestern domains of Satsuma and Higo, with some sympathizers from neighboring domains. The conflict was the first major military challenge faced by the new conscript army, and although the central government prevailed, it was only at enormous cost in blood and treasure.

Satsuma was one of the largest and most powerful domains in Japan, and it had been central to the campaign to unseat the Tokugawa. Yet, for the samurai of Satsuma, the outcome of the Meiji Restoration had been deeply disappointing. Their status privileges lost, they found themselves ignored by the new leadership in Tokyo. Their leader, Saigō Takamori, one of the most romantic and inspiring leaders of the era, had been ousted from the government in 1873. Their daimyo had lost his status as one of the most powerful political figures in Japan. And their military prowess had been disregarded, their former dominance superseded by an army of peasant conscripts. In February 1877, after uncovering a supposed government plot to assassinate Saigō, thousands of ex-samurai gathered for a march on Tokyo with a list of demands for the restoration of their privileges and a purge of perceived corruption in the central government. After seizing the weapons in the government arsenal, the rebels marched on Kumamoto castle, which was defended by a force of 4,400 imperial troops. The central government responded by sending a huge army of some 90,000 men. Fighting continued throughout March, until on April 12 the imperial army launched a full-scale assault, finally liberating the besieged castle. The war dragged on until the end of September, culminating in the bloody battle of Shiroyama, in which most of the remaining rebel forces were wiped out, and Saigō killed.

Koume began writing about the rebellion in early March. On March 9 she wrote: "In Higo [Kumamoto], the governor [and garrison] are in the castle, surrounded on all sides. They're using up their food supplies and are truly in a difficult situation." She added that "the newspapers are on sale daily on the corner of 1-chōme, but when things are not going well for our side, publication is suspended. And sometimes the content changes during the day." By now, newspapers were well established as the main vehicle for communicating news, replacing the diverse communications networks of the Tokugawa era. But Koume did not trust them, believing (correctly in many cases) that the government was using them for its own ends. A few weeks later, on May 22, she commented: "Newspapers are not to be relied on."

On March 17 Koume wrote: "Bought a newspaper for 2 *sen*. News of the battle for Kumamoto in Higo. The imperial army is trying to break out [of the castle]. We still don't know who will win. They are holed up in the castle and have very little food. Those who venture out are killed. It's a very sad situation." And on March 23: "The dead bodies and wounded are being brought to Kobe by ship. There have been twenty-three ships full of wounded. Five thousand heads have arrived, with the names attached to their ears. Yesterday 120 people from Kishū were mobilized to help nurse the wounded.... Anyone who goes to help the wounded will get 40 *sen* a day." According to Koume, among the wounded being sent back to Wakayama were patients who were bedridden, and others who could only crawl. "No matter how it ends, we are walking on thin ice." Koume also reported that some people who had signed contracts to rent rooms in the family's rental properties had been called up; they would be vacating their lodgings and going to the front to fight.

On April 6 Koume once again reported on the uncertain outcome of the battle for Kumamoto castle. She wrote that there were as many as four hundred dead from Kishū. "A head came back yesterday of a fellow from Kajibashi. More are expected. In addition, ears pickled in salt are coming back, with names tagged on them. Many are incorrect."

Faced with a shortage of soldiers, the government began a recruitment drive to augment the conscript forces. Kishū domain's well-trained military made Wakayama an appealing target for this effort. The army persuaded the ex-daimyo, Mochitsugu, to return to Wakayama from Tokyo and give a series of talks encouraging men to sign up. Koume describes one such event, on April 4. The daimyo held the gathering at the mansion of Lord Miura, one of his chief retainers. It was announced in advance that the former daimyo would be handing out gifts. Yūsuke and some of his friends attended. After Mochitsugu delivered an address celebrating the unification of Japan under the emperor, the audience of several hundred was asked to line up to receive the handout from the daimyo. Each received two sheets of paper, one announcing a plan for Mochitsugu to support the poor and elderly with financial aid, the other containing a statement by the famous scholar Fukuzawa Yukichi exhorting the people not to incite unrest. Koume reported that "some people mistakenly thought that his lordship would give them money, and now they are complaining. They are saying they took time off work to attend and so they lost 10 *sen*. And all they got was this paper, which they may as well use to wipe their asses."

On April 14 Koume wrote: "They are now conscripting soldiers. They had been asking for volunteers, and offering them 30 yen, but only a very few enlisted, so in the end the government began conscripting men directly. All men over 17 and under 40 are eligible. They are not paying them even one yen. They say that just here in Kishū, they have conscripted eight thousand men." On April 16 Koume added that "the daimyo has been asked to persuade many men to join the army. But absolutely no one wants to, and it doesn't look as though his goal will be met." She noted: "The samurai have been treated as though they're of no use to anyone, and it's unreasonable to try to use them just in an emergency."

Koume's descriptions reveal some of the bitterness of the samurai class. But they also show the social and political transformation that had taken place in Wakayama during the decade. For a crowd of dissatisfied townsmen to complain about the actions of the daimyo would have been unthinkable a decade earlier—as would a congregation of such people in one of the great aristocratic mansions. And Koume's crude dismissal of the high-flown sentiments expressed in the scrolls distributed by the daimyo hints at an earthy democratic spirit in the air.

Koume reported one other incident of disruption from the war. On May 23 a detachment of soldiers was billeted in Wakayama. "They did all sorts of damage with their swords. Shinpei of the *nagaya* was working for a used clothing shop. He was sent to retrieve the futons [the army] had rented. They were very badly damaged. Some had excrement on them. Others when they unwrapped them had pieces missing. It is a big loss. They are asking the officials to buy them new ones. There were six or seven hundred futons. Rice bowls, bottles, and lamps were strewn all over the place. Since they were so rough, [the authorities] had them accompanied to Osaka."

Wakayama itself remained peaceful. Despite economic and other constraints, Koume was probably more able to do the things she enjoyed during this period than at any other in her life. Koume had always loved the theater and other popular entertainments, but she only once recorded attending a theatrical performance during the years 1837 to 1867. In the six surviving years between 1876 and 1883, she mentions more than sixty visits, often with her grandchildren or with Kano's mother, Kise.[12]

The performances were generally in the kabuki tradition, portraying stirring tales of love and war but also dramatizations of the lives of famous spiritual and political leaders. They generally included intervals of music and dancing as well as acting. For example, on December 12, 1876, Koume "got up at 4:00 a.m., lit a fire and cooked rice, washed, did up my hair, etc., until it got light." She left the house at 6:30 and met Kise and some of her family members at the theater. The cost of entry was 0.05 yen, with a surcharge of 0.06 yen for front-row seating. Tsune came soon after, with her younger siblings. The main performance was a reenactment of the life of the great ninth-century Buddhist monk Kōbō Daishi. Koume was familiar with the actors, who were probably from an Osaka troupe. She was particularly impressed by their onstage transformations. The actor Koenji, for example, was transformed on stage from an elderly court lady into a young country girl. Another actor, who was being chased by half a dozen ruffians, was lifted up into the air to make his escape and floated above the audience into the backstage area. The actor playing Kōbō Daishi, too, did a dramatic change into a female dragon, slipping off his kimono to reveal another covered in scales underneath. He then performed a lovely dance on the "flower path" boardwalk through the audience, before disappearing backstage. Koume declared the whole performance to be "very well done."

The performances generally lasted from morning till night. For Koume, they combined multiple pleasures. She got to dress up in some of her beautiful kimonos; she could spend the day with her grandchildren; she could also enjoy the company of her friend Kise; and she could enjoy the poetry, drama, and skills in music and dance of the performers. Kise died around 1880, and soon after that the grandchildren started getting married and leaving the house, leaving Koume with fewer opportunities to attend performances.

PAINTING IN RETIREMENT

Despite her relative freedom as the retired mistress of the house, Koume's life closed in a little after the death of her husband in 1871. With Yūsuke now the family head, Kano took on many of the social and financial duties that had belonged to Koume. Perhaps it was a relief for her in some ways, but Koume clearly missed the financial independence that she had enjoyed as the Kawai household manager. Koume remained involved in the management of some aspects of the family's finances, including the rental properties, and she kept 0.50 yen a month of the rent money for herself.[13] But she felt the lack of spending money. She had always enjoyed shopping for fine clothes and household items, but now she could not afford to buy anything for herself. On December 6, 1876, Kano invited her on a shopping expedition together with Mrs. Naitō. But, Koume wrote, "I have no money so I didn't go. Instead, I stayed home and sewed socks for o-Shige."

Nor was Koume the only family member short of funds. With a wife, mother, and four children to support, unstable employment, and rapid devaluation of his samurai stipend, Yūsuke too must have struggled to maintain the family's lifestyle. In this situation, any contribution that family members could make was surely welcome. For Koume, doing her bit to support the family business was nothing new. As the diary picks up after an eight-year gap, Koume was making herself useful as a teacher. Her main students at this time were two girls called Ayame and Masue. Masue was a serious art student, while Koume was teaching reading and writing to Ayame as well as painting.

On June 22 Kano's brother-in-law Noguchi Junnosuke called on Koume with an exciting offer. The Mizuno, one of the highest-ranking families of Kishū domain, were looking for a tutor for their young daughter Sada. With Noguchi's help, Koume obtained the position.[14] Starting on July 1, Koume went most weekdays to the Mizuno mansion near the Omotebashi gate of the castle to teach reading, writing, and drawing to her young pupil. On her first day, Sada showed her the books she was reading, as well as her abacus (which Koume admitted she could not help her with), and then the two of them played with a "ring of knowledge" (*chienowa*) puzzle—these typically involved trying to assemble and disassemble a set of interlinked iron rings.[15] Koume often stayed late into the day painting for Sada's grandmother, who was in need of company and entertainment.

The Mizuno family treated Koume with great courtesy, offering her meals, lending her books and interesting collectors' items, and sending their servants to accompany her in wet weather. She clearly enjoyed her connection to this exalted family, but Koume also found her job tiring at times. On September 11, for example, she had finished teaching at the Mizuno and was on her way home when a servant came running after her and asked her to come back and draw some pictures in Sada's copybook. "I agreed. I would have done it on my next visit, but they said I should come now." Arriving home much later than she had planned, she had to deal with a houseful of visitors and then attend a dinner party. And the next day, after teaching at Mizuno, she arrived home hot and exhausted. "It was so hot I thought I would just rest, but Hikosaburō was there, so I changed and made him noodles."

Several times, the Mizuno sent a servant to tell Koume not to come because Sada was indisposed. Sometimes these were genuine complaints such as the heatstroke she suffered on July 25, but at others—for example, the day she needed to rest after spending the previous day at the theater—they suggest a typical child's reluctance to be burdened with dull studies when a world of play was waiting.

One thing that was very welcome about Koume's new job was the salary. The Mizuno paid her 2 yen a month—a good income for a part-time teacher, considering that Yūsuke only made 4 yen working full time at the Nishimura school. But the Mizuno were unreliable as employers: on September 4 she commented, "They gave me a tray of food after our class. But no word about my salary." The next day she was on her way home from the Mizuno when a servant caught up with her. "They had forgotten to pay me my salary." The servant gave her an envelope containing the money. Then, for reasons that Koume was never able to discover, the Mizuno abruptly laid her off. On November 15 a servant came from the family shortly before Koume set off to teach. He asked her to stop coming until further notice. At the time, Koume assumed this meant a break of a few days. But the summons to begin the classes again never came. On November 26 she went to the Mizuno house with a gift of sweets, to see if she could find out what was going on. The grandmother came out to greet her but told her she was too busy to talk. She asked Koume to wait until they sent word. Unable to protest, Koume exchanged polite courtesies with the old lady and went home. She never heard from the Mizuno family again.

Koume continued teaching. Ayame and Masue studied with her for the next several years, and Koume also taught many of her son's students, particularly after Yūsuke abandoned teaching in schools and began to focus exclusively on his private teaching from the end of the 1870s. From this point on, Koume often sat with Yūsuke's students, teaching reading and writing to some, and drawing and painting to others. On May 16, 1880, Yūsuke gave an exam to his students. "Many children came. Fusanosuke had a fight with the boy from the bathhouse, so I painted for them to calm them down. Then they all came upstairs and drew lots [for the paintings]. There were sixteen of them." Incidentally, this incident also points to the democratization of education in the new era: Yūsuke would probably not have taught the children of a bathhouse keeper in the Tokugawa era.

Koume worked with other teachers, particularly her patron and close family friend, Ichikawa Hiroshi. The Kawai family's ties to the Ichikawa stretched all the way back to the 1840s, and there are hundreds of mentions of them throughout the diary. Ichikawa Hitoshi was the same generation as Hyōzō and Koume. He was a scholar, a poet, and a fellow-teacher at the domain school. By the 1870s Hitoshi's son Hiroshi was the family head. Like Yūsuke, Hiroshi became an elementary school teacher in 1876.[16] Later, like Yūsuke, he started his own private academy. The exact relationship between Yūsuke and Ichikawa's academy is unclear, but both Koume and Yūsuke often went there to offer instruction or to paint with the students. For example, on June 11, 1877, Koume attended a school event to celebrate the autumn colors.[17] After a picnic lunch, she sat with the students and did seven paintings of autumn flowers, to which the students added poems. The event was in the gassaku (collaborative) tradition that Koume had valued so much in her years as a scholar's wife. But rather than the intangible capital accruing to Koume and Hyōzō in the Edo era, Koume's work on this occasion was part of the financial economy of the Kawai household. Yūsuke received cash income for sharing Ichikawa's teaching work, part of which he gave to Koume.[18]

Koume's work as a teacher was partly to help Yūsuke, and partly for a little extra income for herself. But most of her effort went into her painting. The years between 1876 and 1882 (when the diary ends) were a period of extraordinary artistic activity for Koume. In her diary there are almost one hundred references to painting in each of the six years recorded by the diary, with many projects extending over days or weeks.[19] It is tempting to attribute this intense activity to Koume's greater leisure as a widow relieved from her duties as wife and mother and finally free to pursue her lifelong love of painting and poetry. But it would be wrong to see Koume as a retired lady pursuing her passion. Although she was by now in her mid-seventies, Koume worked as hard as she ever had in her life. And her work was driven primarily by financial need.

Now that she had lost her husband, Koume was seldom invited to the creative gatherings that had been such an important part of his cultural circle. But she still received numerous commissions and requests. Some of these came from close friends and family members, and as she always had, Koume painted in the knowledge that the reward would be largely intangible. Other requests were from students, for whom she painted samples and copy-books. But most came from her patrons, who commissioned large numbers of paintings from her either for their personal use or for sale to the community of art lovers in Wakayama and the surrounding region.

Most prominent among Koume's patrons was Ichikawa Hiroshi. Through the late 1870s and into the 1880s, Ichikawa used his wide contact network to find commissions for Koume, who painted in a wide variety of genres and media for his friends and acquaintances. For example, on November 14, 1876,

> After noon, I worked on *tanzaku* [rectangular paper used for poetry and painting] paintings of Yō Kihi [Yang Guifei, a famous beauty of Tang-era China] requested by Ichikawa. Three paintings. In the early afternoon I went to Ichikawa to temporarily mount the paintings, and while [the glue] dried I painted a woman in a rice field as well as a Daruma [stylized image of Bodhidarhma]. Finished by the evening. Then I did another *tanzaku* with autumn leaves and cherry blossoms. When it got dark, they gave me sake. They also offered me food, but I didn't eat. Their maid accompanied me home as far as Omotebashi.[20]

On November 16 a letter from Ichikawa asked her to bring over some paintings she had been doing for a third party, and to stay overnight and do more painting. Koume had been planning to quietly mount the paintings at home, but instead she went to the Ichikawa house and worked on paintings of roses, bamboo, daffodils, pinks, lotus, dandelions, and field horsetails. She worked all through that day and the next. On November 17: "In the morning, I was asked to paint a pine in front of the rising sun, in gold on silk. I complied. Then I was called to lunch. I was planning to go home, but instead I painted the [portrait] I had promised, then five or six other paintings, as well as quickly painting some masks on folding fans." She finally was able to go home late in the day.[21]

Ichikawa was placing Koume's work with new owners throughout the area. Sometimes Koume mentioned the name or location of the ultimate owner, though often she painted in bulk for Ichikawa to place the paintings in his own time. And he paid Koume for her work. Shortly before she went home from her overnight stay with Ichikawa, "a traveling saleswoman called Yasuno came [to the Ichikawa house], offering a purple-lined silk crepe kimono for 2.30 yen." Koume knocked the price down to 2 yen and bought the kimono. While this was a common thing for her to do in her prime, she very seldom bought clothes after becoming a widow. Clearly, she was in the mood to indulge herself a little. She added: "I used my own money for this. I had been told I would receive two silver coins [probably 0.25 yen each] in wages." This is one of the most explicit acknowledgments Koume makes that she was being paid by Ichikawa for her work. Just a month later, on December 26, 1876, she wrote: "Ichikawa came over, and as always he gave me two shu, or half a yen. Three of his students contributed 0.10 yen each."[22] Koume mentions receiving the same sum of money from Ichikawa, 0.50 yen, on two other occasions in her diary. At other times, she received smaller amounts of money from Ichikawa, or small gifts.[23]

Ichikawa was not the only patron who acted as commissioning agent for Koume's work. Sakai Baisai, another old family friend who was himself an artist, also sometimes requested work. For example, on August 26, 1878, Koume received a letter from Baisai asking her to paint six sliding screens (*fusuma*) for an acquaintance of his in Yamada village. Baisai specified that four were to be of chrysanthemums and two of plum blossoms, in black ink or in pale colors.[24] Later in the year, on October 31, Sakai Kiyoshi (whose relationship to Baisai is unclear) sent a servant to pick up several paintings he had commissioned from Koume. In a letter, Sakai wrote, "Since I am not planning to keep them myself, please name your price." Koume reflected: "I had no choice but to say how much, so I said 0.12 yen per painting. [The servant] immediately handed over the money and left. It certainly made me feel dirty (*hiretsu*), but that's the world we now live in, so what can I do?" Since Koume had done six black ink paintings for Sakai, she was paid 0.72 yen.[25]

In October 1880 Koume traveled to Nango village, a half day's walk from Wakayama, where she spent more than two weeks working on a total of twenty-five *fusuma* screens for Sugiyama Sagorō, at the request of Tsuji Kenzaemon, a Nango resident who was a close friend of the Kawai family. She painted flowers of the four seasons, lucky gods, and other scenes for the *fusuma*. Koume was also in charge of the delicate and time-consuming job of stretching the paper over the screens. And while she was staying with the Sugiyama family, she received many visits from the villagers and their children, who often asked her to do small paintings.

She was busy from morning till night and ended up staying much longer than she had originally planned. Koume did not mention payment at the time, but the following year, on March 20, she had a visit from Kenzaemon, who gave her a bolt of white cloth and 1 yen "as payment for the *fusuma* I did for him last year."[26]

On June 10, 1881, Koume discussed another commission in Nango village, this time at the request of another old friend, Miwa Saizō (this is probably the same person she called Saijirō when she painted a portrait of his parents), on behalf of the priest of Eishōji temple. The main hall of the temple was being rebuilt, and the priest wanted Koume to paint 180 ceiling panels. In this case, the negotiation was transparent, and purely financial. Koume asked for 0.05 yen per panel, but she accepted the temple's counteroffer of 0.03 yen. It is unclear if Koume ever completed the commission, but the total fee for the project, 5.40 yen, would have been substantial even at this low rate per panel.[27]

Between 1878, when she had found asking for money to be "dirty," and 1881, when she negotiated this contract, Koume's views on cash payment seem to have undergone a transformation. Since her patrons were old family friends, it is easy to see why Koume might have felt uncomfortable with the commercialization of her work. In the past, Koume had painted for the samurai community mainly in exchange for intangible or in-kind compensation, rather than for money. It must have been difficult for her to discuss money transactions with those same people. Painting for cash became acceptable for Koume, however, partly because she needed the money but also because her friends were in turn selling her work to people she did not know. As she herself wrote, this commercial economy was the new world in which she lived.

Indeed, by the 1880s Koume seems to have had a clear expectation of payment for her labor. Several times she referred to payments she received for her work as a "wage" (*chin*).[28] When she failed to receive an expected payment, she was embittered. On August 27, 1882, for example, "Kusano came to thank me for the paintings. . . . He gave me fifteen sweets and two hundred sheets of paper. . . . He had promised to give me 1 yen, but that's all he brought. . . . There's nothing I can do about it. It's a big loss."[29] In another entry, Koume complained: "I have been painting for many people, but I haven't even made one *sen* [0.01 yen]. It's charity."[30]

The members of the Kawai family's ex-samurai community were the hardest to work with. While some, like Ichikawa, clearly understood the economic importance for Koume of her work, there remained an awkwardness around the question of money, and a tendency for others to undervalue Koume's work. Koume's identity as a female artist in the bunjinga tradition, whose practitioners had always prided themselves on their remove from the sordid commerce of the marketplace, made it all the harder for her to ask for money.

But Koume also found a market in the burgeoning commercial culture of the Meiji era. Increasingly, she became involved in commercial ventures with residents of the townsmen's quarters, as well as with ex-samurai who had gone into business for themselves. These ventures also led her into a variety of new types of painting.

From the late 1870s, Koume began drawing stencil designs for embroidered cloth (*oshi-e*). She mostly worked with a Mr. Aoyama, producing large numbers of drawings and working with seamstresses to create the finished product. For example, on April 12, 1878, Koume spent the day drawing humorous pictures, including one of a baby raccoon dog (*tanuki*) carrying a flask of sake, and one of a monkey stealing peaches. The next day some of Aoyama's workers came and worked on embroidering the designs onto cloth. Koume added her own touches to the finished cloth, painting it to embellish the work. She also worked on painting cloth to stretch over paper or wooden boxes (*haribako*).[31]

On April 26, 1878, Take, one of the women living in the Kawai rental houses, came to Koume to ask her to paint the curtain (*noren*) of a rickshaw the family had acquired. Koume spent much of the day painting an imaginative design. Take had asked her to include the character for bamboo (*take*), so Koume wrote a poem and painted it on the cloth:

> Takenoko mo / nori idete koso / chiyo no kage
> If you ride / the bamboo shoot / you will have eternal shade.[32]

Above the poem she painted a bolt of lightning in black and indigo, as well as a pair of bamboo stilts, and, below she painted a humorous image of a dwarf.

On May 31, 1880, Suzuki Yoshiemon came over to ask Koume to paint a pair of *noren*—it is not clear if this was for a business or for his home. Koume undertook the commission and delivered it on June 4. On July 12 the Suzuki family gave her 0.50 yen for the *noren* and three other paintings she had executed for them.[33]

Clearly, Koume was painting for a living. And she was extremely busy with it. Her output during the six years from 1876 to 1882 was enormous, and it increased as time went on. Koume mentioned her painting activities 225 times between 1876 and 1878, and 318 times between 1880 and 1882, the final year of the diary.[34] Undoubtedly she loved painting, but often her descriptions made it sound more like work than pleasure. Koume describes staying up late at night painting; working to finish paintings even though she felt unwell; working with frozen hands in the winter; struggling to mount paper as her glue froze; and tearing up drafts as she struggled to get a painting right for a client. For example, on March 10, 1877, she wrote, "Since yesterday I have been working on the painting requested by Yoshiyama Suitei, on paper of 5 to 6 *sun* [15–18 cm], but it just won't come out well. I tore one draft I did into pieces. Oh dear, it's hard." Four days later, she wrote, "Today I finished the three small paintings requested by Yoshiyama. They came out much worse than I expected. It was cold so that the glue froze."[35] In a particularly woeful entry, she recounted:

> Worked on my painting of pine trees that I'm supposed to send to Ichikawa tomorrow. But I couldn't do it. I was disgusted with myself, so I drank seven and a half cups of sake all at once. Kano came home from Naito, and I listened to her [while she told me about family problems], but then I began to feel sick as well as drunk. [Later] I picked up the brazier to carry it downstairs, but I dropped it, and the hot ashes scattered everywhere. When Kano heard the noise she came up, and she pushed me out of the way and stomped on the embers.[36]

In August 1882 an exciting request was delivered to the seventy-eight-year-old Koume. She was summoned to the prefectural offices, where an official invited her to submit some works of art to the Domestic Painting Competitive Exhibition (Naikoku Kaiga Kyōshinkai) to be held in Ueno Park in Tokyo starting October 1. The official showed her the call for contributions: "These days the fashion is for Western art, oil paintings and things foreign, and Japanese art is being completely abandoned.... His Majesty is concerned that people have become ignorant of the way things used to be, and so we are asking traditional painters such as the Kanō family, painters in the Chinese style, and Utagawa Toyokuni and painters in the Maruyama style and others to contribute to the exhibition." Excited at the invitation, Koume responded, "I will submit two paintings, one of a court lady looking at flowers, the other of peonies, orchids and crab apple blossoms. I paint in the bunjinga school, having learned painting under Nogiwa Hakusetsu, who was a student of Noro Kaiseki."[37]

Both were subjects she had painted many times, but she took her commission very seriously, painting multiple drafts and having her work professionally mounted before she was satisfied enough to submit it at the end of August. From September to December, Koume wrote many entries about the exhibition in her diary. She was excited to think of her work being exhibited in the Ueno Park exhibition hall, and she also had to deal with all sorts of paperwork coming out of the prefectural office.

The exhibition was widely reported in the press. It featured the work of 2,480 artists. The emperor visited the exhibition on October 24, and the publicity brought huge crowds to view the show (at a second exhibition held two years later, soldiers had to be brought in to control the crowds).[38] The exhibitors included some of Japan's most celebrated

FIGURE 7.3 Hiroshige III, *Ueno kōenchi naikoku kangyō hakurankai bijutsukan no zu* (Art Exhibition Hall at Domestic Industrial Exposition), 1877. Collection of National Institute of Japanese Literature, Tokyo. Public domain image reproduced from Wikimedia: https://commons.wikimedia.org/wiki/File:Tokyo-Ueno-Park-National-Industrial-Exhibition-Museum-Hiroshige-III-1877.png.

artists, and prizes were awarded to twenty-nine exhibitors. One celebrity artist, Kawanabe Kyōsai, shocked the judges by putting a price tag of 100 yen on a black ink painting of a crow.[39]

Koume's artwork, however, was not so avidly received. On December 22, 1882, she reported, "I went to the prefectural office. My works were indeed exhibited at the prize show [in Tokyo]." But "The ink painting was sold for 0.50 yen, while the painting of the court lady will come back [to Wakayama]. The price was very low. It barely covers the cost of the paper."[40]

The concern of the organizers of the Domestic Painting Competitive Exhibition that traditional Japanese arts had fallen into decay turned out to be misplaced. The early Meiji years opened new possibilities for professional artists in the literati style, including women. The boom in education including Chinese studies, the continuing rise in incomes of the commercial and farming classes, and the spread of printed materials including primers on Chinese poetry and painting contributed to the popularity of bunjinga painting in the years after the Meiji Restoration. Far from falling into decay, its practitioners experienced a boom in interest and demand, accompanied by what Yurika Wakamatsu calls "commercialism and commodification on a scale never witnessed before."[41] Indeed, one critic commented of this period that anyone with a little knowledge of Chinese culture thought they could paint "landscapes, orchids, or bamboos, by merely smearing paper with India ink."[42]

Although most professional artists in the bunjinga style continued to be male, some women were able to take advantage of the "wide-open atmosphere" of new possibilities for women in the early Meiji period.[43] Okuhara Seiko, who had a studio and academy in Tokyo, was so popular that "an article in the newspaper *Yūbin hōchi shinbun* proclaimed that two things had come to be sold nonstop in Tokyo since the Meiji Restoration of 1868: Hōtan, a medicine for intestinal problems that was said to prevent cholera, and paintings executed by Okuhara Seiko."[44]

Whether or not she was aware of these trends, Koume worked hard to establish herself as a professional artist through the late 1870s and early 1880s, and she was consistently in demand as a painter in the bunjinga style, as well as in a variety of other genres. She expected to be paid, and, increasingly she was rewarded in cash for her work. But her age, gender, and class background hampered her efforts. At best, she was able to eke out a modest income. The evidence from the diary is very partial, but it appears that Koume was earning around 0.12–0.13 yen for a single painting, and 0.50 yen for sets of paintings that might take from one to several days to execute. Adding up the fragmentary references to payment, it seems reasonable to conclude that Koume was making between 2 and 4 yen a month from her painting. Koume's income could not compare with that of Okuhara Seiko or other celebrity female artists of the time. Nor, indeed, was she able to earn as much as the artisans and craftsmen living in the townsmen's quarters. Koume's income was more comparable to that of a female textile factory worker.[45]

Koume was able engage in these semiprofessional painting activities because of the profound changes that were taking place in her own society. The social contract, in which she had accepted her role as a mostly unpaid cultural producer in exchange for the intangible capital accruing to herself and her husband in a world of status and privilege, had disappeared together with the lost world of the samurai elite. In the new world of equal rights and the privileging of commercial development, Koume had new opportunities to pursue her painting as a professional activity. Indeed, the world she now lived in at times demanded that she set a price on her services.

The evidence of the diary suggests, however, that her ability to professionalize her work was only partial. The one salaried job she took, as art teacher to the daughter of the wealthy Mizuno family, lasted only a few months before being abruptly terminated without explanation. As an artist, Koume was sometimes able to negotiate directly for monetary payment for her work. But more often, she expressed her frustration at the difficulties she encountered monetizing her efforts. Those frustrations were particularly evident when she was dealing with former members of her samurai circle, who tended to still see her as a scholar's wife, producing art for the sake of intangible benefits, and who failed to acknowledge her need to provide for herself.

GO-BETWEEN

Koume made one other major contribution to her family in the final years covered by her diary. In 1880 Kano and Yūsuke's eldest daughters turned eighteen (Yone) and sixteen (Tsune). Early in the year the family decided to seek marriages for both of them. Koume played a prominent role in both marriages, representing the family in initial discussions, investigation of candidates, and negotiations with go-betweens.

On January 26, 1880, the family received a proposal from "one of Kuroda's tenants, as well as a woman called Ume," to marry Yone to Enomoto Kankichi. It is unclear why the family would allow its tenants to get involved in such a matter, but in any case, "[Kuroda] Ushinosuke [Kano's brother] said we should not accept.... Kise went to inform them." The next day, "in the evening O-Yae [Ushinosuke's wife] came to talk about a marriage proposal. She proposed Hattori Tatsunojō." This time, the discussions went well. On February 7 Koume reported that "This morning Kuroda [Ushinosuke] came over, as well as Sugihara [Hattori's representative], and they broadly concluded the marriage negotiations. Hattori has asked to be allowed [to marry Yone]. He has agreed not to insist on meeting Yone in person. He says it's enough just to show him a photograph." The Kawai family gave 15 yen to Ushinosuke, to pass on as payment to Sugihara for his services as go-between.

On February 10 Kano took Yone to get her hair done, in preparation for having her photograph taken at a studio in Kitamachi. They were planning to give the photo to Sugihara to be passed on to Hattori, but "it did not come out as well as they expected." Instead, on the fourteenth they arranged for an encounter between Yone and Hattori. "Today word came from Kuroda that if we took Yone out into the street in front of our house, Sugihara would bring Hattori and they would walk past. [The Kuroda family] asked her to come over first for a bath, so Kano took her over there. Then they were planning to put on her make-up and bring her home." But as it turned out, Hattori got off work early that day, and he asked to move up the time for the encounter. A flustered Yone came running home from the Kuroda, and Kano quickly dressed her up for the encounter. Hattori promised that "tomorrow he will give his final answer." On the same day, Hattori handed over a chart showing his family lineage, to ensure that the Kuroda and Kawai families understood exactly what kind of new connections they would be making.

A final round of family discussion followed before the marriage was settled. From initial overture to finalization of the marriage took less than three weeks. Bride and groom had never met each other, and the Koume family knew little about Hattori or his family, other than what they had learned in their brief investigation. As far as the diary indicates, Yone herself was not consulted about the choice of a husband into whose family she would move for the rest of her life.

There followed a week of intense preparations. On February 21, 1880, Yūsuke hired a cook to prepare a wedding banquet, and at five in the evening, Hattori and Sugihara came, as well as the Kuroda family and other close friends and relatives. Yone joined them, dressed in elaborate formal clothing. The dinner lasted until eleven, when the Kawai family ordered a rickshaw to take Hattori home. The following day, the family accepted visitors who came to offer congratulations. The final few days before Yone's move were spent preparing her trousseau, which included cotton-padded futons, two clothes chests, a mirror and stand, sewing accessories, and three brand new kimonos. On February 28 the trousseau was dispatched to the Hattori house, carried by eleven men, who then returned to the Kawai house and drank "a large amount of sake, first 2 shō and then another 2 shō, altogether 4 shō (7.2 liters). They danced, playacted, and ate." The next day Yone moved to her new home and her new life. Her family accompanied her in three rickshaws. The Hattori family entertained them with an elaborate meal accompanied by dancing and shamisen music. Two years later, Yone presented Koume with her first great-grandchild, Kazu. Baby Kazu was only four years younger than her uncle Hidesuga, who was born in 1878.

With Yone safely married off, the family's attention turned to Tsune. Tsune's affair turned out to be much more difficult than that of her older sister. Over the next eighteen months, Koume recorded proposals for more than thirty candidates. None of them worked out. The candidates came from a wide range of social backgrounds: samurai, farmers, merchants, civil servants, and policemen. Some were quickly dismissed. Others seemed attractive, and in one or two cases the family entered serious discussions. On February 23, 1881, Koume commented: "Kusumi, Tatsumi, Oki, the person from Edo, and the rice merchant Tanaka, altogether five families are asking for Tsune. Tanaka is the least attractive. He has an unpleasant appearance, and he's always coming over here to ask about the matter, so that we can't get anything done."

In mid-1881 the family thought that they had a resolution. For over a year the family had been having inconclusive discussions with a Mr. Katayama, a Wakayama native who now lived in Tokyo. In his thirties,

Katayama was at least twice Tsune's age, but the family do not seem to have considered that an obstacle (though they were a little concerned about his attachment to his mother, with whom he still lived). On July 16 it seemed as though all sides had come to an agreement, and the marriage was to go ahead. The next day, however, the go-between, Koume's old friend Tsuji Bungo, came to tell the Kawai family of an unfortunate misunderstanding. Tsuji and the Kawai family thought that, since the couple would later move back to Wakayama, Katayama had agreed to take Tsune without sending a trousseau up to Tokyo. But Katayama was now saying that "it would look much better if [Tsune] brought these things, and items such as mirror stands and sewing equipment were very expensive in Tokyo, so we should send them from here." The negotiations remained at an impasse, and just four days later, Katayama announced his forthcoming marriage to another girl.

Finally, in August, Tsuji Bungo brought the Kawai family another candidate, Maeda Toyohide. Perhaps the family was exhausted by all the previous negotiations and dramas, but this time the proceedings went surprisingly smoothly. On September 2 a meeting was arranged between the prospective couple. Tsune was carefully prepared: her hair was made up, and she was dressed in a beautiful kimono—borrowing some of her accessories from Koume. A few days later, on September 8, word came from the Maeda family that they would like to go ahead with the marriage, and the next day Yūsuke went to Iwasaki Kedayū to borrow 80 yen, at 18 percent, "to pay for the preparations to send Tsune to Maeda Toyohide this month." The marriage contract called for a trousseau consisting of five trunks full of wedding goods, and Yūsuke posted a 500-yen bond to guarantee its delivery.

The marriage negotiations involving Tsune show us how important the negotiations over the trousseau could be. The contract was a binding legal document, with a large amount of money at stake. In Wakayama, at least, trousseaus were typically measured in "ropes" (*tsuri*), referring to the rope hung on a long pole to carry a large wooden trunk. One "rope" meant one trunk, so the true measure was the number of full trunks in the trousseau.[46] Even this was a notional measure, though, as Tsune's actual trousseau contained well over a dozen trunks.

On September 10 Koume's granddaughter Mikiyo carried an inventory of the trousseau over to the go-between, and the next day two representatives of the Maeda family came to take delivery of a part of the trousseau. The goods included mirror stands, kimono, obi, embroidery, fans and other accessories, as well as money gifts for the groom's father, mother, and grandmother. The bridal party then set off in rickshaws to a restaurant for a wedding banquet. Koume commented "The food was rather expensive, but plentiful." She concluded: "It has all ended happily." Finally, the seventeen-year-old Tsune set off in a formal wedding procession to the Maeda home on September 21. The family hired a dozen retainers to accompany the bride. "They emerged from the gate singing. A large crowd came to watch." The procession included a public display of the remainder of the trousseau, packed into more than a dozen boxes and trunks of lacquer and smooth white wood. The celebrations continued with a formal visit the next day, and a "five days returning" ceremony on the twenty-fifth, at which twenty-five guests enjoyed food and musical entertainment, while the bride and groom's families exchanged elaborate compliments.

The dramas over Tsune's marriage were just beginning, however. Two months after her wedding, on November 26, Tsune came to visit her family. She said she had come to practice the shamisen. She was accompanied by her servant Tami, but then she sent the servant away, telling her to come and fetch her in two or three days. "Gradually, [Tsune] told us that Toyohide had been a little angry with her. He did not hit her, but he told her to go home for a bit." The next day Koume went to meet with Maeda Toyohide's representative, a man named Kakutani, from whom "she heard some difficult things." Kakutani promised on November 29 to go to Maeda, "listen to his innermost thoughts," and try to make things better. But the conversation did not go well, and on the thirtieth Koume concluded that "there is nothing to be done. Ushinosuke too is feeling terrible. On our side, we have run out of things to say." Koume never clarified what exactly had happened, or who was at fault. The separation became a divorce, and Tsune was once again in need of a husband.

In 1882 the family once again began entertaining proposals. On March 31 they received a proposal to marry her to Orito Tokutarō. On April 14 Ichikawa came over to report on the candidate: "He is a person of good character, but he lives with his stepmother and her three children, so the circumstances are not very convenient." Ichikawa recommended they withdraw from the discussions. On April 19, however, the go-between organized a meeting between Orito and Tsune, and Orito was said to be pleased. But on April 21 Tsuji Bungo reported on his further investigation of Orito. It was problematic. "He had a pretty bride, whose family had promised a trousseau of seven trunks. He took her on a trip to Awa [Tokushima prefecture, in Shikoku], but she died there. He buried her on the spot, telling her parents he had held a fine funeral for her." Orito then demanded the as yet undelivered seven trunks from her parents. The parents were said to be deeply suspicious. "If this is true then it's very bad." The Kawai family decided to turn the offer down.

By June 12, however, they were once again considering Orito. It is not clear what made them change their minds, but by the nineteenth an agreement had been made, and on June 21 the family held the formal marriage ceremony, then went to a restaurant in Kukenocho for a celebration dinner. On June 23, just two weeks after the initial approach, Tsune once again left home to start a new marriage with a stranger. The family provided a wedding procession of a dozen retainers, accompanied by lanterns, ceremonial umbrellas, and songs by a *geiko* called Kumae. On the twenty-fourth the Kawai family visited Tsune, and the next day the Kuroda family reported that she was still doing well. They had gone up to her room on the second floor and given her several gifts as well as 2 yen to buy whatever she wanted. She had seemed happy. "With that, I can ease my mind," reported Koume.

Once again, though, Tsune's marriage foundered near the outset. Orito was expected by tradition to pay a visit to the Kawai family in the days after his marriage, particularly on the fifth day, when a family celebration was the norm. But although they prepared food and drink for him, Orito never showed up. On June 29 Koume wrote: "For the last three or four days we have been waiting with fish and sake in case Orito comes to visit, but he has not come." It was soon clear to the family that something had gone wrong. But Koume never explained the circumstances, and although she mentioned several times that Tsune wanted to return to her family, the situation remained unresolved in January of the next year, at which point the diary itself came to an end. Now in her seventy-ninth year, Koume was getting too old and tired to keep it going.

There is much of interest in the case of Tsune. Why was the family so anxious to marry her off even though she was so young? What went wrong with her first husband, Maeda Toyohide? Why did they choose two much older men for her, both with past marriages and both with known red flags? And why did the arrangements go so badly wrong? Tsune is of interest also because her son, Shiga Yasuharu, devoted much of his life to preserving Koume's record. It was he who transcribed and published the Koume diary. Without him, Koume's diary might still be sitting undiscovered in a family storehouse. Today the Society for the Enjoyment of Koume's Diary is the main group working to preserve Koume's legacy. The one family member active in the society, Shiga Junko, is Yasuharu's granddaughter. Because of that link, we know that Tsune eventually married Shiga Kusunosuke, who came from a middle-ranking samurai family. We know that she was his second wife (his first had died at the age of thirty, leaving him with three children). And we know that they stayed married and had two children of their own, including Yasuharu.

In the years before her marriages, it is hard to find anything in the diary that hints at trouble ahead. Tsune seems like a very normal girl of her class. She ran errands for her mother and grandmother; she helped out occasionally taking care of the schoolchildren; she played with her Kuroda cousins; she learned to play the shamisen, to sew, and to work the abacus. She wore nice clothes that the family bought for her. And she went often to the theater, sometimes with her sisters and cousins, and sometimes with her grandparents. Tsune did not have all the opportunities that Koume had enjoyed. Like Koume, she grew up in a scholarly household and surely absorbed some of the learning and culture of the educated elite. But she did not have a famous poetry or painting teacher, nor did she have the chance to remain in the house she grew up in as Koume had. How did it feel for Tsune, in the midst of her carefree childhood, to be suddenly married off with barely any say in the matter, first to a man twice her age (though that marriage was called off at the last minute), and then, after the failure of her first marriage, to another much older man? Why were Koume and Kano willing to believe that "Tsune seems happy" when she clearly was not?

Koume was a woman who surely understood the frustrations and limitations imposed by her gender, even as she created a position for herself in Wakayama society that in some ways transcended those limitations. How did it feel to see her granddaughters disposed of like dolls? Unfortunately, if Koume had an opinion, she was too discreet to record it in her diary.

SUNSET

Through much of her life, Koume was remarkably healthy. She often had colds and sometimes complained of tiredness and hangovers, but she seems to have had no serious illness throughout the middle years of her life, and into her old age. But by 1876 Koume was seventy-two years old, and she was starting to feel her age. When she accompanied Yūsuke to his new job in Nishikawa village, she complained that "my feet hurt terribly."[47]

On December 2, 1876, Koume slipped and fell while drawing water from the well in the back garden. "I landed on my hip. I was lying there when the retired Mrs. Wada came in through the garden." Koume is brave about her accident—she does not mention it for the next several days. But on December 10 she writes: "In the evening O-Yae came. She said tomorrow her mother is going to the theater, and would I please join her? But my right leg, which I fell on the other day, is still not better, so I refused. Today is the ninth day [since the accident]. That's not the only time I fell. Some time back I fell and hurt my hand, and at this time of year it still hurts. In any event, my health is not good. But I can do seated work as usual."

Koume's complaints about ill health and accidents increased over the coming years. On March 15, 1877, she lamented: "My legs are unsteady. Today I didn't go upstairs. I just stayed under the *kotatsu* [heated sitting area]." And on May 8 she wrote: "Today my back hurt, and it was a little hard to walk." Because of her difficulty walking, Koume got a rickshaw to join a group of women on a visit to the Tsuwada shrine, but when she tried to pay, she dropped her wallet and had to fumble for the coins. She commented: "When you get old you get dull and stupid in everything."

When she was most frustrated with herself, Koume tended to drink more. On September 27, 1877, she was out visiting with friends and got much too drunk. "I couldn't stand up ... and I lost my umbrella. I'm thoroughly fed up with myself. I got home and went straight to bed." Koume also complained of deafness, which was aggravated by her increasingly frequent colds. For example, on July 19, 1878, she wrote: "For the last three days I haven't been able to hear well. . . . All I hear is a buzzing in my ears."

On September 12, 1881, "in the night, I don't know what time, I suddenly felt ill. I went to the toilet and had diarrhea. I went back to lie down, but then I suddenly felt nauseous and ran to the veranda, where I vomited. Meanwhile it kept coming out like water." Koume lay down after each bout but had to run to the toilet at least four more times. She tried wrapping cloth diapers around her middle, but they didn't work well. Koume spent the next four days in bed, drinking only tea and boiled water. She had to miss Tsune's wedding dinner as a result.

And the following year, on June 15, 1882, just as her family were engrossed in last-minute negotiations with Orito Tokutarō (he would marry Tsune on June 23), Koume had another accident:

> Early this morning I tried waking everyone, but no one got up, so I went down to try and make some rice soup. But nothing had been started. Meanwhile I remembered that I wanted to wash a pair of socks and two hand towels. I was just trying to put my loincloth in the tub, when I lost my balance and fell. I hit my backbone. I couldn't utter a word. I was lying there when Tsune came down. She helped me up and called for Kano, who came down and helped me up to my usual sleeping place. I hit the bone behind my solar plexus, and it hurt terribly. I can't move my body. Now it doesn't hurt any more. I'm lying on my stomach in a good position.

One consequence of Koume's fall was that she was unable to go to the bathroom for the next three days. She was able to urinate in a bed-pan, but she wasn't able to defecate until she could walk to the toilet on the eighteenth. "Today for the first time I went to the toilet. It's been five days since I pooped but nothing came out. I'm not eating as much as usual." And two days later, "I'm still feeling the same. I'm a little better, but my backbone still hurts, and I can't move freely."

On February 6, 1883, a letter arrived for Yūsuke from the office of the ex-daimyo, Tokugawa Mochitsugu. It informed him that since his mother was entering her eightieth year, his lordship had prepared a gift for her. Koume was asked to come and collect it two days later at 10:00 a.m., or, if she was unable to go, to send a representative. On the morning of the eighth, however, Koume reported:

> Heavy snow overnight. Around two feet. . . . We had ordered a rickshaw, but they came to tell us it wouldn't come. We asked around elsewhere, but today is New Year's Day according to the old calendar, so they have

all taken the day off. There wasn't a single man available. It's impossible [for me] to walk, so we were wondering what we should do when a letter came from the Tokugisha [the ex-daimyo's office]. The gist of it was that it would be fine to send a representative [in Koume's place], but that everyone had already come [to collect their gifts], so we should send someone immediately. Yūsuke set off right away.

The letter also contained an elegant poem:

> This passing body cannot even leave a *ninoji* footprint [the *ninoji* is written 二 and resembles the imprint made by a *geta* clog in the snow]
> Having known the great snow on this morning of an abundant year.

The gifts, when Yūsuke carried them back, consisted of a set of porcelain dishes, a painting of hollyhocks (the Tokugawa family crest), and a brocade cloth in the celebratory colors of red and white, as well as several more congratulatory poems.

This milestone in Koume's long life was also the beginning of its final phase. Koume lived for another six years, but the light shone by her diary over her long and interesting life now went dim. After the excitement of the recognition by the ex-daimyo, there are only two other entries in the diary for the whole of 1883. In 1884 Koume wrote an account of the ceremony commemorating the thirteenth anniversary of Hyōzō's death. Other than that, there are only a few entries from the month of January, and then the diary falls altogether silent.

Kawai Koume died on November 2, 1889, a month before her eighty-fifth birthday.

CONCLUSION

Kawai Koume's diary is one of a very small number of surviving firsthand accounts of the daily life of a lower-ranking samurai woman.[1] Yet, as a record of female experiences of the final decades of the Tokugawa era and the early years of Meiji, it has been largely overlooked. Donald Keene, the only other English-language scholar to write about the diary, dismissed it as overly focused on mundane domestic matters and "unlikely to retain the attention of a modern reader for very long." Japanese scholars have used Koume's diary selectively, but none has yet seen her as worthy of foregrounding in a book-length study (the one book on the life of Koume, the late Abe Takeshi's excellent *The Wonderful World of Kawai Koume*, was written by a retired advertising executive who was drawn to Koume by her love of sake).[2] For the most part, the flame of Koume's legacy is kept alight by a group of local historians, of which Abe Takeshi was a member: the Society for the Enjoyment of Koume's Diary (Koume Nikki wo Tanoshimu Kai). Most of them are far more knowledgeable than I can ever hope to be about Wakayama's history and culture, and about the local details of Koume's life. But this book is not intended to be a work of local history. In twenty years of writing biographies of little-known Japanese individuals across 150 years of history, my hope has always been to fulfill the broader aspirations of microhistory, to "serve as an allegory for the culture as a whole" (Jill Lepore); or to take "the lines branching out" from a person's life and point them "towards the general" (Istvan Szijarto).³ What are the lines that branch out from Koume's life? And what insights do they offer into the broader history of the era surrounding Japan's Meiji Restoration?

LIVING HISTORY AWAY FROM THE CENTER

Although Koume often wrote about events of national consequence, those events mostly took place outside her domain, often in places far distant from Kishū. Koume's personal experiences of history, however, were local. Her greatest concerns were those that most closely affected her family. Some of those—such as the death of a beloved grandchild—had little or nothing to do with historical events as they are commonly understood. Yet they represented the reality of Koume's lived experience as much as did the great political upheavals of her time. Of course, even in a provincial city before the era of mass communication and mass mobilization, it is hard (and undesirable) to completely separate the private sphere of family joys and sorrows from the march of historical events. The private tragedy of Kikue's death may have been affected by the cholera epidemic, which was caused in part by the loosened restrictions on trade and shipping as a result of Japan's foreign treaties. And medical practice in Wakayama was influenced by Japan's position in the global community of knowledge.

Koume filtered events, both near and distant, by the impact they had on her family and her immediate community. Rising prices and economic hardship, whether caused by crop failure, foreign trade, or military mobilization, affected Koume and her family deeply and personally. Thanks to its privileged access to the domain's tax rice, Koume's family was largely protected from price increases in their staple. Nevertheless, it suffered from the reductions and forced loans imposed on it by the domain, and from the general rise in commodity and labor prices that accompanied the inflation. The general hardship also affected the Kawai family. Koume often expressed compassion for the victims, recounting stories such as the one in which a father killed his own children in despair. "When the price of rice is high," she comments, "all sorts of things can happen." And Koume had to deal with a steady stream of supplicants—family members and acquaintances—in need of a handout.

Word of political events in Edo and other distant parts of Japan arrived in Kishū as a swirl of rumors. Reporting on them, Koume often framed the events in dark and ominous terms, writing of portents such as dual suns in the sky, earthquakes, or floods, and predicting dark days ahead. It was as though the dramatic events taking place in distant parts of the country were comparable to celestial phenomena over which Koume had absolutely no control, and in the face of which she could only pray "that we will get through this unharmed."

But as events came closer to home, Koume's focus sharpened, and her perspective became more immediate and practical. The arrival of the Perry expedition produced a flood of reporting in Koume's diary, much of it misinformed, and most of it highly alarmist. But when the domain called on its retainers to protect their own coastline, Koume and her family jumped into action. Hyōzō's quest to buy armor; the expenses and debts he incurred; the urgent planning for coastal defense; Hyōzō's work on a memorial to the daimyo, to be passed on to the government in Edo; and Hyōzō's mobilization for coastal defense: these were immediate, real, and visible to Koume. This was her experience of the crisis. There was drama enough here. Political purges, assassinations, military mobilization, foreign ships, floods, and epidemics fill the pages of the diary. These events, many of which centered on the administrative center of Wakayama castle, shaped Koume's understanding of her changing world, and she and her family in turn played their part in shaping that world through their military service, political advising, participation in the rituals of the domain, and acquiescence and support for the ruling elite. Koume and her family were caught up in national events, but their motives and actions were local.

Scholars have long debated the motive forces of the Meiji Restoration. Did its origin lie in the actions of low-ranking samurai concentrated in the southwestern domains, who created a coalition based on emperor-centered nationalism that overthrew the Tokugawa and established the movement's leaders as the leading statesmen of the new era? Was it in the intellectuals who developed powerful critiques of shogunal rule and embraced theories of direct action in support of an imperial "restoration"?

Was it in the eruption of spontaneous protests and rebellions by peasants and other oppressed classes throughout Japan—a Japanese-style French revolution? Or was it, rather, in the activism and financial power of wealthy peasants and merchants who supported and financed the anti-Tokugawa movement: a Japanese version of the Marxist bourgeois revolution? Still other scholars have emphasized the agency and collective importance of diverse small-scale actors: women motivated by the powerful emperor-centric ideologies circulating throughout Japan; small-scale entrepreneurs mobilized by the new opportunities opened up by foreign trade; and well-informed townsmen galvanized by vibrant communications networks.[4]

Given this wide choice of actors, it would be surprising not to find a role for Koume and her family in the Restoration drama. But her agency in political affairs is hard to pin down. Only very occasionally did Koume express a clear opinion on political matters. Those she did express tended toward conservatism. When Ōshio Heihachirō launched his quixotic attack on the merchants and government officials of Osaka, Koume expressed no awareness that her interests as a financially precarious low-ranking bushi might have been aligned with his. Ōshio was, rather, a rebel whom the samurai of Wakayama might be called on to hunt down. Koume was much more concerned about the destruction of property and the threat to public order than about the cause espoused by Ōshio. When the domain issued orders to arrest Ōshio, stating that "no difficulty will be made if he is cut down on the spot," Koume recorded the order without comment.

On the other hand, when the Date family—who subsequently were lauded as visionary leaders and activists in the reformist cause—were purged, Koume expressed satisfaction at the removal of what she—reflecting the propaganda of her domain—perceived as a corrupt politician. And when the reformist administrator Tsuda Izuru was dismissed from his post, she once again aligned herself with the conservative faction, calling his dismissal *"medetashi"* (good news). Even when her close friend Tanaka Zenzō, who was another reforming administrator, was murdered, Koume expressed no regret for him as a political leader—only as a friend. It seems, in fact, that her concerns about possible further loss of income under the policies proposed by Tsuda and Tanaka outweighed any recognition she may have had of their necessity for the domain. Neither, when activist samurai from Chōshū and other domains fomented disturbances in Kyoto, did Koume express any sympathy for their cause, lamenting rather the breakdown of law and order.

Does this mean that Koume had no sympathy for the imperial cause? In her diary, Koume never mentions the movement to restore political power to the emperor, nor the ideologies of the activists, nor the nativist philosophies underpinning them. This was in spite of the fact that the head of one of the leading schools of nativist thought, Motoori Ōhira, was Koume's own teacher. It is indeed remarkable, given the Kishū origins and the daimyo's patronage of the Motoori family, that "national learning" with its implications for the role of the emperor did not become more embedded in Kishū's political consciousness. In Mito, the home of another influential school of nativist thought, many bushi of all ranks embraced the philosophy and the activism it implied—with dire consequences for the domain.[5] Kishū domain went so far as to establish a school of national learning under the umbrella of the Gakushūkan. But for most bushi this never translated into political activism.

One reason may have been the Motoori family's extreme caution with regard to the politicization of their teaching. Norinaga required his students to take an oath that "I will not engage in any unusual behavior with respect to the world at large, nor involve myself in any matters that might excite public opinion." And although Norinaga often disparaged Confucian learning as one of the "evil customs of the Chinese barbarians," he also preached strict obedience to the powers that be, even if they are fundamentally unjust: "Obeying the official laws set down in each era and following the dictates of social custom immediately equal the Way of the gods."[6] Since Koume's teacher Motoori Ōhira was on the domain's payroll, preaching sedition would indeed have been suicidal. Another factor may have been the fact that the majority of the Motoori school's students were not the children of samurai, but of merchants and wealthier farmers, and a third factor may have been that for most students of the Motoori school, the teaching was more about esthetics and the love of poetry than about its possible political implications.[7] For Koume, it was culturally liberating since it helped open the door to her participation in the mostly male-dominated world of scholarly creative production. There is no evidence that it influenced her political views.

Why was it, though, that in spite of the dense flow of information on new ideas, Koume expressed no sympathy for the reformist agendas or imperial ideologies of the activists? Her conservatism, I believe, was born of the balance of her privilege. All the evidence from her diary points to Koume's lifelong commitment to the welfare of her own family. The Kawai may have suffered at times from economic insecurity, but they had far more to lose than to gain from political upheaval. Koume and Hyōzō remained loyal to the Kishū Tokugawa family, which in turn was deeply entangled with the fortunes of the Tokugawa shogunate (indeed, during the most critical years of unrest, the shogun was a former daimyo of Kishū). Certainly, that entanglement carried heavy costs at times, for the domain and for its retainers. Its efforts at coastal defense, followed by its repeated mobilizations for campaigns fought in the Kinai area and beyond, upended the lives of the Kawai family and most of their closest friends.

Nevertheless, rather than sympathize with movements that aimed to disrupt the status quo, throughout her long life Koume remained loyal to the people and institutions that nurtured her: the domain (until its collapse), her extended family, and her network of scholarly and artistic friends and connections. In the late 1860s, when Kishū itself was threatened by the civil war brewing in Kyoto, Koume expressed her solidarity with the daimyo. When he was on his reluctant way through the snow to take up the fight on behalf of the shogun, Koume wrote, "We are worried that his lordship will get cold and ill in his palanquin, and his arrival in Kyoto will be delayed."

Koume had every reason to remain loyal to the system that had nurtured her. Despite their relatively low income, Koume and Hyōzō had enjoyed a highly privileged position as members of the stipendiary samurai class and of the domain's cultural elite. Their position guaranteed them an income paid from the tax rice of the peasants, as well as the respect of the populace as members of the ruling samurai status group, and the prestige accruing to eminent cultural figures. They were undoubtedly beneficiaries of the system, and they saw no reason to encourage its downfall. Perhaps they were disillusioned with the policies, or the incompetence, or the perceived corruption, of key political actors; but where, and when, have people not been fed up with their politicians? Whatever the motives that prompted activist women such as Matsuo Taseko and Kurosawa Tokiko to leave their homes and walk to Kyoto (in one case to join the "revere the emperor, expel the barbarian" movement, and in the other to submit a poetic memorial denouncing the shogun's policies to the emperor; both are the subjects of English-language biographies), Koume showed no sign of sharing them.[8]

On the other hand, Koume does, during the course of the 1850s and 1860s, show some signs of an emerging national consciousness. The arrival of aggressive foreigners on Japanese shores forced Koume and Hyōzō to consider their identity in relation to the foreign powers, which were determined to negotiate closer relations with a "Japan" that turned out to be partly imaginary. When Perry threatened the government in Edo with bombardment by his "black ships," Koume wrote (or possibly copied) a nationalist poem:

> If they stop hiding in shadows and come into the light of the land
> Of the rising sun, they will melt, those ships from America.

And when Ii Naosuke placed the Mito daimyo Tokugawa Nariaki under house arrest, Koume protested that Nariaki's "only concern was the welfare of the nation." Here, Koume used the phrase "*tenka kokka*," combining the concepts of a "national house" (meaning all the domains) with that of "all under heaven," meaning the realm of Japan.[9] Did Koume have a strong sense of "Japan" as a nation before this, or did it take the arrival of a foreign "other" to form a consciousness of national identity? Koume's diary offers little direct evidence, but it does repeatedly show awareness of a variety of national networks: trade, the movement of people, the relationship between Edo and Wakayama, the circulation of news and information, the transferability of art and poetry from one domain to another, and the broad sense of belonging, strengthened by her own daimyo's family ties, to the Tokugawa realm. Watanabe Hiroshi proposes five conditions for the self-perception of Japan as a nation, all of which, he argues, were met by the latter half of the Tokugawa era: political union under a universally acknowledged ruler; economic integration, with national markets and a common currency; active networks for the circulation of people and information, including highways and information networks; cultural integration, with a common language (especially written) and broadly similar customs; and, paradoxically, Japan's relative isolation from the global community, which created a strong "us" versus "other" mentality.[10] Many of these conditions are visible in the everyday interactions recorded in Koume's diary.

Koume's national consciousness is also evident in her xenophobia, which she displays repeatedly as she laments the foreigners' greed, drunkenness, lust, and uncouth behavior. There is no evidence that she ever personally encountered a foreigner, and it is possible that her xenophobia was the result of this lack of contact. The foreigners remained a frightening unknown, about whom all sorts of horrifying stories continued to swirl.

Koume seldom expressed direct political opinions, and when she did, it was usually to condemn personal greed on the part of politicians, and to express shock and disapproval of the growing forces of rebellion. More often, though, she betrayed a sense of powerlessness. What difference would her opinions make? And what actions could she take if she were to embrace a political view? When their lord was called on to support the shogunate in its climactic struggles against the southwestern domains, Koume and Hyōzō's primary concern was the welfare of their own family members (some of whom had been summoned to fight), and then the welfare of their daimyo and domain. As to the best course to take to ensure Japan's future security: like most Japanese (and indeed like their own daimyo), they probably had no idea. Koume, her husband, and her son did their duty as loyal retainers of Kishū domain. When called on to fight, they fought. And when the Tokugawa system collapsed, they adapted as best they could.

Her reporting, however, did betray an abiding cynicism about political affairs, and a willingness to mock even those she admired or considered friends. Repeatedly, in the wake of a major political event, Koume would report on satirical poems or riddles circulating in the major cities. These were not limited to the great cities of Edo, Osaka, and Kyoto. Wakayama had its own industry of scurrilous verse. Koume clearly relished these, often transcribing them word for word. As much as the opinions they expressed, Koume enjoyed these diatribes for their humor and their clever word play. "They are well done," she commented, "but certainly insolent."[11]

Despite her loyalty to the Tokugawa family and system, Koume witnessed their complete collapse at the beginning of 1868. Her diary from the period no longer survives, so we may never know how she responded to the dramatic collapse of the 260-year-old political structure. But when it reopens in 1876, she and her family were struggling to reinvent themselves. The new political order that emerged in the aftermath of the Meiji Restoration severely tested Koume's loyalty. Kishū domain was disbanded, and its daimyo moved to Tokyo. All the privileges that Koume had taken for granted during the Tokugawa era had now vanished.

Koume's family, which (in the absence of work-related supplements) had been economically marginal even during the Tokugawa era, became even more threatened. Once Yūsuke's stipend converted to a bond in 1876, the interest amounted to only 4 yen a month. Added to the income from rental properties, the family's income probably did not exceed 8 yen per month. With the inflation of the late 1870s, the purchasing power of the family's income continued to decline.

By this time, Koume was an old woman, and she was even less likely to become personally involved in political affairs. But by the same token, she was that much readier to express her contempt for the politicians who were running the prefecture and nation. When the Meiji government came to Wakayama to recruit ex-samurai volunteers for the military in its battle against the Satsuma rebels, Koume commented bitterly that "the samurai have been treated as though they're of no use to anyone, and it's unreasonable to try and use them just in an emergency." And, in a shocking reversal, she commented that the paper handed out by the ex-daimyo, who had come specially to Wakayama to participate in the recruitment effort, might as well be used "to wipe their asses." This is an extraordinary comment to make on the former daimyo of the domain, to whom Koume had offered such loyalty through much of her long life.

WORK AND FAMILY

Laurel Ulrich, in her classic study of an eighteenth-century New England midwife, used the analogy of a piece of checkered woven linen to describe the intersecting lives of the men and women of Hallowell, Maine, where Martha Ballard lived. "Think of the white threads as women's activities, the blue as men's, then imagine the resulting social web. Clearly, some activities in an eighteenth-century town brought men and women together. Others defined their separateness."[12] The white threads in Ulrich's portrait reveal a vibrant social and economic world of women, in which Martha managed important financial and nonfinancial transactions, sold and bartered woven cloth, traded in dozens of items from "hoggs lard" to wooden shingles, hired and trained helpers, and attended hundreds of families in childbirth, sickness, and death. Martha Ballard's social and economic activities were mostly separate from those of her husband, who was a not very successful surveyor. But in the public and archival records of the era, it is the men's economic, social, and political lives that have survived. The lives of the women must be carefully excavated from incomplete and tantalizing records that hint at more than they tell. Such is Martha Ballard's diary, and so it is for Kawai Koume. In a world in which nonfinancial capital and noncash exchange were as important as workplace and salary, Koume was an essential contributor to the family economy, and her diary is an important witness to her complex web of activities and connections.

Koume's family was not, of course, in New England. As Mary Elizabeth Berry and Marcia Yonemoto have pointed out, the *ie* (family or house) in Tokugawa-era Japan had different legal and social contexts, and different meanings, from families in other East Asian societies, let alone in Europe or North America—as well, of course, as considerable variety within Japan.[13] Most important, for samurai families, the family was the vehicle for succession to hereditary rank, occupation, and stipend, across generations. The rules of samurai society allowed only one male heir to inherit these privileges (and the responsibilities that went with them), so the provision of a competent male heir was of paramount importance. In Koume's family, this led to two successive generations of adoption into the family of muko heirs.

The family was also the training ground for the production of competent successors to its occupation: scholarship and teaching. In this sense it resembled the family-centered schools that dominated the cultural establishment in Japan. These schools depended on maintaining their reputation as exclusive sites of learning, based on their faithful transmission of a cultural lineage from generation to generation. While the Kawai family did not have the same unique brand as well-known schools like the Hayashi in Edo and the Motoori in Wakayama, it did succeed in transmitting its status as a respected site of Confucian learning, as well as its occupational status as salaried teachers, across four generations spanning the entire history of the Gakushūkan domain school.

The Kawai family was also a site of performance, identified in several recent studies as crucial to the maintenance of the Tokugawa social order.[14] As family head, Hyōzō performed the rituals of attendance at the castle, "enquiring after the daimyo's health," and presiding over public events such as the celebration of the twice-yearly Confucian *sekiten* (Ch: *shi-dian*) ritual. The family also performed its status through its observance of appropriate formalities for participation in scholarly and temple gatherings, cultural events, weddings and funerals, etc.

As the daughter of the Kawai family and wife of a muko husband, and as a cultural figure in her own right, Koume was assured a prominent role in the performance of some of the family's public-facing activities, as well as in household management and decision-making within the family. As a wife within the patriarchal family system, she also uncomplainingly performed the gendered role of the "inner" person, whose responsibilities encompassed the private and domestic sphere: acting as guardian of the home, ensuring the smooth and harmonious functioning of the household, caring for her aged mother, and raising her only child. As a result, Koume appeared in public far less than the men in her household. A survey by Namakura Sumiko has identified only sixty-four times when Koume mentions leaving the house in the eight surviving years (some partial) of the diary between 1849 and 1867: an average of about once per month.[15]

Nevertheless, as Yonemoto has argued, living a gendered role within a patriarchal system was not the same as suffering from "patriarchal domination."[16] Yoshida Yuriko proposes that a patriarchal division between the male "outer" and the female "inner" world of the family was more likely to exist in bushi families, owing to the economic monopoly of the male stipendiary family head.[17] This may have been true of the Rai family, which Yoshida studies, but it does not reflect the experiences of Kawai Koume.[18] Within the bounds of the gendered expectations of her rank and society, Koume enjoyed wide freedom to chart her own course in both the private and public spheres. She was a vital participant in the daily life of her family, her position made all the more central by her status as the wife of a muko, and as a respected artist and participant in the domain's cultural community. Although she stayed at home much more than her husband and son, Koume's education, artistic skills, and status as a birthright Kawai allowed her to interact with the family's social networks as an equal. Moreover, unlike wives described in several other family histories, Koume was not overburdened by the "women's work" of sewing, cooking, cleaning, washing, or child-rearing. She clearly prioritized household management over household labor, and she was able to create ample space in her daily life for the social and cultural activities on which she pinned much of her personal identity and self-worth.

More than anything, the family, for Koume and Hyōzō, was an economic, social, and cultural unit to which all members must contribute for their own advancement and well-being. Throughout the long years of her recorded life, Koume never stopped working to this end. She performed her duties as mother and grandmother. She was a teacher. She was the manager of a busy household. She entertained guests, ensured supplies were always available, managed repairs and renovations, shopped for herself and other household members, cooked, pickled vegetables, distilled fruit liquors, and prepared gifts for auspicious occasions in the lives of friends, colleagues, and family. She occasionally spun thread, sewed kimonos, washed clothes, and bought and distributed raw cotton, without ever allowing these tasks to dominate her life. She drew and painted, for patrons, friends, and family members; managed the family finances, borrowing when necessary and lending when possible; recorded the daily events in the life of her family, as well as news and information about the domain and further afield; managed servants and helpers; and managed and nurtured the complex social networks that were so vital to the family's well-being and advancement. She was helped in these efforts by her cooperative and generally harmonious relationship with her husband—a relationship that feels more like a partnership of equals than a site of patriarchy.

SAMURAI FAMILIES IN THE MEIJI RESTORATION

The Tokugawa regime bestowed special privileges on the bushi status group. Of the four "classes" created by Tokugawa ideology, the samurai were the only group who were clearly distinguished—by physical appearance, legal rights, feudal ties, and hereditary incomes based on a share of tax rice—from the others. And yet, if there is one thing I have learned from this project, it is the impossibility of making any meaningful generalization about the samurai as a group. It embraced immense diversity of occupation, social status, economic wealth, lifestyle, philosophy, educational level, moral code, and life experience. The Kawai family received a stipend ranging from 20 to 50 koku, depending on the career stage of the family head. Did that represent wealth or poverty? In Nakatsu domain, where Fukuzawa Yukichi grew up, it represented enough wealth to "read the Confucian Classics and the Books of History, study military strategy, practise horsemanship, spearmanship and swordsmanship, and generally indulge in all the branches of art and learning which were considered at the time to be cultured and noble." In Mito domain, retainers with nominal incomes under 100 koku were encouraged to undertake side employments to help make ends meet. In Edo, a stipend under 35 koku might force a retainer into a variety of menial occupations to add a little income. Even families whose income level clearly put them above the poverty line were often forced into poverty by their chronic indebtedness, which afflicted a large portion of the samurai population.

Koume and Hyōzō appear to have lived reasonably comfortably on their income, though they, too, were often in debt. But Koume's diary reveals the complexity of any assessment of their wealth. Hyōzō's stipend, paid in rice at the domain's granaries, was always less than the nominal amount. Its conversion into currency was further complicated by the vagaries of the rice and silver markets, the compulsory loans to the domain, and the need to repay existing debts. Moreover, the diary makes it clear that a large portion of the household economy was in the form of noncash exchange: gifts of food and sake bestowed and received; agricultural produce as payment for teaching services; "thank you" gifts for Koume's paintings; and a complex accounting of obligation and exchange that underpinned the smooth functioning of the Kawai household under Koume's management. Were the family members privileged, or was their samurai status a hindrance to a fuller economic life? Were they undertaking side employments, or were they merely doing favors for their friends? Were they to be envied or pitied? The unsatisfactory answer is that their privilege was real, but so was their precarity.

In the aftermath of the Meiji Restoration, Koume's son Yūsuke was forced to adapt to a complete upheaval in the world he had expected to inherit. With the abolition of the domain, the school that had employed four generations of Kawai men closed, leaving Yūsuke jobless. Soon after, his stipend was converted to a limited-term bond, leaving him with an annual interest payment that quickly lost its value. And his status-based privileges were abolished. With four children, including two marriageable daughters, and a wife and a mother to support (and two more children still to come), Yūsuke was undoubtedly in a hard place. Kishū domain had been one of the three great Tokugawa branch houses, so perhaps there was some reason to accept hardship after the defeat of the Tokugawa. Other loyalist domains, such as Aizu, which fought the imperial forces to the bitter end, suffered far worse penalties. By contrast, samurai in the victorious anti-Tokugawa domains had far more reason to feel disgruntled at their loss of privilege, and it was in those domains where resentment erupted into protest and rebellion.

The new leaders well understood the importance of the samurai, and the possible consequences of their disbandment. If the ex-samurai were unable to adapt to the new world in which they found themselves, they might (and indeed they did) rebel against the new government. On the other hand, if they could be put to work in the new system, they could be vital contributors to the development of a modern nation. As Iwakura Tomomi wrote, the former samurai were "the most useful group in society and should be called the spirit of the state. . . . In order that we may compete with foreigners and create flourishing conditions, it is necessary to use the samurai."[19] The new government initiated a number of programs to provide training and useful employment for ex-samurai, in the hope that they would "transform themselves into government officials, bureaucrats, petty-traders, capitalists, professional soldiers, farmers, craftsmen, industrial workers, publicists, priests, teachers, anything in short but *samurai*."[20] The government's budget for support for former samurai peaked at around three million yen in the early 1880s.[21]

How successfully did the ex-samurai adapt? The question is not only an economic one. Historians have long debated the role of the samurai in the Meiji Restoration and in the era of autocracy and militarism that followed. Was the Restoration a failed bourgeois revolution, in which a coalition of merchants and landowners used the samurai as a useful tool to achieve the overthrow of the feudal regime, only to find themselves marginalized by a new samurai oligarchy? Was it, rather, a changing of the guard among feudal elites, with the samurai class conversely using the merchants to secure their power in the modernizing state, and going on to create the absolutist "emperor system"? Or was it a mixture of the two, led by a coalition of "feudal remnants" composed of militaristic samurai autocrats, monopolistic merchant barons, and oppressive village landlords: what E. H. Norman called the "union of the yen and the sword"?[22]

There is ample data to support the dominance of the Meiji state at all levels by a samurai elite. Of 450 top administrative positions appointed between 1868 and 1877, former samurai held 399. And in an 1880 study of thirty-seven thousand government officials of all levels, 74 percent were held by ex-samurai. Some professions, such as policing, were almost entirely dominated by ex-samurai.[23] Ex-samurai also formed the backbone of the new entrepreneurial class that drove Japan to such economic success in the coming decades. Earl Kinmonth found that despite their status-based privileges, former samurai embraced the entrepreneurial spirit embodied in Samuel Smiles' concept of "self-help," and many went on to strive for personal and national advancement despite having few assets beyond education and motivation.[24] Samurai from lower-ranking backgrounds may have been even more motivated than those from the higher ranks, since the former had never expected a life of ease and were more willing to embrace new (and foreign) ideas and learning.[25]

Yet, scholars have long acknowledged that a very large proportion of the former samurai were poorly equipped to adapt to their loss of privilege, or to thrive in the modern state. They remained, to use Norman's phrase, "feudal warriors stranded in a modern society."[26] Stories abound of samurai starting new enterprises only to fail due to their lack of commercial skills; sinking into the most marginal of trades; or falling into complete destitution. One possible explanation for the anomaly of ex-samurai both constituting the new ruling class, and also falling into the lowest ranks of society, is the disconnect between status (*mibun*)—the prevalent concept in the Tokugawa era—and class, which is a Western construct of the nineteenth and twentieth centuries. Most scholars, even within the Marxist framework that dominated Japanese scholarly analysis in the middle decades of the twentieth century, recognized the wide class distinctions within the samurai status group. Even before the Meiji Restoration, many families of samurai status had, by the mid-nineteenth century, effectively fallen into the urban proletariat; others, even if of low rank, used their education and leadership skills to thrive in the Meiji state.²⁷

Quantitative studies have found little correlation, however, between the class (i.e., income and rank) of Tokugawa-era samurai and their subsequent economic success or failure in the Meiji state. Hamana Atsushi, for example, has analyzed the data for Gifu prefecture in an 1883 government survey of ex-samurai incomes and wealth. Out of eighty-three wealthy families with stipends of 200 koku or more during the Tokugawa period, only thirty (36 percent) remained wealthy in 1883. Twenty-six (31 percent) were classified as "poor" or "extremely poor." Similarly, in a study of Sasayama domain (now Hyogo prefecture), Hirota Teruyuki found that of 161 wealthy samurai families in the Tokugawa period, 34 had fallen into the lowest income bracket by 1883.²⁸ Of the total sample of 2,504 former samurai households in Gifu prefecture, 66 percent were "poor" or "extremely poor" by 1883. The majority (54 percent) had either lost or sold the government bonds they had been issued in lieu of their stipend a few years earlier. While 22 percent were in professions such as government service or teaching, 35 percent described themselves as "unemployed," and 15 percent declared themselves destitute, receiving no income whatever.²⁹ Anecdotally, high-ranking samurai were said to lack the basic skills needed to earn a living or start a business. The phrase "samurai business practices" (*shizoku no shōhō*) was mocking slang for incompetence.³⁰

But education continued to be a path to success, and the children of former samurai who excelled in the new school system more commonly found their way into some corner of the ruling elite. When it came to excelling, the children of ex-samurai had the advantage of a well-educated family background and good local connections, with the result that they often dominated the elite educational institutions of the new prefectures, as they had in the old domains.³¹ Former samurai also dominated the scholarly elite. In 1882, for example, forty-eight of sixty-seven members of the Tokyo Imperial University faculty were former samurai.³²

Again, the experience of the Kawai family seems to embrace these contradictions. Yūsuke's losses from the Restoration were both real and painful. But his education and experience also afforded him an opportunity to thrive in the new system, as new schools competed for teachers. Even when his Chinese classical education shut him out from the state's modernizing curriculum, Yūsuke was able to pivot one more time, taking advantage of the strong interest among the emerging commercial middle class in classical accomplishments, and opening his own academy. Two generations later Koume's great-grandson Shiga Yasuharu was still a member of Wakayama's scholarly elite, and the family retained its place in the middle class. Of the three living descendants I have been able to identify, one is a retired English teacher in the Wakayama school system, and one retired as a top executive in one of Japan's largest corporations. Hidesuga, the heir to the family name, moved to Tokyo, where he worked for Japan's largest shipping company, NYK. His son worked for the Takashimaya department store. Hidesuga's great granddaughter is a housewife, still living in the Tokyo area. Despite the immense upheavals of the past 150 years, the family appears to remain firmly in the educated middle class.

ART AND GENDER

Koume's art was one of her most vital contributions to the social and cultural economy of her family. Throughout her long life, Koume never stopped producing art. Although she prioritized her duties as a wife and mother over her painting, she retained her identity as an artist above all else, and during her long life she established a secure position in the world of Wakayama's cultural elite. Trained in the Chinese bunjinga or "literati" style, she produced work in a wide variety of contexts. The literati tradition embraced the ideal of the "passionate amateur." Painters in this tradition cultivated a scholarly and intellectual image, in which excessive attention to detail was frowned on as too commercial. Rather, literati artists admired spontaneity, warmth, humor, and an embrace of the inspiration that could be found in good company, beautiful surroundings, and the free flow of sake. At the core of Koume's work in this tradition was the culture of the scholarly community of Wakayama. This community incorporated art it into its social and cultural life through collaborative parties at which Koume's art was embellished with poetry and calligraphy by Hyōzō and his colleagues.

For a female artist from the samurai class like Koume, the literati esthetic offered opportunities to establish a reputation as an active participant in the cultural life of the domain. Male artists could secure positions as officials in the domain hierarchy, or they could establish themselves as independent professionals. For Koume, those avenues were closed. Instead, she developed her reputation as an amateur, who painted for pleasure and gave away much of her work to friends, family members, and more distant members of the community. It is tempting, then, to think of Koume's work merely as a hobby or a feminine accomplishment.

To do so, though, would be to misunderstand the meaning of Koume's art. For Koume, painting was work. It cannot be separated from her broader participation in the family's household economy and management. Through painting, Koume could contribute to the economy of gift exchange and, at times, cash or in-kind payment. She could also help her husband burnish his cultural credentials as he established his position as one of the leading cultural figures in the domain.

Koume's work as a painter extended beyond the artistic gatherings of the Wakayama scholarly community. She painted for a wide variety of other constituents, including samurai patrons, students, friends, and even tenants and servants and their families. Most often, she painted in response to specific requests. Sometimes she fulfilled these requests out of friendship or obligation. But often, the requests were a form of patronage. Well-connected friends commissioned Koume to paint for them and then placed her paintings with third parties in and beyond Wakayama. Her patrons clearly recognized that Koume's work for them was a form of labor, and they offered compensation. Usually that was in the form of gifts, such as cloth, fish, and sake. But occasionally she sold her work for readily exchangeable gifts or for cash.

After the Meiji Restoration, Japan's social and economic conditions changed significantly, particularly for the bushi class. While some scholars have pointed to the disruption and resistance created by this era of change, others have emphasized the new sense of potential, particularly for women who mobilized to call for changes in their status and legal rights.[33] For Koume, the new era brought the challenges of lost status, widowhood, and economic insecurity. As she had throughout her life, Koume accepted the status quo. She was not an activist, nor, in her diary at least, did she articulate a vision of new opportunities. Outwardly, her life appeared to be that of a dignified widow, pursuing elegant accomplishments in her old age. But once again, she refused to be defined by labels of status, gender, or age. Driven by economic need and loyalty to her family, she worked extraordinarily hard to produce works of art that would be valued and compensated accordingly. Despite the enormous challenges for someone of her age, class background, and gender, she moved toward establishing herself as a self-supporting, professional artist.

What were those challenges? The one salaried job Koume took, as art teacher to the daughter of the wealthy Mizuno family, was insecure and lasted only a few months. As an artist, Koume struggled at times to obtain reasonable compensation for her efforts. Her frustrations were particularly evident when she was dealing with former members of her samurai circle, who tended still to see her in terms of her role as a scholar's wife producing art as an elegant hobby, and who failed to acknowledge her need to provide for herself. Her samurai background and her gender remained obstacles to the fulfilment of her aspirations.

Yet the fact remains that faced with the loss of much that had made her life comfortable and pleasant, Koume confronted the challenges of the brave new world of the Meiji state mostly without complaint. Many were the days when she painted in the cold, her hands barely able to feel the brush, the glue she used to mount her paper coming unstuck from the cold. She painted furiously, sometimes completing dozens of sketches in a day, other times painting and repainting the same work until she was satisfied that she had it right. She persevered out of determination and need. And, increasingly, she was able to establish a stable place for herself in the commercial economy of artistic production. Kawai Koume never achieved wealth or fame, nor did she stake a claim as an activist pushing against the boundaries of social custom or political ideology. Nevertheless, her work seems more like the trailblazing of a pioneer than the leisurely pastime of a retired old lady.

NEWS AND INFORMATION IN A TURBULENT ERA

As much as she was a household manager and an artist, Koume was a faithful chronicler of the lives of her family members, as well of events in the Wakayama community and beyond. For someone who seldom left the house, even more rarely left the boundaries of the castle town, and never, as far as we know, left her domain, Koume was extraordinarily well informed. We see her in her diary absorbing, reporting on, interpreting, and transcribing news and information from a wide variety of sources: news and gossip received by word of mouth from visitors, shopkeepers, and servants; letters from Kyoto, Osaka, and Edo; dramatized human-interest stories circulating in the town; official communications from the castle; satirical verses, lampoons, and broadsheets; and, later in the 1860s, newspapers.

All or parts of eighteen years of Koume's diary survive, over a period of forty-eight years between 1837 and 1885. We know that there was more: a prewar publication listed at least seven more years that were in existence at the time.[34] Probably the diary was divided between family members, and some of it lost in the American bombing of the city. We do not know when Koume started keeping her diary; perhaps as early as her teen years, when she married Hyōzō. The surviving volumes are evidence enough that the diary was a lifelong project for Koume.

Diary-keeping was a common activity in nineteenth-century Japan. Many male family heads took charge of family diaries, which in some cases extended over generations. In them, they recorded the day-to-day business of their family enterprises, whom they met and what they discussed, as well as mundane matters like the weather, the prices of commodities, and the state of local affairs. Women's diaries were also quite common, but few have been published, and most of those are literary journals, in which women wrote elegantly about their travels or their cultural activities. Koume's diary is unusual in that it includes much of the content one would expect to find in a diary kept by the (male) household head. Her unusually broad education, as well as her status as the wife of an adopted husband, may help explain this.

The diary is not only about Koume and her activities. She saw herself as chronicler of all her family's affairs, and of events in the wider world that might affect her family. Each day, Koume had to process a dense flow of information passing through her household, in written or printed materials circulating in Wakayama, or passed on by visitors and family friends, or relayed to her by her husband and son. The diary is both an account of the receipt of information, and a reference source for that information, on everything from the price of rice and fish to the activities of the shogun in distant Edo. In its pages, Koume describes the daily flow of rumor, official communications, gossip, satire and lampoons, and other information that passed through the household.

Koume's diary vividly illustrates the rich information culture in which Koume and her family lived their daily lives. Many scholars have written of the explosion in print culture during the Edo period.[35] Koume grew up surrounded by books, and she was an avid reader and writer throughout her life. Many of the books in the Kawai household were scholarly works on Chinese literature and philosophy, or collections of classical poetry and literature. But Koume also mentions a variety of more popular genres, such as "picture books" (*ehon*), referring to the popular illustrated woodblock-printed books known as *kusazōshi*, *akahon*, or *kibyōshi*; well-known popular tales such as the *Akō gishiden* (Tales of the loyal samurai of Akō domain); books of famous places in Kishū and other parts of Japan; Rai San'yō's famous history of Japan, *Nihon Gaishi*; books for women such as the *Onna takarabako* (Women's treasury); books about the city of Edo; reports on the conditions in the West published by the Dutch merchant colony in Nagasaki (*Oranda fūsetsusho*); Ōta Nanba's miscellany *Ichiwa Ichigon*; and the best-selling adventure story of Satomi and the Eight Dogs (*Nansō Satomi hakkenden*).

In addition to books, literate Japanese encountered an enormous variety of ephemeral publications: *kawaraban* and *chobokure* broadsheets; circulating commentary and lampoons such as *senryū*, *kyōka*, *rakusho*, and *fūshi*; *ukiyoe* prints; advertisements and handbills; theater programs; images of *kami* and *hotoke* divinities; and lists ranking sumo wrestlers, actors, *onsen* resorts, soy sauce makers, etc. Many of these circulated clandestinely. *Kawaraban*, for example, were usually published anonymously, and they were sold by street vendors (*yomiuri*) wearing wide-brimmed hats to hide their identity. Their scale of production and distribution are impossible to measure, but Koume was certainly reading and copying them in Wakayama.[36]

Available documents show us that leading merchants, well-informed townsmen, and those living in post stations on the busy highways were able to obtain a far-reaching and comprehensive grasp of the news across the whole of Japan. The rice brokers of Osaka, for example, used both relay couriers and a hand-signal network (at night they used flashing lanterns) to obtain timely information that might affect rice prices.[37] In Edo, the bookseller Sudō Yoshizō collected and distributed in his journal enormous amounts of information on political and other events (subsequently published as *Fujiokaya nikki*). Sudō's diary expanded as the volume and circulation of news increased. He produced one volume per year through the 1840s, but by the 1860s each year was filling twelve volumes.[38] Similarly, Tsugami Etsugorō, a shipping broker in Miyaura town, Chikuzen province (now Fukuoka prefecture), kept a detailed and wide-ranging diary of events taking place all over Japan.[39] Maruyama Yasunari also describes the movement of lampoons and satirical verses along the highway, suggesting that they were being passed on and transcribed as they spread across the country.[40] According to Ono Hideo, the turbulent events that rocked Japan in the 1850s and 1860s unleashed a flood of underground materials. The main consumers were low-ranking samurai and wealthier townsmen from the merchant classes. But increasing literacy was constantly expanding their reach.[41]

Many of these materials, and the information and opinions they contained, reached Koume and her husband. Koume's diary shows a remarkably broad grasp of current events and political developments, and the information flowing in was generally quite accurate, even when it came from far away. The diary reveals the family's acute interest in the political events of the time, and it offers some hints as to Koume and Hyōzō's reactions. The tumultuous upheavals of the late Tokugawa and early Meiji eras, which are recorded in the diary, affected the Kawai family more or less directly. In many cases, the events described were distant and, while shocking, may not have suggested direct consequences for the family. But the diary also describes the political assassination of one of the family's closest friends; the mobilization of the domain's menfolk, including Hyōzō and their son Yūsuke, for military service; the dire financial straits of their own domain as it struggled to meet its military obligations; and the radical reforms of the Meiji era, which included the abolition of the domain school in which four generations of the Kawai family had taught.

Did this dense flow of information circulating on a national scale create political agency among its consumers? Even Koume, who seldom expressed political opinions, was moved to comment disapprovingly on the arrest of Tokugawa Nariaki, an event that took place 600 kilometers away in Mito. Undoubtedly, increasing education and access to news and information enhanced people's political awareness and enabled a politically engaged public. Whether or not this helped propel the Meiji Restoration, it surely was a prerequisite for the national Popular Rights Movement of the Meiji era.[42] But for Koume, I would argue that news and information enabled a different kind of agency. Koume's diary was a repository of information and knowledge about the affairs of her own family, the Wakayama community, the domain, and the country. Its breadth and range attest to her confident position in her own household, her strong work ethic, her high level of literacy and cultural attainment, and her mastery of huge quantities of information. Her command of this rich repository in turn added to her authority and her ability to advance the status and well-being of her family.

WHO WAS KAWAI KOUME?

Any project that sets out to chronicle a life must eventually reckon with the meanings of that life. As a historian, one can find such meanings in the intersections between an individual's life and the larger historical issues of the time. How was the Restoration era experienced in a provincial castle town? What was Koume's agency as a samurai wife? What were the meanings of "family" for her, and what was her role? What was her political consciousness? How did she and her family adapt to the new conditions of the Meiji era? I have tried to answer these questions in this book. But Koume herself showed only occasional interest in such questions. What did Koume's life mean to *her*?

Only once, late in her life, in her seventy-fourth year, did she reflect on the course of her life. Over the course of a few days, she read through some of the old volumes of her diary. On April 19, 1877, she wrote: "Yesterday and today I have been examining my diary, looking at it bit by bit from the time I was born [*sic*]. I would like to make a copy. My legs are shaky these days, but my spirit is still strong." On the twenty-third, she commented again that she would like to use the diary to write about the events of her life: "I would like to write about matters from the time of the Bunka era [1804–1818].... Now I have a little leisure. I don't know how much time I have left, and once I am gone no one will know about these things." Koume seems to be looking to the diary itself to lend meaning to her life, as a chronicler of the times through which she had lived.

History has more than fulfilled Koume's aspiration to be remembered by future generations for the record she left. The diary was a constant in Koume's life for the five decades or more during which she wrote her daily entries, and even during her own lifetime, it was her window onto a wider world, allowing her to participate in events near and far, and to claim a space of autonomy and significance within her communities. But although it was an important reality of Koume's daily life, surely her most meaningful daily reality was her work as a wife, mother, artist, and household manager. In this, I think, she was no different from most of us. Her diary vividly illustrates the powerful meanings these activities had for Koume. They gave her life much of its structure, and they grounded her identity in a set of communities, most of them local to Wakayama.

The families we build and nurture are one of the enduring sources of meaning and happiness for human beings. The circumstances of Koume's birth and education conspired to give her unusual authority within her own family. As the wife of a muko husband, she lived her entire life in her natal home and retained a strong voice in its management. By some accounts, she chose her own husband. As a respected artist, she was able to participate in activities otherwise reserved for men. And her diary bears witness to the harmonious and trusting relationship she and Hyōzō enjoyed, as the two of them shared the large amounts information passing through their home each day.

Community was another daily reality. Although Wakayama was the eighth largest city in Japan, Koume and her husband Hyōzō lived most of their lives within two small subsets of Wakayama society: lower-ranking samurai retainers, and members of the small scholarly elite. This group numbered no more than a few hundred families: more a village than a city. Within their immediate social network, Koume and Hyōzō's connections were deep and intense. Its members relied on each other for social interaction, economic support, mutual assistance, and solidarity in dealing with other segments of the domain's social and political structure. As in a village, mobility in and out of the group was limited, and its members did all they could to build constructive and enduring ties through gift exchange, shared rituals of celebration and loss, cultural interactions, and the free flow of sake as a social lubricant. Throughout her life, Koume was deeply connected to the overlapping communities of her extended family and close family friends, of Hyōzō's workplace, of the scholarly and artistic networks of the city and domain, and of the broader community of servants, helpers, merchants, and townsmen. She interacted intensively with each of these communities on a daily basis, to the point that her home was as much a communal gathering place as it was a private space.

And Koume's cultural production was the other great reality of Koume's daily life. Like her diary, Koume's art offered a window onto a wider world, expanding the possibilities for involvement and meaningful contribution beyond the prescribed women's sphere of motherhood and household management. Koume was both talented and hard-working, and she was enormously invested in her work as an artist. In addition to the pleasure and satisfaction of the work itself, Koume's painting brought validation and respect from the communities that she valued so much. We may remember Koume primarily as a diarist, but I have no doubt that in her own mind, she was first and foremost an artist.

These realities, which gave so much meaning to Koume's life, were tested by the events of her lifetime, both public and private. She managed her household through shortage and plenty, through epidemic, flood, and earthquake. She endured the loss of a beloved grandchild, and of her own mother and husband. She helped support her family as its men were called up for military service; as they struggled to find the money for weapons and armor; and as needy relatives came begging at the door for financial and other forms of aid. Koume lived to see the certainties of her world shaken by political upheaval, purges, rebellion, war, and revolution. Ultimately, she witnessed the dismantling of many of the building blocks of her family's economic and cultural life: Hyōzō's lifelong scholarship abandoned by the domain; the domain school, where four generations of her family had taught, closed; the privileges of the bushi class abolished; the domain itself abolished, and the daimyo sent to live in Tokyo. Through all these upheavals, Koume never lost her sense of mission to support her family, nor her sense of belonging to her family network and her cultural community.

Above all, Koume held on to her identity as an artist. Throughout her life, she continued painting. Her work covered a wide variety of genres, extending far beyond the "literati" pigeonhole. And it served a range of constituents, from the gassaku creators of the scholarly community, to friends needing a portrait of a loved one; to patrons looking to place Koume's work in the local art market; to family members wanting something for their wall, or a decoration for their furniture or clothing; to students, servants, rental house dwellers, and other acquaintances from the town. Koume's art was an essential component of her contribution to her family's social economy. And, in the brave new world of the Meiji era, it was Koume's own lifeline to a measure of economic security and well-being. It was, I think, the key to her identity and sense of purpose. But, more than that, it was her own call to action. More than the call to expel the barbarians or revere the emperor, more than political reform, nation-building, or the struggle for women's rights, art, for Koume, represented the power to improve her own personal status and economic well-being, and to contribute to the cultural and economic lives of those she cared about the most: her family, her community of scholars and friends, and the town where she spent her entire life.

NOTES

PREFACE AND ACKNOWLEDGMENTS

1. Abe Takeshi, *Bakumatsu Kishū Kawai Koume no wandafuru wārudo* (Kyoto: Aunsha, 2013).

INTRODUCTION

1. Going forward, I will use Japanese dates, with the Gregorian year in parentheses, for all dates up to Japan's adoption of the Gregorian calendar in 1873. The Japanese used a twelve-month calendar, but it was usually about one month behind the Gregorian. There are many online converters, most of which require Japanese input capability. I use https://maechan.net/kanreki/.
2. Kawai Koume, Shiga Yasuharu, and Murata Shizuko, *Koume nikki: Bakumatsu Meiji o Kishū ni ikiru*, vol. 2, Tōyō bunko 268 (Tōkyō: Heibonsha, 1974), 36–37 (Bunkyū 4/7/18). I have cut some intermediate passages for concision and to improve the flow of the translation.
3. Donald Keene, *Modern Japanese Diaries: The Japanese at Home and Abroad as Revealed Through Their Diaries* (New York: Columbia University Press, 1999), 270.
4. Andy Alaszewski, *Using Diaries for Social Research* (Thousand Oaks, Calif.: Sage, 2006), 1–2.
5. Hiraku Shimoda, *Lost and Found: Recovering Regional Identity in Imperial Japan* (Cambridge, Mass.: Harvard University Press), 3. See also Kären Wigen, *The Making of a Japanese Periphery, 1750–1920* (Berkeley: University of California Press, 1995); Maren Annika Ehlers, *Give and Take: Poverty and the Status Order in Early Modern Japan* (Cambridge, Mass.: Harvard University Asia Center, 2018); and David Luke Howell,

Geographies of Identity in Nineteenth-Century Japan (Berkeley: University of California Press, 2005).

6. Anne Walthall, *The Weak Body of a Useless Woman: Matsuo Taseko and the Meiji Restoration*, Women in Culture and Society (Chicago: University of Chicago Press, 1998); Laura Nenzi, *The Chaos and Cosmos of Kurosawa Tokiko: One Woman's Transit from Tokugawa to Meiji Japan* (Honolulu: University of Hawai'i Press, 2015); Amy Stanley, *Stranger in the Shogun's City: A Woman's Life in Nineteenth-Century Japan* (London: Vintage, 2020); Mary Elizabeth Berry and Marcia Yonemoto, *What Is a Family? Answers from Early Modern Japan* (Oakland: University of California Press, 2019).
7. Bettina Gramlich-Oka, *Thinking like a Man: Tadano Makuzu (1763–1825)* (Leiden: Brill, 2006).
8. Edwin McClellan, *Woman in the Crested Kimono: The Life of Shibue Io and Her Family* (New Haven, Conn.: Yale University Press, 1985); Yamakawa Kikue, *Women of the Mito Domain: Recollections of Samurai Family Life*, trans. Kate Wildman Nakai (Tokyo: University of Tokyo Press, 1992).
9. Walthall, *Weak Body*, 59. The author is quoting Patricia Buckley Ebrey, *The Inner Quarters: Marriage and the Lives of Chinese Women in the Sung Period* (Berkeley: University of California Press, 1993), 9.
10. Amy Stanley, "Maidservants' Tales: Narrating Domestic and Global History in Eurasia, 1600–1900," *American Historical Review* 121, no. 2 (2016): 447.
11. Walthall, *Weak Body*, 6.

1. GROWING UP IN KISHŪ DOMAIN

1. Abe Takeshi, *Bakumatsu Kishū Kawai Koume no wandafuru wārudo* (Kyoto: Aunsha, 2013), 248–49.
2. The Kii family survives to this day. The current head, Kii Toshiaki, is the eighty-first-generation family head.
3. The lots were 16 by 19 *ken*, about 29 by 35 meters. The houses averaged 100 *tsubo*, or 330 square meters. Abe Takeshi, *Bakumatsu Kishū Kawai Koume*, 34.
4. Abe Takeshi, 34–35.
5. Abe Takeshi, 122–32.
6. Kawai Koume, Shiga Yasuharu, and Murata Shizuko, *Koume nikki: Bakumatsu Meiji o Kishū ni ikiru*, vol. 2 (Keio 3/8/11) (Tokyo: Heibonsha, 1974), 180.
7. "Aizu han no mibun seido (3): buke yashiki," http://www4.plala.or.jp/bakumatsu/aidu/aidu-kiso-bukeyashiki.htm, accessed November 4, 2017. Samurai housing in Edo was more generous. Kozo Yamamura notes that in Edo, retainers with fiefs of 200–300 koku (equivalent to 70–100 koku in rice stipend) were allocated lots of 600 tsubo, about twice the size of the Kawai family property. Kozo Yamamura, *A Study of Samurai Income and Entrepreneurship; Quantitative Analyses of Economic and Social Aspects of the Samurai in Tokugawa and Meiji, Japan* (Cambridge, Mass.: Harvard University Press, 1974), 15.

1. GROWING UP IN KISHŪ DOMAIN   255

8. There is little firm evidence for the samurai population of Wakayama castle town in the late Tokugawa period. Estimates range (sometimes in the same book) from 1,200 to over 10,000. See, for example, Mio Isao, *Jōkamachi Wakayama hyakuwa* (Wakayama: Uji Shoten, 2001), 105 and 27. My estimate of 1,200 is based on a detailed map of Wakayama produced in 1855, which lists every samurai family by name. It shows no more than a thousand samurai houses in the city. There were certainly more families eligible for military service, but they do not seem to have lived in the samurai quarters of the town.
9. The population of Wakayama in the first Meiji period census of 1886 was 54,865. Unlike Edo, Wakayama did not see any significant outflow of population in the years around the Meiji Restoration.
10. Based on a surviving map from the Ansei period (1853–1859), the townspeople's districts totaled about three square kilometers. I am assuming a townspeople population of about 45,000–50,000. Manhattan has a population density of 28,000 people per square kilometer, but the majority live in high-rise buildings.
11. Buyō Inshi, *Lust, Commerce, and Corruption: An Account of What I Have Seen and Heard*, trans. Mark Teeuwen et al. (New York: Columbia University Press, 2017), 248–49.
12. A study of housing in Wakayama city at the turn of the eighteenth century found that in one neighborhood, only 24 out of 142 residential units were owner-occupied. The rest were rentals, owned in many cases by landlords who lived in other parts of the city. Mio Isao, *Jōkamachi Wakayama hyakuwa*, 127–28.
13. Mio Isao, 128–30.
14. David Howell distinguishes *eta*, who "disposed of animal carcasses, worked with leather, and performed various police and jailhouse duties" from *hinin*, who "begged, served as village and urban-ward guards, and also performed police and jailhouse duties." Koume, however, seems to use *hinin* as a catch-all catgory. David Luke Howell, *Geographies of Identity in Nineteenth-Century Japan* (Berkeley: University of California Press, 2005), 28–29.
15. Wakayama Jinken Kenkyūjo, *Wakayama no burakushi. Tsūshi hen*, ed. Wakayama no Burakushi Hensankai (Tokyo: Akashi Shoten, 2015), 230. See also Fujimoto Seijirō, *Jōkamachi sekai no seikatsushi: botsuraku to saisei no shiten kara* (Tokyo: Seibundō, 2014).
16. Wakayama Jinken Kenkyūjo, *Wakayama no burakushi*, 213.
17. Tsukada Takashi, *Kinsei mibunsei to shūen shakai* (Tokyo: Tōkyō Daigaku Shuppankai, 1997). See also Maren Annika Ehlers, *Give and Take: Poverty and the Status Order in Early Modern Japan* (Cambridge, Mass.: Harvard University Asia Center, 2018), chap. 2. Howell goes so far as to argue that "the benefits of membership in an official outcaste group may well have outweighed the burden of the extra measure of contempt that accompanied it." Howell, *Geographies of Identity*, 32.
18. Wakayama Jinken Kenkyūjo, *Wakayama no burakushi*, 105. See also Hayashi Noriaki and Ichikawa Kunitoshi, eds., *Burakushi ni manabu: Kishūhan rōbangashirake monjo o yomu*, Jinken bukkuretto (Wakayama: Wakayama Jinken Kenkyūjo, 2003).

19. Wakayama Shishi Hensan Iinkai, *Wakayama Shishi*, vol. 2, *Kinsei* (Wakayama-shi: Wakayama-shi, 1989), 467–69.
20. Wakayama Shishi Hensan Iinkai, 460–62.
21. On scholars' audiences with the Kishū daimyo, see Iwasaki Takehiko, "Kishū hangaku to shomin kyōiku," ed. Wakayama Shiritsu Hakubutsukan (Wakayama: Wakayamashi Kyōiku Iinkai, 1990), 8–9.
22. Wakayama Shishi Hensan Iinkai, *Wakayama Shishi*, 2, Kinsei, 466.
23. Howell, *Geographies of Identity*, 24–26.
24. For analyses of status groups and their historiography, see Howell, chap. 2. See also Ehlers, *Give and Take*, introduction.
25. Basil Hall Chamberlain, *Things Japanese; Being Notes on Various Subjects Connected with Japan for the Use of Travellers and Others*, 4th ed. (London, Yokohama: J. Murray Kelly & Walsh, 1902), 424.
26. Marcia Yonemoto, *The Problem of Women in Early Modern Japan* (Berkeley: University of California Press, 2016), 2.
27. Yonemoto, 164.
28. Yonemoto, 166.
29. Yonemoto, 171–72.
30. Quoted in Yonemoto, 178.
31. Ray A. Moore, "Adoption and Samurai Mobility in Tokugawa Japan," in *The Samurai Tradition*, ed. Stephen R. Turnbull (Tokyo: Japan Library, 2000); G. William Skinner, "Conjugal Power in Tokugawa Japanese Families: A Matter of Life or Death," in *Sex and Gender Hierarchies*, ed. Barbara D. Miller (Cambridge: Cambridge University Press, 1993); Wakita Osamu, "Bakuhan taisei to josei," in *Nihon joseishi*, ed. Joseishi Sōgō Kenkyūkai (Tokyo: Tōkyō Daigaku Shuppankai, 1982). The data are summarized in Marcia Yonemoto, "Adoption and the Maintenance of the Early Modern Elite: Japan in the East Asian Context," in *What Is a Family? Answers from Early Modern Japan*, ed. Mary Elizabeth Berry and Marcia Yonemoto (Oakland: University of California Press, 2019), 58.
32. Quoted in Wakayama Kenshi Hensan Iinkai, *Wakayama Kenshi. Kinsei* (Wakayama-shi: Wakayama-ken, 1990), 871.
33. Yabuta Yutaka and Yanagiya Keiko, *Mibun no naka no josei*, *"Edo" no hito to mibun* (Tokyo: Yoshikawa Kōbunkan, 2010), 3–4. The game is "New sugoroku game for instructions in female success" (Shinpan musume teikin shusse sugoroku). See also https://library.u-gakugei.ac.jp/digitalarchive/pdf/honji-sugoroku1.pdf (accessed December 1, 2020).
34. Anne Walthall, *The Weak Body of a Useless Woman: Matsuo Taseko and the Meiji Restoration* (Chicago: University of Chicago Press, 1998), 59.
35. Amy Stanley, *Stranger in the Shogun's City: A Woman's Life in Nineteenth-Century Japan* (London: Vintage, 2020).
36. Howell, *Geographies of Identity*, 43.
37. Iwasaki Takehiko, "Kishū hangaku to shomin kyōiku," 9.

38. Abe Takeshi, *Bakumatsu Kishū Kawai Koume*, 223.
39. Iwasaki Takehiko, "Kishū hangaku to shomin kyōiku," 9.
40. Quoted in Ronald Dore, *Education in Tokugawa, Japan* (Berkeley: University of California Press, 1965), 140.
41. Peter F. Kornicki, "Women, Education, and Literacy," in *The Female as Subject: Reading and Writing in Early Modern Japan*, ed. Peter F. Kornicki, Mara Patessio, and G. G. Rowley (Ann Arbor: Center for Japanese Studies, University of Michigan, 2010), 9, 11.
42. Yamakawa Kikue, *Women of the Mito Domain: Recollections of Samurai Family Life*, trans. Kate Wildman Nakai (Tokyo: University of Tokyo Press, 1992), 22, 24–27, 30.
43. See Suzuki Yuriko, "Jusha josei no seikatsu," in *Josei no kinsei*, ed. Hayashi Reiko (Tokyo: Chūō Kōronsha, 1993).
44. Koume is listed as one of Ōhira's 337 recorded students. Abe Takeshi, *Bakumatsu Kishū Kawai Koume*, 241.
45. Yutaka Yabuta, *Rediscovering Women in Tokugawa Japan* (Cambridge, Mass.: Harvard University, Edwin O. Reischauer Institute of Japanese Studies, 2000), 5–9.
46. Matthias Hayek and Annick Horiuchi, *Listen, Copy, Read: Popular Learning in Early Modern Japan* (Leiden: Brill, 2014), 83.
47. Walthall, *Weak Body*, 32–33.
48. Kawai Baisho and Shiga Yasuharu, *Bunkyū sannen jūgun nichiroku: Tenchūgumi* (Wakayama-shi: Miyai Heiandō, 1982), 79–80.

2. A YEAR OF CALAMITIES

1. Francis Hall, F. G. Notehelfer, and Cleveland Public Library, John G. White Department, *Japan Through American Eyes: The Journal of Francis Hall, Kanagawa and Yokohama, 1859–1866: from the Cleveland Public Library, John G. White Collection of Orientalia* (Princeton, N.J.: Princeton University Press, 1992), 301.
2. For the number of sake shops (in 1837), see Abe Takeshi, *Bakumatsu Kishū Kawai Koume no wandafuru wārudo* (Kyoto: Aunsha, 2013), 103; on sake coupons, see 175–78.
3. "Edo jidai no shitsū no chiryō ha?," https://www.dent-kng.or.jp/museum/ja/hanohaku03/; and "Edo jidai no ha no chiryō," https://www.familiar-shika.com/post-3164/, accessed April 11, 2022.
4. Abe Takeshi, *Bakumatsu Kishū Kawai Koume*, 334.
5. Based on conversion at ten *to* per koku, and sixty monme per *ryō*.
6. Marc-Antoine Longpré et al., "Sulfur Budget and Global Climate Impact of the A.D. 1835 Eruption of Cosigüina Volcano, Nicaragua," *Geophysical Research Letters* 41, no. 19 (2014): 6667–75. The Babajuan eruption is disputed: see Christopher S. Garrison, Christopher R. J. Kilburn, and Stephen J. Edwards, "The 1831 Eruption of Babuyan Claro That Never Happened: Has the Source of One of the Largest Volcanic Climate Forcing Events of the Nineteenth Century Been Misattributed?," *Journal of Applied Volcanology* 7, no. 1 (2018): 1–21.

7. Harold Bolitho, "The Tempo Crisis," in *The Cambridge History of Japan*, vol. 5: *The Nineteenth Century*, ed. Marius B. Jansen (Cambridge: Cambridge University Press, 1989), 118.
8. Ann Bowman Jannetta, "Famine Mortality in Nineteenth-Century Japan: The Evidence from a Temple Death Register," *Population Studies* 46, no. 3 (1992): 429.
9. Nakazawa Benjirō, *Nihon beika hendōshi* (Tokyo: Kashiwa Shobō, 2001).
10. Fujita Teiichirō, "Shiryō shōkai: Tenpōki Wakayamahan kakyū bushi nyōbō no nikki—1," *Shakai kagaku* 5, no. 1 (1974): 212. Tenpō 8/4/5 (May 9, 1837).
11. Wakayama Kenshi Hensan Iinkai, *Wakayama kenshi. Kinsei* (Wakayama-shi: Wakayama-ken, 1989), 789.
12. Abe Takeshi, *Bakumatsu Kishū Kawai Koume*, 384–86.
13. Abe Takeshi, 382.
14. The price was a quarter ryō. Based on 4,000 mon to the ryō, and 60 monme to the ryō.
15. Abe Takeshi, *Bakumatsu Kishū Kawai Koume*, 267.
16. Abe Takeshi, 72.
17. Fujita Teiichirō, "Shiryō shōkai," Tenpō 8 (1837)/3/8, 207–8.
18. E.g., Kawai Koume, Shiga Yasuharu, and Murata Shizuko, *Koume nikki: Bakumatsu Meiji o Kishū ni ikiru*, vol. 1 (Kaei 2/9/1) (Tōkyō: Heibonsha, 1974), 7.
19. Quoted in Kozo Yamamura, "The Increasing Poverty of the Samurai in Tokugawa Japan, 1600–1868," *Journal of Economic History* 31, no. 2 (1971): 401n.66.
20. Quoted and translated in Kozo Yamamura, *A Study of Samurai Income and Entrepreneurship; Quantitative Analyses of Economic and Social Aspects of the Samurai in Tokugawa and Meiji, Japan* (Cambridge, Mass.: Harvard University Press, 1974), 44.
21. Abe Takeshi, *Bakumatsu Kishū Kawai Koume*, 75.
22. Abe Takeshi, 73.
23. Anne Walthall and M. William Steele, *Politics and Society in Japan's Meiji Restoration: A Brief History with Documents* (Boston: Bedford/St. Martin's, Macmillan Learning, 2017), 9. For a fuller analysis of Ōshio's philosophy, see Tetsuo Najita, "Ōshio Heihachirō," in *Personality in Japanese History*, ed. Albert M. Craig and Donald H. Shively (Berkeley: University of California Press, 1970).
24. Translated in Walthall and Steele, *Politics and Society*, 39–40.
25. I have drawn on two accounts of the rebellion and battle: Ivan Morris, *The Nobility of Failure: Tragic Heroes in the History of Japan* (London: Secker and Warburg, 1975), 207–8; and Yonekura Isamu, "The Revolt of Oshio Heihachiro: Rebel with a Cause," *East* 7, no. 10 (1971): 20–27.
26. Abe Takeshi, *Bakumatsu Kishū Kawai Koume*, 395.
27. Abe Takeshi, 396–97.
28. Translated in Walthall and Steele, *Politics and Society*, 39.
29. Adam Johann von Krusenstern and Richard Belgrave Hoppner, *Voyage Round the World, in the Years 1803, 1804, 1805, & 1806 by Order of His Imperial Majesty Alexander the First, on Board the Ships Nadeshda and Neva, Under the command of Captain A. J. von Krusenstern* (London: C. Roworth for J. Murray, 1813), 244–50. Goreglyad

has October 26: V. N. Goreglyad, "The Manuscript of 'Kankai Ibun' in the Collection of the St. Petersburg Branch of the Institute of Oriental Studies," *Manuscripta Orientalia* 3, no. 2 (1997): 58–67.
30. Krusenstern and Hoppner, *Voyage Round the World*, 85–86.
31. Goreglyad, "Manuscript of 'Kankai Ibun,'" 66n.5.
32. Translated in Goreglyad, 59.
33. Yamaue Sachiko, "Kawai Koume to 'Kankai ibun,'" *wōku shiryō*, Koume Nikki wo Tanoshimu Kai, 2014.
34. David Luke Howell, "Foreign Encounters and Informal Diplomacy in Early Modern Japan," *Journal of Japanese Studies* 40, no. 2 (2014): 298.
35. Constantine Nomikos Vaporis, *Voices of Early Modern Japan: Contemporary Accounts of Daily Life During the Age of the Shoguns* (Santa Barbara, Calif.: Greenwood, 2012), 115–17. For a detailed description of Mito villagers' encounters with foreign ships, see Howell, "Foreign Encounters."

3. IN THE SHADOW OF THE BLACK SHIPS

1. Andō Seiichi, *Wakayamaken no rekishi*, Kenshi Shirīzu (Tokyo: Yamakawa Shuppansha, 1970), 160.
2. Inoue Yasuo, *"Koume nikki" ni miru Kishū no bakumatsu* (Wakayama: privately published, 2017).
3. Andō Seiichi, *Wakayamaken no rekishi*, 156–58.
4. Abe Takeshi, *Bakumatsu Kishū Kawai Koume no wandafuru wārudo* (Kyoto: Aunsha, 2013), 416.
5. Quoted in Okazaki Hisahiko, *Mutsu Munemitsu and His Time*, trans. Noda Makito (Tokyo: Japan Publishing Industry Foundation for Culture, 2018), 38.
6. Okazaki Hisahiko, 35.
7. Inoue Yasuo, *"Koume nikki,"* 14.
8. Suyama Takaaki, *"Koume nikki" oyobi "Zakki" ni mirareru bakumatsu no Kishū: Harutomi no shi to Kaei no seihen* (Wakayama: Wakayama Monjokan, 1994).
9. Luke Shepherd Roberts, *Performing the Great Peace: Political Space and Open Secrets in Tokugawa Japan* (Honolulu: University of Hawai'i Press, 2012), 82–83.
10. M. William Steele, "Goemon's New World," in *Alternative Narratives in Modern Japanese History* (London: RoutledgeCurzon, 2003), 5. See also Iwashita Tetsunori, *Bakumatsu Nihon no jōhō katsudō: "Kaikoku" no jōhōshi* (Tokyo: Yūzankaku Shuppan, 2000), 109–35.
11. Quoted in Steele, "Goemon's New World," 6.
12. Ōta Tomiyasu, "Perī raisenki ni okeru nōmin to kurofune jōhō shūshū: Musashinokuni Kawagoehan nanushi no baai," *Saitama kenritsu monjokan kiyō*, no. 5 (1991): 24–54.
13. Abe Takeshi, *Bakumatsu Kishū Kawai Koume*, 436–39.
14. Reproduced in Kawai Baisho and Kunioka Denjirō, *Isenki* (Wakayama: Kii Kyōdo Shiryō Bunken Hanpukai, 1929).

15. Horiuchi Shin, *Nanki Tokugawashi*, vol. 3 (Wakayama: Nanki Tokugawashi Kankōkai, 1932), 33.
16. Kawai Koume, Shiga Yasuharu, and Murata Shizuko, *Koume nikki: Bakumatsu Meiji o Kishū ni ikiru*, vol. 1 (Kaei 6/12/8) (Tokyo: Heibonsha, 1974), 135. I have used Donald Keene's translation in his *Modern Japanese Diaries: The Japanese at Home and Abroad as Revealed Through Their Diaries* (New York: Columbia University Press, 1999), 274–75.
17. Abe Takeshi, *Bakumatsu Kishū Kawai Koume*, 253.
18. A chronology prepared by Koume's great-grandson shows them departing in 1857 and staying until early 1858. Kawai Koume, Shiga Yasuharu, and Murata Shizuko, *Koume nikki: Bakumatsu Meiji o Kishū ni ikiru*, vol. 3 (Tokyo: Heibonsha, 1974), 279.
19. Abe Takeshi, *Bakumatsu Kishū Kawai Koume*, 336. Hyōzō regularly attended the meetings of the Shiga group, the Yamamoto group, the Tamiya group, and the Natsume group.
20. Abe Takeshi, 336. In 1859 Hyōzō lectured at the Kanō mansion thirty-nine times, and he lectured twelve times each to the Miura and Andō families.
21. Abe Takeshi, 334–35.
22. Koyama Yasunori, *Wakayamaken no rekishi*, Kenshi (Tokyo: Yamakawa Shuppansha, 2015), 245.
23. Abe Takeshi, *Bakumatsu Kishū Kawai Koume*, 345.
24. Ann Bowman Jannetta, *The Vaccinators: Smallpox, Medical Knowledge, and the "Opening" of Japan* (Stanford, Calif.: Stanford University Press, 2007).
25. Inoue Yasuo, "Koume nikki," 32.
26. Kélina Gotman, *Choreomania: Dance and Disorder* (New York: Oxford University Press, 2018).

4. WORK AND FAMILY

1. Yoshida Yuriko, *Kinsei no ie to josei* (Tokyo: Yamakawa Shuppansha, 2016), 155, 163–65.
2. I am grateful to Yamaue Sachiko for her reminiscences of this type of sushi preparation as a child, and also for sharing her mother's experiences, which date back to the days before refrigeration.
3. Andō Seiichi, "Gyūniku to Kishūhan," *Nihon rekishi* 537, no. 2 (1993): 57–58.
4. Harada Nobuo, *Edo no shokuseikatsu* (Tokyo: Iwanami Shoten, 2003), 38–40. See also Hans Martin Krämer, "'Not Befitting Our Divine Country': Eating Meat in Japanese Discourses of Self and Other from the Seventeenth Century to the Present," *Food & Foodways* 16, no. 1 (2008): 38–39.
5. Harada Nobuo, *Edo no shokuseikatsu*, 40–41.
6. Fukuzawa Yukichi, *The Autobiography of Fukuzawa Yukichi*, trans. Kiyooka Eiichi (Tokyo: Hokuseido Press, 1960), 59.
7. Andō Seiichi, "Gyūniku to Kishūhan," 58.
8. See, for example, the entry for Bunkyū 1 (1861)/5/24.

4. WORK AND FAMILY   261

9. Kawai Koume, Shiga Yasuharu, and Murata Shizuko, *Koume nikki: Bakumatsu Meiji o Kishū ni ikiru*, vol. 2 (July 1, 1876) (Tokyo: Heibonsha, 1974), 243–44.
10. Abe Takeshi, *Bakumatsu Kishū Kawai Koume no wandafuru wārudo* (Kyoto: Aunsha, 2013), 315.
11. Constantine N. Vaporis, "Samurai and Merchant in Mid-Tokugawa Japan: Tani Tannai's Record of Daily Necessities (1748–54)," *Harvard Journal of Asiatic Studies* 60, no. 1 (2000): 205–27.
12. Isoda Michifumi, *Bushi no kakeibo: "Kaga-han gosan'yōmono" no Bakumatsu Ishin*, Shinchō shinsho (Tokyo: Shinchōsha, 2003), 55–57.
13. Fujita Teiichirō, "Koume nikki Kōka 5-nen no jō—1," *Dōshisha shōgaku* 26, no. 2 (1974): 1–22.
14. Morgan Pitelka, *Spectacular Accumulation: Material Culture, Tokugawa Ieyasu, and Samurai Sociability* (Honolulu: University of Hawai'i Press, 2016), chap. 3; Morimoto Masahiro, *Nihon chūsei no zōyo to futan*, Rekishi kagaku sōsho (Tokyo: Azekura Shobō, 1997); Martha Chaiklin, *Mediated by Gifts: Politics and Society in Japan, 1350–1850* (Leiden: Brill, 2016).
15. Yamakawa Kikue, *Women of the Mito Domain: Recollections of Samurai Family Life*, trans. Kate Wildman Nakai (Tokyo: University of Tokyo Press, 1992), 19.
16. Koizumi Kazuko, "Kaji no jinsei," in *Josei no kinsei*, ed. Hayashi Reiko, Nihon no kinsei (Tokyo: Chūō Kōronsha, 1993), 193–94.
17. Yoshida Yuriko, *Kinsei no ie to josei*, 170–71.
18. In the ninth month of Bunkyū 1 (1861), for example, Koume and Hyōzō bought at least 40 kg of raw cotton, which they spun through the ninth and tenth months.
19. Fukuzawa Yukichi and Carmen Blacker, "Kyūhanjō," *Monumenta nipponica* 9, no. 1/2 (1953): 313.
20. Yamakawa, *Women of the Mito Domain*, 15–16.
21. Kären Wigen, *The Making of a Japanese Periphery, 1750–1920* (Berkeley: University of California Press, 1995), 86–87.
22. Ujiie Mikito, *Hatamoto gokenin: Odoroki no bakushin shakai no shinjitsu*, vol. 22, Rekishi shinsho (Tokyo: Yōsensha, 2011), 94–95.
23. Isoda Michifumi, *Kinsei daimyō kashindan no shakai kōzō* (Tokyo: Tōkyō Daigaku Shuppankai, 2003), 295–97.
24. Yamakawa, *Women of the Mito Domain*, 17.
25. Kawai Koume, Shiga Yasuharu, and Murata Shizuko, *Koume nikki: Bakumatsu Meiji o Kishū ni ikiru*, vol. 1 (Kaei 4/7/25) (Tokyo: Heibonsha, 1974), 72.
26. For drinking, see Kawai, Shiga, and Murata, vol. 1, 21 (Kaei 2/11/15) and 76 (Kaei 6/1/5). For the bath, see 53 (Kaei 4/4/15). For theatrical performance, see 5 (Kaei 2/8/19).
27. Ōoka Toshiaki, *Bakumatsu kakyū bushi no enikki: sono kurashi to sumai no fūkei o yomu* (Tokyo: Sagami Shobō, 2007).
28. According to Yamaue Sachiko, the painting was not one of those originally painted for the temple but was donated more recently (personal communication, January 25, 2021).
29. Kawai Baishō and Shiga Yasuharu, *Bunkyū sannen jūgun nichiroku: Tenchūgumi* (Wakayama-shi: Miyai Heiandō, 1982), 83.

5. WAR AND REVOLUTION

1. Koume breaks down the rice income into "owned fields" (*arita*), 13 koku, and "Nagusa [county]" rice, 13 koku plus 7 koku, for a total of 33 koku, implying an average price of 217 monme. It is not clear if she is referring to notional income or actual rice received. Prices fluctuated widely during the year, between 200 and 400 monme per koku.
2. Abe Takeshi, *Bakumatsu Kishū Kawai Koume no wandafuru wārudo* (Kyoto: Aunsha, 2013), 152–53.
3. Kawai Koume, Shiga Yasuharu, and Murata Shizuko, *Koume nikki: Bakumatsu Meiji o Kishū ni ikiru*, vol. 2, 79 (Keiō 1/3/26) (Tokyo: Heibonsha, 1974), 6.
4. Reiko Tanimura, "Practical Frivolities: The Study of Shamisen Among Girls of the Late Edo Townsman Class," *Japan Review* 23, no. 23 (2011): 73–96.
5. John Reddie Black, *Young Japan: Yokohama and Yedo, 1858–79*, vol. 2 (New York: Oxford University Press, 1968), 84–85.
6. Kawai, Shiga, and Murata, *Koume nikki*, vol. 2, 287 (Man'en 2/10/17).
7. See Simon Partner, *The Merchant's Tale: Yokohama and the Transformation of Japan* (New York: Columbia University Press, 2017). Kōshūya Chūemon, the protagonist, was one of the merchants who did well from the cotton trade.
8. Kawai, Shiga, and Murata, *Koume nikki*, vol. 2, 157–58 (Keio 3/5/2).
9. For a fuller discussion of comets and their perception in late Tokugawa Japan, see Laura Nenzi, "Caught in the Spotlight: The 1858 Comet and Late Tokugawa Japan," *Japan Forum* (Oxford, England) 23, no. 1 (2011): 1–23.
10. Seishin Ninpo Dojo (blog), https://seishinninpodojo.wordpress.com/2011/07/04/tenchugumi-a-rebellion/.
11. Wakayama Kenshi Hensan Iinkai, *Wakayama kenshi. Kinsei* (Wakayama-shi: Wakayama-ken, 1990), 878–79; Kawai Baisho and Shiga Yasuharu, *Bunkyū sannen jūgun nichiroku: Tenchūgumi* (Wakayama-shi: Miyai Heiandō, 1982), 46–47. The former gives a figure one thousand men; the latter, five hundred.
12. Kawai and Shiga, *Bunkyū sannen jūgun nichiroku*, 53–54, 65.
13. Kawai, Shiga, and Murata, *Koume nikki*, vol. 2, 33 (Bunkyū 4/6/26).
14. Kawai, Shiga, and Murata, vol. 2, 32–33 (Bunkyū 4/6/25).
15. Conrad D. Totman, *The Collapse of the Tokugawa Bakufu 1862–1868* (Honolulu: University Press of Hawaii, 1980), 138. See also Kawai, Shiga, and Murata, *Koume nikki*, vol. 2, 67–68 (Genji 2/1/24).
16. Totman, *Collapse of the Tokugawa Bakufu*, 154.
17. Inoue Yasuo, *"Koume nikki" ni miru Kishū no bakumatsu* (Wakayama: privately published, 2017), 61–69.
18. Totman, *Collapse of the Tokugawa Bakufu*, 155.
19. Inoue Yasuo, *"Koume nikki,"* 59–61.
20. Partner, *Merchant's Tale*, 153.
21. Abe Takeshi, *Bakumatsu Kishū Kawai Koume*, 305.
22. Abe Takeshi, 487–88.
23. Kawai, Shiga, and Murata, *Koume nikki*, vol. 2, 206 (Keiō 3/11/18).

24. Kawai, Shiga, and Murata, vol. 2, 207–8 (Keiō 3/11/24).
25. Abe Takeshi, *Bakumatsu Kishū Kawai Koume*, 357.

6. THE ARTIST'S LIFE

1. Yonezawa Yoshiho and Yoshizawa Chū, *Japanese Painting in the Literati Style*, trans. Betty Iverson Monroe (New York: Weatherhill/Heibonsha, 1974), 19–21.
2. James Cahill, *Scholar Painters of Japan: The Nanga School* (New York: Asia Society; distributed by New York Graphic Society, 1972), 15–16.
3. Melinda Takeuchi, *Taiga's True Views: The Language of Landscape Painting in Eighteenth-Century Japan* (Stanford, Calif.: Stanford University Press, 1992).
4. Cahill, *Scholar Painters of Japan*, 48.
5. Yonezawa Yoshiho and Yoshizawa Chū, *Japanese Painting*, 127–28.
6. Yurika Wakamatsu, "Painting in Between: Gender and Modernity in the Japanese Literati Art of Okuhara Seiko (1837–1913)," PhD dissertation, Harvard University, 2016, 2.
7. Yukio Lippit, "Urakami Gyokudō: An Intoxicology of Japanese Literati Painting," in *Dialogues in Art History, from Mesopotamian to Modern: Readings for a New Century*, ed. Elizabeth Cropper (Washington, D.C.: National Gallery of Art, 2008), 169.
8. Lippit, 167.
9. Lippit, 169, 167. See also Kōno Motoaki, "Nihon bunjinga shiron," *Kokka* 1207 (1996): 5–13.
10. Ernest F. Fenollosa, *Epochs of Chinese and Japanese Art: An Outline History of East Asiatic Design*, vol. 2 (New York: Frederick A. Stokes, 1912), 164–65.
11. Matthias Hayek and Annick Horiuchi, *Listen, Copy, Read: Popular Learning in Early Modern Japan* (Leiden: Brill, 2014), 323–26.
12. Kawai Koume, Shiga Yasuharu, and Murata Shizuko, *Koume nikki: Bakumatsu Meiji o Kishū ni ikiru*, vol. 1 (Kaei 4/3/11) (Tokyo: Heibonsha, 1974), 46.
13. Kawai, Shiga, and Murata, 1, 46.
14. Kawai, Shiga, and Murata, painting for lady-in-waiting vol. 1, 35 (Kaei 4/1/22); folding fan, 36 (Kaei 4/1/27); Gassaku event, 45 (Kaei 4/3/8); Kusumotoya, 47 (Kaei 4/3/20); sixtieth birthday, 48–49 (Kaei 4/3/25); request to return paintings, 57 (Kaei 4/5/11); Taya paintings, 64 (Kaei 4/6/13); gift to Toyo, 70 (Kaei 4/7/15).
15. The Kishū retainers were mobilized in 1853 for a possible war against the United States; in 1863 to combat the Tenchūgumi rebellion; several times during the 1860s to quell unrest in Kyoto; and in 1866–1868 for the two campaigns against Chōshū domain.
16. For the full text, in modern kanji with introductory essay, see Ishii Kendō and Yamashita Tsuneo, *Edo hyōryūki sōshū: Ishii Kendō korekushon* (Tokyo: Nihon Hyōronsha, 1992), 65–603.
17. Kondō Takashi, *Kawai Koume no sakuhin to gagyō*, ed. Hara Yōko (Wakayama: Koume Nikki wo Tanoshimu Kai, 2019), 9–12.
18. Interview with Patricia Fister, November 26, 2019.

19. Wakayama Shiritsu Hakubutsukan, *Jōkamachi Wakayama no eshitachi: Edo jidai no Kishū gadan* (Wakayama: Wakayama Shiritsu Hakubutsukan, 2016), 57.
20. Abe Takeshi, *Bakumatsu Kishū Kawai Koume no wandafuru wārudo* (Kyoto: Aunsha, 2013), 335.
21. There are numerous references to fish prices throughout the diary, varying with size, quality, and rate of inflation. For an example of prices of top-quality fish, see Kawai, Shiga, and Murata, *Koume nikki*, vol. 1, 178 (Ansei 6/6/18).
22. Kawai Koume, Shiga Yasuharu, and Murata Shizuko, *Koume nikki: Bakumatsu Meiji o Kishū ni ikiru*, vol. 2 (Genji 1/8/13) (Tokyo: Heibonsha, 1974), 41; (Genji 1/3/5), 16.
23. Timon Screech, "Owning Edo-Period Paintings," in *Acquisition: Art and Ownership in Edo-Period Japan*, ed. Elizabeth Lillehoj (Warren, Conn.: Floating World Editions, 2007), 23–51. Screech gives one example of a pair of screens by Soga Shōhaku that sold in 1770 for over 2,000 monme, but he describes this as an exceptional price.
24. In 1845 Hakusetsu held an official position of "Oban ishi" and received a "10-man fuchi" salary equivalent to 18 koku. Wakayama Prefectural Museum News, http://kenpakunews.blog120.fc2.com/blog-entry-676.html, accessed 6/30/2020.
25. Patricia Fister, *Japanese Women Artists, 1600–1900* (New York: Spencer Museum of Art/Harper & Row, 1988), 103.
26. Wakamatsu, "Painting in Between."
27. See Matthew Fraleigh, "Kanshibun in the Late Edo Period," in *The Cambridge History of Japanese Literature*, ed. Haruo Shirane (Cambridge: Cambridge University Press, 2015), 465–70.
28. Kawai, Shiga, and Murata, *Koume nikki*, vol. 2, 158 (Ansei 6/4/3).

7. ACROSS THE DIVIDE

1. Wakayama Kenshi Hensan Iinkai, *Wakayama Kenshi. Kin-gendai* (Wakayama-shi: Wakayama-ken, 1989), 18–20.
2. Wakayama Kenshi Hensan Iinkai, 51–61.
3. Wakayama Kenshi Hensan Iinkai, 31–40.
4. Wakayama Kenshi Hensan Iinkai, 296–300.
5. Wakayama Kenshi Hensan Iinkai, 305–6.
6. Kawai Koume, Shiga Yasuharu, and Murata Shizuko, *Koume nikki: Bakumatsu Meiji o Kishū ni ikiru*, vol. 1 (Kaisetsu) (Tokyo: Heibonsha, 1974), 299.
7. Margaret Mehl, *Private Academies of Chinese Learning in Meiji Japan: The Decline and Transformation of the Kanguku Juku* (Copenhagen: NIAS, 2003), 31–34.
8. Kawai Koume, Shiga Yasuharu, and Murata Shizuko, *Koume nikki: Bakumatsu Meiji o Kishū ni ikiru*, vol. 3 (Meiji 11/9/2) (Tokyo: Heibonsha, 1974), 37–38.
9. Shindo Motokazu, "The Inflation in the Early Meiji Era—History of Inflation in Japan," *Kyoto University Economic Review* 24, 2 (1954): 46.
10. Kawai Koume, Shiga Yasuharu, and Murata Shizuko, *Koume nikki: Bakumatsu Meiji o Kishū ni ikiru*, vol. 2 (Meiji 9/10/27) (Tokyo: Heibonsha, 1974), 259.

11. For 1860s dollar exchange rates, see Simon Partner, *The Merchant's Tale: Yokohama and the Transformation of Japan* (New York: Columbia University Press, 2017), 7. For Meiji prices and exchange rates, see Coin-walk.site, http://sirakawa.b.la9.jp/Coin/J077.htm#E01 (accessed June 1, 2020). For 1865 income and rice price, see Kawai, Shiga, and Murata, *Koume nikki*, vol. 2 (Genji 2/12/30), 131.
12. According to Abe Takeshi, Koume mentioned visits to the theater ten times between 1837 and 1867, but sixty-six times between 1876 and 1883. Forty-three of those were between 1876 and 1880. Abe Takeshi, *Bakumatsu Kishū Kawai Koume no wandafuru wārudo* (Kyoto: Aunsha, 2013), 160.
13. Abe Takeshi, 494.
14. Koume does not state which branch of the Mizuno family she is working for. This interpretation is from Abe Takeshi, 499.
15. *Nihon daihyakka zensho = Encyclopedia Nipponica 2001* (Tokyo: Shōgakkan, 2001). Electronic edition accessed through JapanKnowledge.
16. Koume, Shiga, and Murata, *Koume nikki*, vol. 3 (9/26/1878), 42.
17. Kawai, Shiga, and Murata, vol. 2 (6/11/1877), 314.
18. For example, on September 29, 1877, Yūsuke received monthly tuition of 0.15 yen from a student. He divided the fee with Koume, giving her 0.06 yen. Kawai, Shiga, and Murata, vol. 2 (9/29/1877), 334.
19. Abe Takeshi, *Bakumatsu Kishū Kawai Koume*, 516.
20. Kawai, Shiga, and Murata, *Koume nikki*, vol. 2 (11/14/1876), 270.
21. Kawai, Shiga, and Murata, vol. 2 (11/16/1876), 270.
22. Kawai, Shiga, and Murata, vol. 2 (12/26/1876), 277.
23. Kawai, Shiga, and Murata, vol. 3 (4/13/1882), 209–10.
24. Kawai, Shiga, and Murata, vol. 3 (8/27/1878), 36.
25. Kawai, Shiga, and Murata, vol. 3 (10/31/1878), 47.
26. Kawai, Shiga, and Murata, vol. 3 (3/20/1881), 128.
27. For a discussion of this commission, see Takeuchi Yoshinobu, "Kawai Koume no gagyō ni tsuite no gonin," *Wakayama Chihōshi kenkyū* 63 (2012): 26–30.
28. See, for example, Kawai, Shiga, and Murata, *Koume nikki*, vol. 3 (3/17/1882), 204.
29. Kawai, Shiga, and Murata, vol. 3 (8/27/1882), 243.
30. Kawai, Shiga, and Murata, vol. 3 (5/31/1882), 220.
31. Kawai, Shiga, and Murata, vol. 3 (4/12/1878), 16.
32. Kawai, Shiga, and Murata, vol. 3 (4/26/1878), 19.
33. Kawai, Shiga, and Murata, vol. 3 (5/31/1880), 82; (6/4/80), 82; (7/12/80), 91.
34. Abe mentions this trend. My own count is higher than Abe's. Abe Takeshi, *Bakumatsu Kishū Kawai Koume*, 511.
35. Kawai, Shiga, and Murata, *Koume nikki*, vol. 2 (3/10/1877), 290.
36. Kawai, Shiga, and Murata, vol. 3 (1/7/1881), 114–15.
37. Kawai, Shiga, and Murata, vol. 3 (8/15/1882), 239–40.
38. Rosina Buckland, *Painting Nature for the Nation: Taki Katei and the Challenges to Sinophile Culture in Meiji Japan* (Leiden: Brill, 2013), 3. See also Miwa Hideo, "Naikoku kaiga kyōshinkai," in Kokushi Daijiten (accessed through JapanKnowledge).

39. *Yomiuri shinbun*, November 15, 1881, 1.
40. Kawai, Shiga, and Murata, *Koume nikki*, vol. 3 (12/22/1882), 265.
41. Yurika Wakamatsu, "Painting in Between: Gender and Modernity in the Japanese Literati Art of Okuhara Seiko (1837–1913)," PhD dissertation, Harvard University, 2016, 15; Buckland, *Painting Nature*, 43–95; Matthew Fraleigh, "Kanshibun in the Late Edo Period," in *The Cambridge History of Japanese Literature*, ed. Haruo Shirane (Cambridge: Cambridge University Press, 2015), 465–70.
42. Quoted in Buckland, *Painting Nature*, 100.
43. See David L. Howell, "The Girl with the Horse-Dung Hairdo," in *Looking Modern: East Asian Visual Culture from Treaty Ports to World War II*, ed. Jennifer Purtle (Chicago: Center for the Arts of East Asia, 2009), 204.
44. Wakamatsu, "Painting in Between," 171. According to Wakamatsu, 196, a price-list published in 1882 states that the going rate for a painting by Seiko was 7 yen.
45. According to the standard compendium of long-term statistics, carpenters in 1885 earned an average 5.675 yen for a twenty-five-day working month. Female textile workers earned 2.825 yen. Sōmuchō Tōkeikyoku, *Nihon chōki tōkei sōran*, vol. 4 (Tokyo: Nihon Tōkei Kyōkai, 1987), 228–31, chart 16-1.
46. I am grateful to Mr. Inoue Yasuo for this insight.
47. Kawai, Shiga, and Murata, *Koume nikki*, vol. 3 (3/12/1876), 231.

CONCLUSION

1. For others, see Yoshida Yuriko, *Kinsei no ie to josei* (Tokyo: Yamakawa Shuppansha, 2016); Suzuki Yuriko, "Jusha josei no seikatsu," in *Josei no kinsei*, ed. Hayashi Reiko (Tokyo: Chūō Kōronsha, 1993), 146–55; Mega Atsuko, *Buke ni totsuida josei no tegami: Binbō hatamoto no Edo-gurashi* (Tokyo: Yoshikawa Kōbunkan, 2011).
2. Abe Takeshi, *Bakumatsu Kishū Kawai Koume no wandafuru wārudo* (Kyoto: Aunsha, 2013).
3. See Jill Lepore, "Historians Who Love Too Much: Reflections on Microhistory and Biography," *Journal of American History* 88, no. 1 (2001): 129–44; István Szijártó, "Four Arguments for Microhistory," *Rethinking History* 6, no. 2 (2002): 209–15.
4. For low-ranking samurai, see Marius B. Jansen, *Sakamoto Ryōma and the Meiji Restoration* (Princeton, N.J.: Princeton University Press, 1961). For intellectuals, see Harry D. Harootunian, *Toward Restoration: The Growth of Political Consciousness in Tokugawa Japan* (Berkeley: University of California Press, 1970). For peasant protests, see George M. Wilson, *Patriots and Redeemers in Japan: Motives in the Meiji Restoration* (Chicago: University of Chicago Press, 1992). For Marxist interpretations, see *Meiji ishinshi*, vol. 1, *Nihon shihon shugi hattatsushi kōza* (Tokyo: Iwanami Shoten, 1932). For female actors, see Anne Walthall, *The Weak Body of a Useless Woman: Matsuo Taseko and the Meiji Restoration* (Chicago: University of Chicago Press, 1998). For entrepreneurs, see Simon Partner, *The Merchant's Tale: Yokohama and the Transformation of Japan* (New York: Columbia University Press, 2017). For communications networks,

see Miyachi Masato, *Bakumatsu ishinki no bunka to jōhō* (Tokyo: Meicho Kankōkai, 1994). There are of course many others.
5. See Yamakawa Kikue, *Women of the Mito Domain: Recollections of Samurai Family Life*, trans. Kate Wildman Nakai (Tokyo: University of Tokyo Press, 1992).
6. Watanabe Hiroshi, *A History of Japanese Political Thought, 1600–1901*, trans. David Noble (Tokyo: International House of Japan, 2012), 250, 248.
7. Richard Rubinger, *Private Academies of Tokugawa Japan* (Princeton, N.J.: Princeton University Press, 1982), 164–65.
8. Walthall, *Weak Body*; Laura Nenzi, *The Chaos and Cosmos of Kurosawa Tokiko: One Woman's Transit from Tokugawa to Meiji Japan* (Honolulu: University of Hawai'i Press, 2015).
9. "Tenkakokuka," entry in *Kadokawa kokugo daijiten*. Accessed via JapanKnowledge, May 24, 2022.
10. Watanabe Hiroshi, *Japanese Political Thought*, 277–78.
11. M. William Steele finds this cynicism to have been extremely widespread in urban society in the late Tokugawa period. See Steele, "Goemon's New World," in *Alternative Narratives in Modern Japanese History* (London: RoutledgeCurzon, 2003), 4–18.
12. Laurel Ulrich, *A Midwife's Tale: The Life of Martha Ballard, Based on Her Diary, 1785–1812* (New York: Vintage, 1990), 75–76.
13. Mary Elizabeth Berry and Marcia Yonemoto, "Introduction," in *What Is a Family? Answers from Early Modern Japan*, ed. Mary Elizabeth Berry and Marcia Yonemoto (Oakland: University of California Press, 2019), 1–20.
14. Luke Shepherd Roberts, *Performing the Great Peace: Political Space and Open Secrets in Tokugawa Japan* (Honolulu: University of Hawai'i Press, 2012). See also Watanabe Hiroshi, *Japanese Political Thought*, chap. 2.
15. Nakamura Sumiko, "Koume no gaishutsu chōsa," undated, Koume Nikki wo Tanoshimu Kai, Wakayama.
16. Marcia Yonemoto, *The Problem of Women in Early Modern Japan* (Berkeley: University of California Press, 2016), 15.
17. Yoshida Yuriko, *Kinsei no ie to josei*.
18. Yonemoto, too, concludes that "gender hierarchies even within elite Japanese families did not conform to the norms and standards of Confucian patriarchy." Yonemoto, *The Problem of Women*, 14.
19. Quoted in Harry D. Harootunian, "The Progress of Japan and the Samurai Class, 1868–1882," *Pacific Historical Review* 28, no. 3 (1959): 259.
20. E. Herbert Norman, *Japan's Emergence as a Modern State: Political and Economic Problems of the Meiji Period* (New York: International Secretariat Institute of Pacific Relations, 1940), 83.
21. See Ochiai Hiroki, *Meiji kokka to shizoku* (Tokyo: Yoshikawa Kōbunkan, 2001).
22. Norman, *Japan's Emergence*, 61; Harootunian, "Japan and the Samurai Class," 255. See also Douglas R. Howland, "Samurai Status, Class, and Bureaucracy: A Historiographical Essay," *Journal of Asian Studies* 60, no. 2 (2001): 353–80. There are, of course, many other interpretations of the Meiji Restoration that pay less attention the role of the samurai.

23. Harootunian, "Japan and the Samurai Class," 260. For police, see Norman, *Japan's Emergence*, 61, 83.
24. Earl H. Kinmonth, *The Self-Made Man in Meiji Japanese Thought: From Samurai to Salary Man* (Berkeley: University of California Press, 1981), 9–43.
25. Hirota Teruyuki, *Marriage, Education and Social Mobility in a Former Samurai Society After the Meiji Restoration* (Oxford: Nissan Institute of Japanese Studies, 1994), 8–9.
26. Norman, *Japan's Emergence*, 83.
27. Howland, "Samurai Status, Class, and Bureaucracy," 363.
28. Hirota Teruyuki, *Marriage, Education and Social Mobility*, 24.
29. Hamana Atsushi, "Meiji shoki kaisō kōzō no kenkyū," in *"Kindai Nihon" no rekishi shakaigaku*, ed. Tsutsui Kiyotada (Tokyo: Bokutakusha, 1990), 39–57. See also Sonoda Hidehiro, Hamana Atsushi, and Hirota Teruyuki, *Shizoku no rekishi shakaigakuteki kenkyū* (Nagoya: Nagoya Daigaku Shuppankai, 1995), 291.
30. David L. Howell, "Early 'Shizoku' Colonization of Hokkaidō," *Journal of Asian History* 17 (1983): 62.
31. Hirota Teruyuki, *Marriage, Education and Social Mobility*, 32–34.
32. Harootunian, "Japan and the Samurai Class," 261.
33. See, for example, Sugano Noriko, "Kishida Toshiko and the Career of a Public-Speaking Woman in Meiji Japan," in *The Female as Subject: Reading and Writing in Early Modern Japan*, ed. Peter F. Kornicki, Mara Patessio, and G. G. Rowley (Ann Arbor: Center for Japanese Studies, University of Michigan, 2010); Marnie S. Anderson, "Women's Agency and the Historical Record: Reflections on Female Activists in Nineteenth-Century Japan," *Journal of Women's History* 23, no. 1 (2011).
34. Abe Takeshi, *Bakumatsu Kishū Kawai Koume*, 28–29.
35. See, for example, Mary Elizabeth Berry, *Japan in Print: Information and Nation in the Early Modern Period* (Berkeley: University of California Press, 2007), 31.
36. Peter F. Kornicki, *The Book in Japan: A Cultural History from the Beginnings to the Nineteenth Century* (Leiden: Brill, 1998), 63–64. See also Ono Hideo, *Kawaraban monogatari: Edo jidai masukomi no rekishi* (Tokyo: Yuzankaku, 1985); Yajima Takanori and Suzuki Tōzō, *Edo jidai rakusho ruijū*, 3 vols. (Tokyo: Tōkyōdō, 1985).
37. Maruyama Yasunari, *Jōhō to kōtsū*, vol. 6, Nihon no kinsei (Tokyo: Chūōkōronsha, 1992), 22–23.
38. Yoshihara Ken'ichirō, *Edo no jōhōya: Bakumatsu shominshi no sokumen*, NHK bukkusu (Tokyo: Nippon Hōsō Shuppan Kyōkai, 1978), 17–18.
39. Maruyama Yasunari, *Jōhō to kōtsū*, vol. 6, 52.
40. Maruyama Yasunari, vol. 6, 44–46.
41. Ono Hideo, *Kawaraban monogatari*, 226–42. For transcriptions, see Gankyū Inshi, *Edo kawaraban hayariuta hachijisshu: Ōsaka Daigaku Ninchōji Bunko zō*, Zokuyō sōsho (Tōkyō: Taihei Shooku, 2000).
42. Miyachi argues that the informed public enabled by the spread of news and information was indeed a catalyst for the Restoration. Miyachi Masato, *Bakumatsu ishinki no bunka to jōhō*.

BIBLIOGRAPHY

Abe Takeshi. *Bakumatsu Kishū Kawai Koume no wandafuru wārudo*. Kyoto: Aunsha, 2013.
Alaszewski, Andy. *Using Diaries for Social Research*. Thousand Oaks, Calif.: SAGE, 2006.
Anderson, Marnie S. "Women's Agency and the Historical Record: Reflections on Female Activists in Nineteenth-Century Japan." *Journal of Women's History* 23, no. 1 (2011): 38–55.
Andō Seiichi. "Gyūniku to Kishūhan." *Nihon rekishi* 537, no. 2 (1993): 57–58.
——. *Wakayamaken no rekishi*. Kenshi Shirīzu. Tokyo: Yamakawa Shuppansha, 1970.
Berry, Mary Elizabeth. *Japan in Print: Information and Nation in the Early Modern Period*. Berkeley: University of California Press, 2007.
Berry, Mary Elizabeth, and Marcia Yonemoto. "Introduction." In *What Is a Family? Answers from Early Modern Japan*, ed. Mary Elizabeth Berry and Marcia Yonemoto, 1–20. Oakland: University of California Press, 2019.
——. *What Is a Family? Answers from Early Modern Japan*. Oakland: University of California Press, 2019.
Black, John Reddie. *Young Japan: Yokohama and Yedo, 1858-79*. Oxford in Asia Historical Reprints. Vol. 2. New York: Oxford University Press, 1968.
Bolitho, Harold. "The Tempo Crisis." In *The Cambridge History of Japan*. Vol. 5: *The Nineteenth Century*, ed. Marius B. Jansen, 116–67. Cambridge: Cambridge University Press, 1989.
Buckland, Rosina. *Painting Nature for the Nation: Taki Katei and the Challenges to Sinophile Culture in Meiji Japan*. Japanese Visual Culture. Leiden: Brill, 2013.
Buyō Inshi. *Lust, Commerce, and Corruption: An Account of What I Have Seen and Heard*, trans. Mark Teeuwen, Kate Wildman Nakai, Fumiko Miyazaki, Anne Walthall, and John Breen. Translations from the Asian Classics. New York: Columbia University Press, 2017.
Cahill, James. *Scholar Painters of Japan: The Nanga School*. New York: Asia Society; distributed by New York Graphic Society, 1972.
Chaiklin, Martha. *Mediated by Gifts: Politics and Society in Japan, 1350-1850*. Brill's Japanese Studies Library. Leiden: Brill, 2016.

Chamberlain, Basil Hall. *Things Japanese; Being Notes on Various Subjects Connected with Japan for the Use of Travellers and Others*. 4th ed. London: J. Murray Kelly & Walsh, 1902.

Dore, Ronald. *Education in Tokugawa, Japan*. Berkeley: University of California Press, 1965.

Ebrey, Patricia Buckley. *The Inner Quarters: Marriage and the Lives of Chinese Women in the Sung Period*. Berkeley: University of California Press, 1993.

Ehlers, Maren Annika. *Give and Take: Poverty and the Status Order in Early Modern Japan*. Harvard East Asian Monographs. Cambridge, Mass.: Harvard University Asia Center, 2018.

Fenollosa, Ernest F. *Epochs of Chinese and Japanese Art: An Outline History of East Asiatic Design*. Vol. 2. New York: Frederick A. Stokes, 1912. https://doi.org/9781933330266.

Fister, Patricia. *Japanese Women Artists, 1600–1900*. New York: Spencer Museum of Art/ Harper & Row, 1988.

Fraleigh, Matthew. "Kanshibun in the Late Edo Period." In *The Cambridge History of Japanese Literature*, ed. Haruo Shirane, 465–70. Cambridge: Cambridge University Press, 2015.

Fujimoto Seijirō. *JōKamachi sekai no seikatsushi: Botsuraku to saisei no shiten kara*. Tokyo: Seibundō, 2014.

Fujita Teiichirō. "Koume nikki Kōka 5-nen no jō—1." *Dōshisha shōgaku* 26, no. 2 (1974): 1–22.

——. "Shiryō shōkai: Tenpōki Wakayamahan kakyū bushi nyōbō no nikki—1." *Shakai kagaku* 5, no. 1 (1974): 196–215.

Fukuzawa Yukichi. *The Autobiography of Fukuzawa Yukichi*, trans. Kiyooka Eiichi. Tokyo: Hokuseido Press, 1960.

Fukuzawa Yukichi and Carmen Blacker. "Kyūhanjō." *Monumenta nipponica* 9, no. 1/2 (1953): 304–29.

Gankyū Inshi. *Edo kawaraban hayariuta hachijisshu: Ōsaka Daigaku Ninchōji Bunko zō*. Zokuyō sōsho. Tokyo: Taihei Shooku, 2000.

Garrison, Christopher S., Christopher R. J. Kilburn, and Stephen J. Edwards. "The 1831 Eruption of Babuyan Claro That Never Happened: Has the Source of One of the Largest Volcanic Climate Forcing Events of the Nineteenth Century Been Misattributed?" *Journal of Applied Volcanology* 7, no. 1 (2018): 1–21.

Goreglyad, V. N. "The Manuscript of 'Kankai Ibun' in the Collection of the St. Petersburg Branch of the Institute of Oriental Studies." *Manuscripta Orientalia* 3, no. 2 (1997): 58–67.

Gotman, Kélina. *Choreomania: Dance and Disorder*. New York: Oxford University Press, 2018.

Gramlich-Oka, Bettina. *Thinking like a Man: Tadano Makuzu (1763–1825)*. Brill's Japanese Studies Library. Leiden: Brill, 2006.

Hall, Francis, F. G. Notehelfer, and Cleveland Public Library, John G. White Department. *Japan Through American Eyes: The Journal of Francis Hall, Kanagawa and Yokohama, 1859–1866: From the Cleveland Public Library, John G. White Collection of Orientalia*. Princeton, N.J.: Princeton University Press, 1992.

Hamana Atsushi. "Meiji shoki kaisō kōzō no kenkyū." In *"Kindai Nihon" no rekishi shakaigaku*, ed. Tsutsui Kiyotada. Tokyo: Bokutakusha, 1990.

Harada Nobuo. *Edo no shokuseikatsu*. Tokyo: Iwanami Shoten, 2003.

Harootunian, Harry D. "The Progress of Japan and the Samurai Class, 1868–1882." *Pacific Historical Review* 28, no. 3 (1959): 255–66.

———. *Toward Restoration: The Growth of Political Consciousness in Tokugawa Japan*. Publications of the Center for Japanese and Korean Studies. Berkeley: University of California Press, 1970.

Hayashi Noriaki and Ichikawa Kunitoshi, eds. *Burakushi ni manabu: Kishūhan rōbangashirake monjo o yomu*, Jinken bukkuretto. Wakayama: Wakayama Jinken Kenkyūjo, 2003.

Hayek, Matthias, and Annick Horiuchi. *Listen, Copy, Read: Popular Learning in Early Modern Japan*. Brill's Japanese Studies Library. Leiden: Brill, 2014.

Hirota Teruyuki. *Marriage, Education and Social Mobility in a Former Samurai Society After the Meiji Restoration*. Nissan Occasional Paper Series. Oxford: Nissan Institute of Japanese Studies, 1994.

Horiuchi Shin. *Nanki Tokugawashi*. Vol. 3. Wakayama: Nanki Tokugawashi Kankōkai, 1932.

Howell, David Luke. "Early 'Shizoku' Colonization of Hokkaidō." *Journal of Asian History* 17 (1983): 40–67.

———. "Foreign Encounters and Informal Diplomacy in Early Modern Japan." *Journal of Japanese Studies* 40, no. 2 (2014): 295–327.

———. *Geographies of Identity in Nineteenth-Century Japan*. Berkeley: University of California Press, 2005.

———. "The Girl with the Horse-Dung Hairdo." In *Looking Modern: East Asian Visual Culture from Treaty Ports to World War II*, ed. Jennifer Purtle, 203–19. Chicago: Center for the Arts of East Asia, 2009.

Howland, Douglas R. "Samurai Status, Class, and Bureaucracy: A Historiographical Essay." *Journal of Asian Studies* 60, no. 2 (2001): 353–80.

Inoue Yasuo. *"Koume nikki" ni miru Kishū no bakumatsu*. Wakayama: privately published, 2017.

Ishii Kendō and Yamashita Tsuneo. *Edo hyōryūki sōshū: Ishii Kendō korekushon*. 6 vols. Tokyo: Nihon Hyōronsha, 1992.

Isoda Michifumi. *Bushi no kakeibo: "Kaga-han gosan'yōmono" no Bakumatsu Ishin*. Shinchō Shinsho. Tokyo: Shinchōsha, 2003.

———. *Kinsei daimyō kashindan no shakai kōzō*. Tokyo: Tōkyō Daigaku Shuppankai, 2003.

Iwasaki Takehiko. "Kishū hangaku to shomin kyōiku," ed. Wakayama Shiritsu Hakubutsukan. Wakayama: Wakayamashi Kyōiku Iinkai, 1990.

Iwashita Tetsunori. *Bakumatsu Nihon no jōhō katsudō: "Kaikoku" no jōhōshi*. Tokyo: Yūzankaku Shuppan, 2000.

Jannetta, Ann Bowman. "Famine Mortality in Nineteenth-Century Japan: The Evidence from a Temple Death Register." *Population Studies* 46, no. 3 (1992): 427–43.

———. *The Vaccinators: Smallpox, Medical Knowledge, and the "Opening" of Japan*. Stanford, Calif.: Stanford University Press, 2007.

Jansen, Marius B. *Sakamoto Ryōma and the Meiji Restoration*. Princeton, N.J.: Princeton University Press, 1961.

Kawai Baisho and Kunioka Denjirō. *Isenki*. Wakayama: Kii Kyōdo Shiryō Bunken Hanpukai, 1929.

Kawai Baisho and Shiga Yasuharu. *Bunkyū sannen jūgun nichiroku: Tenchūgumi*. Wakayamashi: Miyai Heiandō, 1982.

Kawai Koume, Shiga Yasuharu, and Murata Shizuko. *Koume nikki: Bakumatsu Meiji o Kishū ni ikiru*. Tōyō Bunko 256. Vol. 1. Tokyo: Heibonsha, 1974.

———. *Koume nikki: Bakumatsu Meiji o Kishū ni ikiru*. Tōyō Bunko 268. Vol. 2. Tokyo: Heibonsha, 1974.

———. *Koume nikki: Bakumatsu Meiji o Kishū ni ikiru*. Tōyō Bunko 284. Vol. 3. Tokyo: Heibonsha, 1974.

Keene, Donald. *Modern Japanese Diaries: The Japanese at Home and Abroad as Revealed Through Their Diaries*. New York: Columbia University Press, 1999.

Kinmonth, Earl H. *The Self-Made Man in Meiji Japanese Thought: From Samurai to Salary Man*. Berkeley: University of California Press, 1981.

Koizumi Kazuko. "Kaji no jinsei." In *Josei no kinsei*, ed. Hayashi Reiko. Nihon No Kinsei 32. Tokyo: Chūō Kōronsha, 1993.

Kondō Takashi. *Kawai Koume no sakuhin to gagyō*, ed. Hara Yōko. Wakayama: Koume Nikki wo Tanoshimu Kai, 2019.

Kōno Motoaki. "Nihon bunjinga shiron." *Kokka* 1207 (1996): 5–13.

Kornicki, Peter F. *The Book in Japan: A Cultural History from the Beginnings to the Nineteenth Century*. Leiden: Brill, 1998.

———. "Women, Education, and Literacy." In *The Female as Subject: Reading and Writing in Early Modern Japan*, ed. Peter F. Kornicki, Mara Patessio, and G. G. Rowley, 7–38. Michigan Monograph Series in Japanese Studies. Ann Arbor: Center for Japanese Studies, University of Michigan, 2010.

Koyama Yasunori. *Wakayamaken no rekishi*. Kenshi. Tokyo: Yamakawa Shuppansha, 2015.

Krämer, Hans Martin. "'Not Befitting Our Divine Country': Eating Meat in Japanese Discourses of Self and Other from the Seventeenth Century to the Present." *Food & Foodways* 16, no. 1 (2008): 33–62.

Krusenstern, Adam Johann von, and Richard Belgrave Hoppner. *Voyage Round the World, in the Years 1803, 1804, 1805, & 1806 by Order of His Imperial Majesty Alexander the First, on Board the Ships Nadeshda and Neva, Under the Command of Captain A. J. Von Krusenstern*. London: C. Roworth for J. Murray, 1813.

Lepore, Jill. "Historians Who Love Too Much: Reflections on Microhistory and Biography." *Journal of American History* 88, no. 1 (2001): 129–44.

Lippit, Yukio. "Urakami Gyokudō: An Intoxicology of Japanese Literati Painting." In *Dialogues in Art History, from Mesopotamian to Modern: Readings for a New Century*, ed. Elizabeth Cropper, 167–87. Studies in the History of Art. Washington, D.C.: National Gallery of Art, 2008.

Longpré, Marc-Antoine, John Stix, Cosima Burkert, Thor Hansteen, and Steffen Kutterolf. "Sulfur Budget and Global Climate Impact of the A.D. 1835 Eruption of Cosigüina Volcano, Nicaragua." *Geophysical Research Letters* 41, no. 19 (2014): 6667–75.

Maruyama Yasunari. *Jōhō to kōtsū*. Nihon no kinsei. Vol. 6. Tokyo: Chūōkōronsha, 1992.

McClellan, Edwin. *Woman in the Crested Kimono: The Life of Shibue Io and Her Family*. New Haven, Conn.: Yale University Press, 1985.

Mega Atsuko. *Buke ni totsuida josei no tegami: Binbō hatamoto no Edo-gurashi*. Tokyo: Yoshikawa Kōbunkan, 2011.

Mehl, Margaret. *Private Academies of Chinese Learning in Meiji Japan: The Decline and Transformation of the Kanguku Juku*. Nordic Institute of Asian Studies Monograph Series. Copenhagen: NIAS, 2003.
Meiji ishinshi. Vol. 1: *Nihon shihon shugi hattatsushi kōza*. Tokyo: Iwanami Shoten, 1932.
Mio Isao. *Jōkamachi Wakayama hyakuwa*. Wakayama: Uji Shoten, 2001.
Miyachi Masato. *Bakumatsu ishinki no bunka to jōhō*. Tokyo: Meicho Kankōkai, 1994.
Moore, Ray A. "Adoption and Samurai Mobility in Tokugawa Japan." In *The Samurai Tradition*, ed. Stephen R. Turnbull. Key Papers on Japan. Tokyo: Japan Library, 2000.Morimoto Masahiro. *Nihon chūsei no zōyo to futan*. Rekishi kagaku sōsho. Tokyo: Azekura Shobō, 1997.
Morris, Ivan. *The Nobility of Failure: Tragic Heroes in the History of Japan*. London: Secker and Warburg, 1975.
Najita, Tetsuo. "Ōshio Heihachirō." In *Personality in Japanese History*, ed. Albert M. Craig and Donald H. Shively, 155–79. Berkeley: University of California Press, 1970.
Nakamura Sumiko. "Koume no gaishutsu chōsa." Undated. Koume Nikki wo Tanoshimu Kai, Wakayama.
Nakazawa Benjirō. *Nihon beika hendōshi*. Tokyo: Kashiwa Shobō, 2001.
Nenzi, Laura. "Caught in the Spotlight: The 1858 Comet and Late Tokugawa Japan." *Japan Forum* (Oxford, England) 23, no. 1 (2011): 1–23.
———. *The Chaos and Cosmos of Kurosawa Tokiko: One Woman's Transit from Tokugawa to Meiji Japan*. Honolulu: University of Hawai'i Press, 2015.
Nihon daihyakka zensho = *Encyclopedia Nipponica 2001*. Tokyo: Shōgakkan, 2001.
Norman, E. Herbert. *Japan's Emergence as a Modern State: Political and Economic Problems of the Meiji Period*. I.P.R. Inquiry Series. New York: International Secretariat Institute of Pacific Relations, 1940.
Ochiai Hiroki. *Meiji kokka to shizoku*. Tokyo: Yoshikawa Kōbunkan, 2001.
Okazaki Hisahiko. *Mutsu Munemitsu and His Time*, trans. Noda Makito. Japan Library. Tokyo: Japan Publishing Industry Foundation for Culture, 2018.
Ono Hideo. *Kawaraban monogatari: Edo jidai masukomi no rekishi*. Tokyo: Yuzankaku, 1985.
Ōoka Toshiaki. *Bakumatsu kakyū bushi no enikki: Sono kurashi to sumai no fūkei o yomu*. Tokyo: Sagami Shobō, 2007.
Ōta Tomiyasu. "Perī raisenki ni okeru nōmin to kurofune jōhō shūshū: Musashinokuni Kawagoehan nanushi no baai." *Saitama kenritsu monjokan kiyō*, no. 5 (1991): 24–54.
Partner, Simon. *The Merchant's Tale: Yokohama and the Transformation of Japan*. New York: Columbia University Press, 2017.
Pitelka, Morgan. *Spectacular Accumulation: Material Culture, Tokugawa Ieyasu, and Samurai Sociability*. Honolulu: University of Hawai'i Press, 2016.
Roberts, Luke Shepherd. *Performing the Great Peace: Political Space and Open Secrets in Tokugawa Japan*. Honolulu: University of Hawai'i Press, 2012.
Rubinger, Richard. *Private Academies of Tokugawa Japan*. Princeton, N.J.: Princeton University Press, 1982.
Screech, Timon. "Owning Edo-Period Paintings." In *Acquisition: Art and Ownership in Edo-Period Japan*, ed. Elizabeth Lillehoj, 23–51. Warren, Conn.: Floating World Editions, 2007.

Shimoda, Hiraku. *Lost and Found: Recovering Regional Identity in Imperial Japan.* Cambridge, Mass.: Harvard University Press.

Shindo Motokazu. "The Inflation in the Early Meiji Era—History of Inflation in Japan." *Kyoto University Economic Review* 24, no. 2 (1954): 39–59.

Skinner, G. William. "Conjugal Power in Tokugawa Japanese Families: A Matter of Life or Death." In *Sex and Gender Hierarchies*, ed. Barbara D. Miller. Publications of the Society for Psychological Anthropology, xix. Cambridge: Cambridge University Press, 1993.

Sōmuchō Tōkeikyoku. *Nihon chōki tōkei sōran.* Vol. 4. Tokyo: Nihon Tōkei Kyōkai, 1987.

Sonoda Hidehiro, Hamana Atsushi, and Hirota Teruyuki. *Shizoku no rekishi shakaigakuteki kenkyū.* Nagoya: Nagoya Daigaku Shuppankai, 1995.

Stanley, Amy. "Maidservants' Tales: Narrating Domestic and Global History in Eurasia, 1600–1900." *American Historical Review* 121, no. 2 (2016): 437–60.

———. *Stranger in the Shogun's City: A Woman's Life in Nineteenth-Century Japan.* London: Vintage Books, 2020.

Steele, M. William. "Goemon's New World." In *Alternative Narratives in Modern Japanese History*, 4–18. London: RoutledgeCurzon, 2003.

Sugano Noriko. "Kishida Toshiko and the Career of a Public-Speaking Woman in Meiji Japan." In *The Female as Subject: Reading and Writing in Early Modern Japan*, ed. Peter F. Kornicki, Mara Patessio, and G. G. Rowley. Michigan Monograph Series in Japanese Studies, ix. Ann Arbor: Center for Japanese Studies, University of Michigan, 2010.

Suyama Takaaki. *"Koume nikki" oyobi "Zakki" ni mirareru bakumatsu no Kishū: Harutomi no shi to Kaei no seihen.* Wakayama: Wakayama Monjokan, 1994.

Suzuki Yuriko. "Jusha josei no seikatsu." In *Josei no kinsei*, ed. Hayashi Reiko, 146–55. Tokyo: Chūō Kōronsha, 1993.

Szijártó, István. "Four Arguments for Microhistory." *Rethinking History* 6, no. 2 (2002): 209–15.

Takeuchi, Melinda. *Taiga's True Views: The Language of Landscape Painting in Eighteenth-Century Japan.* Stanford, Calif.: Stanford University Press, 1992.

Takeuchi Yoshinobu. "Kawai Koume no gagyō ni tsuite no gonin." *Wakayama Chihōshi kenkyū* 63 (2012): 26–30.

Tanimura, Reiko. "Practical Frivolities: The Study of Shamisen Among Girls of the Late Edo Townsman Class." *Japan Review* 23, no. 23 (2011): 73–96.

Totman, Conrad D. *The Collapse of the Tokugawa Bakufu 1862–1868.* Honolulu: University Press of Hawaii, 1980.

Tsukada Takashi. *Kinsei mibunsei to shūen shakaii.* Tokyo: Tōkyō Daigaku Shuppankai, 1997.

Ujiie Mikito. *Hatamoto gokenin: Odoroki no bakushin shakai no shinjitsu.* Rekishi shinsho. Vol. 22. Tokyo: Yōsensha, 2011.

Ulrich, Laurel. *A Midwife's Tale: The Life of Martha Ballard, Based on Her Diary, 1785–1812.* New York: Vintage Books, 1990.

Vaporis, Constantine N. "Samurai and Merchant in Mid-Tokugawa Japan: Tani Tannai's Record of Daily Necessities (1748–54)." *Harvard Journal of Asiatic Studies* 60, no. 1 (2000): 205–27.

———. *Voices of Early Modern Japan: Contemporary Accounts of Daily Life During the Age of the Shoguns*. Voices of an Era. Santa Barbara, Calif.: Greenwood, 2012.

Wakamatsu, Yurika. "Painting in Between: Gender and Modernity in the Japanese Literati Art of Okuhara Seiko (1837–1913)." PhD dissertation, Harvard University, 2016.

Wakayama Jinken Kenkyūjo. *Wakayama no burakushi. Tsūshi hen*, ed. Wakayama no Burakushi Hensankai. Tokyo: Akashi Shoten, 2015.

Wakayama Kenshi Hensan Iinkai. *Wakayama Kenshi. Kin-gendai*. Wakayama-shi: Wakayama-ken, 1989.

———. *Wakayama Kenshi. Kinsei*. Wakayama-shi: Wakayama-ken, 1990.

Wakayama Shiritsu Hakubutsukan. *Jōkamachi Wakayama no eshitachi: Edo jidai no Kishū gadan*. Wakayama: Wakayama Shiritsu Hakubutsukan, 2016.

Wakayama Shishi Hensan Iinkai. *Wakayama Shishi*. Vol. 2. *Kinsei*. Wakayama-shi: Wakayama-shi, 1989.

Wakita Osamu. "Bakuhan taisei to josei." In *Nihon joseishi*, ed. Joseishi Sōgō Kenkyūkai, 1–30. Tokyo: Tōkyō Daigaku Shuppankai, 1982.

Walthall, Anne. *The Weak Body of a Useless Woman: Matsuo Taseko and the Meiji Restoration*. Women in Culture and Society. Chicago: University of Chicago Press, 1998.Walthall, Anne, and M. William Steele. *Politics and Society in Japan's Meiji Restoration: A Brief History with Documents*. Bedford Series in History and Culture. Boston: Bedford/St. Martin's, Macmillan Learning, 2017.

Watanabe Hiroshi. *A History of Japanese Political Thought, 1600–1901*, trans. David Noble. Ltcb International Library Selection. Tokyo: International House of Japan, 2012.

Wigen, Kären. *The Making of a Japanese Periphery, 1750–1920*. Berkeley: University of California Press, 1995.

Wilson, George M. *Patriots and Redeemers in Japan: Motives in the Meiji Restoration*. Chicago: University of Chicago Press, 1992.

Yabuta, Yutaka. *Rediscovering Women in Tokugawa Japan*. Occasional Papers in Japanese Studies. Cambridge, Mass.: Harvard University, Edwin O. Reischauer Institute of Japanese Studies, 2000.

Yabuta Yutaka and Yanagiya Keiko. *Mibun no naka no josei. "Edo" no hito to mibun*. Tokyo: Yoshikawa Kōbunkan, 2010.

Yajima Takanori and Suzuki Tōzō. *Edo jidai rakusho ruijū*. 3 vols. Tokyo: Tōkyōdō, 1985.

Yamakawa Kikue. *Women of the Mito Domain: Recollections of Samurai Family Life*, trans. Kate Wildman Nakai. Tokyo: University of Tokyo Press, 1992.

Yamamura, Kozo. "The Increasing Poverty of the Samurai in Tokugawa Japan, 1600–1868." *Journal of Economic History* 31, no. 2 (1971): 378–406.

———. *A Study of Samurai Income and Entrepreneurship; Quantitative Analyses of Economic and Social Aspects of the Samurai in Tokugawa and Meiji, Japan*. Harvard East Asian Series. Cambridge, Mass.: Harvard University Press, 1974.

Yamaue Sachiko. "Kawai Koume to 'Kankai ibun.'" *Wōku shiryō*. Koume Nikki wo Tanoshimu Kai, 2014.

Yonekura Isamu. "The Revolt of Oshio Heihachiro: Rebel with a Cause." *East* 7, no. 10 (1971): 20–27.

Yonemoto, Marcia. "Adoption and the Maintenance of the Early Modern Elite: Japan in the East Asian Context." In *What Is a Family? Answers from Early Modern Japan*, ed. Mary Elizabeth Berry and Marcia Yonemoto, 47–67. Oakland: University of California Press, 2019.

———. *The Problem of Women in Early Modern Japan*. Asia: Local Studies/Global Themes. Berkeley: University of California Press, 2016.

Yonezawa Yoshiho and Yoshizawa Chū. *Japanese Painting in the Literati Style*, trans. Betty Iverson Monroe. Heibonsha Survey of Japanese Art. New York: Weatherhill/Heibonsha, 1974.

Yoshida Yuriko. *Kinsei no ie to josei*. Tokyo: Yamakawa Shuppansha, 2016.

Yoshihara Ken'ichirō. *Edo no jōhōya: Bakumatsu shominshi no sokumen*. NHK bukkusu. Tokyo: Nippon Hōsō Shuppan Kyōkai, 1978.

INDEX

Abe Ise no Kami (Kishū domain elder), 76
Abe Takeshi (historian), 13, 227, 265n12, 265n34
adoption, 14, 56, 65, 108, 124, 128, 129; of Hyōzō, 121, 246; of Kanae, 12–13, 40; of son-in-law (*muko yōshi*), 12–13, 30, 31–32, 121, 236, 237, 246; and status of women, 31–32, 246, 250
Aizawa Seishisai (scholar), 142
Aizu domain, 18, 146, 147, 151, 240
Aki domain, 162
Akō gishiden (Tales of the loyal samurai of Akō domain), 247
Andō, Lord, 149, 160
Andō family, 24, 79
Andō Naohiro, 175
Andō Naotsugu, 14
Aoyama Kiku, 110, 114
Arima Son'an (medical doctor), 84
Arisugawa, Prince, 162
artisans, 28, 29, 32
artists, 164–88; and gender, 8, 167, 182–88, 243–45; stipends for, 15. *See also* Kawai Koume, as artist; paintings
Asano Yoshinaga, 14

Bailey, M. Buckworth (newspaper editor), 161
Ballard, Martha (diarist), 235–36
Bankoku shinbun (News of the world), 161
beriberi, 149–51
Berry, Mary Elizabeth (historian), 236
Book of Filial Piety, 44
Britain, xviii; Japanese relations with, 60, 61, 83, 91; ships from, 72, 138, 142, 147
bunjinga (*wenrenhua*; literati painting), 37–38, 164–67, 216; as amateur style, 166–67, 186, 243; and commercial economy, 213; and copying *vs.* spontaneity, 171; and Domestic Exhibition, 215; and *gassaku* events, 167–73; in Kishū domain, 164, 165

Cahill, James (historian), 165
calendar: traditional, 139, 196, 225; Western, xix, 195, 253n1
calligraphy, 15, 38, 164, 166, 243. *See also gassaku*
Chamberlain, Basil Hall, 30
Chaos and cosmos of Kurosawa Tokiko, The: One Woman's Transit from Tokugawa to Meiji (Nenzi), 9

China, 31, 38, 60
Chinese studies: in Edo period, 33–34, 35, 239, 247; in education, 33–34, 35, 37, 44, 171, 239, 242; and Gakushūkan, 80, 194, 231, 236; and painting, 164–67, 171, 210, 214; in post-Meiji period, 198, 199–200, 216, 242–43. *See also* Confucianism
cholera, 83–84, 85, 91–92, 93, 228; and dancing, 86, 89–90; and Koume, 84, 85
Chōshū domain: civil war in, 148–49; and foreigners, xviii, 147–49; *vs.* Kishū, 154, 263n15; and Meiji Restoration, 162; military of, 145, 148–49, 151; in post-Meiji period, 189–90, 192; and pre-Meiji unrest, xix, 1, 153, 161, 230–31; revolutionary factions in, 141–51
Christianity, 138
Chronicle of the Foreign Ships (*Isenki*), 76
Chūbei (servant), 43
civil service examinations, 33
clothing, 104, 133, 135–36, 238; as investment, 70, 104, 128; in paintings, 173, 177, 178, 182; pawning of, 51, 105, 128, 157; purchase of, 52, 102, 117, 122, 127–28, 211, 219; and status, 28, 134
Confucianism: in education, 33–34, 35, 44, 171, 239; in Gakushūkan, 80, 194, 231, 236; and gender roles, 237, 267n18; *vs.* national learning, 231; neo-, 33–34, 54; and status, 28, 236
currency, xv–xiv, 92, 233, 239; and gift exchange, 98, 184

Date Chihiro (Kishū administrator), xviii, 69, 99, 141, 155, 190, 230; and Kaei purge, 65–66
Date Gorō, 141
Date Munemitsu. *See* Mutsu (Date) Munemitsu (Meiji statesman)
Daughter of the Samurai, A (Sugimoto Etsu), 6
Defoe, Daniel, 4
diaries, 3–4, 246, 248

divination, 111; and bad omens, 89–90, 138–40, 156–59, 229
domains: abolition of, xix, 163, 192; economies of, 115, 149; and foreign threat, 73, 75, 152; and national identity, 233; and post-Meiji unrest, 202, 240; and pre-Meiji unrest, 141–42, 145–46, 149, 151, 161. *See also particular domains*
Domestic Painting Competitive Exhibition (Naikoku Kaiga Kyōshinkai; 1882), 214–16
Dutch studies, 60, 80, 198, 247. *See also* Netherlands
Du Yu (Chinese scholar), 126

earthquakes, xviii, 77–78, 90
Echizen domain, 162
economy: of artistic production, 8, 113, 115–16, 167, 186, 243, 245, 266n44; cash, 7, 53, 108–9, 193, 200; and foreign trade, 59–61, 75, 83, 92, 99, 127, 136, 137–38, 160, 228, 230, 233, 262n7; and frugality, 69, 134–35; inequality in, 61, 64–65; inflation in, 93, 132–38, 139–41, 142, 200, 201, 228–29, 235, 247, 264n21; and Kawai family, 228–29, 235; post-Meiji, 200, 201, 212–13, 217, 243, 245, 266n45; pre-Meiji, 6, 62–65; and pre-Meiji unrest, 54, 58, 139–41, 142, 143; reforms of, 63–65, 154–55, 190, 191, 228; and taxation, 28, 48, 53, 62–65, 191, 193, 232, 238; of Wakayama, 10, 16–18, 20–22, 96. *See also* currency; gift exchange; household economy; rice; stipends
education, 33–39; Chinese studies in, 33–34, 35, 37, 44, 171, 239, 242; Imperial Rescript on, xix; and information, 248–49; of Koume, 37–38, 164, 166, 237, 246; new techniques in, 34; post-Meiji, xix, 193–94, 198, 199–200, 209, 216, 239–40, 242–43, 248; and research, 34–35; and status, 33–34, 38, 39, 231; of women, 35–39. *See also* Gakushūkan

Egawa Gennosuke (Gakushūkan scholar), 79
Ema Saikō (artist), 186
embroidery (*oshi-e*), stencil designs for, 213
emperor, Japanese: and Meiji Restoration, 162, 229, 231, 241; and pre-Meiji unrest, 141–42, 145, 153, 161; return of domains to, xix, 163, 192. *See also particular rulers*
Endō Ichirō, 98, 104–5, 109, 185
Enomoto Kankichi, 218
Enomoto Seizaemon, 74
epidemics, 48, 49; beriberi, 149–51; cholera, 83–84, 85, 86, 89–92, 93, 228
eta (outcastes), 132, 255n14. *See also hinin*
Etō Shinpei (rebel leader), 202
ex-samurai, 191–93, 238–43, 251; and education, 199, 242; government bonds for, xix, 7, 200, 201, 235, 240, 242; and Koume, 205, 212–13, 217; and military, 202, 203, 205, 235; and post-Meiji unrest, 202–5, 240; social status of, 240, 241, 242

famine, 132–38; and Kawai household economy, 52–53; and Koume, 49; Tenpō (1837), xvii, 46–49, 53–54, 61; in Wakayama, 46–49
farmers, 5, 28, 29, 53, 120; and foreigners, 99, 136; and Kawai family, 30, 38–39, 200; in military, 74, 143, 191, 203; and nightsoil collection, 38–39, 200; post-Meiji, 193, 194, 199, 240; and rebellion, 55, 56, 57, 61, 64–65, 143, 230; taxation of, 28, 48, 53, 64, 191, 193, 232; wealthy, 38, 57, 231. *See also* landowning class
Fenollosa, Ernest (art critic), 167
Fister, Patricia (art historian), 182
foreigners: attacks on, 90, 92–93; and Chōshū, xviii, 147–49; cultural influence of, 99, 101; expulsion of, 1, 142–43; and ex-samurai, 240; hostility towards, 136–38, 142; and Koume, 72, 75, 76, 91, 179, 228, 233, 234; and pre-Meiji unrest, 151, 152, 160; and Satsuma domain, 142–43;

threat of, 58–61, 70–78, 141; and Tokugawa shogunate, 75, 83, 92–93, 141–42, 149; trade with, 59–61, 75, 83, 92, 99, 127, 136, 137–38, 160, 228, 230, 233, 262n7. *See also particular countries*
France, 83, 142, 147
Frank, Anne, 4
Fujiokaya nikki (Sudō Yoshizō), 248
Fujita Ryōkichi, 105
Fukuoka domain, 202
Fukuzawa Yukichi (Meiji intellectual), 30, 99, 114, 204, 239

Gajin shūkai zu (painting; Illustration of a gathering of people of taste; Noro Kaiseki), 168
Gakushūkan (domain school), xvii, xviii, 35; abolition of, xix, 193, 194, 248, 251; and black ships, 74; community of, 107–8; Confucian learning in, 80, 194, 231, 236; decline of, 79–81; and Kawai Shunsen, 15, 33; and national learning, 80, 231
gassaku (combined work of poetry, calligraphy, and painting), 109, 166, 179, 209, 251; gatherings for, 167–73
gazetteers, xvii, 35
gender roles: and artists, 8, 167, 182–88, 243–45; Confucianism on, 237, 267n18; and marriage, 223; in post-Meiji period, 216; in samurai class, 6–7, 30–31, 94–95, 120, 237, 267n18; and status, 30–33; and stipends, 31, 237
gift exchange: *vs.* cash economy, 98, 108–9, 113, 128, 184, 194, 217, 236, 239; and celebrations, 48, 82; of food and drink, 2, 44, 53, 96, 97–98, 118; in household economy, 7, 46, 101, 102, 104, 107–10, 122, 236, 239; and Koume, 109, 122, 184, 188, 238, 244; and recycling, 109–10; of sake coupons, 41, 42–43, 81, 82, 98, 109, 112, 185; and side employment, 112; and social networks, 40, 44, 65, 107–10, 250
Gion Nankai (artist), 165

Gonshichi (servant), 100, 101, 105, 116–17
Gramlich-Oka, Bettina (historian), 9
Greater Learning for Women (*Onna Daigaku*), 36, 38

Hagi domain, 202
Hall, Francis (diarist), 42
Hamana Atsushi (historian), 242
haribako (decorative boxes), 113
Hashimoto Chūbei (follower of Ōshio Heihachirō), 57
Hattori Kazu (great-grandchild), 219
Hattori Tatsunojō (Tatsunosuke; husband of Kawai Yone), xiii, xx, 218–19
Hayashi school, 33
Hayashi Shinkai (diarist), 73
Heco, Joseph (newspaper editor), 161
Higo domain, 202, 203
hinin (nonpeople, outcastes), 23–24, 47, 48, 255n14, 255n17
Hirata Atsutane (scholar), 142
Hirota Teruyuki (historian), 242
Hisano, Lord of Tanba, 155
Hizen domain, 192
Hori Chikasada (daimyo of Iida domain), 114
Horinouchi Makoto, 80
horse racing, 129–30
household economy, 49–53; and aid to relatives, 50–51; and cash, 7, 43, 44, 49–51, 52, 95, 96, 98, 101, 103–5, 113–14, 127, 128, 209; financial management of, 101–7, 122, 127, 200–1, 206–9, 230, 235, 238, 251; food in, 95–101, 103–4; and gardening, 112; gift exchange in, 7, 46, 101, 102, 104, 107–10, 122, 236, 239; and homemade goods, 53, 113, 122; and housework, 110–12; and indebtedness, 50–53, 104–5; and Koume's art, 164, 182–88, 244, 245; Koume's management of, 7, 10, 237, 238, 250, 252; in post-Meiji period, 206–9; rice in, 49–53, 95–96, 102, 104; sake in, 52–53, 104; servants in, 110–12, 116–18; and side employment, 112–16, 127, 261n18; women's management of, 7, 94–95
household registration system (post-Meiji), 192–93
Howell, David (historian), 28, 33, 61, 255n14, 255n17
Hyakunin Isshu (poetry collection), 36

Ichikawa Hiroshi (patron of Koume's art), 209, 210–11, 212, 214, 221
Ichikawa Hitoshi (patron of Koume's art), 126, 175, 185, 199, 209
Ichiwa Ichigon (Ōta Nanba), 247
Iida domain, 114–15
Ii Naosuke, 83, 233
Ikeda family (neighbors of Kawai family), 44
Ike no Taiga (artist), 165, 167, 171
Imagawa Letter for Women, 36, 38
Imai Zuian (medical doctor), 85
indebtedness: and family, 134; and household economy, 50–53, 74, 101, 102, 104–5, 107; of Kishū domain, 63, 64; of samurai, 105–6, 239; and servants, 118; and side employment, 113–14, 115. *See also* pawnshops
information economy, 8, 245–49; and broadsheets, 18, 46, 66, 72, 152, 246, 247; and famine, 46; on foreigners, 72–73, 233; and gift exchange, 107; and Kaei purge, 66–67; and Koume, 120, 121–22, 231, 233; and Meiji Restoration, 230, 268n42; and newspapers, 161, 203, 246; and pre-Meiji unrest, 58, 161
Inuyama family (Kaga domain retainers), 106
Investigation of the Commentary of Zuo (*Saden kōchō*; Kawai Hyōzō), xviii, 44, 108, 126, 160–61, 251
Isoda Michifumi (historian), 106, 115
Itō Taizō, 79
Iwahashi family (friends of Kawai family), 108

INDEX 281

Iwahashi Kusumatsu, 103
Iwahashi Tetsunosuke, 67, 68
Iwahashi Tōsuke, 100
Iwahashi Tōzō, 79
Iwakura Tomomi (Meiji statesman), 240
Iwasaki Kedayū, 220

Japanese language, 3, 37
Jinmu, emperor, 162
Journal of the Plague Year (Defoe), 4

kabuki theater, 205–6
Kaei purge (1852), 62–70
Kaibara Ekiken (author of *Greater Learning for Women*), 110
Kaigai shinbun (newspaper), 161
Kanamiya Gohei (merchant), 54
Kanamori Genzaemon (beriberi victim), 149
Kanbai ensō bijinzu (Beautiful woman gazing at plum blossoms through a round window; Kawai Koume), 179, 181–82, 183
Kanō, Lord, 155
Kanō family, 79
Katsu Kaishū (shogunal administrator), 5
Kawaguchiya Saburō (rice broker), 49
Kawai family, xiii, xvii–xx; and economy, 228–29, 235; and famine, 48–49; and farmers, 30, 38–39, 200; finances of, 101–7, 122, 127, 200–1, 206–9, 230, 235, 238, 251; household economy of, 49–53; marriages in, 217–23; and military, 74, 148, 229, 232, 248; post-Meiji status of, 189–209, 243, 251; pre-Meiji status of, 28–33, 39, 121, 237; and religious ceremonies, 118–19; servants of, 116–18; side employments of, 112–13, 115–16, 261n18; stipends of, xviii, xix, 18, 22, 28, 30, 40, 49–53, 103, 104, 112, 116, 127, 184, 194, 200, 232, 235, 239, 240; and students, 16, 35, 40, 41, 43, 95, 100, 107, 111, 116, 118
Kawai Harue (grandchild), xiii

Kawai Hidesuga (grandson), xiii, 124, 219, 243
Kawai Hyōzō (husband), xiii, xvii, xviii, 238; adoption of, 121, 246; and cholera, 83–84; death of, xix, 195, 206, 226; and foreigners, 74–75, 76; and Gakushūkan, 79–81; and gift exchange, 109; illness of, 86–87, 89; and Koume's art, 243; marriage of, 39–40; and military, 148, 229; paintings by, 173, 174; and politics, 61, 67, 248; and pre-Meiji unrest, 143, 144, 155, 234; relationship with Koume of, 43, 78, 120–23, 184, 250; retirement of, xix, 127; and sake, 53, 100, 101; social life of, 42, 45, 46, 65, 131, 167, 260n19; stipend of, xviii, xix, 49–53, 104, 116, 127, 184, 232, 239; students of, 41, 43, 44, 95, 112, 118; teaching career of, 44, 95, 112–13, 115–16, 124–25, 127, 260n20; and *Zuo Commentary*, xviii, 44, 108, 126, 160–61, 251
Kawai Iwaichirō. *See* Kawai Yūsuke
Kawai Iwakuma (grandson), xiii, 111, 124
Kawai Kanae (Kitamura Kanae; father), xiii, xvii, 12–13, 32, 40
Kawai (Kuroda) Kano (daughter-in-law), 111, 124, 125, 135, 195, 214; and daughters' marriages, 218, 225; in post-Meiji period, 206, 207
Kawai Kikue (granddaughter), xiii, 78, 81–82, 124; illness and death of, 84–88, 93, 228, 251
Kawai Koume, xiii, 249–52; on bad omens, 89–90, 138–40, 156–59, 229; birth of, xvii, 13, 15; as chronicler, 249–50; conservatism of, 230–32; diary of, 1–11, 223; excursions of, 82, 129–31, 171–72, 195–98; as go-between, 217–23; illnesses and death of, xx, 224–26; marriage of, 39–40; in post-Meiji period, 206–17, 244–45; relationship with Hyōzō of, 78, 120–23, 184, 250; and sake, 100–1, 224, 227; as teacher, 207–9, 238

Kawai Koume, as artist: and cash payments, 113, 185, 187–88, 212–13, 216, 244; and Domestic Painting Competitive Exhibition, 214–16; education of, 37–38, 164, 166; and *gassaku* gatherings, 167–73; and gender discrimination, 167, 182, 187–88, 250; and household economy, 10, 110, 120–21, 122, 164, 182–88, 244, 245; paintings by, 122–23, 169–73, 175–77, 178, 251; patrons of, 185, 210–12, 244, 252; professional status of, 185, 188, 209–17, 245; recipients of work of, 173, 175; side employments of, 113, 115–16; social status of, 32, 237, 243–45, 250; styles of, 164, 173–82, 251–52. See also *Strange Things Heard in Foreign Lands*
Kawai Mikiyo (granddaughter), xiii, 195, 220
Kawai Shichirō (Matsushita Hikoemon; uncle), xiii, 13, 108, 146
Kawai Shige (granddaughter), xiii, 195
Kawai Shunsen (grandfather), xiii, 12–13, 16, 25, 35, 39–40; and Gakushūkan, xvii, 15, 33; status of, 28, 29–30
Kawai Tatsuko (mother), xiii, xvii, 41, 43, 45, 49, 100, 117, 125, 169; death of, xix, 126; and *muko* system, 12–13, 32; as poet, 35, 126
Kawai (Okamoto) Tomi (aunt), xiii
Kawai Tsune (granddaughter), xiii, 124, 195, 198, 206; marriages of, 217, 219–23, 225
Kawai Yone (granddaughter), xiii, 124, 128, 131, 135, 195; marriage of, 217–19
Kawai Yūsuke (Iwaichirō; son), xiii, 5, 125, 126, 130, 224; birth of, xvii, 123; childhood of, 41, 43, 44, 45, 49, 50; and cholera, 83–84, 85; and daughters' marriages, 219, 220; and domain, 68, 78; and earthquake, 77; and foreigners, 74, 75; and household economy, 50, 102; and Koume's 80th birthday, 225–26; marriage of, xviii, 78; and medical care, 84; and military, 74, 148; name change of, xvii, 67, 78; painting by, 173; in post-Meiji period, 194–200, 206–9, 239–40, 242–43; and religious activities, 119; and sake, 45, 100; stipend of, 194, 200, 207, 235, 240; teaching career of, xix, xx, 127, 194–200, 208–9, 265n18
Kawanabe Kyōsai (artist), 159, 216
Keene, Donald (historian), 227
Kii family, 14, 254n2
Kii Toshiaki, 254n2
Kiku no zu (Painting of chrysanthemums; Kawai Koume), 169–71
Kinmonth, Earl (historian), 241
Ki no Tsurayuki (poet), 4
Kishi Junnosuke (Gakushūkan scholar), 80
Kishi Kakunosuke, 67
Kishū domain, xvii, xviii, xix, 6, 12–15; *bunjinga* in, 164, 165; cholera in, 83–84; and Chōshū, 147–48, 149, 263n15; and famine, 47–48; finances of, 63, 190; and foreigners, 71, 73–74, 76, 138, 263n15; Kaei purge in, 62–70; military of, 143–45, 146, 191–92, 204, 232, 263n15; and national learning, 231; in post-Meiji period, 189–90, 204–5, 235, 240; and pre-Meiji unrest, 143–44, 146, 151–52, 229, 234; reform in, 63–64, 190–92; scholarly community of, 8, 167, 184; taxation in, 62–63; uprising in (1823), 64–65. See also Tokugawa Mochitsugu
Kitamura family, xiii, 108, 110
Kitamura Kanae. See Kawai Kanae
Kōbō Daishi, 206
Koeppen, Carl (Prussian military specialist), 191
Koiku (servant's sister), 117–18
Kōmei, Emperor, xix, 141, 142, 147
Kondō Takashi (art historian), 182
Kōno Motoaki (art historian), 166
Korea, 31, 60
Kōshūya (Shinohara) Chūemon (Yokohama merchant), 5, 262n7
Kōyama Kunikiyo (governor of Wakayama Prefecture), 192
Kozo Yamamura (historian), 254n7

Krusenstern, Johann von (Russian ship's captain), 59
Kuge Umanosuke (Gakushūkan scholar), 79
Kumamoto domain, 202–3, 204
Kumano, paintings of, 165
Kumano shrines lending office (*Kumano sanzan kashitsuke*), 63, 64
Kuroda family (relatives by marriage), 218
Kuroda Jinbei, xix, 78, 81, 84, 88, 140; illness and death of, 125–26
Kuroda Kan, 82, 84
Kuroda Kano. *See* Kawai (Kuroda) Kano
Kuroda Kise, xx, 84, 87, 126, 128, 205–6
Kuroda Kojirō, 128
Kuroda O-Yae, 158, 218, 224
Kuroda Ushinosuke, 125–26, 148, 218, 221
Kurosawa Tokiko, 232
Kuwayama Gyokushū (artist), 165
Kuwayama Shigeharu (deputy of Toyotomi Hideyoshi), 14

landowning class, 29, 64–65, 193, 196, 240
Lepore, Jill (historian), 227
Lippit, Yukio (art historian), 166, 167
literacy, 248, 249; of women, 36, 38, 187. *See also* education

Maeda Toyohide (husband of Tsune), xiii, xx, 220–21, 222
Manzai no zu (Illustration of Manzai performers; Koume and Hyōzō), 172–73, 174
Maruyama Yasunari (historian), 248
Matsudaira Saburōtarō (Gakushūkan scholar), 80–81
Matsudaira Sadanobu (shogunal administrator), 36
Matsuo Taseko (poet), 33, 232
Matsushita family (relatives by adoption), xiii, 108
Matsushita Hikoemon (Kawai Shichirō; uncle), xiii, 13, 108, 146
Matsushita Kōnosuke (business leader), 182

Matsuzaka (town), 13
McClellan, Edwin (translator), 9
medical care, 43, 45–46, 48, 82, 84–88, 111, 228. *See also* epidemics
Mehl, Margaret (historian), 200
Meiji, Emperor, xix, 214, 215
Meiji Restoration (1868), xix, 6, 161–63; causes of, 229–30, 240–41; effects of, 5, 9, 162, 189–206; and lower-ranking samurai, 7–8, 229, 241–42; and role of emperor, 162, 229, 231, 241; unrest leading up to, xix, 1, 3, 54, 58, 139–46, 149, 151–63, 229, 230–31, 235
merchants, 21–22, 26, 117; accounting skills of, 103; education of, 38, 80, 187, 199, 231; and foreign trade, 136, 137–38; and information networks, 247–48; and Meiji Restoration, 230, 240–41; popular anger at, 55–56, 64–65, 140; status of, 28, 29, 30, 32; wealthy, 22, 24, 28, 53, 55–56, 61, 63, 64–65, 140, 165, 186, 187, 248; wives of, 30, 38, 39, 94, 120
military: of Chōshū, 145, 148–49, 151; compulsory conscription for, 191, 192, 193, 204–5; and ex-samurai, 202, 203, 205, 235; farmers in, 74, 143, 191, 203; foreign, 60, 61, 143, 161, 190; and Kawai family, 28, 74, 143, 144, 148, 229, 232, 248; of Kishū, 73, 143–45, 146, 191–92, 204, 232, 263n15; Koume on, 145–46, 147–48; in post-Meiji period, 7, 189–90; reform of, 141, 145, 148, 154–55, 190–91; training for, 74, 80
Mito domain, 1, 83, 248; and foreigners, 61, 92, 233; and national learning, 231; side employment in, 114, 239; women of, 6, 9, 36, 110, 116
Miura, Lord, 74, 109, 146, 204
Miura family, 24, 79
Miwa Bunko fubo no zu (Portrait of Miwa Bunko's parents; Kawai Koume), 178–79, 180
Miwa Saizō (Saijirō; family friend), 179, 212
Miyachi Masato (historian), 268n42
Mizuno, Lord, 160

Mizuno family, 24, 207–8, 217, 245
Mizuno Sada (student of Koume), 207–8
Mizuno Shigenaka, 14
Mizuno Tadanaka, 69
Mizuno Tamon (Gakushūkan governor), 126, 143, 144–45, 146
Mizuno Tōbei (Kishū administrator), 140–41
Moore, Ray (historian), 32
Mōri Daizen (Takachika; daimyo of Chōshū), 149, 153
Mori Ōgai (diarist), 9
Mōri Takachika. *See* Mōri Daizen
Moriya Kane (sister-in-law), 106
Moriya Nao, 134
Moriya Rihachi, 85, 133–34
Moriya Shōbei (brother-in-law), 106, 133
Moriya Shōsuke, 50, 106
Morrison (ship), 61
Motoori Norinaga (scholar), 142, 231
Motoori Ōhira (poetry teacher of Koume), xvii, 37, 231
Motosaki Bōsuke (cholera victim), 85
Murata Seifū (Edo-era social commentator), 51
music, 38, 68, 166, 167, 205, 206, 219, 221; koto, 37, 39, 128–29, 131
Mustard Seed Garden Manual of Painting, 165
Mutsu (Date) Munemitsu (Meiji statesman), 141, 184, 190

Nagasaki, 59, 60, 61, 82, 83, 247
Nagasawa Seiemon, 70
Naitō Jingozaemon (cousin of Hyōzō), 74
Nakai, Kate (historian), 9
Nakatsu domain, 114, 239
Nakura Hachizō (medical doctor), 85
Namakura Sumiko (chairperson of the Society for the Enjoyment of Koume's Diary), 237
national identity, 61, 76–77, 229, 233–34
national learning, 37, 80, 142, 231
nativism, 231

Nenzi, Laura (historian), 7, 9
Netherlands, 60, 83, 142, 147
newspapers, 161, 203, 246
New Year festival, 42, 67, 111–12, 119, 128, 225
night soil contracts, 38–39, 200
Nihon Gaishi (Rai San'yō), 247
Niida Genichirō (Gakushūkan scholar), 110
Nishikawa Sukenobu (artist), 32
Nishikawaya Haru (family friend), 129
Nishikawaya Tsuneno (family friend), 129
Nishimura elementary school, 195–98, 208
Nishiyama diary, 5
Nogawaya Yahei (rice merchant), 140
Nogiwa Hakusetsu (artist), 37, 166, 186, 215, 264n24
Nogiwa Saichō, 103
Noguchi Junnosuke, 207
Noguchi Junsuke (Gakushūkan scholar), 161
Norman, E. H. (historian), 241
Noro family, 108
Noro Kaiseki (artist), 165, 166, 167, 187, 215
Noro Seikichi (Gakushūkan scholar), 91–92, 119, 173

Ogyū Sorai (scholar), 34
Okamoto Banji (uncle), xiii
Oka Shōgorō (Okayama domain retainer), 115
Okuhara Seiko (artist), 186–87, 216, 217, 266n44
One Hundred Types of Women (Nishikawa Sukenobu), 32
Onna takarabako (Women's treasury), 247
Ono Hideo (historian), 248
Orito Tokutarō (husband of Tsune), xiii, xx, 221–22, 225
O-Shika (servant), 45
Ōshio Heihachirō insurrection (Osaka; 1837), xvii, 53–58, 142, 230
Ōta Nanba (Edo-era author), 247
Ōta Tomiyasu (historian), 73
Owari domain, 147, 149, 151
Ozaki Sekijō (Oshi domain retainer), 119

paintings: *bijinga* (images of beautiful women) in, 182; Chinese, 164–67, 171, 210, 214; copying of, 175, 177; by Koume, 122–23, 169–73, 175–77, 178, 251; of Kumano, 165; market for, 186, 243, 245; prices of, 167, 266n44; as side employment, 113, 115–16. See also *bunjinga*; *gassaku*; Kawai Koume, as artist
papermaking, 114–15
pawnshops, 50–53, 104–5, 127, 128, 157
Pepys, Samuel (diarist), 4
periodicals, 161, 203, 246, 247
Perry, Matthew (U.S. naval commodore), xviii, 70–77, 229, 233
poetry: Chinese, 37; in education, 33–34, 36, 37–38; on foreigners, 76, 91; *haikai*, 169; on horse racing, 130; by Hyōzō, 122; and Koume, 110, 122, 135, 172, 213, 233; for Koume's eightieth birthday, 226; and painting, 166, 243; on pre-Meiji unrest, 57–58, 66, 152; romantic, 40; satirical, 51–52, 58, 66–67, 72, 152, 156, 234, 246, 248; and scholarly community, 38, 231; and Tatsuko, 35, 126; *waka*, 37; and women, 33, 36, 186. See also *gassaku*
politics, 138–51; and bad omens, 138–40; and inequality, 53–58; information on, 248, 249; and Koume, 6, 8, 57–58, 60, 61, 65, 66, 69–70, 122, 141, 145–47, 149, 162, 228–35, 249; and women, 33, 36
Popular Rights Movement, 249
Portugal, 101
priests, 14, 21, 29, 44, 65, 88, 131, 240; and Kawai family, 118–19, 131, 168–69, 173, 212. See also temples
print culture, 38–39, 72, 165, 171, 216, 247–49. See also information economy
Problem of Women in Early Modern Japan, The (Yonemoto), 30–31

Rafudōsen (Koume's pseudonym), 182
Rai family, 237
Rai O-Tō (sister of San'yō), 37
Rai San'yō, 94, 247
Rai Shizuko (mother of San'yō), 37, 94, 111, 120, 121
Rai Shunsui (father of San'yō), 94, 120, 121
rebellions: and farmers, 55, 56, 57, 61, 64–65, 143, 230; and foreigners, 136–38, 147–49, 151, 152, 160; and Meiji Restoration, xix, 1, 3, 54, 58, 139–46, 149, 151–63, 229, 230–31, 235; post-Meiji, 202–5, 240; and revolutionary factions, 141–51; and Satsuma, xx, 146, 147, 151, 153, 161, 235; and *sonnō jōi*, 142, 232, 252; Tenchūgumi (rebel faction), 143–45, 263n15. See also Ōshio Heihachirō insurrection
Record of Women's Great Treasures (*Onna Chōhōki*), 38–39
reform: administrative, 189–90; economic, 63, 154–55, 190, 191, 228; in education, xix, 248; in Kishū, 63–64, 190–92; and Koume, 230–32; military, 141, 145, 148, 154–55, 190–91; and pre-Meiji unrest, 152–53; and reduction of stipends, 154–55, 190, 191, 228
religious ceremonies, 135–36; and cholera, 85, 86, 88, 89, 92; and Kawai family, 118–19. See also priests; temples
Rezanov, Nikolai (Russian diplomat), 60
rice: fluctuating prices of, 46–47, 52, 55, 57, 127, 132–33, 228, 247–48, 262n1; in household economy, 49–53, 95–96, 102, 104, 262n1; and information, 247–48; and sake, 52–53; stipends paid in, 28, 49–50, 52, 62, 94, 104, 127, 200, 228, 232, 239, 254n7; taxes paid in, 62–63, 232, 238
Roberts, Luke (historian), 68–69
Russia, 59–63, 77, 83, 91, 175, 177

Saga domain, 202
Saigō Takamori (rebel leader), 203
Sakagami Tatsu (Sogyoku; artist), 187
Sakai Baisai (family friend), 98–99, 129, 146, 156, 162, 185, 211
Sakai Haru, 156
Sakai Kiyoshi, 211

286 INDEX

Sakai Tsuneno, 129, 131, 156
Sakanishi Sōroku (Kishū domain military officer), 143
sake: coupons for, 41, 42–43, 81, 82, 98, 109, 112, 185; distillation of, 101; in household economy, 52–53, 104; and Koume, 100–1, 224, 227; and rice, 52–53; and social activities, 100, 104, 168, 243, 250; and Yūsuke, 45, 100
Sakichi (servant), 130, 157
samurai (*bushi*): and adoption, 236; and art, 129, 164, 166, 186, 243–44, 245; business skills of, 103, 106, 241–42; debts of, 105–6, 239; diversity of, 29, 239, 241–42; education of, 33, 248; family names of, 192; finances of, 51–52, 116; and foreigners, 73–74, 90, 92; and frugality, 134–35; and gender roles, 6–7, 30–31, 94–95, 120, 237, 267n18; and gift exchange, 108–9; housing lots for, 18, 254n7b; lower-ranking, 3, 7–8, 18, 25, 28, 54, 57, 61, 90, 92, 105–6, 114, 229, 241, 248, 250; and Meiji Restoration, 3, 7–8, 162, 229, 240; and military, 28, 73, 74, 114, 143–44; and national learning, 231; in pre-Meiji unrest, 54–58, 61, 235; and reform, 141, 154; side employments of, 112–15, 239; status of, 28–33; in Wakayama, 18–19, 255n8; and Wang Yangming, 54–55. *See also* ex-samurai; stipends
Satomi and the Eight Dogs (*Nansō Satomi hakkenden*; Takizawa Bakin), 39, 247
Satsuma domain: and foreigners, 142–43; and Meiji Restoration, 162; in post-Meiji period, 189–90, 192, 202–3; and pre-Meiji unrest, xix, xx, 146, 147, 151, 153, 161, 235
Screech, Timon (art historian), 186
Sekigahara, battle of (1600), 14
Sekiguchi diary, 5
Shibayama Torazaemon (Kishū domain officer), 143
Shiga Junko (descendent of Koume), 223
Shiga Kusunosuke (husband of Tsune), xiii, 223

Shiga Yasuharu (great grandson), 40, 123, 223, 243, 260n18
Shimazu Tadayoshi (Satsuma daimyo), 153
Shin'emon (farmer), 43–44
Shinohara Chūemon. *See* Kōshūya (Shinohara) Chūemon (Yokohama merchant)
Shinpūren attack (Kumamoto castle; 1876), 202–3, 204
Shiroyama, battle of (1876), 203
Skinner, William (historian), 32
smallpox, 82, 198
Smiles, Samuel (British author), 241
social activities: expenses for, 81–82; during famine, 49; and gift exchange, 107–8, 109; *vs.* housework, 111; for Kikue, 81–82; and Koume, 45, 120, 121, 122, 125, 128–29, 166, 237, 250–51; male-only, 45, 186; in post-Meiji period, 198, 209; and sake, 100, 104, 166, 168, 243, 250; at temples, 45, 82, 118–19, 122, 129, 131, 135, 168–69, 196, 198, 237. *See also gassaku*
social networks: of Gakushūkan, 40, 42, 107–8, 184; and *gassaku* gatherings, 167–73, 243, 251; and gift exchange, 7, 107–10, 250; of *hinin*, 23; and Koume, 2, 8, 38, 40, 53, 60, 95, 101, 120, 228, 237–38, 250–51, 252; and Koume's painting, 116, 120, 184, 185, 210, 212, 243–44; and sake, 104, 250; scholarly, 38, 40, 42, 79, 104, 107–8, 126, 229, 231, 232, 236–38, 242–44, 250–51; of Tatsuko, 126; of Wakayama, 60, 79, 104, 126, 153, 184, 243, 249, 250
social status: *vs.* class, 241–42; and education, 33–34, 38, 39, 187, 231; of ex-samurai, 240, 241, 242; and gender roles, 30–33; and inequality, 53–58; of Koume, 32, 237, 243–45, 250; markers of, 28, 134, 237; and marriage, 39, 219; of merchants, 28, 29, 30, 32, 187; in post-Meiji period, 189–209, 243, 251; in pre-Meiji period, 28–33, 39, 121, 237; and side employment, 113–15

Society for the Enjoyment of Koume's Diary (Koume Nikki wo Tanoshimu Kai), viii–ix, 223, 227
Soga Shōhaku (artist), 264n23
sonnō jōi (revere the emperor and expel the barbarian), 142, 232, 252
Spring and Autumn Annals, 44
Stanley, Amy (historian), 7, 9, 10, 33
Steele, William (historian), 72, 267n11
stem family model, 31
stipends: for artists, 15; in cash, xx, 200, 239; conversion to bonds of, xix, 7, 200, 201, 235, 240, 242; for daimyo, 192; and gender, 31, 237; and gift exchange, 108; of Kawai family, xviii, xix, 18, 22, 28, 30, 40, 49–53, 103, 104, 112, 116, 127, 184, 194, 200, 232, 235, 239, 240; reductions of, 50, 52, 62, 63, 70, 144–45, 154–55, 190, 191, 228; in rice, 28, 49–50, 52, 62, 94, 104, 127, 200, 228, 232, 239, 254n7; and side employment, 114–15, 239
Stranger in the Shogun's City: A Japanese Woman and Her World (Stanley), 9
Strange Things Heard in Foreign Lands (*Kankai ibun*; Ōtsuki Gentaku et al.), xvii, 58–61; background of, 58–61; Koume's paintings in, 175, 177, 178
Sudō Yoshizō (bookseller and diarist), 248
Sugihara (go-between), 218, 219
Sugimoto Etsu (samurai wife), 6
Sugiyama Sagorō (patron of Koume's art), 211
Supplemental Gazetteer of Kii (*Kii zoku fudoki*), xvii, 35
Suzuki Kantarō, 153
Suzuki Yoshiemon (patron of Koume's art), 213
Suzuki Yoshitarō, 82
Szijarto, Istvan (historian), 228

Takahashi Saburoemon, 41, 42
Takizawa Bakin (Edo-era author), 39
Tale of Genji, The (*Genji monogatari*), 39, 175

Tamaki Nui (Kumano shrine priest), 65, 66, 69
Tamiya Heishirō (Gakushūkan scholar), 80–81
Tamiya Shūhaku (medical doctor), 45–46
Tanaka family, 108
Tanaka Hisano (Zenzō's mother), 154
Tanaka Kyūemon, 68
Tanaka Zenzō (Gakushūkan scholar and Kishū domain administrator), xix, 2, 70, 100, 146, 172, 230; murder of, 152, 154–56
Tani Tannai (Tosa domain retainer), 105–6
taxation, 62–65; of farmers, 28, 48, 53, 64, 191, 193, 232; and rice, 62–63, 232, 238
temples, 12, 14, 20, 23, 88, 212; donations to, 44; social activities at, 45, 82, 118–19, 122, 129, 131, 135, 168–69, 196, 198, 237
Tenchūgumi (Heaven's Wrath Band) rebellion, 143–45, 263n15
Thinking Like a Man: Tadano Makuzu (Gramlich-Oka), 9
Toba-Fushimi, Battle of (1868), xix, 151, 162, 189
Toda Kinzaemon, 134
Toda Korekiyo, 134
Tokugawa family, 6, 234–35
Tokugawa Harutomi (Kishū daimyo), xvii, 15, 25, 30, 35, 63–69; death of, xviii, 62, 67–68
Tokugawa Iemochi (Yoshitomi), xviii, 14, 15, 82, 83, 142, 149; death of, xix, 151
Tokugawa Iesada, 83
Tokugawa Ieyasu, 14, 31
Tokugawa Ieyoshi, 71–72
Tokugawa Keiki (Hitotsubashi), 152
Tokugawa Mochitsugu (Kishū daimyo), xix, 82, 147, 149–51, 160, 225; in post-Meiji period, 189–90, 192, 204, 235
Tokugawa Nariaki, 83, 233, 248
Tokugawa Narikatsu, 62
Tokugawa Nariyuki, 62

Tokugawa shogunate: and bad omens, 139–40; bureaucracy of, 25, 31, 33, 69, 80, 115, 164; and Chōshū, 146–48, 149; fall of, 5, 151–63; and foreigners, 75, 83, 92–93, 141–42, 149; isolation policy of, 61, 71; and Kawai family, 232; rebellions against, xix, xx, 1, 54–58, 61, 141–53, 161, 229, 230–31, 234, 235; and revolutionary factions, xviii, 141–51
Tokugawa Yorinobu, 14
Tokugawa Yoshikatsu, 147
Tokugawa Yoshimune, 14, 63
Tokugawa Yoshinobu, xix, 83, 153, 161–62, 189
Tokugawa Yoshitomi, 62, 69
Tokura Ryōzō (student), 118
Tominaga family, 108
Tomiya O-Take (beggar), 133
Tomiya Zensuke, 133
Tosa domain, 105, 153, 162, 179, 192
Tosa nikki (Ki no Tsurayuki), 3, 4
Toyo (servant), 117–18, 175
Toyotomi Hidenaga, 14
Toyotomi Hideyoshi, 14
Treasure Box of Greater Learning for Women, 38
Treasury of Various Mundane Matters (Kaibara Ekiken), 110–11
treaty ports, 83, 90, 99, 149. See also Nagasaki
Tsuda Matatarō (Tsuda Izuru; Kishū domain administrator), 152, 155, 156, 190–92, 230
Tsugami Etsugorō (diarist), 248
Tsuji Bungo (family friend), 158, 220, 222
Tsuji Kenzaemon, 211–12
Tsuji Takano (daughter of Bungo), 158
Tsukayama Gakuzō (Gakushūkan scholar), 126, 173
Tsuneno (*Stranger in the Shogun's City*), 5, 10, 33

Uchimura Matajūrō, 43, 74
Ujiie Mikito (historian), 115

ukiyo-e prints, 177, 186, 247
Ulrich, Laurel (historian), 235
Umemoto Asakitsu, 83–84
Umemoto Asanosuke, 79
Umemoto family (birth family of Hyōzō), 134
Umemoto Hisano, 84
Umemoto Hyōzō. *See* Kawai Hyōzō
Umemoto Keizō, 146
Umemoto Tōshirō, 54
Umemoto Yae, 125, 126
United States (U.S.), 147, 263n15; black ships from, 70–77; Civil War in, 136; Japanese relations with, xviii, 60–61, 77, 83, 91
U.S.-Japan Treaty of Amity and Commerce (1854), 77
U.S.-Japan Treaty of Amity and Friendship (1858), xviii
U.S.-Japan Treaty of Kanagawa (1854), xviii
Utagawa Toyokuni (artist), 214

Vaporis, Constantine (historian), 105
volcanic eruptions, 46, 257n6

Wada Jintatsu (student), 118
Wada Yoshirō, 146
Wakamiya-maru (ship), 59
Wakayama, vii–viii, xvii; bunjinga in, 164; cholera in, xviii, 83–84, 86; City Museum of, 177; districts of, 15–24; earthquake in, 77–78; economy of, 10, 16–18, 20–22, 65, 96; famine in, xviii, 46–49; and foreigners, 1, 60, 71; history of, 6, 13–14, 227; housing in, 18, 22, 254n7b, 255n12; information in, 6, 246; and national politics, 229, 230; population of, 18, 20, 255nn8–10; in post-Meiji period, 193–94, 202, 204, 205; and pre-Meiji unrest, xviii, 1, 64, 152, 153–54, 155, 235; social classes in, 22–24; social networks in, 60, 79, 104, 126, 153, 184, 243, 249, 250
Wakayama castle, 2, 8, 12, 14, 15, 21, 24–27
Wakita Osamu (historian), 32

Walthall, Anne (historian), 7, 9, 10, 40
Wang Yangming (philosopher), 54–55, 142
Watanabe Hiroshi (historian), 233
Watanabe Ikkaku, 71
Weak Body of a Useless Woman, A: Matsuo Taseko and the Meiji Restoration (Walthall), 9
Western learning, 60, 80, 160–61, 198, 199, 200, 247
Wigen, Kären (historian), 114, 115
Woman in the Crested Kimono (McClellan), 9
women: as artists, 8, 167, 182–88, 243–45; education of, 35–39; and household economy, 7, 94–95; literacy of, 36, 38, 187; and Meiji Restoration, 230, 232–33; merchant, 30, 38, 39, 94, 120; and poetry, 33, 36, 186; and popular fiction, 39, 247; in post-Meiji period, 216, 244–45; roles of, 94–95, 235–38; samurai, 6–7, 30–31, 94–95, 120, 237, 267n18; status of, 30–33, 246, 250; in Wakayama castle, 26
Women of Mito Domain (Yamakawa Kikue), 6, 9
Wonderful World of Kawai Koume, The (Abe Takeshi), 227

Xie He (art theorist), 171

Yamada Shōzaemon, xiii
Yamaguchi Hyōma, 70

Yamakawa Kikue (memoirist), 6, 9, 36, 110, 114, 116
Yamamoto family (Gakushūkan scholars), 108
Yamamoto Hikojūrou, 74
Yamamoto Kanzō, 126
Yamamoto Shōtarō, 79, 119
Yamanaka Tokunosuke, 70
Yamanaka Toshinobu (Kishū domain administrator), 65, 67, 69
Yamaue Sachiko (member of the Society for the Enjoyment of Koume's Diary), 260n2, 261n28
Yasoichirō (colleague), 87, 90, 100
Yasubei (servant), 70, 111, 112, 117, 118
Yasujirō (servant), 195, 196, 197
Yatsuzuka Magosaburō (family friend from Kokawa village), 130–31
Yokohama, 83, 90
Yonemoto, Marcia (historian), 7, 30–31, 236, 237, 267n18
Yosa Buson (artist), 167
Yoshida Shōin (scholar and activist), 142
Yoshida Yuriko (historian), 94, 111, 120, 121, 237
Yoshiyama Suitei (patron of Koume), 214
Yurika Wakamatsu (art historian), 216
Yūsuke, xix

Zuo zhuan (*Sashiden*; *Commentary of Zuo*), xviii, 44, 108, 126, 160–61, 251

GPSR Authorized Representative: Easy Access System Europe, Mustamäe tee
50, 10621 Tallinn, Estonia, gpsr.requests@easproject.com

www.ingramcontent.com/pod-product-compliance
Lightning Source LLC
Chambersburg PA
CBHW022037290426
44109CB00014B/884